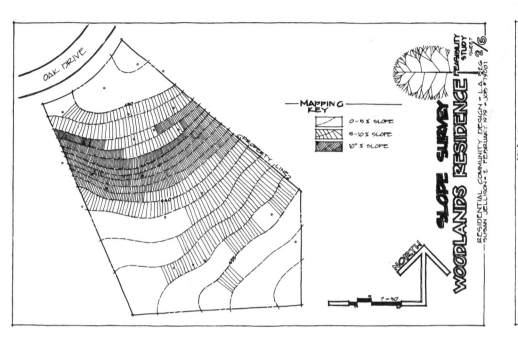

SLOPE SURVEY — WOODLANDS RESIDENCE — FEASIBILITY STUDY — SHEET 2/6

RESIDENTIAL COMMUNITY DESIGN · LA 22G · SUSAN JELLISON · 2 FEBRUARY 1979 · JOB #9001

MAPPING KEY
0–5% SLOPE
5–10% SLOPE
10%+ SLOPE

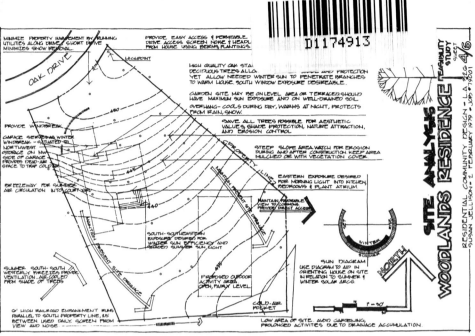

SITE ANALYSIS — WOODLANDS RESIDENCE — FEASIBILITY STUDY — SHEET 4/6

RESIDENTIAL COMMUNITY DESIGN · LA 22G · SUSAN JELLISON · 2 FEBRUARY 1979 · JOB #9001

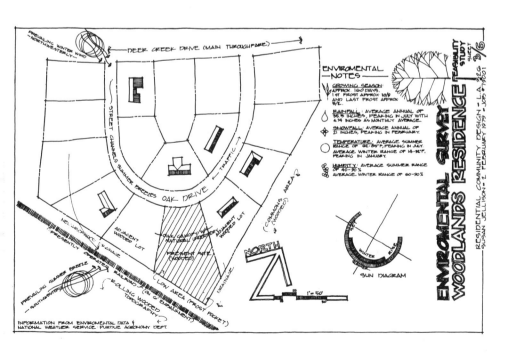

ENVIROMENTAL SURVEY — WOODLANDS RESIDENCE — FEASIBILITY STUDY — SHEET 3/6

RESIDENTIAL COMMUNITY DESIGN · LA 22G · SUSAN JELLISON · 2 FEBRUARY 1979 · JOB #9001

ENVIROMENTAL NOTES

INFORMATION FROM ENVIROMENTAL DATA & NATIONAL WEATHER SERVICE, PURDUE AGRONOMY DEPT.

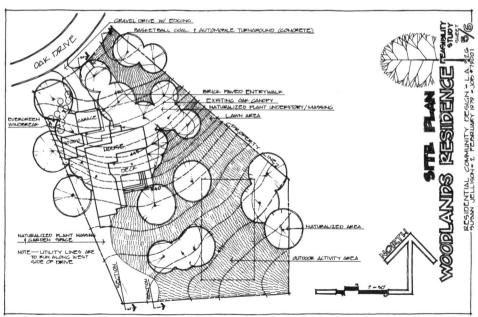

SITE PLAN — WOODLANDS RESIDENCE — FEASIBILITY STUDY — SHEET 5/6

RESIDENTIAL COMMUNITY DESIGN · LA 22G · SUSAN JELLISON · 2 FEBRUARY 1979 · JOB #9001

RESIDENTIAL LANDSCAPES

Graphics, planning, and design

RESIDENTIAL LANDSCAPES

Graphics, planning, and design

Gregory M. Pierceall, ASLA

Purdue University

WAVELAND
PRESS, INC.

Prospect Heights, Illinois

For information about this book, write or call:

Waveland Press, Inc.
P.O. Box 400
Prospect Heights, Illinois 60070
(708) 634-0081

Copyright © 1984 by Gregory M. Pierceall
1994 reissued by Waveland Press, Inc.

ISBN 0-88133-788-9

Printed in the United States of America

7 6 5 4 3 2 1

This text is dedicated to my understanding and loving wife Harriet and to our scallawag daughter Hillary.

Contents

Preface

Landscape design as it relates to residential site develop-
ment is a space and activity definer within which clients live, relax,
and recreate. Design proposals are not an end unto themselves but
a means of creating a setting that is useful and pleasing, reflecting
the site, client, and surrounding influences. Design ideas are refined
through a systematic thought process and expressed in plans that
are in turn used to implement actual site developments. Landscape
designs are only as alive and dynamic as the imaginations of the
client and designer.

Residential Landscapes: Graphics, Planning, and Design is a reference for individuals involved in the design and development of
plantings and constructed features for residential sites. Homeowners, landscape nurserymen, landscape contractors, landscape maintenance firms, and landscape architects individually and collectively
are involved in landscape design. The homeowner's involvement in
landscape design can be as a consumer or designer, while the other
individuals are professionals in the larger landscape industry.

To a landscape architect, landscape design is a specialty area as well as an extension of other more primary planning services provided to clients. The student landscape architect initially applies planning and design principles to smaller sites such as residential properties and then progresses to larger scale design situations such as park, recreation, housing and urban developments. Landscape nurserymen, contractors, and maintenance firms as part of the landscape industry are also involved with landscape design. As professionals, they not only produce and sell plants and construction materials but install and care for landscape designs beyond the design stages of development. As specialists within their fields, these landscape industry individuals are often called on to make recommendations that influence landscape designs.

The graphic, planning, and design concepts used to present planting and construction ideas for residential sites are the focus of this text. Illustrations and actual residential case study examples are used to communicate the graphic, planning, and design information. Part One is an introduction to landscape design and the landscape industry. Chapter 1 focuses on a typical residential entry problem and illustrates some of the graphic, design, and planning considerations involved in a design proposal. Site design and the landscape industry are discussed in Chapter 2. The graphics used to communicate landscape design proposals as well as the equipment, processes, and procedures required are discussed in Part Two. Chapters 3, 4, 5, 6, and 7 include descriptions and illustrations of the tools, drawings, and presentation methods available in the development of design proposals. Part Three, Chapters 8 and 9, focuses on the planning process and design principles used in landscape design. Finally, Part Four, which includes Chapters 10, 11, 12, and 13, involves the changing character of residential landscape design and case studies illustrating the graphics, planning, and design of selected residential properties. The renovation of an existing landscape site, the planning of a new residential property, and the planning and design of multifamily housing are project illustrations used. The summary in Chapter 14 is followed by a glossary of terms and appendices.

This text represents my interest and experience in residential landscape design and my experiences as a landscape contractor, landscape architect, and educator. Graphics, planning, and design information have been combined in this single volume as a means of communicating their interrelationships in developing a design proposal. The case studies used illustrate the various graphic, planning, and design concepts relative to a residential site development. No matter what the scale or complexity of a proposal, an understanding of these concepts provides the necessary theoretical basis to communicate a design idea. In the thought sequence from ideas to drawings to development, graphics, planning, and design are only a means to make an idea reality.

The Cover Illustration

A residential landscape provides not only the setting or location for a residence, but an opportunity to physically and visually extend indoor activities outdoors. While sunlight, winds, and other climatic influences may limit the use of outdoor spaces, these same influences, if moderated, can be stimulating and enjoyable. Landscape design at the residential scale of development is an exciting focus of endeavor as each proposal relates to a specific site, residence, surrounding area, and client need. Residential landscape design is the selection of construction materials and plantings to furnish the site's "outdoor rooms."

As seen in the cover illustration, landscape development is a physical and visual extension of the structure and the client's activities. The outdoor spaces and uses are established by the location of adjoining interior rooms, and the functional benefits plantings, and the constructed features provide. The existing trees provide a frame and focus. The deck and planters define the limits of the active use of the space, while the ground plantings add visual interest and limit physical movement off the deck. The area is alive with the dynamics of seasonal change as evidenced by the various flowers, leaves, and textures of the plantings and reflects the changing patterns of sun, shade, and shadows. Comfortable chairs and client artwork further detail and personalize the space. The only design element missing in the scene is the client, the homeowner—the user of the space.

Acknowledgements

With the completion of this text, I would like to recog-
nize and thank everyone who has contributed to the content and
development of this endeavor. My appreciation and thanks are extended to those who encouraged me in the profession of landscape
architecture, my wife Harriet, my parents, and my in-laws, Mr. and
Mrs. William I. Smith. I also extend my thanks to Marion J. Wiswell,
J. R. Cline, Mrs. William Braker, Herbie Beyler, Alan and Barbara
Bennett, and Professors G. D. Coorts and I. Hillyer for their concern
and encouragement. To the numerous residential landscape design
clients that have trusted my judgment and expertise in the practice
of landscape design and to the many students and colleagues with
whom I have shared ideas and they their thoughts regarding landscape design, I send a special thanks.

For their review and direction during the manuscript's early
planning, I thank Professors William R. Nelson of the University of
Illinois and Will Hooker of North Carolina State University. For their
review of the intermediate manuscript, I thank Thomas C. Wang at
the University of Michigan, John Wott at the University of Washing-

Acknowledgements

ton, and Jim Perry at Mississippi State University. And for their review of the final manuscript, I thank Norman Booth of Ohio State University and again John Wott of the University of Washington.

For their constant encouragement and counsel, I thank Herbie Beyler, Ginger Smith, Dan Krall, and Leeta Hickman. To all the students who freely gave their projects as examples in the text, I extend my sincere appreciation. To the Ted Baker Group in Coral Gables, Florida, and Altums Landscaping and Eagle Creek Nurseries of Indianapolis, Indiana, my thanks for their contributions. Thanks go to Raymond Paul Strychalski and Thomas G. Kramer for sharing their skills in the development of some of the graphics. And to the production staff of Printing Services at Purdue, thanks for their cooperation and efficiency in the handling of the many blackline prints and PMTs. Special thanks are extended to Barbara J. Yeoman who typed all the drafts of the manuscript and to whom is due special recognition for her reading of "hieroglyphics," otherwise known as my handwriting. Lastly, I would like to thank the technical and production staff of Reston Publishing Company, especially Beth Eldred and Catherine Rossbach for their ever present advice and encouragement during the manuscript's development. Also thanks to Bob Nash for his initial direction and to Camelia Townsend for the final guidance in the production of this text.

A N INTRODUCTION TO LANDSCAPE DESIGN

ONE

*R*esidential landscape design

*R*esidential **landscape** and **landscape design** are **terms** often used to describe the setting, areas, developments, and activities associated with a home. Foundation plants were once and, in some instances, are still the only concern in a homeowner's mind. However, many changes are now occurring. Today's landscapes include more attached housing, and there is a need for (residential or home) sites that are functional besides being attractive. As homes and landscapes get smaller in response to increasing housing demands and increases in energy and construction costs, landscape designs are becoming extensions of indoor activities and functions. While increased numbers of decks and patios bring interior activities outdoors, shade trees protect exterior and interior spaces from the sun's heat and thus reduce cooling needs.

Landscape design should function as a space and activity definer within which the client and his or her personal needs determine the site's development. Landscape design is not an end unto itself, but a setting for homeowners to live, relax, and recreate. Landscape design is a logical thought process that combines landforms, vegetation, and constructed features into functional and attractive settings reflecting the site, surroundings, climate, and client needs.

The residential landscape is usually considered to be the physical and visual areas surrounding a single-family home. Opportunities for relaxation, recreation, and entertaining in home landscapes have not always been enjoyed as an extension of indoor activities. The concept of the "outdoor room" in site design evolved in the 1950s. The genius of a California landscape architect, Thomas Church, in conjunction with the homeowner's need for more usable space and the comfortable western climate of California, provided the impetus for this indoor/outdoor landscape garden concept (Laurie 1975, p. 45). Today, as we evaluate the design concepts used in residential landscapes, we realize they have changed dramatically from the large villas and lavish landscape gardens of the nineteenth century (Figure 1-1). Changing lifestyles, more informal entertaining preferences, smaller households, and a need to conserve natural and energy resources have influenced the forms and functions of housing and its associated landscapes. More homeowners are now aware that the orientation of a site, the residence's design, and the surrounding influences affect the utility and comfort of use areas both inside and out (Figures 1-2 and 1-3).

Site development and landscape design concepts have changed from an era when landscaping was considered as an art form and status symbol to current times when residential site design must provide for a more functional and attractive home environment (Figure 1-4). Rather than design proposals that show the diversity and complexity of available plantings and construction materials, today's landscape designs reflect more simple schemes that use the site, its surroundings, climatic influences, and client needs as design determinants. Just as the landscape designers of the past proposed plans which suited the environment and social context in which they practiced, today's landscape designers must apply new technologies, practices, and considerations.

For the landscape designer, the residential design process includes the planning and design of landscape plantings and construction features. The designer also educates the client as to the functional and aesthetic benefits of a planned site development. As shown in Figure 1-5, the designer sees the planting quite differently from the homeowner. Homeowners typically have limited perceptions of landscape design because the aesthetic benefits of plants in site development and landscape design are more easily recognized than the functional benefits they provide. Shading, reducing glare, buffering winds, and directing breezes are some of the functional benefits plants can provide in almost any landscape proposal.

A site inventory and a site analysis are used to identify and define the functional and aesthetic considerations of landscape design. A *site inventory* identifies the site's existing features, and a *site analysis* evaluates the site's limits and opportunities for development. The site, its surroundings, and climate, client's needs, physical room relationships, and the physical and visual character of the residence within its surroundings are design determinants identified through design.

Landscape design based upon site and client considerations has long been accepted by landscape architects as a means to propose functional, aesthetic, and buildable landscape developments. Homeowners and novice designers often overlook site and client considerations because their experience and knowledge often are in the design of plant and construction materials rather than in planning.

FIGURE 1-1

The Tower Grove country house, built in 1851 in St. Louis, Mo., is an example of the estate or villa type development. Historically, this style was the focus of landscape architectural planning and design.

FIGURE 1-2(a)

In this rear yard space, the deck, overhead lattice, and permanent benches provide an additional outdoor living space adjoining the living/dining area, as seen in Figure 1-2b. (Designer: Gregory W. Schlink)

FIGURE 1-2(b)
Living/dining area. (Designer: Raymond Paul Strychalski)

FIGURE 1-3

The space adjoining a residence can serve many functions. The sun, breezes, sights, and sounds that are associated with outdoor space make the landscape a dynamic place to recreate, relax, and entertain. (Designer: Raymond Paul Strychalski)

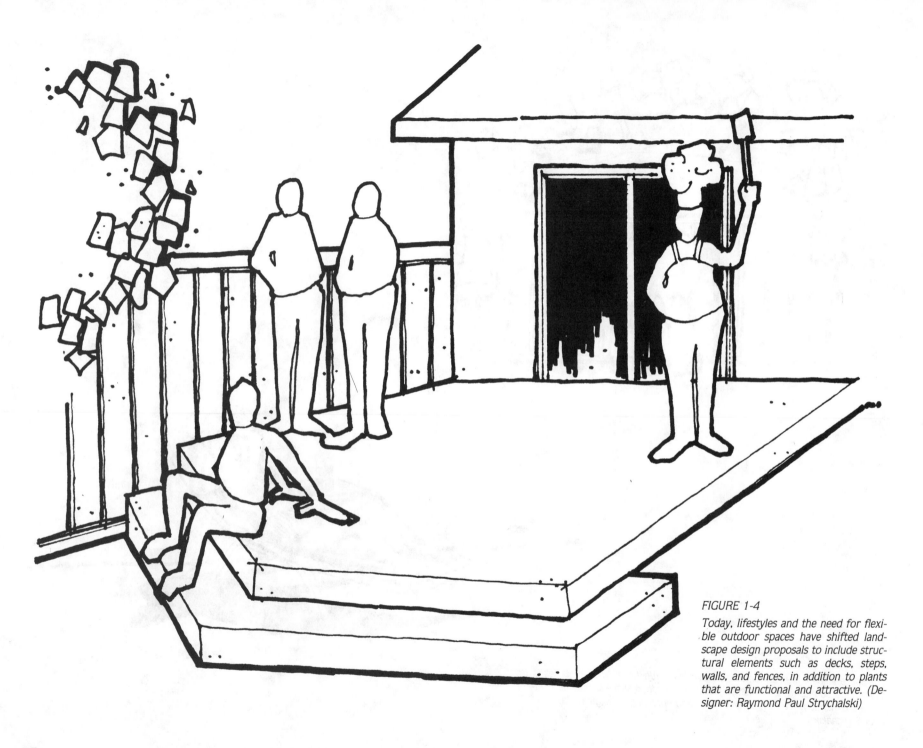

FIGURE 1-4

Today, lifestyles and the need for flexible outdoor spaces have shifted landscape design proposals to include structural elements such as decks, steps, walls, and fences, in addition to plants that are functional and attractive. (Designer: Raymond Paul Strychalski)

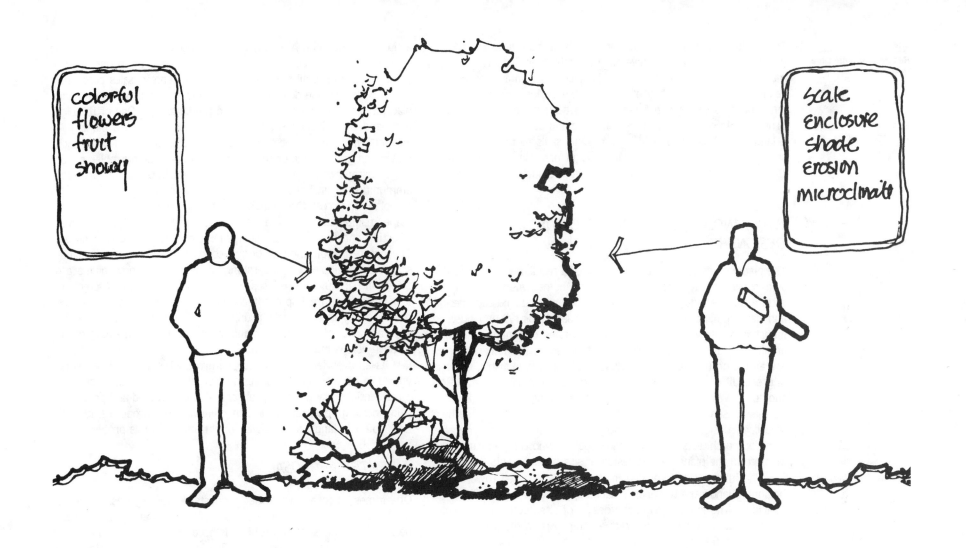

FIGURE 1-5

When evaluating a site and in the selection of plantings, the designer must adhere to the client's needs, in addition to the underlying principles and elements found in good compositions. (Designer: Raymond Paul Strychalski)

The designer may understand the individual materials but lack an understanding of how to develop them into a unified site development (Figure 1-6). The practice of landscape design as a profession requires an understanding of the site, the region, client, and planning concepts to develop functional and aesthetic landscape design proposals. In concert with these planning and design considerations, a landscape designer should have graphic skills to record and present existing site information and design proposals. Graphics help the designer to visualize and communicate ideas to clients and themselves.

WHY LANDSCAPE DESIGN AND LANDSCAPE DESIGNERS?

The planning, design, and development of a residential landscape design involves many different people, from homeowners to landscape architects. The industry that has developed around landscape design and development is often called the "green industry" or landscape industry. Nurserymen, sales people, landscape designers, landscape architects, landscape contractors, and landscape maintenance firms are all integral parts of this industry. Within this industry, there is a great difference of opinion concerning what landscape design should be. While each specialty area has a definite expertise, there is no real consensus as to the goals and objectives to be satisfied by a landscape design. To add to the confusion, many states register landscape architects and thus legally define who can and cannot be involved in the planning and design of site developments.

The information provided in this text is oriented towards the beginning landscape designer. A *landscape designer* is defined as an individual who is engaged in the design of site development involving minimal landform design, with an emphasis on site plantings and constructed features. According to this general definition, a landscape designer can be a landscape architecture student, a landscape contractor, or a semi-pro homeowner. Thus, *landscape design* is an activity that involves the range of professionals in the landscape industry (Figure 1-7). Even though specific areas within the landscape industry do not propose designs, they produce, sell, and service landscapes, and an awareness of design is important at all levels.

At the production end of the landscape industry, knowledge of landscape design provides background to select, produce, and merchandise plant materials that are desirable for use in site development. With trends toward reduced maintenance and smaller sites, ground covers and native plants are increasingly more important in a site's development. Also, smaller sites necessitate a range of small trees rather than trees that mature with forest proportions. At the point of sales in retail nurseries and garden centers, sales personnel can provide valuable design assistance in identifying the cultural and placement requirements for plants in the landscape. One of the biggest landscape problems caused by novices is placing a plant in a location where it cannot survive and mature. Spacing a plant such that it can grow is one of the major landscape design problems. For the landscape contractor, knowledge of landscape design provides ammunition against the concept that landscape design is exclusively the planting across the foundation of a home. Lastly, for the landscape maintenance firms, an awareness of landscape design gives direction and focus to the management of plants once established. The greatest application of design concepts, in the case of a landscape, is developing an understanding of why and how plants are placed in particular site spaces. For example, uses such as screening and enclosures are important components of a design but can be destroyed by inappropriate pruning. Also, an understanding of the natural habits of growth of plants assists in the maintaining of attractive versus manicured plants.

As an overview of the concepts, procedures, and techniques involved in developing typical residential landscape design proposals, a residential entry planting proposal will be discussed and presented using basic graphic techniques. In reviewing the proposals, identify how you as a landscape designer might approach this problem.

AN ENTRY PROPOSAL

Oftentimes when a homeowner requests design services, the focus of the plan that is evolved centers on the main entry of the residence. Thus, this specific problem is used as an introduction to the planning, design, and graphic considerations used in developing a landscape design proposal.

The Problem

The site includes a small home on a narrow property adjoining a four-lane, one-way street. The 30-year-old plus home had been purchased by its residents as their "first" home. In their request for a design proposal, they indicated a desire for a plan that could be phased over five years. Their design objectives were to create a more inviting entry, screen the street from the living room views, and break away from the concept of a typical foundation planting.

FIGURE 1-6

The landscape designer has to understand design and the external conditions necessary for plant growth before a scheme is proposed. (Designer: Raymond Paul Strychalski)

Minnesota

North Carolina

Maryland

Indiana

Arizona

FIGURE 1-7

In these five residential entry designs, the settings created reflect the client's preferences, site location and regional conditions. Each entry has been designed to be aesthetically pleasing and functional. Plant material reflect the regional conditions of nature, vegetation, climate and construction materials.

As can be seen in Figure 1-8a, the existing site conditions were inventoried and used as the basis for design recommendations and proposals. A separate site evaluation is also shown as a basis for development of the final design proposals (Figure 1-8b). At this time, design process is not fully defined except as a logical thought process. Chapter 8 includes an explanation of design process with case study examples using the process in Chapters 11, 12, and 13.

Site Inventory and Analysis

When completing a site survey, slides or photographs help define the physical site, the residence, and surroundings in addition to plans and notes. Slides taken during the on-site visit not only help to refresh or identify site areas forgotten, but can be used for sketching elevations, etc., of design proposals. When slides are taken, they can be projected onto a sheet of paper so that the basic outlines of the residence and site features can be traced. Then, as the proposal develops, the additions of plants and other features can be sketched in. Figures 1-9 (a) and (b) show how a slide can be traced to produce a line drawing.

The actual site inventory information that should be reviewed and recorded during an on-site visit is as follows. En route to the site, mentally note the neighborhood character of architectural styles and landscape as a basis of evaluating the existing conditions of the site. Upon arrival at the site, determine what are primary versus secondary approaches to the residence. This is helpful when aligning the actual proposal you develop. Review the site's boundaries with the client. An assumed property line may cause problems later in the design process. While recording actual site dimensions and the location of fixed features, such as the house, walks, walls, and so forth, list any questions that arise for discussion later. For instance, if the entry walk is narrow or cracked, question the client as to replacement and/or relocation options. Review the site's landform and define level and sloping areas. Landforms not only affect a site's use, but its surface drainage. If retaining walls are failing or drainage problems are noted, discuss these basic elements while on site.

After the fixed elements are located, next locate existing planting relative to measurements taken already. Locating a tree relative to the corner of the house or sidewalk is easier and less confusing than referencing it back to a property line. While locating plants, also note the approximate spread, trunk diameter, species, and condition. These considerations can be helpful later when you design

FIGURE 1-8(a)

Photographs of existing site conditions in conjunction with plans or maps help define and record the base information prior to the development of a design proposal. As seen in the photos, a viewer passing by has constantly changing vantage, as does the resident looking out into the landscape. Photos not only record existing features, but can be used to outline changes to be proposed. (Designer: Gregory M. Pierceall)

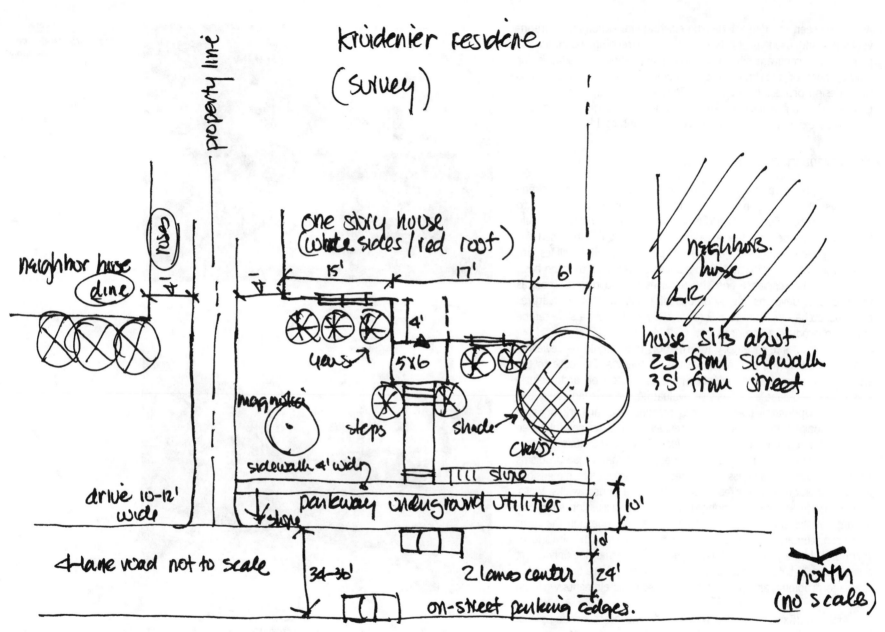

kruidenier residene
(survey)

one story house
(white sides / red roof)

neighbor huse
dine

roses

15'   17'   6'

4'

5x6

years

magnolia

steps   shade

cross.

sidewalk 4' width

drive 10-12' wide

slope

parkway underground utilities.

neighbors.
huse
LR

house sits about
25' from sidewalk
35' from street

10'

10'

1 lane road not to scale

34-36'

2 lanes center   24'

on-street parking edges.

north
(no scale)

FIGURE 1-8(b)

If a site or plot plan is not available, grid paper is often used to identify existing features that may be included in the landscape design and development. After the on-site inventory, these rough field notes are refined into a scaled drawing. (Designer: Gregory M. Pierceall)

with or consider relocation of existing vegetation. Besides the record of information, try to determine how a plant may contribute or detract from the site. If a deciduous tree is located to the south of a residence, try to determine if it can provide or has the potential to provide shade in summer. If an evergreen tree were in the same location, it may not provide shade to cool the house in summer and may block valuable sun in the winter. Take note of any existing plants that have the potential of being litter problems; for example, any plants that have branches which break easily in winter, fruit that litters or disease and insect problems. Existing vegetation is one of the important inventory elements to review because these plants are the basic elements that help create spaces and subspaces within a site in conjunction with landforms and constructed features.

After the landform, fixed features, and vegetation have been defined, an inventory of views into and out from the site are recorded. Views are important in understanding how people see and move with the site and residence. Even though the landscape is separated from interior spaces by walls, we visually and physically relate interior rooms to the outdoors through windows and doors. Site development considers both views off site looking in and interior views looking out. At the entry area, the primary view is the door. When approaching the site as a guest, this is what you are looking for, while in the backyard the usual primary views are related to activities within the space. In regions where the natural landscape is more dramatic or evident (mountainous areas or valleys), a visual link between the site and regional features may also be desirable.

In conjunction with visual movement and site design, physical movement is important as well. Access for autos, within and off the site, is also an inventory consideration. Primary access onto the site is usually associated with vehicular access from the street. Access points also may include pedestrians moving from the sidewalk onto the site. An evaluation of the connection of these access points to the entry and rear yard is desirable. The primary entry walk would be to the front door. It should be at least 4' wide and of a permanent surface for safety and ease of maintenance. A secondary walk may include access from the drive to the rear yard. This link is normally related to the garage end of the house to provide easy movement of supplies from drive and garage to the rear yard. If the property has a rear alley or garage access to the rear yard, this secondary connection may not be needed. Through definition of existing or desirable physical movement on the site, the location of plantings and surfacings can better be determined.

After the physical and visual site considerations are recorded, an evaluation of the site's surroundings and determination of climatic influences are noted. While a site's surroundings are not part of the actual design, adjoining plantings or constructed features can influence the design proposal. Existing shade trees can influence the cultural situations on neighboring sites. Fences, walls, or structures can impact the feeling of enclosure and establish edges that influence design decisions.

Parallel to the site inventory, a client inventory is completed to understand the client's needs, priorities, perceptions, and preferences. During this discussion stage, the designer develops an understanding of the needs to be satisfied and the impact of physical limits of the site has on the activities desired. After the client's needs, often called the *design program,* are established, an evaluation of the site inventory data can proceed. From this analysis, the designer determines the opportunities and limitations of the site situation relative to the client's desires.

FIGURE 1-9(a)

While photos help define what is existing on a site and provide a record of this inventory, line drawings [Figure 1-9(b)] are often used to show proposed changes.

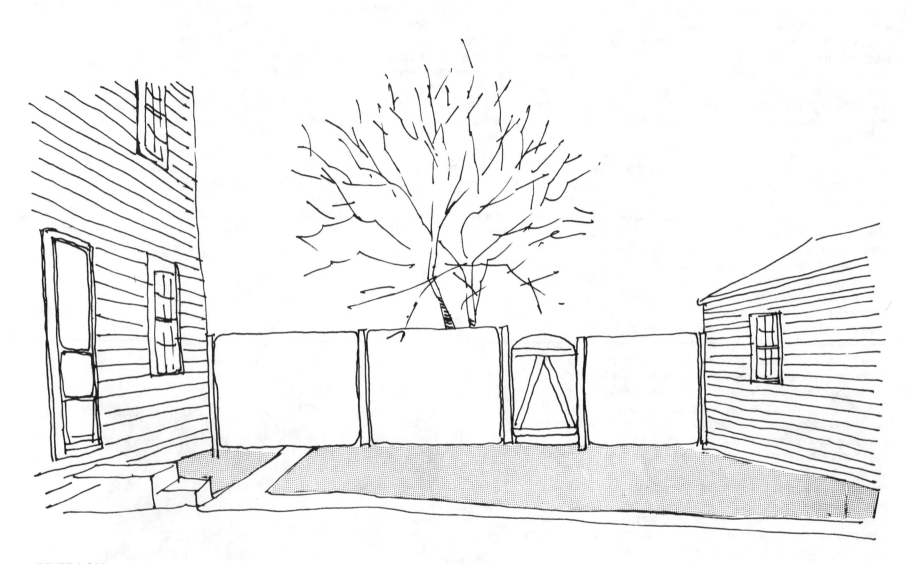

FIGURE 1-9(b)

In this line drawing, the photo showing existing site conditions as seen in Figure 1-9a in the form of a slide was projected onto paper and the basic lines traced to provide an outline for the design proposal. This method of sketching saves times and is easier than constructing a technical perspective drawing. For the average residential design proposal, a simple sketch such as this is adequate to present design ideas. (Designer: Gregory M. Pierceall)

The Site and Clients

The existing main entry on the north side of the house includes a planting of seven small Japanese yews, one small star magnolia, and a mature Japanese lilac tree of medium size. The ground surface is in turf, and the ground slopes slightly towards the sidewalk and street. The public sidewalk parallel to the house is separated from the street by a wide grassed parkway which serves as the right-of-way for underground utilities—gas, electricity, and water. The primary guest entry walk is the one that presently exists. It runs directly to the front door. This entry sequence includes two steps at the public sidewalk edge and four steps up to the stoop. Then an additional step is required from the stoop to reach the interior's finished floor. These level changes add up to seven steps. With each step 6" high, the interior floor is approximately 3.5' higher than the public sidewalk.

Any design proposals should evaluate these level changes because they affect a visitor's approach to the entry and also define how views will be affected as the residents look out towards the street. Because these level variations, both inside and out, influence views and access while entering and leaving the residence, the entry area steps could use simplification and screening plants. With the views from inside the house being elevated, the perspective of traffic and residences across the four-lane street is greater. Any designs proposed should consider the need to create privacy and enclosure for the interiors from the street traffic and neighbors. The drive access to the garage is to the east of the residence and is shared with the adjoining residence. To the west, the residences are of similar scale and style having typical lawns and foundation plantings.

The clients are both professional people with active schedules; thus, design solutions should provide an opportunity for reduced maintenance after the establishment time required for new plantings. No budget limitation was established at the design time, yet this does not mean the proposals recommended should not be realistic in terms of the conditions or design situation. Budget is a factor in most design situations. While working within a budget, do not try to develop the entire site on a minimal amount of resources. By planning the entire scheme, plantings can be phased and will result in a designed landscape, not a scattering of plants. For this client, the overall planting and construction concepts are most important. As a budget and the availability of materials are defined, a phasing schedule and selection of plant sizes and materials for the actual installment can be determined.

The Design Objectives

The entry proposals included are illustrations of how four landscape architecture design students interpreted this design problem. The examples are concepts of plantings and landscape construction that could occur. Each of the proposals includes a reduced plan of the existing conditions rather than the site inventory and analysis shown. The proposals are site specific and reflect the regional influences of climate, plant availability, and construction materials. If the same proposals were developed in a different region of the country, they would reflect the inherent site, surroundings, and local climatic variations. A site's microclimate (the climatic variations on site), the interplay of sun, winds, shadow patterns and local landforms, soil types and plant species and construction materials influence design proposals. As to other visual considerations of design proposals, regional differences of style, building materials, colors, and plants available further influence the overall types, textures, and forms of plant and construction materials developed in a design.

Each example included has attempted to address the need for a more physically and visually unified entry. Some planting masses would be desirable to the northeast corner of the entry to separate the windows and entry from the views of the street. Their need is for better primary access and secondary access from the public sidewalk and driveway where the residents or guests may park and have a more direct access to the front door. Elimination of the turf between the house and sidewalk to create a courtyard-type space is desirable. This would visually extend views and break up the symmetry of the existing entry.

Because the entry is on the north side of the house, it is shaded somewhat in the winter by the house and is colder in the winter due to the predominant northerly winter winds. Due to the limited space and the existing Japanese lilac tree to the northwest of the site, no evergreen plantings are possible as a windbreak for winter winds. If the space had been larger, an evergreen buffer could have been included to modify the cold northerly winds and provide some separation from the street.

The Proposals

The first proposal uses diagonals as a theme to break the rectangular character of the site and residence (Figure 1-10). The diagonals also relate to the view a guest might have moving west on the one-way street. The mass planting of small, multitrunked trees and evergreen ground cover provides a focus and screen for the living

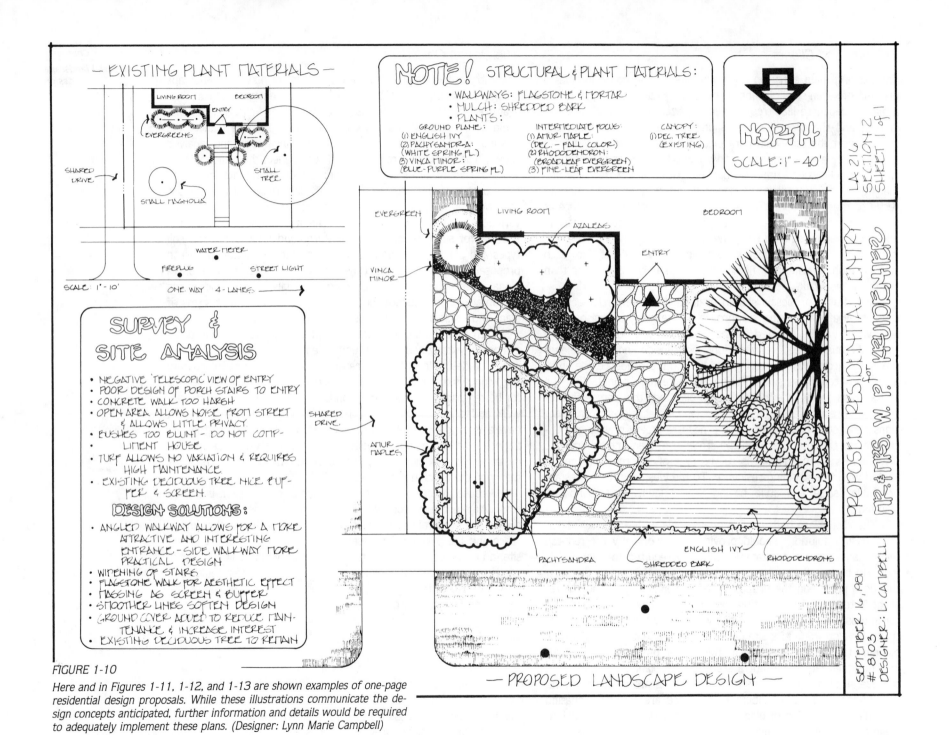

– EXISTING PLANT MATERIALS –

LIVING ROOM | BEDROOM

ENTRY

EVERGREENS

SHARED DRIVE

SMALL TREE

SMALL MAGNOLIA

WATER METER

FIREPLUG | STREET LIGHT

SCALE: 1" = 10'

ONE-WAY 4-LANES

NOTE! STRUCTURAL & PLANT MATERIALS:
- WALKWAYS: FLAGSTONE & MORTAR
- MULCH: SHREDDED BARK
- PLANTS:

GROUND PLANE:
(1) ENGLISH IVY
(2) PACHYSANDRA:
  (WHITE SPRING FL.)
(3) VINCA MINOR:
  (BLUE-PURPLE SPRING FL)

INTERMEDIATE FOCUS:
(1) AMUR MAPLE:
  (DEC. - FALL COLOR)
(2) RHODODENDRON:
  (BROADLEAF EVERGREEN)
(3) FINE-LEAF EVERGREEN

CANOPY:
(1) DEC. TREE
  (EXISTING)

NORTH

SCALE: 1" = 40'

EVERGREEN | LIVING ROOM | BEDROOM

AZALEAS

ENTRY

VINCA MINOR

AMUR MAPLES

SHARED DRIVE

SURVEY & SITE ANALYSIS

- NEGATIVE 'TELESCOPIC' VIEW OF ENTRY
- POOR DESIGN OF PORCH STAIRS TO ENTRY
- CONCRETE WALK TOO HARSH
- OPEN AREA ALLOWS NOISE FROM STREET & ALLOWS LITTLE PRIVACY
- BUSHES TOO BLUNT – DO NOT COMPLIMENT HOUSE
- TURF ALLOWS NO VARIATION & REQUIRES HIGH MAINTENANCE
- EXISTING DECIDUOUS TREE NICE BUFFER & SCREEN.

DESIGN SOLUTIONS:
- ANGLED WALKWAY ALLOWS FOR A MORE ATTRACTIVE AND INTERESTING ENTRANCE – SIDE WALKWAY MORE PRACTICAL DESIGN
- WIDENING OF STAIRS
- FLAGSTONE WALK FOR AESTHETIC EFFECT
- MASSING AS SCREEN & BUFFER
- SMOOTHER LINES SOFTEN DESIGN
- GROUND COVER ADDED TO REDUCE MAINTENANCE & INCREASE INTEREST
- EXISTING DECIDUOUS TREE TO RETAIN

PACHYSANDRA | SHREDDED BARK | ENGLISH IVY | RHODODENDRONS

– PROPOSED LANDSCAPE DESIGN –

PROPOSED RESIDENTIAL ENTRY
for
MRS. W. P. KREIDEMIER

SEPTEMBER 16, 1981
8103
DESIGNER: L. CAMPBELL

FIGURE 1-10

Here and in Figures 1-11, 1-12, and 1-13 are shown examples of one-page residential design proposals. While these illustrations communicate the design concepts anticipated, further information and details would be required to adequately implement these plans. (Designer: Lynn Marie Campbell)

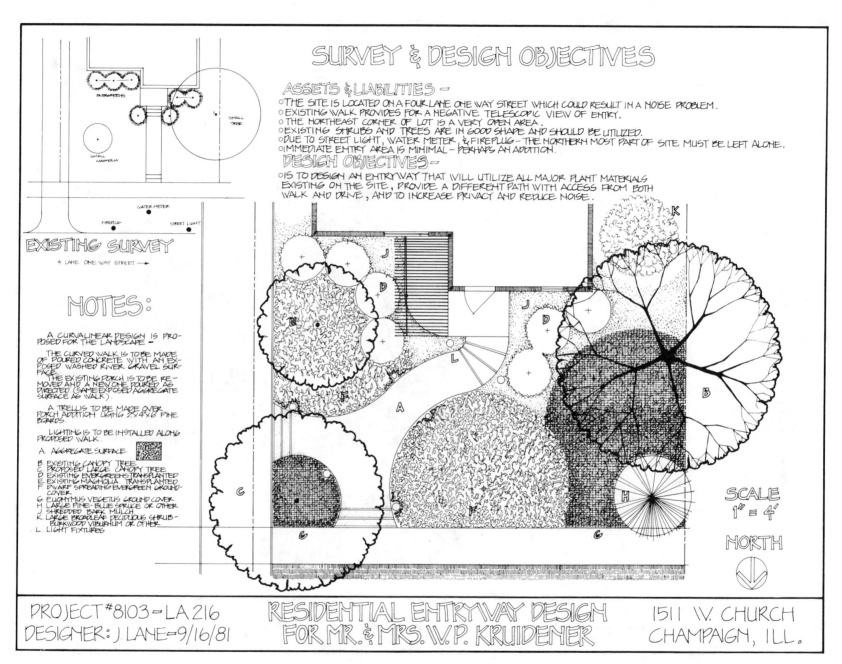

SURVEY & DESIGN OBJECTIVES

ASSETS & LIABILITIES –

- THE SITE IS LOCATED ON A FOUR LANE ONE WAY STREET WHICH COULD RESULT IN A NOISE PROBLEM.
- EXISTING WALK PROVIDES FOR A NEGATIVE TELESCOPIC VIEW OF ENTRY.
- THE NORTHEAST CORNER OF LOT IS A VERY OPEN AREA.
- EXISTING SHRUBS AND TREES ARE IN GOOD SHAPE AND SHOULD BE UTILIZED.
- DUE TO STREET LIGHT, WATER METER, & FIREPLUG – THE NORTHERN MOST PART OF SITE MUST BE LEFT ALONE.
- IMMEDIATE ENTRY AREA IS MINIMAL – PERHAPS AN ADDITION.

DESIGN OBJECTIVES –

- IS TO DESIGN AN ENTRYWAY THAT WILL UTILIZE ALL MAJOR PLANT MATERIALS EXISTING ON THE SITE, PROVIDE A DIFFERENT PATH WITH ACCESS FROM BOTH WALK AND DRIVE, AND TO INCREASE PRIVACY AND REDUCE NOISE.

(inset, upper left)
EVERGREENS
SMALL TREE
SMALL MAGNOLIA
WATER METER
FIREPLUG
STREET LIGHT

EXISTING SURVEY

4 LANE ONE WAY STREET →

NOTES:

A CURVALINEAR DESIGN IS PROPOSED FOR THE LANDSCAPE –

THE CURVED WALK IS TO BE MADE OF POURED CONCRETE WITH AN EXPOSED WASHED RIVER GRAVEL SURFACE.

THE EXISTING PORCH IS TO BE REMOVED AND A NEW ONE POURED AS DIRECTED (SAME EXPOSED AGGREGATE SURFACE AS WALK).

A TRELLIS TO BE MADE OVER PORCH ADDITION USING 2 X 4 X 6 PINE BOARDS.

LIGHTING IS TO BE INSTALLED ALONG PROPOSED WALK.

A. AGGREGATE SURFACE
B. EXISTING CANOPY TREE
C. PROPOSED LARGE CANOPY TREE
D. EXISTING EVERGREENS TRANSPLANTED
E. EXISTING MAGNOLIA TRANSPLANTED
F. DWARF SPREADING EVERGREEN GROUND-COVER
G. EUONYMUS VEGETUS GROUND COVER
H. LARGE PINE – BLUE SPRUCE OR OTHER
J. SHREDDED BARK MULCH
K. LARGE BROADLEAF DECIDUOUS SHRUB – BURKWOOD VIBURNUM OR OTHER
L. LIGHT FIXTURES

SCALE
1" = 4'

NORTH

PROJECT #8103 – LA 216
DESIGNER: J. LANE – 9/16/81

RESIDENTIAL ENTRYWAY DESIGN FOR MR. & MRS. W.P. KRUIDENER

1511 W. CHURCH
CHAMPAIGN, ILL.

FIGURE 1-11
Design proposal. (Designer: John Lane)

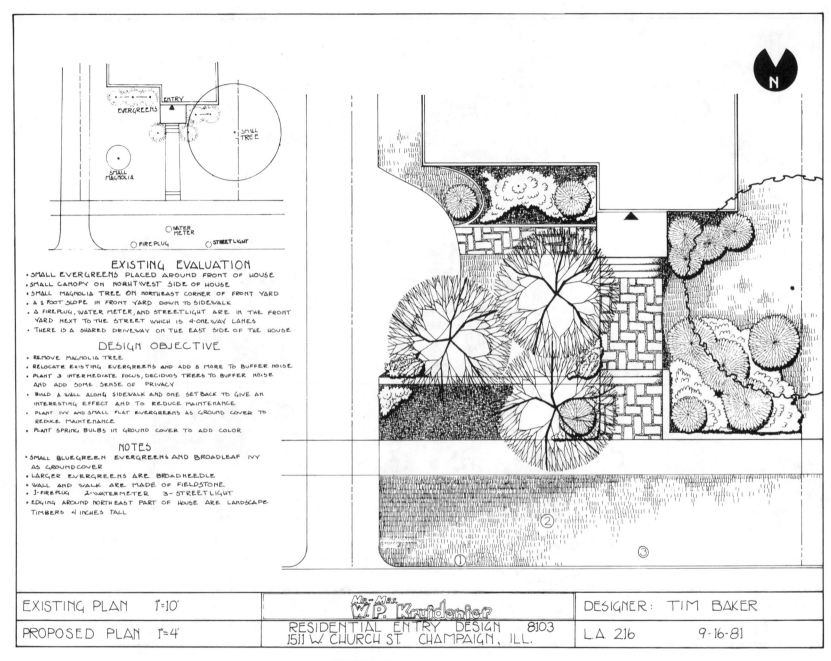

EXISTING EVALUATION

- SMALL EVERGREENS PLACED AROUND FRONT OF HOUSE
- SMALL CANOPY ON NORHTWEST SIDE OF HOUSE
- SMALL MAGNOLIA TREE ON NORTHEAST CORNER OF FRONT YARD
- A 1 FOOT SLOPE IN FRONT YARD DOWN TO SIDEWALK
- A FIREPLUG, WATER METER, AND STREETLIGHT ARE IN THE FRONT YARD NEXT TO THE STREET WHICH IS 4-ONE WAY LANES
- THERE IS A SHARED DRIVEWAY ON THE EAST SIDE OF THE HOUSE

DESIGN OBJECTIVE

- REMOVE MAGNOLIA TREE
- RELOCATE EXISTING EVERGREENS AND ADD 8 MORE TO BUFFER NOISE
- PLANT 3 INTERMEDIATE FOCUS, DECIDUOS TREES TO BUFFER NOISE AND ADD SOME SENSE OF PRIVACY
- BUILD A WALL ALONG SIDEWALK AND ONE SETBACK TO GIVE AN INTERESTING EFFECT AND TO REDUCE MAINTENANCE
- PLANT IVY AND SMALL FLAT EVERGREENS AS GROUND COVER TO REDUCE MAINTENANCE
- PLANT SPRING BULBS IN GROUND COVER TO ADD COLOR

NOTES

- SMALL BLUEGREEN EVERGREENS AND BROADLEAF IVY AS GROUNDCOVER
- LARGER EVERGREENS ARE BROADNEEDLE
- WALL AND WALK ARE MADE OF FIELDSTONE
- 1-FIREPLUG 2-WATERMETER 3- STREETLIGHT
- EDGING AROUND NORTHEAST PART OF HOUSE ARE LANDSCAPE TIMBERS 4 INCHES TALL

EXISTING PLAN 1"=10'	Mr. and Mrs. W.P. Kruidenier	DESIGNER: TIM BAKER
PROPOSED PLAN 1"=4'	RESIDENTIAL ENTRY DESIGN 8103 1511 W. CHURCH ST. CHAMPAIGN, ILL.	L.A. 216 9-16-81

FIGURE 1-12

Design proposal. (Designer: Tim Baker)

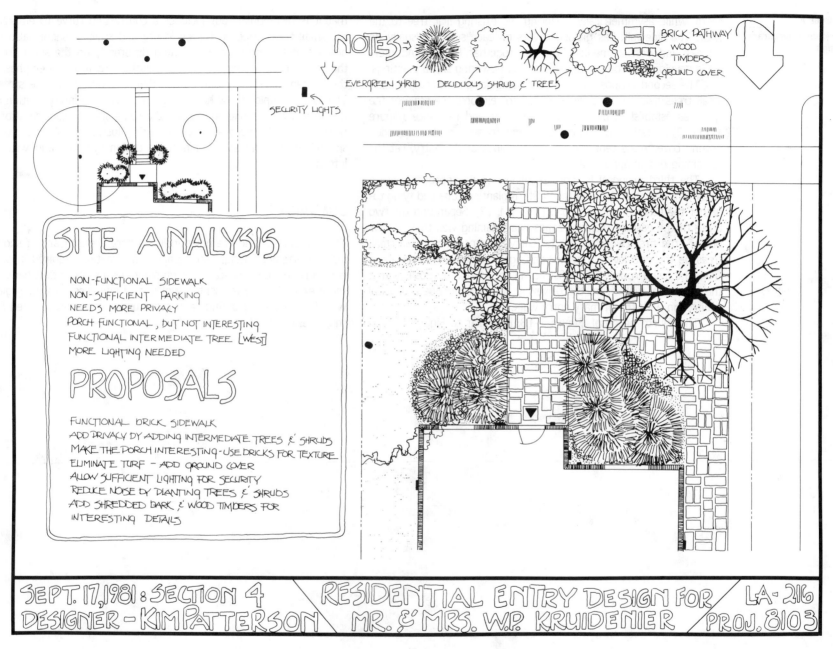

NOTES → EVERGREEN SHRUB   DECIDUOUS SHRUB & TREES

BRICK PATHWAY
WOOD TIMBERS
GROUND COVER

SECURITY LIGHTS

SITE ANALYSIS

NON-FUNCTIONAL SIDEWALK
NON-SUFFICIENT PARKING
NEEDS MORE PRIVACY
PORCH FUNCTIONAL, BUT NOT INTERESTING
FUNCTIONAL INTERMEDIATE TREE [WEST]
MORE LIGHTING NEEDED

PROPOSALS

FUNCTIONAL BRICK SIDEWALK
ADD PRIVACY BY ADDING INTERMEDIATE TREES & SHRUBS
MAKE THE PORCH INTERESTING - USE BRICKS FOR TEXTURE
ELIMINATE TURF - ADD GROUND COVER
ALLOW SUFFICIENT LIGHTING FOR SECURITY
REDUCE NOISE BY PLANTING TREES & SHRUBS
ADD SHREDDED BARK & WOOD TIMBERS FOR
INTERESTING DETAILS

SEPT. 17, 1981 : SECTION 4
DESIGNER - KIM PATTERSON

RESIDENTIAL ENTRY DESIGN FOR
MR. & MRS. W.P. KRUIDENIER

LA-216
PROJ. 8103

FIGURE 1-13
Design proposal. (Designer: Kimberly J. Patterson)

room, while asymmetrically balancing the existing lilac tree to the west. The sidewalk has ground covers on each side to visually tie the east and west segments of the yard together. Background interest is developed through the use of small flowering shrub plantings.

The second proposal uses a curvilinear design theme. Adjoining small trees next to the drive are used to reinforce the scale of the space as established by the size of the lot and residence (Figure 1-11). The design is somewhat symmetrical with the rounded ground cover mass centered on the terminus of the entry, yet the remaining design appears asymmetrical.

The third proposal is more rectilinear in its approach, with a small retaining wall defining the western planting zone and tying together the eastern planting zone (Figure 1-12). Separating the two levels of the eastern planting zones is a retaining wall that "grows out of" the first two steps in the entry sequence. The three small trees tie the two levels together and again screen the street views from the living room. One deficiency in this design proposal is that the secondary walk from the driveway does not provide a physical connection with the primary entry walk.

The fourth proposal, Figure 1-13, is similar to Figure 1-12 in that it is rectangular, but includes a contrasting curve to embrace the small tree proposed for enclosure and scale. It should also be noted that this proposal is oriented differently on the sheet from the other three proposals. This proposal is organized to emphasize the homeowners' view out, rather than the view from the street. The four examples show how design may differ in interpretation of theme and form while addressing the same site/use considerations. Besides exemplifying design schemes, the illustrations show a diversity of sheet organization, landscape design symbols, and written information.

SUMMARY

The illustrations and examples included here are a means of showing the planning, design, and graphic information required in proposing residential landscape design solutions. As you reflect back on these examples, try to identify which local influences in your region would modify the plantings and construction materials selected for these design situations.

Site design and the landscape industry

In practice, the landscape design process is initiated by the homeowner as a request for information and/or services relative to the development of his or her site. As a landscape designer, the information and services provided focus on the client, the site, its surroundings, and other conditions to develop an attractive and useful space. However, not all sites and situations can be designed to accommodate a client's needs or to maximize the desirable and minimize the adverse climatic, surrounding, or site influences. These factors should be considered when making site recommendations or proposals.

SITE DEVELOPMENT CONSIDERATIONS

As seen in the residential entry example in Chapter 1, landscape designers use a design method to record, evaluate, and organize the background information that is needed for a design proposal. Landscape designers need a design sequence that establishes a pathway or direction for the design and explanation of the why and how a

FIGURE 2-1

Typical residential patio area. This photo shows the round patio as it existed prior to the addition of the deck surface, trellis, and new fences. (Photo courtesy of P. Bennett)

landscape design develops. All too often homeowners and designers alike have more experience and knowledge of landscape plants and construction materials than they have of planning and design. This often results in a collection of plants and materials that may not be as attractive or useful as they could be.

Site planning, long the focus of landscape architects, includes the process of evaluating the relationships between a site, structures, people, and landscape plus the composition of landforms, vegetation, and constructed features. As mentioned in Chapter 1, Thomas Church, a prominent residential scale landscape architect of the 1950s, advocated that the landscape garden surrounding a residence should function as an extension of the interior spaces yet be responsive to surrounding and climatic influences. Church, in his design of residential sites, developed three sources of design forms for residential site proposals.

> The first consisted of human needs and the specific personal requirements and characteristics of the client. The second comprised an awareness and knowledge of the technology of materials, construction, and plants, including maintenance and a whole range of form determinants desired from the site conditions and quality. The third was a concern for the spatial expression, which would go beyond the mere satisfaction of requirements and into the realms of fine art (Laurie 1975, p. 45).

Parallel to Church's residential design theories, architectural design trends allowed more physical access to outdoor spaces. These landscape design concepts advocated some 30 years ago were accepted and utilized to design larger estates, homes and sites. In today's society, these same considerations are even more applicable for the development of the typical residential sites. It is the smaller homes and properties of today that can most benefit from application of these concepts that encourage indoor activities to extend into the outdoors. Figure 2-1 and 2-2 show a typical residential property and the increased utility and attractiveness that have resulted through design in the outdoor living area.

FIGURE 2-2

The new decking provides a more efficient entertaining area with less glare and a cooler surface than the concrete. The new fences provide privacy from neighbors, enclose an air conditioning unit, and help tie the deck and trellis elements together. (Photo courtesy of P. Bennett)

As established home sites are remodeled and new housing includes smaller units the changes in shapes, construction methods, and densities can provide new opportunities for the contributions of landscape design. The illusion of spaciousness created by integrating an interior with exterior spaces and the use of smaller plants and new construction features better provide homeowners with more useful and easier to maintain outdoor spaces. These smaller design situations also foster new opportunities for landscape designers and the landscape industry. Existing and new residential sites comprise most of the "landscape" we experience daily. The future of residential landscape design will not be solely in the design of estate gardens but in the design of small quality gardens and landscapes that will create useful and attractive outdoor spaces for people to live. As shown in Figure 2-3, the client needed a more inviting entry and an outdoor entertaining area. With the site's location at the end of a cul-de-sac, the two needs were combined into an entry terrace. The spaces provide both an inviting entry while servicing entertaining needs as an extension of the kitchen to the front of the house.

FIGURE 2-3(b)
The entry/entertaining area as seen from the driveway.

FIGURE 2-3(c)
The entry space as seen from the street.

FIGURE 2-3(a)
The before and after photos show how an entry space can be used as an entertaining area. Not all residential situations would be conducive to this type development. Remember that an entry should be developed considering a guest's and the homeowner's needs.

THE LANDSCAPE INDUSTRY

As a person interested in horticulture, landscape design, or landscape architecture, it is important to understand the specialties within the landscape industry. To best align personal interests and abilities with the appropriate career areas, an understanding of the expertise and knowledge required for each of the landscape professions is necessary. The residential landscape is planned, designed, installed, maintained, and serviced by the landscape industry. Landscape architect, designer, contractor, manager, salesperson, or nurseryman are a few of the professions in the landscape industry involved with the development of site landscapes.

Landscape design is a specialty area within the fields of landscape architecture and landscape contracting. As a means to define the similarities and differences between the practice of landscape architects and landscape designers, brief descriptions of each follow.

Landscape Architects

A *landscape architect* is a practitioner of the design profession of landscape architecture (Horticultural Research Institute 1971). *Landscape architecture* is the art of arranging land and the objects upon it for human use and beauty (H.R.I. 1971). A landscape architect's expertise is in the design of facilities on the land. As an example, a family planning to build a home might hire a landscape architect to make siting recommendations in locating a home, drive, walks, walls, and other construction or planting features on a site (*American Nurseryman*, DeTurk and Hamilton, June 1978).

In the formal education of a landscape architect, the primary objective is training in design process and as a consultant in site planning and landscape design. Landscape architects provide advice and recommendations to clients regarding site feasibility studies, design alternatives, and design solutions for a range of specific site situations and activities, not exclusively residential scale design. The *skills* required in the practice of landscape architecture include a competency in graphic communication, such as drafting, sketching, lettering, and rendering, and the composition of "graphic information." *Expertise* is required in planning and design processes for site development and information and in native and ornamental plants, soils, climate, and construction methods. *Knowledge* is needed in verbal and written presentation methods, as well as business practices associated with design professionals, including familiarity with contracts and project specification writing.

Training in landscape architecture may take four to five years depending on university requirements. Schools that do offer landscape architecture usually are accredited by the national ASLA. Attendance in an accredited program is often a requirement for practice and registration in many states. Registration or licensure is a legal definition of who can practice a specific profession, in this case landscape architecture. Qualifications are determined by specific requirements regarding training, education, apprenticeship, examination, or a combination of these. Holding a license represents a legal right to engage in an activity otherwise prohibited by law. There are two main types of licensure laws: (1) a *Practice Act* which defines what work can be performed by a qualified landscape architect; and (2) a *Title Act* which states that the title of Landscape Architect may not be used by persons not qualified or without a license (*ASLA Members Handbook* 1983). For further information regarding an individual state's licensure requirements, contact your local ASLA state chapter or the National Headquarters of the American Society of Landscape Architects. See Appendix 2 for added details.

Many institutions may provide landscape architecture or landscape design courses yet may not be accredited by the American Society of Landscape Architects (ASLA) to offer a landscape architectural degree. Selection of an institution should then relate to your eventual professional goals for practice. Further information regarding L.A. schools, degrees, and accreditation can be received by writing the ASLA. See Appendix 1 for further address information.

LANDSCAPE ARCHITECTURE PRACTICE. The practice of landscape architecture can be on an individual basis or as a team member in a private company or public/governmental agency. Landscape architects may be generalists and perform a variety of services from residential landscape design to larger scale site planning proposals such as commercial, institutional, or statewide projects. Other avenues available in landscape architecture include urban or regional planning, and design/build firms which focus on the design and installation of site developments (Figure 2-4). Teaching is also a specialty area within the profession of landscape architecture. With the intense training and limited number of practitioners, few landscape architects concentrate solely on residential scale landscape design. The cost of design versus the scale of design also makes some landscape architects too costly for homeowners. In the same respect, some landscape architects enjoy the detail of residential design and are affordable (Figures 2-5 and 2-6).

FIGURE 2-4(a)

Main entry to the residence. The landscape development shown in photos (a) to (f) has been designed and installed by a design-build firm. Design-build landscape firms provide comprehensive services including design and implementation. The firm may employ landscape architects and landscape contractors and often produces much of their own plant materials. One advantage of a design-build firm is the ease of communication between design and development. After installation, the design-build firm may also maintain the landscape, which further complements the earlier services provided. (Photos courtesy of Altums Landscape Design, Indianapolis, IN).

FIGURE 2-4(b)

Separate service entry screened from the main entry area.

FIGURE 2-4(c)

Access to the rear yard is provided by a stepping stone path that is defined by lush ground covers and shrub planting.   (Continued)

FIGURE 2-4(d)

Hard to mow edges or planting bed areas are defined by planting edges and mulched in pea gravel or hardwood barks.

FIGURE 2-4(e)

This traditional style residence is complemented by curving beds of ground covers and a simple foundation planting.

FIGURE 2-4(f)

The existing multi-trunked tree has been integrated into the planting through the use of a wooden tree wall and ground covers.

FIGURE 2-5

Often site development requires constructed features such as walks, walls, and fences. In landscape design, these fabricated features are known as site structures.

FIGURE 2-6

Landscape design requires an understanding of plants, their cultural requirements, and site applications, as both aesthetic and functional elements within a landscape.

Landscape Designers

While landscape design can be an emphasis within landscape architecture, it is also associated with the nursery, garden center, and contracting or maintenance professions. *Landscape design,* as defined by the Horticultural Research Institute, is a creative environmental problem-solving process to organize external space and attain an optimum balance of natural factors and human needs (H.R.I. 1971). To the landscape architect, this definition may translate into the selection of components, materials and plants, and their combinations as solutions to limited and well-defined site problems (Laurie 1975). To a landscape designer, one who recommends the selection and location of plants and limited construction features in the landscape, it may simply be the functional and attractive composition of plants and constructed elements in small-scale situations, including residential and commercial sites (Figures 2-7 and 2-8). When used in this text landscape design relates to plant and constructed landscape features for small site developments. At the residential scale of design, the primary design focus is towards the proposal of plantings and constructed features such as pavements, light wooden construction, and site accessories (Figure 2-9). Related to

FIGURE 2-7

Fences and walls can be used in landscape design to provide screening or enclosure. They have the advantage of being immediately effective. If plants are used, screening and enclosure are dependent on the plants' growth and development. (Photos courtesy of Chicago Botanic Garden)

(a)

FIGURE 2-8

Overhead trellis areas can be used to provide shade instead of or in conjunction with shade trees or vines. Early in the development of a site, a trellis and fences can provide shade and enclosure while plants are being established. These structural features can also help extend the building construction materials into the landscape and provide a more unified relationship between building and landscape. (Photo (a) courtesy of Chicago Botanic Garden; Photo (b) courtesy of University Green, Houston, TX)

(b)

(Before)

(After)

FIGURE 2-9

Topography, the lay of the land, is a basic consideration in any site's development. In this before and after example, the slope was retained by a timber retaining wall that also serves as a walkway. (Photos courtesy of May-Mak Plant Farm, Raleigh, NC)

the proper establishment of plants and installation of constructed features is landform development or finish grading. *Finish grading* is the final manipulation of the site's landform for proper drainage and base of landscape features. Since the landscape designer is likely to be selected for his/her talents in planting design, site grading may be handled by a landscape architect or a general contractor (Figure 2-10).

Landscape design or landscape contracting courses are available in many two-year and four-year degree programs within horticulture and/or applied plant science departments. Selection of an institution and degree program should satisfy an individual's interests and needs yet provide the requirements necessary to practice after graduation.

Landscape design and/or contracting should include training in the identification and culture of woody native and ornamental plants as well as herbaceous materials. Knowledge of the ecological interaction of plants, relative topographic regions, and site environments as they apply to landscape design and plant establishment is also im-

portant. Courses in construction practices, horticulture, and business procedures may also be included in a designated degree program (Figures 2-11 and 2-12).

Education and experience go hand-in-hand whether one's interests are in landscape architecture, landscape design, or landscape horticulture; thus, work study is also a desirable complement to formal training in whatever interest area one pursues.

Landscape designers are often also salespersons, nurserymen, and/or maintenance people but offer design services as well. One potential conflict that can occur when designing, as well as installing, selling, and servicing landscape proposals, is that the design proposal becomes a means to install, sell, and maintain rather than solely an extension of the site, surroundings, and client needs. The services provided by landscape designers and other landscape professionals should be consistent with a code of ethics, as a means of providing the professional services without conflicts of interest. Because of the wide variety of services requested, few landscape designers specialize specifically in design.

FIGURE 2-10

While landforms influence drainage and access, they can also be sculpted to create or define spaces and activities within a site. In the photos shown, the outdoor entertaining area is defined by the gradual slopes carved from a previously unattractive and linear cut out from the house. (Photos courtesy of P. E. DeTurk)

FIGURE 2-11

Landscape design as an activity and space definer often includes the proposal of "outdoor rooms." In this situation, the transition between a family room and the rear yard is made more functional and attractive through a grade-level deck. The posts seen were later developed into a screen for privacy from adjoining neighbors. (Photos courtesy of E. Beyler)

(a)

FIGURE 2-12

Landscape design is the proposal of plantings and construction features for a specific site and client. While development may occur in stages, as seen in photo (a), the designer has to understand the relationship of this single area to the site as a whole, as seen in photo (b). (Photos courtesy of A. Bennett)

(b)

Associated Professional Organizations

Many landscape industry organizations are available to provide information directly related to your professional or personal interests. Included is a partial listing of professional landscape industry organizations; their addresses can be found in Appendix 1.

AAN   American Association of Nurserymen

ALCA   Associated Landscape Contractors of America

ASLA   American Society of Landscape Architects

CELA   Council of Educators in Landscape Architecture

IFLA   International Federation of Landscape Architects

LAF   Landscape Architecture Foundation

LIAC   Landscape Industry Advisory Council

NLA   National Landscape Association

Industry Publications

The landscape industry is also serviced by publications which provide current information concerning trends, products, and other subject matter relative to landscape development. A listing of some of these industry publications follows; addresses can be found in Appendix 1.

Landscape Architecture   An international magazine of regional and land planning, landscape design, construction, and management. Published six times per year.

Garden Design   A quarterly magazine that reflects the diversity of residential landscape architecture and design. This is an offshoot of *Landscape Architecture Magazine.*

Landscape and Turf   A publication that focuses on the landscape industry. Included are planning, design, maintenance, and establishment aspects of site development. Published seven times per year.

American Nurseryman   A bimonthly publication concerning plant production, maintenance, and development areas within the landscape industry.

Weeds, Trees, and Turf   A monthly publication that emphasizes the production, installation, and maintenance of landscapes.

SUMMARY

Landscape design, which involves professionals in landscape architecture and the landscape industry, must include concepts of planning and design, with graphic skills to develop site design proposals that are functional and attractive. Landscape design can be an idea, a drawn plan, or the actual developed site. As you read about residential landscape graphics, planning, and design, put the information in perspective relative to the applications you see in your selected area of interest. The end result of any residential landscape design should be a quality space for its resident. Residential design is responsive to the site, its surroundings, and client in providing a useful and attractive area for both outdoor and indoor enjoyment.

*G*RAPHIC MATERIALS AND CONCEPTS

TWO

*G*raphic equipment, materials, procedures, and processes

Skillful graphic communications are the result of a designer's proficiency in the use of available graphic tools, materials, and reproduction processes. Graphics are used by designers to communicate design ideas and concepts. In the production of drawings, the tools, supplies, and processes are only as effective as an individual designer's skills and creativity. To effectively present information, designers need to interpret the project situation, that is, decide which type of graphics are appropriate, and then use available resources to produce the drawings.

From the beginning to the end of a design problem, designers use a variety of equipment, materials, and techniques to record, evaluate, and develop design proposals. Early design ideas are often sketched out using soft pencils, paper, and markers. Through these inexpensive and informal materials, the designer is allowed maximum flexibility and creativity. As ideas crystalize and are refined, the techniques and materials used to illustrate the ideas become more controlled and defined. Final colored presentations, often the end product of design, are the result of many layers of design sheets and utilize a range of media and techniques. As you review the equipment, materials, techniques, and processes described in this discussion of graphics, please be aware that the resources used in presenting a proposal should be selected relative to individual project requirements and an individual's skills.

EQUIPMENT AND MATERIALS

Pencils

Pencils are one of the basic drawing tools used by all designers. The component parts of a pencil include the lead, casing or shell, and the cap which may or may not include an eraser. The types of leads available include graphite, plastic, and plastic/graphite. The hardness or softness of the leads selected should relate to the line qualities desired. Lead hardness may range from 9H to 6B, with H leads the harder and B leads the softer (Figure 3-1). Harder leads such as 3H or 4H produce thin sharp lines and are used for lettering guidelines and construction drawings. Softer leads such as B or 3B are used to

produce thicker lines that are darker and bolder. They are often used for sketching, lettering, and primary drawing lines. When using the variety of lead hardnesses available, designers should be aware that softer leads, while producing thicker, darker lines, also smear easier and thus require careful presentation and drafting techniques. Harder leads, while producing thin, crisp lines, do not smear and are not as easily erased.

The types of pencils used in design are often identified by the casing or mechanics that enclose and protect the leads. Commonly used pencil casings include wooden, lead holders, or mechanical. The most traditional and least expensive is the *wooden pencil*. Its light weight gives flexibility in line variations and makes it a popular and inexpensive medium. Wooden pencils are sharpened by the use of a knife or sharpener and have a simple casing with no "mechanical parts" that can be broken (Figure 3-2). The *lead holder* type of pencil has a plastic, metal, or combination casing which has interchangeable leads within. Lead holders allow the flexibility of changing lead hardnesses easily and sharpening without wooden shavings (Figure 3-3). Sharpening is achieved by using a variety of *lead pointers*

FIGURE 3-1
Lead hardness chart.

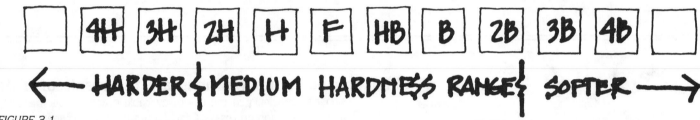

FIGURE 3-2
Wooden pencil. (Illustration by Raymond Paul Strychalski)

FIGURE 3-3
Lead holder. (Illustration by Raymond Paul Strychalski)

rather than pencil sharpeners (Figure 3-4). Lead holders are normally heavier in weight and are more expensive than wooden pencils. The flexibility of interchanging lead hardnesses and specialty leads, such as the *nonprint* leads, makes pencil holders more efficient and reduces the number of pencils needed. (Nonprint lead will be discussed later in the chapter.)

The *mechanical pencil* is similar to the lead holder type in construction, cost, and flexibility, yet requires no sharpening due to the predetermined sizes of leads available (Figure 3-5). Mechanical pencils are available in .3 mm to .9 mm sizes rather than the one diameter size of wooden pencils and lead holders. However, variation in lead thickness limits the opportunity of interchanging one mechanical pencil with another. Selection of a mechanical pencil diameter relative to your drafting needs is important. To help with pencil lead selection, smaller lead sizes, .3 to .5 mm, are often used for lettering guidelines, whereas larger leads, .5 to .9 mm, can be used for the actual final lettering and heavier line work. Graphite and plastic leads are available for use in mechanical pencils. Since no sharpening is required, these leads offer a time savings advantage and lower overall costs.

Other leads available to designers are the *nonprint* and *nonphoto* types. Nonprint leads are purplish in color and are used as guidelines for the layout of information before lettering or final drafting. When original drawings are duplicated, the blueprinting process does not recognize this purple color and the nonprint lines do not "print" while the ink or pencil does. The use of this lead saves time because no erasing is required before duplication. Nonphoto leads are similar to nonprint except they are used in the photographic duplication of information. Caution should be taken when using nonphoto lead for lettering guidelines or layout lines on vellum drawings to be printed. Due to its color, the nonphoto lead may print in the blueprint process and result in lines not desired in the final copy.

Pencils can be used for sketching ideas, guidelines, and layouts or before hard lining occurs with pencils or inking to produce fin-

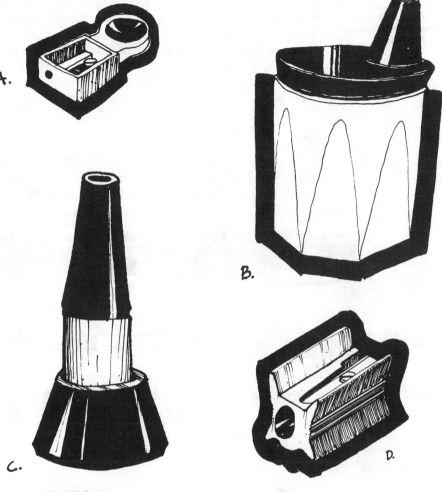

A.

B.

C.

D.

FIGURE 3-4

Lead sharpeners: (a), (b), and (c), are used to sharpen the lead in a lead holder; (d) is a typical sharpener for wooden pencils. (Illustration by Raymond Paul Strychalski)

FIGURE 3-5

Mechanical pencil. (Illustration by Raymond Paul Strychalski)

ished drawings. Construction drawings are normally drafted in pencil since the information included is routinely changed, including specific revisions and/or redesign. Mechanical pencils are used for their thin, consistent lines and for layout and guidelines, not for bold lines which can be produced by using lead holders or wooden pencils. Overall, designers will probably use all three types of pencils in the course of producing a variety of design drawings.

Ink

Ink as a medium is often used for illustrative plans and permanent information. Titles, borders, scales, and north arrows do not change as often during the design process and so may be in ink.

For the most contrast and quality in line, inking or technical pens are used for their consistency, accuracy, and ease of reproduction (Figure 3-6). When inking or technical pens are used, they produce clear, consistent lines flowing through a manufactured point of specific width. This consistent line width is also called *line weight*. Line weights can vary from fine to thick and are identified by metric or other measures (Figure 3-7). Technical pen brands available are numerous and should be selected only after understanding individual features, uses, and costs. When using technical pens, make sure the ink selected is waterproof and nonclogging. Often due to neglect, poor maintenance, or dormancy, ink pens clog, a primary disadvantage and a major cause of dissatisfaction. Reading the instructions and understanding the pen's mechanics, care, and use help

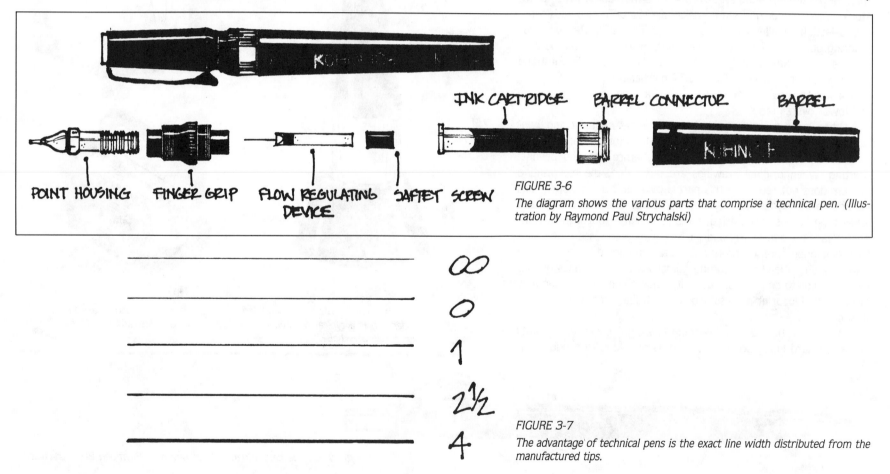

FIGURE 3-6

The diagram shows the various parts that comprise a technical pen. (Illustration by Raymond Paul Strychalski)

FIGURE 3-7

The advantage of technical pens is the exact line width distributed from the manufactured tips.

reduce the clogs and frustrations. Due to their cost, their use of ink, and the extended drafting time required, pens should be used only for finished presentation work. Illustrative site plans may be ink or pencil while sheet titles, borders, and other permanent, nonchanging information should be in ink. Sketching, construction drawings, and guidelines are usually completed in pencil, not ink.

Optional Drawing Tools

If an alternative to using pencils or pens exclusively is needed due to their cost or if a variety of media is required, many options are available. The Pilot, Sharpie, Markette, Design chisel point marker (CPM), all commercial brands, are good alternatives. These less expensive graphic tools produce a variety of line weights and line contrasts (Figure 3-8). While similar to colored markers, these drafting media use a chisel-shaped plastic or felt tip to distribute ink in a fine line or broad stroke. The basic advantage of some of these drawing tools is the variety of points available and their ease of use in sketching. When used on vellum, the line quality and darkness are similar to ink, yet they have less line contrast. These drawing tools can also be used to detail or outline objects on prints in conjunction with colored markers. Dry markers are used to add color to black-line prints. These markers also use felt tips to distribute colored inks for highlighting design drawings. Tips available range from a fine point to broad chisel (Figure 3-9). (Colored markers are discussed further in Chapter 5.)

LINE WEIGHT, CONTRAST, AND LINE QUALITY

In presenting design ideas, designers use lines, textures, and colors to represent the essence of an idea to be proposed. Basic to any graphic presentation of information is the *line drawing*. Line drawings use line and line variations of width and style to define objects. In the production of line drawings, line weight, contrast, and line quality are the main aspects to be considered.

Line Weight

Line weight is defined as a line's width and darkness. When a line drawing is composed of varied line weights, a hierarchy or contrast of dark, wide lines to light, thin lines should be developed. The heavier the line weight, the more important the element being defined.

Wide lines in drawings are used to outline the edges of major forms (such as a house) and to define elements closest to the viewer. Lighter lines in drawings should be used for secondary elements and to add details representing textures. Thinner lines are used to define the edges of lesser forms and to represent objects further from the viewer.

Line Quality

Line quality in a drawing refers to the regularity and clarity of a line. Just as a drawing should include a line hierarchy or contrast that is consistent, line quality also needs to be consistent. Line weights and line quality in drawing are dependent on the designer's drafting technique and skill in the use of the tools.

Pencil line quality is dependent on the hardness of the lead and the drafting technique used. To draft a concise quality line, the designer's pencil is pulled and rotated with consistent pressure. Both hard and soft leads must be pulled and rotated while scoring a line with a straight-edge to maintain a sharp point and consistent line. Figure 3-10 shows the pulling and rotating used to develop consistent lines. Harder leads retain a point longer and require less sharpening than softer leads which require constant pointing to maintain line quality. Line darkness or the opaqueness of a line is also a result of the lead hardness. The softer the lead the darker the line.

Other factors influencing pencil line quality are the drawing surface and the drafting surface. Smoother papers are used for harder leads while rougher papers are used for softer leads. The surface texture of paper is often referred to as its *tooth*. The more tooth a paper has the rougher the surface, the less tooth the smoother the paper. When using pencils, the graphite or lead material is rubbed onto the paper. Harder leads wear down slower with less graphite, thus are better applied to smoother papers. Softer leads which wear quickly need more tooth for the graphite particles to attach. The resiliency of the drafting table or surface also influences pencil line quality. Softer surfaces allow a flexibility between the paper and pencil. Harder surfaces may cause more scoring of the paper rather than a clear graphite line.

Ink line quality is achieved by holding the pen perpendicular to the paper or drawing surface, as shown in Figure 3-11. As mentioned previously, line sharpness or clarity is affected by the drawing surface. When using ink pens, smoother toothed papers or plastic-type drawing surfaces (mylar) should be used.

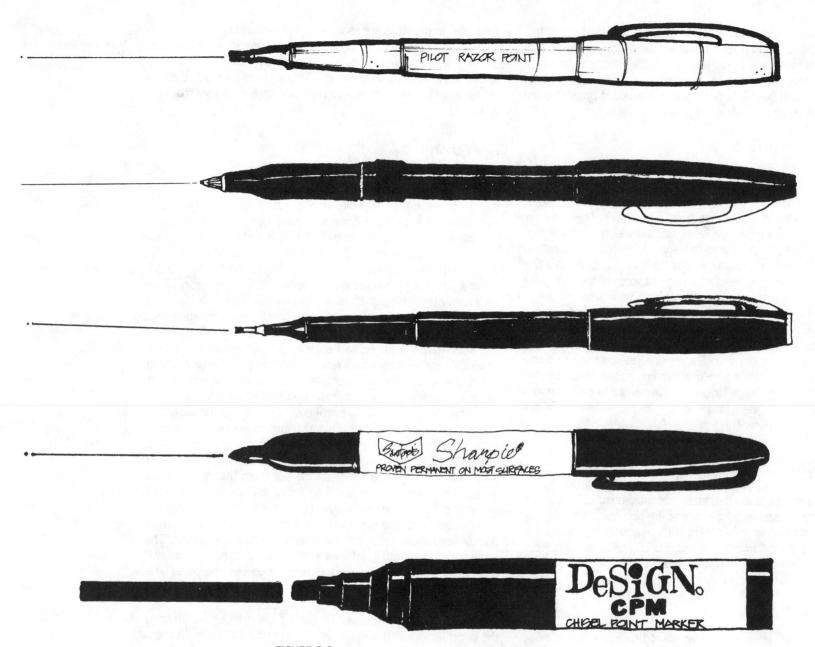

PILOT RAZOR POINT

Sharpie — PROVEN PERMANENT ON MOST SURFACES

DeSiGN. CPM — CHISEL POINT MARKER

FIGURE 3-8

These six drawing tools can be used as options to pencils and technical pens
in presenting design ideas. (Illustration by Raymond Paul Strychalski)

44

FIGURE 3-9

Rendering markers with tips ranging from wide points to nibs. (Illustration by Raymond Paul Strychalski)

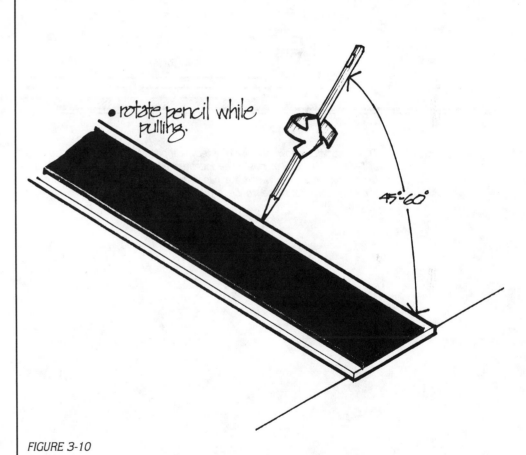

• rotate pencil while pulling.

45°–60°

FIGURE 3-10

Technical skill is needed to produce a clean, consistent line when drafting with a pencil. While pulling the pencil, it is rotated to wear the point evenly and lay an even line. (Illustration by Raymond Paul Strychalski)

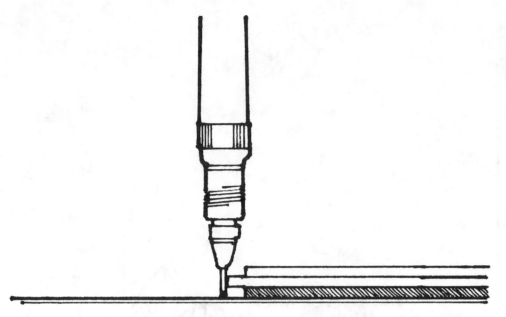

FIGURE 3-11

This illustration shows the use of a technical pen and a ruling edge (such as a T-square or parallel rule). The indented edge of the rule prevents ink from being drawn between the paper and rule. Holding the pen upright allows a consistent line to be produced. (Illustration by Raymond Paul Strychalski)

DRAWING SURFACES

Directly related to the media of leads and ink are drawing surfaces. Graphic ideas can be presented on thin tracing papers, sketching grade papers, quality grade vellums, film (plastic), and illustration boards. In selecting a drawing surface, one should consider the type of drawing, sheet size needed, drawing permanence, costs, and the reproduction process if any to be used.

Tracing Papers

Preliminary thoughts, diagrams, or initial design ideas are often conceptualized on *thin tracing papers*. Their relatively inexpensive cost and transparency allows the freedom of developing many variations by tracing ideas from one sheet to the next. Revisions and final ideas then can be traced through from thin tracing paper to a more permanent drawing surface. Thin tracing paper's major utility is its low cost, transparency, and ease of use throughout the design proposal phase. The papers are available in a variety of roll widths and lengths, such as 12", 24", and 36" widths. For preliminary design, these papers are ideal because of their minimal cost when compared to quality tracing papers. A disadvantage related to the use of these papers is that they are brittle and shred and thus are sometimes called "trash" paper or "bum wad," when preliminary ideas are thrown away. Soft pencils and colored markers are the media most used with these papers to conceptualize ideas. Thin tracing papers can be duplicated in a blueprint machine, but extreme care and caution must be exercised because of their brittleness. The slightest tear often ends up compounding when trash papers are run through the printer. Taking slides is probably the best means of recording and storing drawing information when these less permanent paper media are used.

Sketching grade papers can include sketchbooks, sketch pads, and marker papers. All of these are good for original drawings in ink, black marker, or pencil that are not to be reproduced. Sketching paper and marker papers have similar drawing surfaces, a rough-toothed surface that accepts pencil and markers easily. Marker paper comes in pads 9" × 12" or 18" × 24" and includes a waxed backing that prevents markers from bleeding through the sheets on to desk surfaces. These papers are normally used for preliminary sketches or presentation information that does not require reproduction. Xerox or other means of duplication of these originals is often the best means of recording and storage of this information. An option to marker paper but in a roll rather than a pad is waxed freezer paper. This paper is normally used to wrap frozen foods yet has a similar toothed surface and waxed backing as marker paper. The 18″×50′ roll is an inexpensive alternative to the marker paper pads.

Paper towels while not for formal presentation are another inexpensive media that can be used to illustrate preliminary ideas. To "sketch out" early design concepts, marker-type media work best on paper towels. Due to their small size paper towels are best used for individual project ideas. Later, these sketched ideas can be refined and drawn on more permanent paper if necessary.

Vellum

Quality grade tracing vellums are the papers used in final presentation drawings. The term *vellum* originally was used to describe a type of parchment made from calfskin and used as a writing surface or for book bindings. Today paper vellums are normally 100 percent rag papers and provide a quality transparent surface for finished line work.

When selecting vellums one should consider the proper paper surface in relation to the drafting materials used. Smooth-toothed papers are best used for ink drawings, while rougher toothed surfaces are best for pencil presentations. Vellum whiteness and transparency are also important qualities to consider in the selection of papers. Transparency and whiteness affects the quality of prints produced. Vellum paper sizes range from pads 8½″×11″, 9″× 12″, 11″×17″, and 12″×18″, to rolls 18″, 24″, 36″, and 48″ wide with varying lengths. Pencil and ink used on vellum surfaces provide the most permanence for original drawings. If markers rather than pencil or ink are used on vellum, they often separate and disperse into the paper over time, leaving a faded line and halo effect which destroy the drawing and its permanence.

Another drawing surface available is a sepia. A *sepia* is a piece of vellum which has an emulsion applied to its surface to produce, in essence, another original of a drawing. Sepias are produced as part of the blueprint process and are used when multiple drawings are needed in a presentation. The sepia or sepias produced can then be used to produce prints as would an original drawing. Sepias will be discussed further in the section involving blueprint process later in this chapter.

To provide clearer drawings that accept pencil or ink more evenly, designers may use *pounce* as a surface preparation. Pounce,

a fine granular powder, is sifted into the paper tooth to produce a smoother drafting surface.

Plastic or Film Drafting Surfaces

Drawing surfaces of *film, plastic, or mylar* are the most permanent and durable. These synthetic surfaces accept pencil and ink readily, are waterproof, and harder to damage, thus giving the assurance of permanence and durability. However, there are disadvantages to plastic or film drawing surfaces. For example, they cost much more than paper, and the surface can also be damaged if objects are dropped or drawn across them causing dents or scratches. In the selection and use of plastic drawing surfaces, the cost/benefit ratio relative to the project and the need for permanence must be considered and compared to other drawing surface options.

Boards

Illustration board can also be used as a drawing surface. Illustration board is available in either a toothed surface (cold press) or a smooth surface (hot press) for original line work and drawings. The range of colors and thicknesses provides an excellent surface for durable presentations. If original work is drafted on boards, it cannot be duplicated or revised as easily as can transparent drawing surfaces. Corrections or revisions are almost impossible once drafted because erasing would alter the colored board surface. Illustration boards provide a quality base for drawings yet require precise and accurate drafting skills. Illustration boards can also be used to mount or mat drafted or other presentations.

DRAFTING EQUIPMENT

In combination with the large selection of pencils, inking pens, and papers, designers use a range of other equipment to control, organize, and remove lines in scale drawings. Typical supportive drawing equipment includes a drawing table or board, T-square or parallel-rule, triangles, templates, erasure shields, electric erasers, scales, and lettering guides.

Drawing Boards and Tools

The *drawing table or board* is a squared surface that allows designers to align papers squarely and securely so as to produce drawings

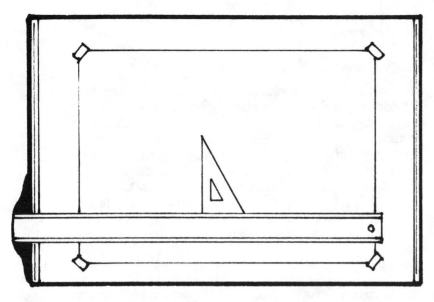

FIGURE 3-12

The top illustration shows the use of a T-square and triangle by a right-handed person. The T-square would be used off the right edge of the board by a left-handed person. The bottom illustration shows the application of a parallel rule which is kept square by the wire guides incorporated in the table. (Illustration by Raymond Paul Strychalski)

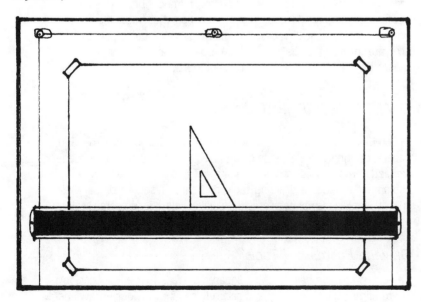

and lines that are parallel and perpendicular to the paper's edges. Drawing boards are normally wooden with metal edges machined to maintain a "square" drawing base. Often a plastic resilient surface is added to the wooden surface to protect the basic board from mechanical injury and to provide a flexible surface for drafting. In conjunction with these drawing surfaces and boards, a *T-square* or *parallel-rule* is used to draft lines that are parallel to the board's square edges. The T-square, as a drafting tool, is used off the left or right square edges of the board to provide perpendicular guides for paper alignment or drafted lines. For right-handed people, the left side of the drawing board is used and for left-handed people the right edge is used. The parallel-rule produces similar line guides, yet is permanently attached to the board whereas T-squares are removable (Figure 3-12).

T-squares and parallel-rules are used primarily for horizontal lines, while *triangles* are used for vertical and diagonal lines. The most frequently used triangles include the 30 degree, 45 degree, 60 degree, and 90 degree triangles. Selection of a triangle and its sizes should reflect the types of angles used in drafting and satisfy the range of project involvements. Triangles come in 6″, 8″, and 10″ lengths and larger, all of which are appropriate for most drawings. When selecting a triangle consider the following: (1) colored triangles are easier to see on desks than clear ones; (2) triangle edges with "cut areas" can be picked up more easily; (3) an inking edge is desirable to prevent ink from running under the plastic edge. See Figures 3-13 and 3-14 for examples of triangles and their use in conjunction with a T-square or parallel-rule.

Templates are used in design to quickly draw shapes commonly used. For example, circular templates are used by some designers to establish the outlines of trees and shrubs before the plant symbol is established and drawn in ink or final pencil (Figure 3-15). If ink is to be the presentation medium, it is used over the lead guidelines, since templates often do not have inking edges. An inking edge is the variation in a ruling edge to reduce the ink blots that often occur under a template or triangle.

A variation of template is an *erasure shield*. Erasure shields are used to control the area that needs to be erased in pencil or ink drawings. The shield, as you might assume, masks desirable lines and leaves exposed the line areas to be erased (Figure 3-16).

A very helpful tool used in conjunction with an erasure shield and sepia drawings is an *electric eraser*. The eraser uses an eraser shaft able to "peel off" lines much easier, efficiently, and faster than

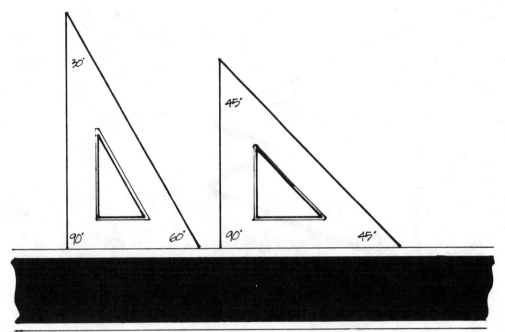

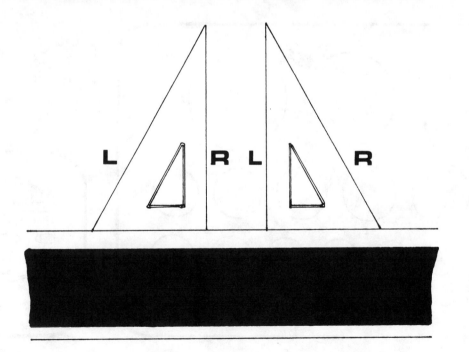

49

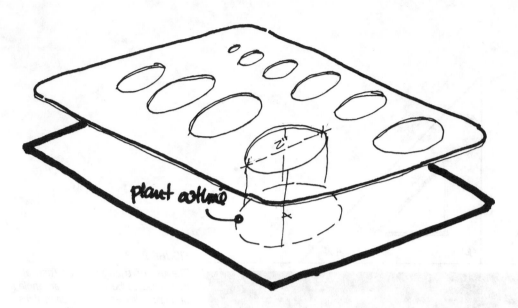

FIGURE 3-15

The most commonly used template is a circle. In the graphic presentation of plants, the spread of a plant is usually drawn as a circle. It is important to remember that the scale of a drawing determines what is being represented. If a two-inch circle is used as an example at 1" = 8', it would represent a 16' wide plant. At 1" = 10', a 20' tree, at 1" = 4', an 8' plant, and at 1" = 1', a 2' plant. (Illustration by Raymond Paul Strychalski)

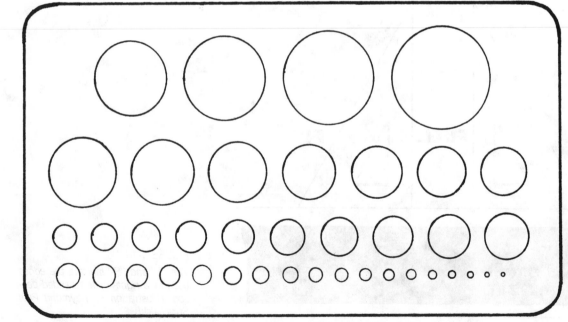

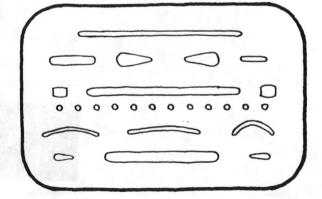

FIGURE 3-16

Erasure shield. (Illustration by Raymond Paul Strychalski)

a common eraser (Figure 3-17). While efficient, the electric erasers are expensive and provide the most benefit when used for their time savings value and not as a necessity.

Scales

Since scaled drawings are representations of actual spaces, designers use a tool called a *scale* to accurately draw plans. Three scales are commonly used in design. An *architects scale* is a rule, one foot in length including scales of $1/16'' = 1'0''$, $1/8'' = 1'0$, $1/4'' = 1'0$, $1/2'' = 1'0$, $3/8'' = 1'$, $3/4'' = 1'0$, $1'' = 1'$, $3/16'' = 1'$, $3/32'' = 1'$, $1\frac{1}{2}'' = 1'$, and $3'' = 1'$. This scale range is most often used for construction drawings and in architecture and interior design projects. A drawing using $1/8'' = 1'$ shows the contractor or workman that $1/8''$ represents one foot in size of the actual project to be constructed. The *engineers scale* is again one foot in length, divided into six scales which are subdivided into 10, 20, 30, 40, 50, or 60 parts to the inch. This scale is commonly used on landscape plans which represent larger site areas. When using an engineers scale, each equal segment can be interpreted as one foot or more depending on the scale drawing needed. As an example, when using the 10 scale, one segment can be read as one foot, thus a scale of $1'' = 10'$ or as $10'$ representing a scale of $1'' = 100'$. The *metric scale*, similar to the engineers scale, includes ratios of 1:100, 1:125, 1:200, 1:500, 1:750, 1:1,000. The ratios on a metric scale relate to a meter. Thus, a scale of 1:100 represents graduations in the length of a meter totaling 100 equal parts. A scale of 1:500 represents a division of 500 equal parts to the meter and so on.

Figure 3-18 shows an architects, engineers, and metric scale. These triangular scales can include as many as 11 different scales. For example, 11 are included on the architects scale, 6 on the engineers scale, and 6 on the metric scale. It is important to mention that scales are precision tools with exact graduations and never should be used as a straight-edge for drafting. Scales may be constructed from wood or plastic, yet plastic scales are most common. Because they are easily cracked or broken if dropped care should be used when handling them. To help relate the concept of scale it is often desirable to measure a drawing area then relate it to the space in which you are drawing. Often floor tiles are one foot square which helps you to visualize the actual space you are reviewing in the plan.

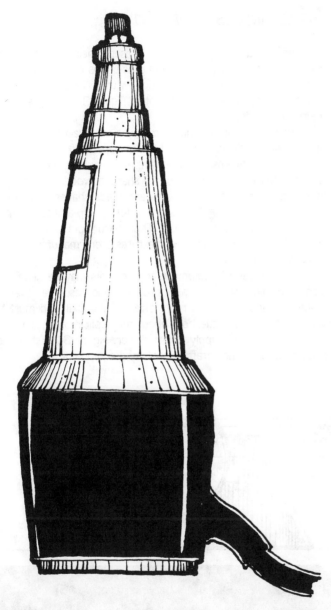

FIGURE 3-17

Electric eraser. The eraser shield can be used with hand-held erasers or in conjunction with an electric eraser. The basic function of the shield is to mask areas not to be erased while defining the area to be removed. (Illustration by Raymond Paul Strychalski)

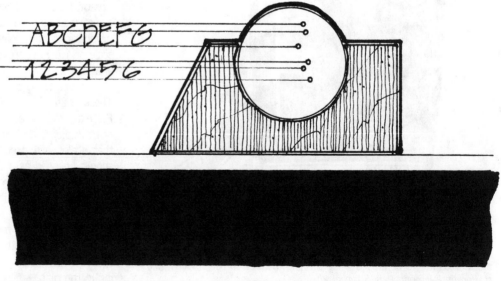

MISCELLANEOUS EQUIPMENT

Another tool that helps designers present sheet information better and more efficiently is a *lettering guide*. This guide is used to draw horizontal guidelines in conjunction with a T-square for lettering and organizing words to form notes. Figure 3-19 shows the use of a lettering guide.

Other tools that designers may use are exacto knives and burnishers. An *exacto knife* is used to cut paper and illustration boards to the proper dimensions. They are also used for models construction, matted presentations, and to sharpen wooden pencils. Exacto knives come in a variety of sizes and blade shapes. *Burnishers* are used in design to apply "press-on" lettering, zip-a-lines, or manufacture visual textures or surfaces. Their hard blunt end is used when transferring lettering, lines, or textures from manufactured sheets to design proposals.

Other pieces of equipment and/or tools may be helpful in design. Becoming aware of new products and resources available to make your job easier and more effective is a skill and must be developed. If you have questions about the application of products, ask your local drafting supply or art dealer. Figure 3-20 shows examples of various other drafting tools and equipment.

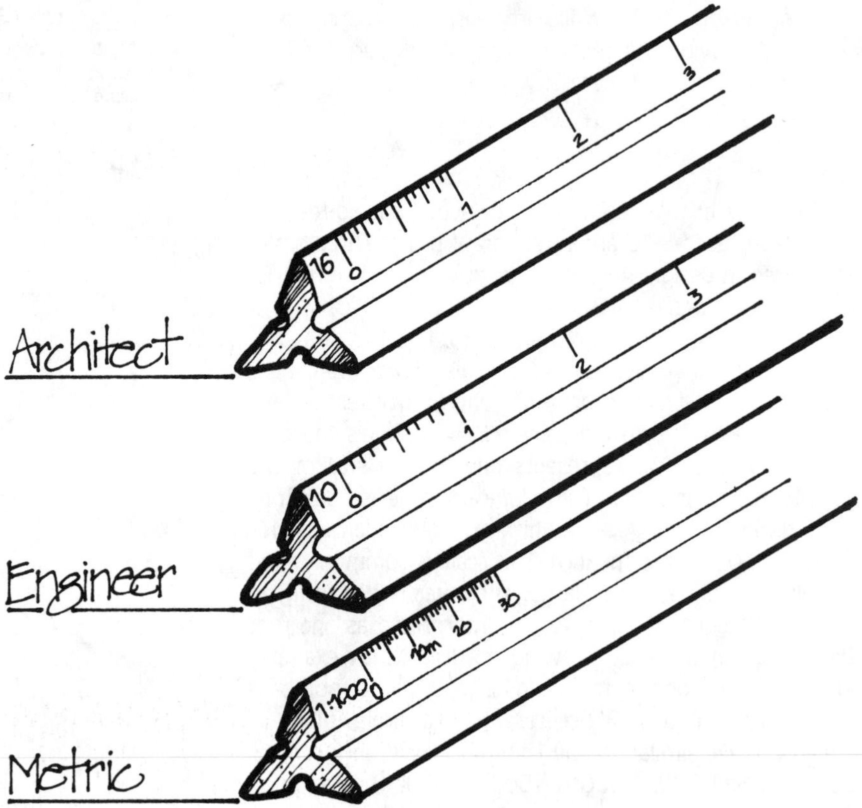

FIGURE 3-18

Scales—architectural, engineering, metric. The scales shown are triangular in shape, allowing the possibilities of six or more scales to be represented on the faces exposed. Scales do come in other configurations such as flat or beveled edges for their ease in carrying. (Illustration by Raymond Paul Strychalski)

FIGURE 3-19

Lettering guides are normally used with a parallel rule or T-square to define guidelines that are in concert with the sheet's edge and other lines on the sheet. Lettering guidelines establish the constancy of letter heights. (Illustration by Raymond Paul Strychalski)

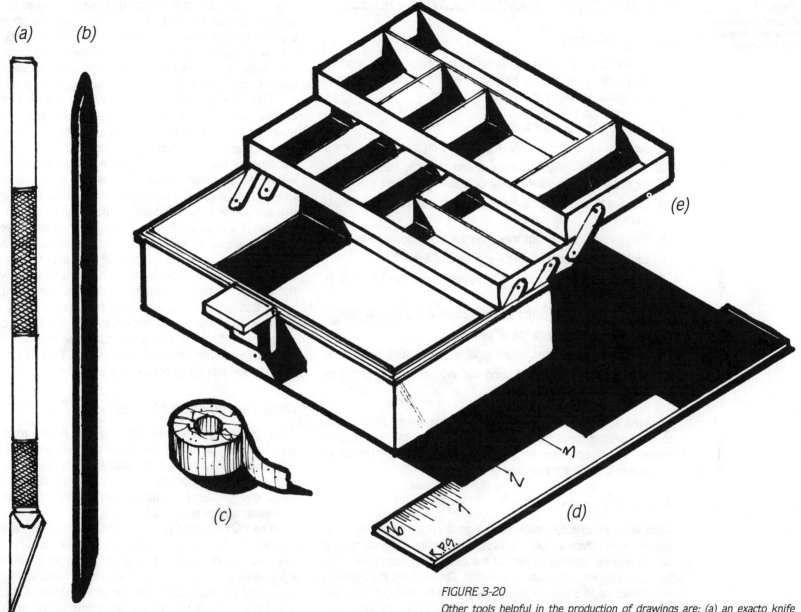

(a)

(b)

(c)

(d)

(e)

FIGURE 3-20

Other tools helpful in the production of drawings are: (a) an exacto knife for cutting paper, etc.; (b) a burnisher for applying pressure-sensitive materials; (c) drafting tape for mounting paper to the drawing board; (d) a metal rule 18" for a cutting edge; and (e) a tackle box to keep drafting and drawing tools together. (Illustration by Raymond Paul Strychalski)

53

DRAFTING SEQUENCE AND DUPLICATING PROCESSES

Drawing Sequence

To prepare finished drawings, designers normally follow a procedure or routine in setting up paper, guidelines, inking steps, and so forth. A typical sequence of steps is as follows:

1. Clean drafting surface and hands.
2. Tape base sheet or preliminary drawing on the drawing board.
3. Tape drafting vellum or mylar sheets over the base sheet and align the paper to locate borders, legend, and title block.
4. Using a T-square or parallel-rule, lay out major horizontal guidelines.
5. Using a triangle, lay out major vertical and diagonal lines.
6. Lay out secondary horizontal and vertical lines.
7. Organize areas for support information such as lettering, labels, and legend.
8. Hard line in ink or pencil major horizontal and vertical lines.
9. Add secondary lines in ink or pencil.
10. Add textures, surfaces, lettering, labels, and legend information.
11. Erase pencil guidelines if using ink and clean up sheet for reproduction (see Figure 3-21).

After this sequence of steps, the designer takes the original drawing to a blueprinter for duplication. After duplication, the designer may render, that is, add color to the plans, and then present the design package to the client for review.

Blueprint Process

Duplication of original vellum drawings is required because a designer never gives original drawings to clients. Original tracings should also be retained as part of the designer's records and to allow for revisions in the future if needed. Traditionally, the blueprint, sometimes called the *diazo process,* was used for duplication of tracings. The *ozalid process* has now replaced the diazo process in reproducing drawings. Basic to the ozalid and diazo processes is the use of a reproduction paper that is coated with a light-sensitive emulsion, usually a chemical compound. When these reproduction papers, in combination with original tracings, are exposed to high intensity light, the areas on the print paper covered by lines of the drawing are not exposed. The areas left have the chemical coating exposed to light which burns off the surface, resulting in a white area when developed. Development of these lines occurs when the print paper and remaining emulsion areas are exposed to ammonia compounds. Figure 3-22 shows the basic printing process.

The emulsion and paper used will determine if the duplicate drawing is a blackline, blueline, brownline, or sepia. Blackline and blueline prints are made of an opaque, toothed paper ideal for colored markers and colored pencil presentations. A sepia, unlike the blacklines or bluelines, is a copy made on transparent or translucent vellum that can then be used for making additional direct copies, either prints or sepias. Sepias are often called *intermediate* drawings and can be made for additive information based on the original drawing. If a sepia will involve erasing information as well as adding new data, a reverse sepia can be used. This allows removal of information on the back and addition of new data to a clean drafting surface (Figure 3-23). Sepia lines can be erased easily with an electric eraser, or sepia eradicator, a chemical solvent. It should be noted that original drawings and print paper when exposed to strong sunlight age quickly and deteriorate. Storage of originals and prints should be away from direct sources of light to reduce yellowing and the disintegration of these papers. Plan files or plan tubes are desirable storage options available.

Other Reproduction Methods

Other duplication processes that might be helpful to designers are photographic methods of reduction and enlargement of drawings. Original drawings, maps, and plans can be photographically enlarged or reduced onto print paper or film. In the case of topographic maps, enlargement or reduction can be extremely important as a time saver and to ensure accuracy.

The *PMT,* or *photographic mechanical transfer,* is a method of reducing large line drawings to $10'' \times 12''$ or $12'' \times 18''$ print sizes. Prints photographed at a $10'' \times 12''$ print size can have an image area $8\frac{1}{2}'' \times 11''$. Thus, they can be used in page-size portfolios and are easy to handle and store (Figure 3-24). These reduced drawings convey the overall effects of the project and may look more attractive as the detail is reduced. Most of the examples in the text are PMTs.

Another method for reducing drawings for portfolios or storage is a *contact negative*. Projects are photographically reduced us-

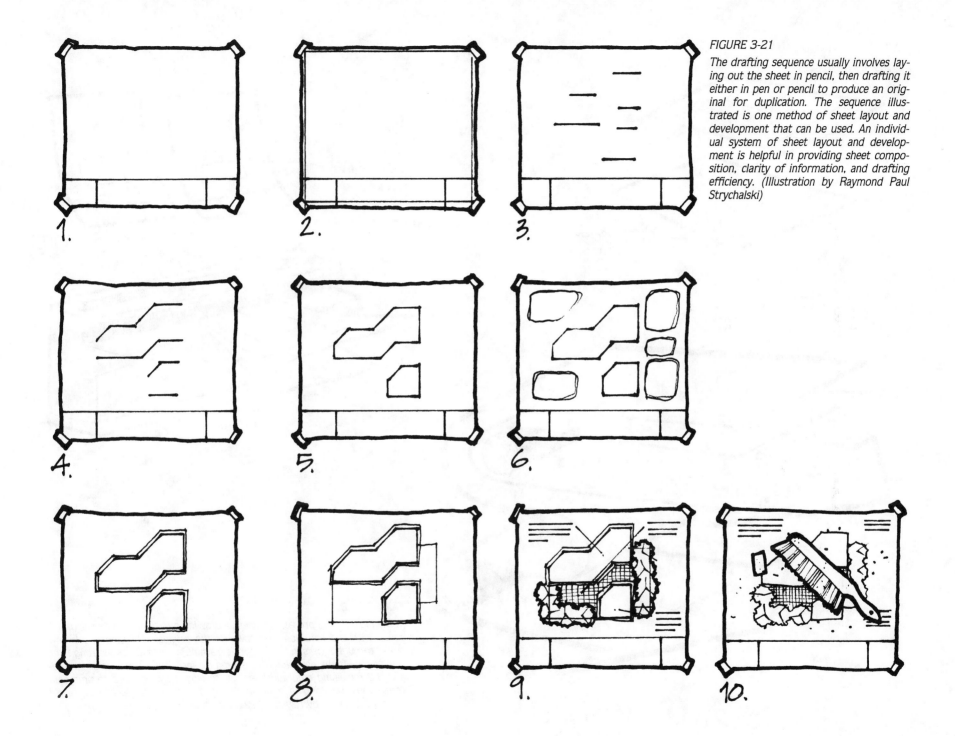

FIGURE 3-21

The drafting sequence usually involves laying out the sheet in pencil, then drafting it either in pen or pencil to produce an original for duplication. The sequence illustrated is one method of sheet layout and development that can be used. An individual system of sheet layout and development is helpful in providing sheet composition, clarity of information, and drafting efficiency. (Illustration by Raymond Paul Strychalski)

1.

2.

3.

4.

5.

6.

7.

8.

9.

10.

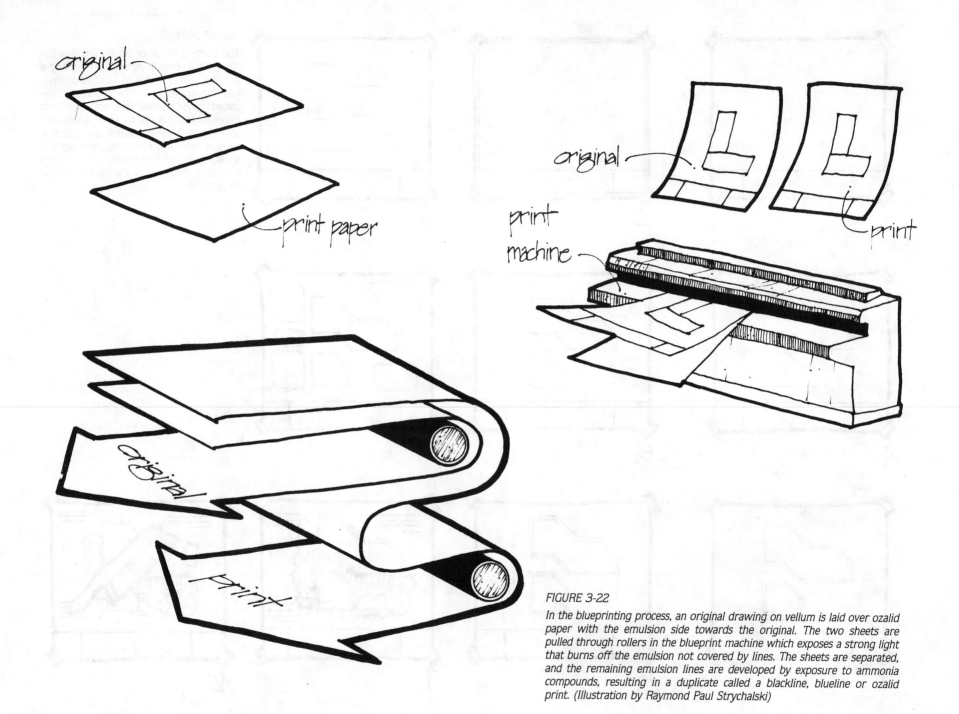

original

print paper

original

print

print machine

original

print

FIGURE 3-22

In the blueprinting process, an original drawing on vellum is laid over ozalid paper with the emulsion side towards the original. The two sheets are pulled through rollers in the blueprint machine which exposes a strong light that burns off the emulsion not covered by lines. The sheets are separated, and the remaining emulsion lines are developed by exposure to ammonia compounds, resulting in a duplicate called a blackline, blueline or ozalid print. (Illustration by Raymond Paul Strychalski)

original/sepia process

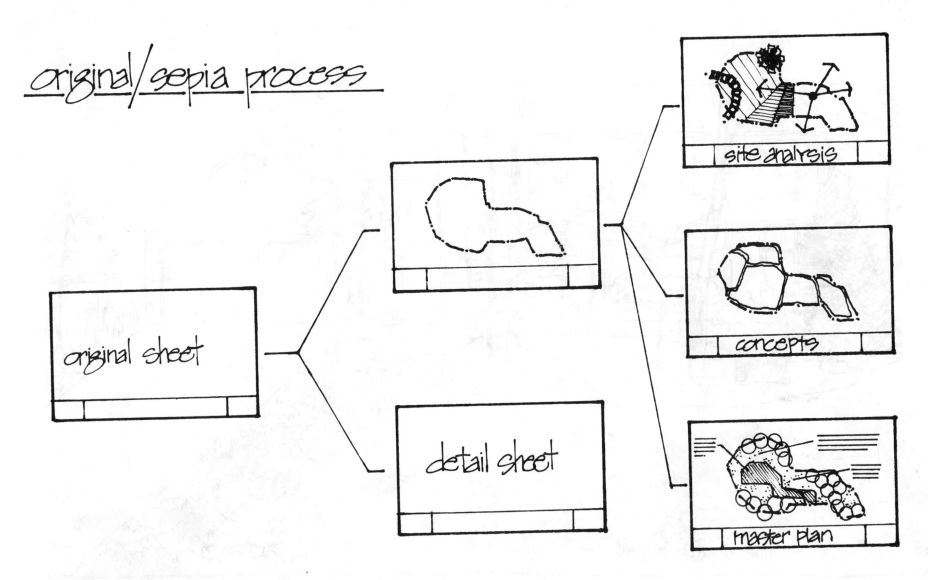

FIGURE 3-23

Sepia prints are used as originals in the drafting process. A sepia is produced from an original drawing on vellum just as an ozalid print. The difference between the blackline or blueline prints and a sepia is the base paper the emulsion is coated on. Blackline or blueline prints use an opaque paper whereas sepias use a vellum-like paper. (Illustration by Raymond Paul Strychalski)

HO. 820

front elevation proposed

FIGURE 3-24

This illustration represents a part of the original drawing before photo-graphically reduced in the PMT (Photographic Mechanical Transfer) process.

FIGURE 3-25

Photographic reduction of plans provides a means of presenting design work without the awkwardness of larger sheet sizes. The PMT (Photographic Mechanical Transfer) shown represents an original drawing 18×24"; PMTs are normally used as a means to record and store design projects and for use in portfolios and presentations. (Designer: Gregory M. Pierceall)

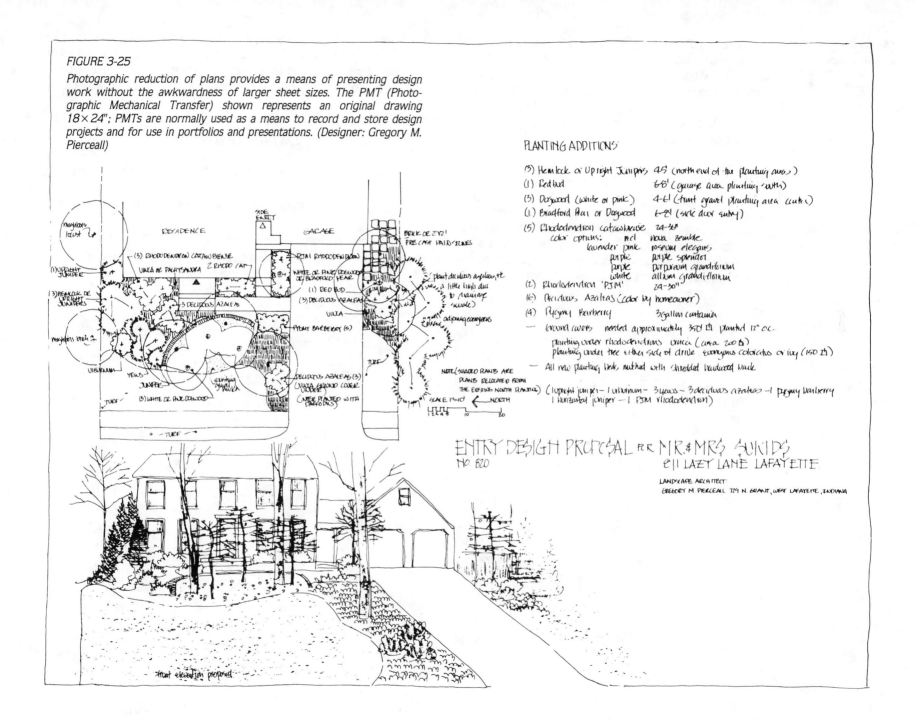

ing an 8″ × 10″ contact negative. This photographic process creates a reverse image of the original drawing with black lines now white and white areas black. These negatives can then be put through a blueprint machine, and the resulting ozalid prints are white lines on dark backgrounds. Figure 3-25 shows a blackline of a PMT reduction in comparison to the same project presented using the contact negative process.

SUMMARY

Graphic production of drawings requires an understanding of the equipment, materials, procedures, and processes used to communicate design ideas. Designers should experiment with a wide range of materials and methods to discover those that are most applicable to the project. Designers should also practice with new techniques and materials to ensure proficiency. The basic requirements of any drawing are accuracy, neatness, and reproducibility. The procedures and techniques used to achieve the drawings are dependent on the drawing required and the style and preference of the designer.

REFERENCES AND READINGS

Ball, John E. *Architectural Drafting.* Reston, VA: Reston Publishing Co., 1981.

Wang, Thomas C. *Pencil Sketching.* New York: Van Nostrand Reinhold Co., 1977.

Lin, Mike. *Economy of Graphics.* Washington, D.C.: ASLA 1979.

Letraset. *Graphic Art Materials Reference Manual.* Paramus, NJ: Letraset Corporation, 1981.

*G*raphic communications

In landscape planning and design graphics are used as a language to describe and present a visual image of our thoughts and ideas. The components of line, form, texture, and color are often used in the same way that an author uses words to stimulate our imagination and thinking. As new ideas arise, graphics are used to record, sketch, and revise concepts as solutions and alternatives to site design problems. Graphics are the most convenient, efficient, economical, and flexible means designers have to communicate and present information. However, they are not an end unto themselves, but only a means to communicate our design intentions. Successful graphic communications are the result of a working understanding of the various concepts, techniques, and drawing styles used in presenting design information.

DRAWING CONCEPTS

To present ideas visually, the criteria used to develop drawings should address *first,* What is to be presented? Will the drawing present planting plans, construction details, or other design information? *Second,* To whom are you communicating the information? Is the drawing for other designers, clients, or contractors? *Third,* How is the information to be used? Are the ideas just preliminary or are they being used in a presentation to the client or to a contractor, or are they for yourself? *Fourth,* What is the expected, accepted, or needed format? Are they, for example, illustrations or construction drawings? (See Figure 4-1.)

As preparation for presenting design projects, always understand the project's focus and the client's needs before selecting graphic techniques. Knowing the site size and being aware of what drawings are needed (such as plans or perspectives) can be a great help in deciding which sheet organization, graphic techniques, and styles to use. Always select a sheet size large enough to present the necessary information and support data (such as title blocks, legend, and labels). Figure 4-2 shows examples of title blocks, sheet information, and organization.

If the initial drawings are to be preliminary, the graphic techniques used should concentrate less on refinement and more on creativity and planning ideas relative to the problem. Refinement of ideas and details can occur later in the final drafting stages of a design. Figure 4-3 shows the progressive refinement of preliminary ideas to final design proposals.

Drawing techniques and styles are often individualized and relate to a designer's skills and the character of the design problem. As a design professional, a time/benefit equilibrium has to be established; that is, the techniques and styles selected should be appropriate and realistic for the scale of the problem and the time and fee framework defined. Remember, more ink requires more time!

GRAPHIC PRESENTATIONS

Landscape design uses graphic techniques that are pictorial, representational, or illustrative in their presentations of information and ideas. Graphics suggest through lines, textures, symbols, and often color the likenesses of objects or scenes in the landscape. In the presentation of drawings, one must understand that design graphics are not photographic, yet use photographic techniques in the composition and presentation of images and ideas on flat, two-dimensional surfaces. As through the lens of a camera, designers select the framing and vantage through which one can view an image or scene. Drawings and graphics should also include the influences of

light and shadows to further illustrate heights, creative depth, and realism.

Through the application of the same concepts of perspective and proportion that are found in photographs, design sketches can create a representation or a feeling of what a proposal could look like once developed. Figure 4-4 shows how in design graphic sketching techniques tend to abstract the essence of a scene or image yet retain its framing, perspective, and character. There is a basic difference between drawings and the photographic reproduction of images. In a drawing the designer interprets and abstracts the image in addition to adding elements which may be proposed; a photograph reproduces the scene exactly as it exists.

Through a variety of illustrations, design drawings, and graphics, designers show how site proposals will look. Typical design illustrations include plans, sections, elevations, and perspectives. Through the use of these illustrations, design proposals can be presented, revised, and constructed on paper long before any actual development occurs. In practice, graphics allow "planning before planting." Rather than planting and replanting until the actual site proposal looks right, planting and construction ideas can be proposed and reviewed on paper before actually being implemented. Landscape design does require the composition of plants in addition to topography, pavements, water, and other site features. While the statement "planning before planting" is used generally, plants are only a portion of a total design proposal. Graphics save time and labor by anticipating needs. It is easier to move plants and make construction decisions on paper than actually doing the work. However, minor design changes do occur during construction due to conditions or influences that could not be anticipated at the time of design or due to client or project changes.

DRAWINGS

In landscape design, landscape architecture, and other landscape industry disciplines, the most widely used drawings include the plan, section, elevation, and perspective. The designer selects the vantage from which to present existing conditions and proposed ideas. Oftentimes to fully communicate a design concept, a plan, section, elevation, and perspective may all be used. With these drawings the entire site and proposals can be envisioned and reviewed in total before the actual development takes place.

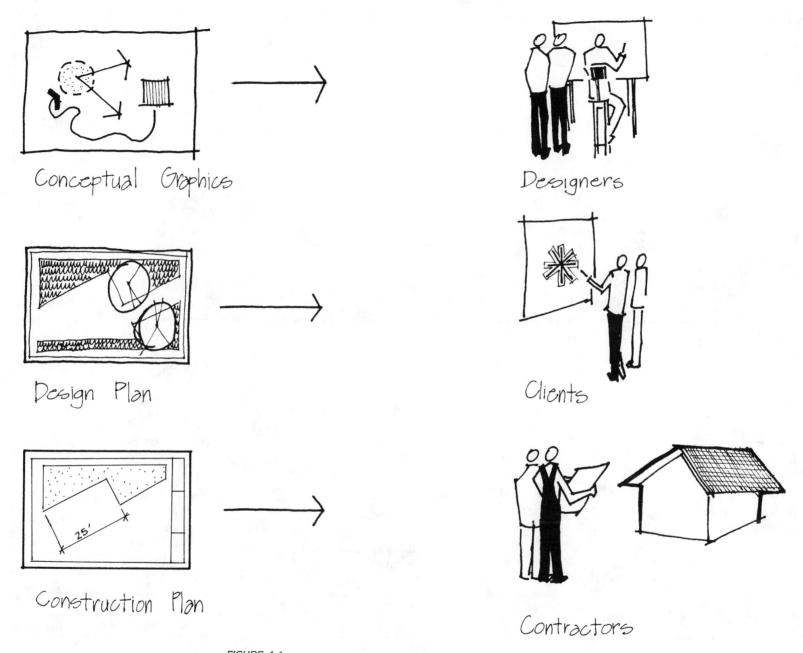

Conceptual Graphics

Design Plan

Construction Plan

Designers

Clients

Contractors

FIGURE 4-1

Always select graphic techniques appropriate to their intended use and the individual user. (Illustration by T. G. Kramer)

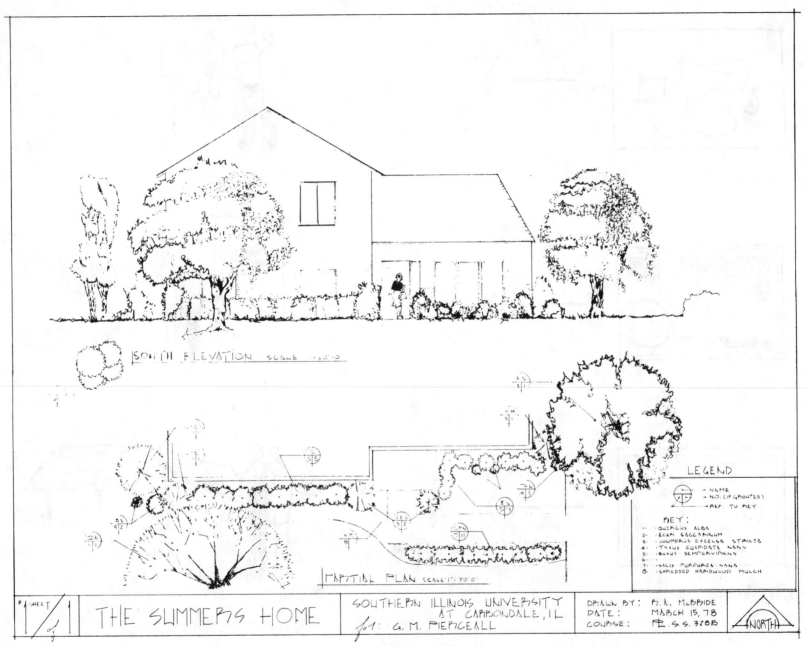

SOUTH ELEVATION SCALE 1'=20'0"

PARTIAL PLAN SCALE 1"=20'0"

LEGEND

= NAME
= NO. (IF GROUPED)
= REF. TO KEY

KEY:
1- QUERCUS ALBA
2- ACER SACCHARINUM
3- JUNIPERUS EXCELSA STRICTA
4- TAXUS CUSPIDATA NANA
5- BUXUS SEMPERVIRENS
6-
7- SALIX PURPUREA NANA
8- SHREDDED HARDWOOD MULCH

THE SUMMERS HOME

SHEET 1 of 1

SOUTHERN ILLINOIS UNIVERSITY AT CARBONDALE, IL
for: G. M. PIERCEALL

DRAWN BY: R. A. McBRIDE
DATE: MARCH 15, 78
COURSE: P.S.S. 320B

NORTH

FIGURE 4-2(a)

The horizontal title block defines the bottom of the sheet and helps tie the sheet composition together. (Designer: R. A. McBride)

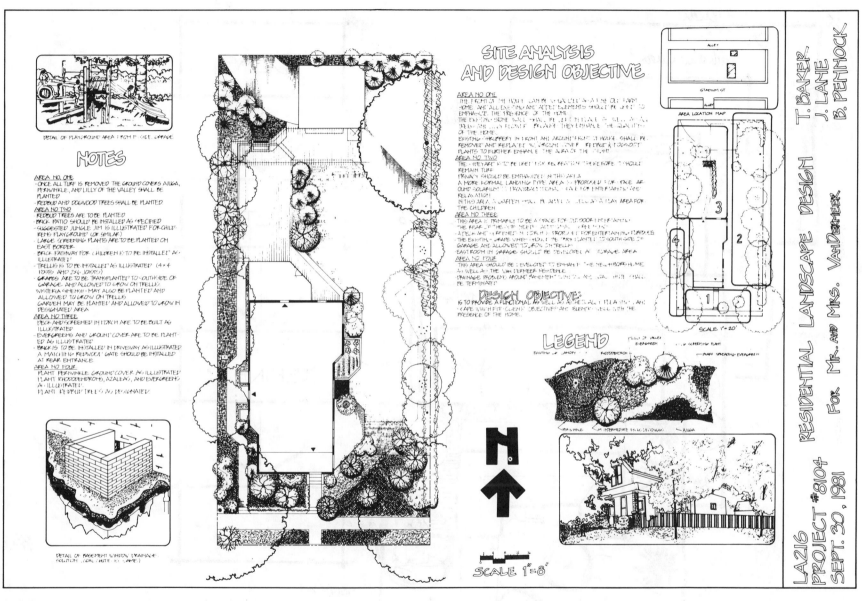

FIGURE 4-2(b)

While the sheet orientation is the same as in Figure 4-2a, the title block here is developed at the right edge. In this format, the sheets binding edge may be on the left edge or at the top of the sheet. (Designer: Baker, Lane, Pennock)

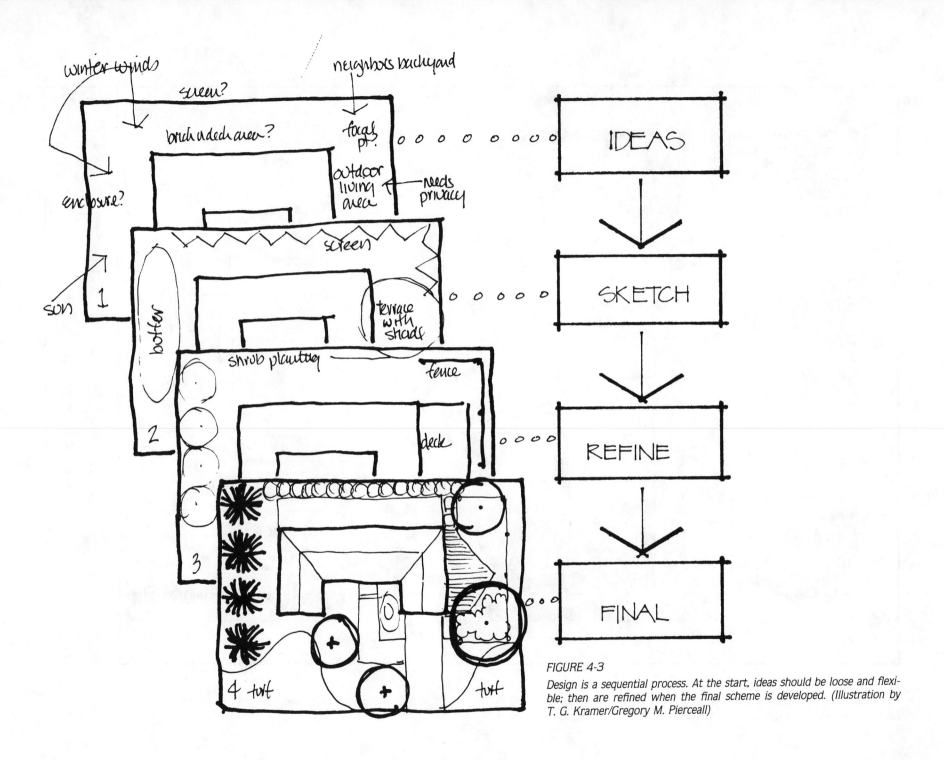

Text labels within the illustration:

winter winds
screen?
neighbors backyard
brick nadded area?
focal pt.
outdoor living area
needs privacy
enclosure?
sun
1

screen
botter
terrace with shade
2

shrub planting
fence
deck
3

4 turf
turf

IDEAS

SKETCH

REFINE

FINAL

FIGURE 4-3

Design is a sequential process. At the start, ideas should be loose and flexible; then are refined when the final scheme is developed. (Illustration by T. G. Kramer/Gregory M. Pierceall)

FIGURE 4-4

In the development and proposal of design ideas, sketches are often used in addition to plans to fully communicate concepts. In the illustrations shown, the plan and sketch were used prior to the planting to show the client how the entry space would look after development. (Designer: Gregory M. Pierceall)

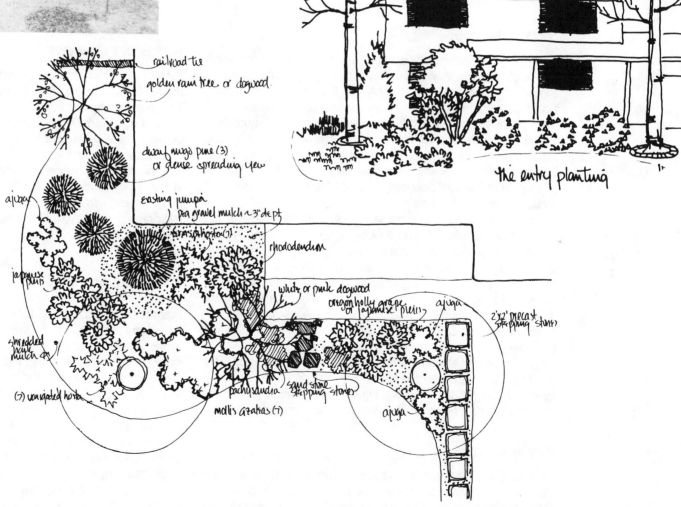

the entry planting

railroad tie

golden rain tree or dogwood.

dwarf mugo pine (3)
or dense spreading yew

existing juniper
pea gravel mulch ~ 3" dept.

terras/hosta (7)

rhododendron

white or pink dogwood

oregon holly grape
or japanese pieris

ajuga

2'x2' precast
stepping stones

ajuga

japanese
pieris

shredded
bark
mulch ~

(7) variegated hosta

pachysandra

sand stone
stepping stones

mollis azaleas (7)

ajuga

Plan Drawings

In a *plan view*, the drawing is developed as if from the vantage of a plane above the site. Horizontal distances can be easily recognized, yet vertical dimensions of objects may be represented only by shadows. Plans are accurate, scaled drawings, usually drawn from on-site surveys or other inventory methods. Property lines, easements, buildings, drives, fences, walks, steps, vegetation, and topography are common components found in plans. Plans allow a designer to work with the entire site in total which often cannot be seen otherwise. Figure 4-5 shows an example of a typical residential site plan.

Section Drawings

Since many site features shown in a plan drawing have both width and height, *section drawings* are used to help communicate details concerning the vertical aspects of objects. A section is a specific vertical plane cut through the site plan. It is a scaled drawing of "a slice" of the site plan drawn at the same scale as the plan drawing. The designer selects a section line across the base plane that best explains major site features. This cut-away view of a selected portion of the plan is viewed from a plane perpendicular to the flat site surface. Thus, section drawings provide a view of horizontal and vertical dimensions together.

Section drawings also show various level changes that may occur on the site plan. They often offer a view of the topography above and below the site surface to show grading into and on top of the existing site grade. Section drawings are also selected to explain existing and proposed grading or level changes such as slopes, steps, walks, fences, developed in master plan proposals. Figure 4-6a shows an example of a section through the plan drawing illustrated in Figure 4-5. Note the reference line on the plan that indicates the exact location the section was taken from.

A variation of the section drawing is the section/elevation. This drawing shows depth behind the primary drawing object and may include shading and/or shadows. Figure 4-6b shows a typical section, and Figure 4-6c shows the same scene as a section/elevation.

Elevation Drawings

Elevations are like sections in that they are drawn from a similar vantage, but they represent a side view of the site plan, not a slice through the proposal. Elements above the ground surface are drawn as if seen by a person looking directly at the scene with no perspective. This view of the site assumes the vantage of an average person standing at the site's ground level. In this drawing, foreground, middleground, and background aspects of the scene and surface details of elements are included. Glass reflections, the form of building, construction materials, and surfaces are also shown. Elevations, in contrast to sections, show more depth and surface detailing of objects and forms, and they seem more realistic. Figure 4-7 shows an example of an elevation drawing taken from the site plan (Figure 4-5). Notice that elements in the foreground are larger and more detailed than those in the middle and background planes. The area between the foreground and middleground plane then is the emphasis of the drawing.

Perspective Drawings

Perspective drawings present images pictorially as would be seen by the naked eye looking through a camera lens or at a photograph. The scene is represented as if the viewer were actually standing in the plan or design. Depth, proportion, and relative distances are included in these drawings to fully convey the volume of a space. Line, textures, and color are added to reinforce the feeling of realism. Objects closest to the viewer are larger and more detailed than those in the background. Thus, the emphasis is on the foreground and middleground elements. Figure 4-8 shows an example of a perspective drawing taken from Figure 4-5. The procedures used in developing one- and two-point perspective drawings can be found in Appendix 4.

In the composition and presentation of drawings, a coordination of lines, textures, shadows, and colors is needed to fully communicate the design concepts proposed. In the production of drawings or illustrations, line is the first element used to establish the framework for textures, shadows, and color. Line is used initially to define areas and forms. Textures using line or tone are added to show detail, indicate surfaces, and often to show shading. Shadows are used to create depth and reinforce the realism of forms and shapes in the drawing. Color is often used to further complement the line weights, textures, and shadows already established. Since clients often are not familiar with plans and sketches, color adds the contrast they need to picture the planes and components within a design. Color helps to communicate design. However, if duplication or photography are to be used for any reason black and white reproductions are less costly than color. Figure 4-9 shows a drawing's progression from line to the stage before color is added.

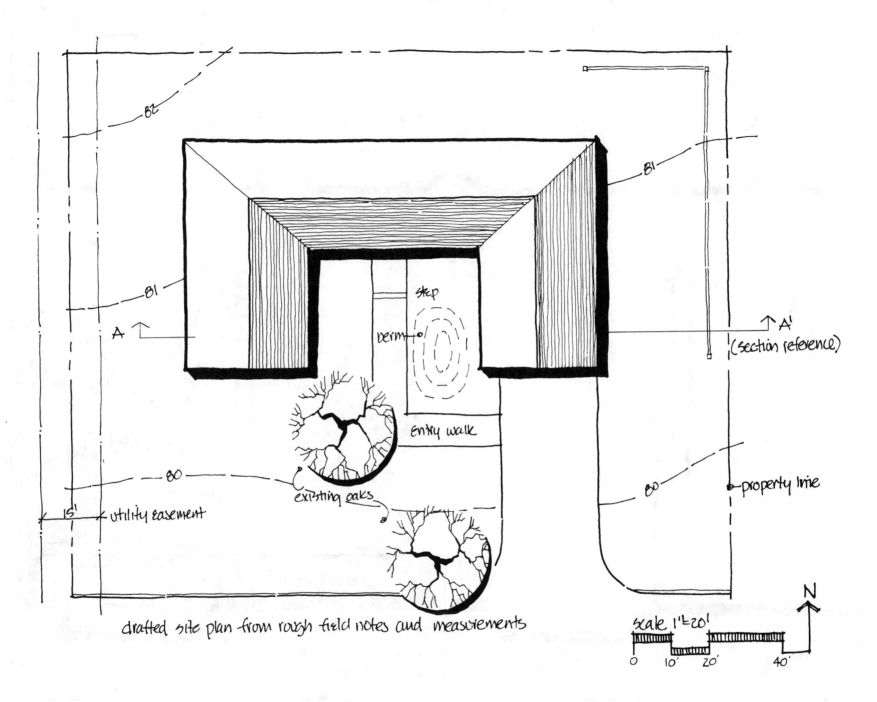

82

81

81

81

A

A'
(section reference)

step

berm

Entry walk

existing oaks

80

80

property line

15'
utility easement

drafted site plan from rough field notes and measurements

scale 1"=20'

0   10'   20'   40'

N

FIGURE 4-5
Freehand drafted residential site plan. (Designer: T. G. Kramer)

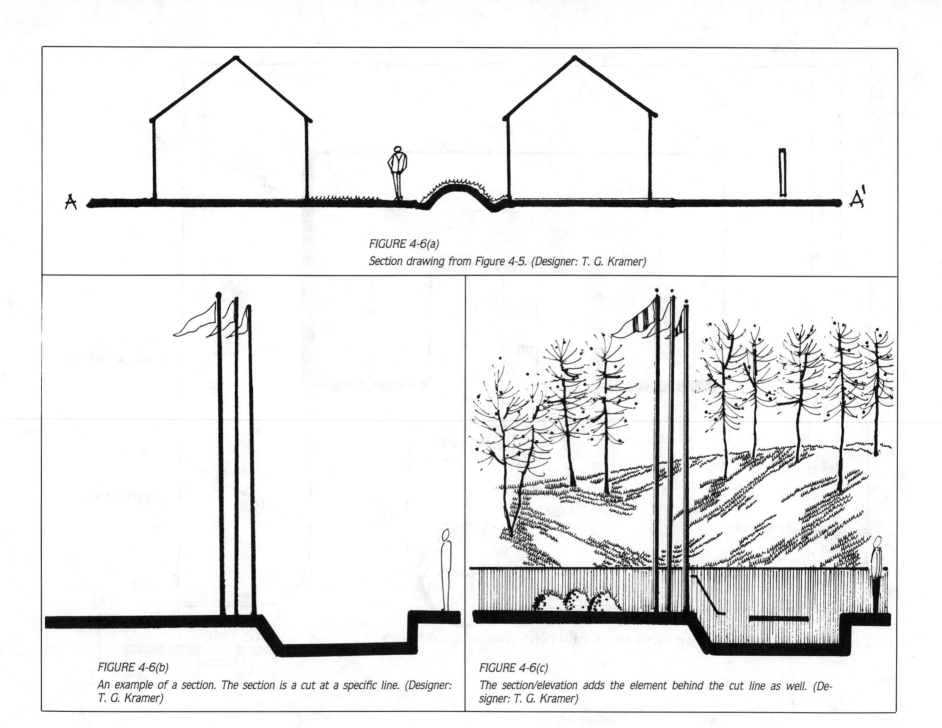

FIGURE 4-6(a)
Section drawing from Figure 4-5. (Designer: T. G. Kramer)

FIGURE 4-6(b)
An example of a section. The section is a cut at a specific line. (Designer: T. G. Kramer)

FIGURE 4-6(c)
The section/elevation adds the element behind the cut line as well. (Designer: T. G. Kramer)

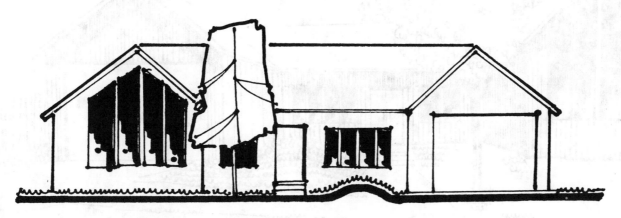

FIGURE 4-7

A typical elevation. Note that the windows are darkened to give a reflective
quality and depth to the drawing. (Designer: T. G. Kramer)

FIGURE 4-8

In this perspective, the same graphic techniques are used as in the elevation, Figure 4-7, yet here more depth and details are shown. Note that the elements closest to the viewer are drawn darker and more detailed than elements further back in the drawing. (Designer: T. G. Kramer)

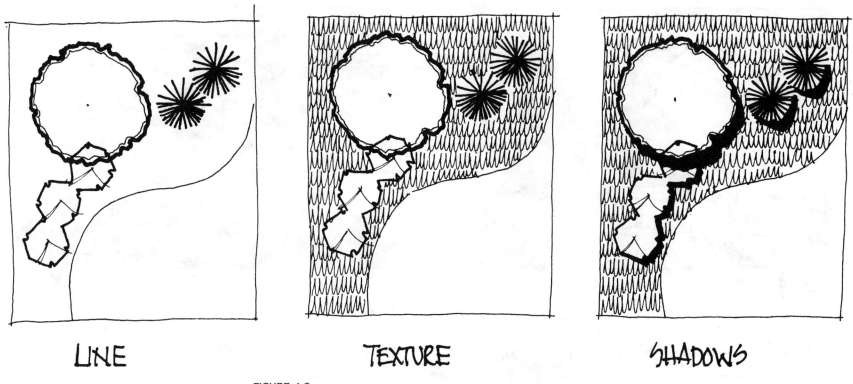

LINE   TEXTURE   SHADOWS

FIGURE 4-9

In a drawing, line, texture, and shadows are the basic elements used to symbolize an actual site space. (Designer: T. G. Kramer)

In plan, elevation, and perspective drawings, the tallest or primary objects, such as buildings, trees, main pavements, or ground surfaces and edges, are presented in heavier line weights. These heavier lines indicate the importance of the objects. Smaller objects or secondary elements, such as turf, planting beds, and stepping stones are normally drawn with thinner line weights and values as they recede into the background. Plan drawings and elevation presentation of plants are shown in Figure 4-10. Note that objects closest to the viewer are drawn with darker line weights and values, which decrease as the eye moves down towards the ground plane. The same concept may be used for its plane contrast as seen in Figure 4-11 of plan and section drawings.

In section drawings, the primary line weights and contrasts are again the outline of major objects and the ground line. Sections not showing textures and secondary elements use less secondary lines. Figure 4-12 compares a typical residential section and a section/elevation.

In elevation drawings, primary lines are used to emphasize middleground elements and the outline of objects. Secondary lines are used for surfaces, textures, and so forth. Figure 4-13 shows the residential example in 4-12 as an elevation.

Perspective drawings use a variety of line weights, values, and contrasts to give depth and proportion to the objects presented. Again, objects closest to the viewer have greater line contrast, detail, and shading than receding elements in the perspective. Figure 4-14 is a perspective showing a residential entry design proposal.

PERSPECTIVES

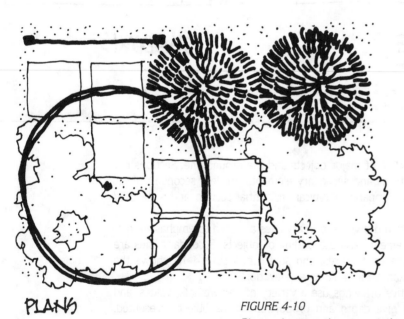
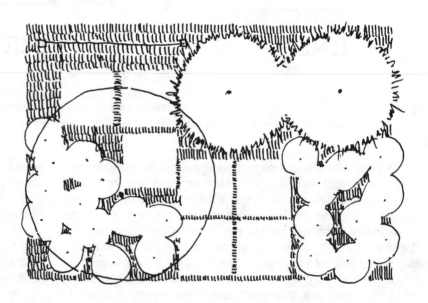

PLANS

FIGURE 4-10

Plan and perspective presentations should support each other. In the examples shown, a variety of line weights and contrasts are used. (Designer: Gregory M. Pierceall)

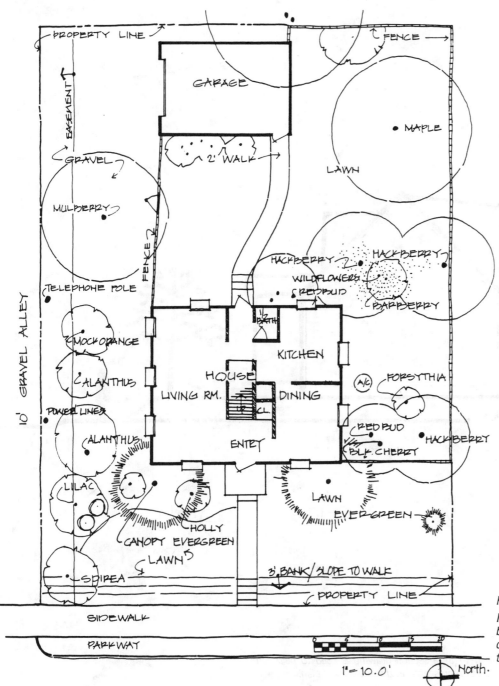

PROPERTY LINE

FENCE

EASEMENT

GARAGE

2' WALK

GRAVEL

LAWN

MAPLE

MULBERRY

FENCE

10' GRAVEL ALLEY

TELEPHONE POLE

HACKBERRY
HACKBERRY
WILDFLOWERS
REDBUD
BARBERRY

MOCKORANGE

CALANTHUS

½ BATH

KITCHEN

POWER LINES

HOUSE

LIVING RM.
DINING
CL.

A/C
FORSYTHIA

ALANTHUS

ENTRY

REDBUD
BLK. CHERRY
HACKBERRY

LILAC

HOLLY

LAWN
EVERGREEN

CANOPY EVERGREEN

LAWN

SPIREA

3' BANK/SLOPE TO WALK

PROPERTY LINE

SIDEWALK

PARKWAY

1" = 10.0'

North.

FIGURE 4-11(a)

In this design proposal, the plan and section are drawn with simple lines because they are being used only as inventory pieces of information. As the design proposal develops, more detail can be used in the plan and elevations to show what changes are to be made. (Designer: Gregory M. Pierceall)

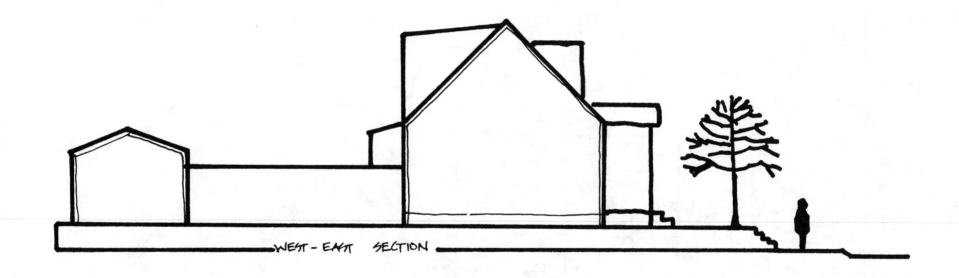

WEST - EAST SECTION

$1" = 10' 0'$

 North

FIGURE 4-11(b)

From the plan in Figure 4-11(a), a section drawing is used to help communicate the vertical aspects represented in the site survey plan.

WEST—EAST SECTION/ELEVATION

North.

FIGURE 4-12

As a contrast to the section drawing in Figure 4-11, the designer's graphic techniques show more details as this is what is to be proposed. Not only is the elevation shown, but details beyond this section of the drawing. The primary emphasis of the drawing is the proposed plantings. (Designer: Gregory M. Pierceall)

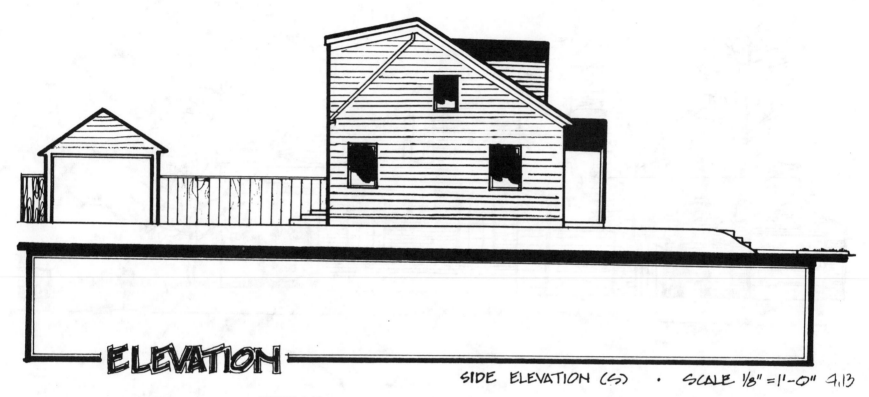

ELEVATION

SIDE ELEVATION (S) • SCALE ⅛" = 1'-0" 4.13

FIGURE 4-13

This architectural elevation shows structural elements such as windows, siding, fences, etc. (Designer: Gregory M. Pierceall)

Residence
Entry Cou[rt]

FIGURE 4-14

This entry perspective was developed to illustrate what a proposed planting would look like before it actually was planted. The drafting time involved would most likely not be justified for the average residential situation. (Designer: Gregory M. Pierceall)

SHADOWS. In plan, elevation, and perspective drawings, shading and shadows help create depth and define the vertical aspects and configuration of the site elements. Without shadows and shading, drawings would look flat and unrealistic. To communicate this feeling of realism in plan, elevation, and perspective drawings, an assumed light source has to be defined and used to establish shadows. A generally accepted rule of thumb is shadows should be drawn to the bottom and/or right edges of a sheet rather than to the top or left. This emphasis relates to the direction plans are read, left to right and top to bottom. This shadowing orientation also places the "visual weight" at the bottom of the drawing where it appears to be more at ease. Sections do not use shading and shadows because they are technical drawings used primarily to express heights and widths in design proposals. The exception to this rule is the *section/ elevation drawing*. Figures 4-15 and 4-16 show examples of shadows in plan and perspective drawings.

DRAWING COORDINATION

When drawing multiple views of the same area or proposal, remember that all drawings should work together in supporting the design concept. Plan, section, elevation, and perspectives should use consistent drawing techniques and styles, line weights, and contrasts to best present the primary components in the design. Figures 4-5 through 4-8 show consistent drawing styles and graphic presentation coordination.

DESIGN ELEMENTS INCLUDED IN DRAWINGS

Line

Line can be produced by pencils, pens, or markers and is one of the basic elements of any landscape design proposal or drawing. Line is the skeleton that defines edges, areas, shapes, and surfaces including textures, shading, shadows, and color included in drawings. Basic line qualities that can be selected, used, and manipulated are line weight, line contrast, and line style. *Line weight* is the hierarchy of line widths within a drawing. When presented, the darkest lines by width should visually be more predominant. These heavier lines should define the primary drawing elements, such as buildings, walls, and walks. Lighter lines are narrower and represent secondary drawing elements such as steps, plantings, edges, and so on. De-

tails such as textures and shading can then be added to line drawings. (See Figure 4-17.)

Value Contrast

All good drawings should include value contrasts to define areas or planes. Line and/or tones of gray can be used to separate visually one area from another. Value contrast should be used in all plan drawings to create the layered character of overlapping elements. In elevation and perspective drawings, value contrast is used to define elements closest to the viewer and separate them from components further away. Figure 4-18a is an example of value contrast using line to establish the planes in the drawing. Figure 4-18b is value contrast using line values to define areas.

Before final drafting, designers should consider the line weights and contrasts that may be developed to achieve a distinct hierarchy of edges and areas. Primary design elements such as buildings, walls, and walks are usually darker and contrast with the lighter lines of planting bed edges, groundcovers, and secondary elements or surfaces. This degree of contrast and drawing clarity is often referred to as *reading*. When a drawing reads, the edge lines and value contrasts create visual depth, which easily identifies the areas and planes to the viewer. Shadows also help define the various levels and details of the drawing. Figure 4-19 shows a comparison of plans and the varying degrees of readability using line and shadows.

Freehand and Drafted Drawing Styles

Drafting style is determined by what is being drawn. The graphic line style selected may use freehand or drafted techniques. *Drafted* styles use exact pencil guidelines which are drawn with a straight-edge for accuracy and clarity. Drafted lines are normally used for design elements that are constructed or are to be built. In presentation drawings, buildings, walks, walls, and fences are drafted lines. All construction drawings are drafted because the actual element being built will be constructed from this information. These documents are also the guides for the estimating and bidding processes prior to the project's implementation.

Freehand styles of drafting use lightly ruled pencil guidelines with all final lines drawn without a straight-edge in either ink or a heavier pencil weight. Freehand drafting lends itself to representing the more natural elements in a site plan such as plant materials, surfaces such as mulch, and ground planes. Realistic textures and time

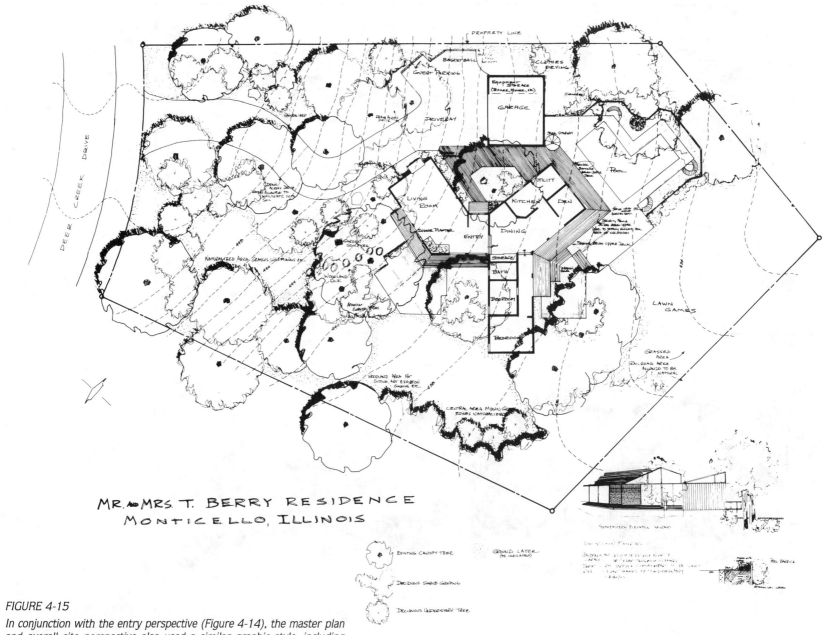

MR. and MRS. T. BERRY RESIDENCE
MONTICELLO, ILLINOIS

EXISTING CANOPY TREE

GROUND LAYER
(AS INDICATED)

DECIDUOUS SHRUB GROUPING

DECIDUOUS UNDERSTORY TREE

FIGURE 4-15

In conjunction with the entry perspective (Figure 4-14), the master plan and overall site perspective also used a similar graphic style, including shading and shadows, thus presenting a unified design package. (Designer: Gregory M. Pierceall)

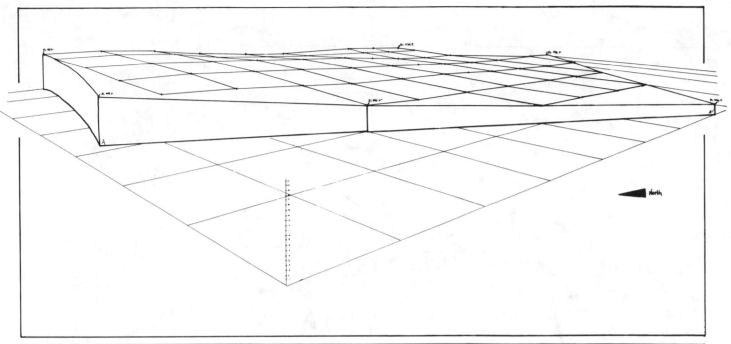

North

Figure 4-16

From the plan in Figure 4-15, a two-point aerial perspective was developed. (Designer: Gregory M. Pierceall)

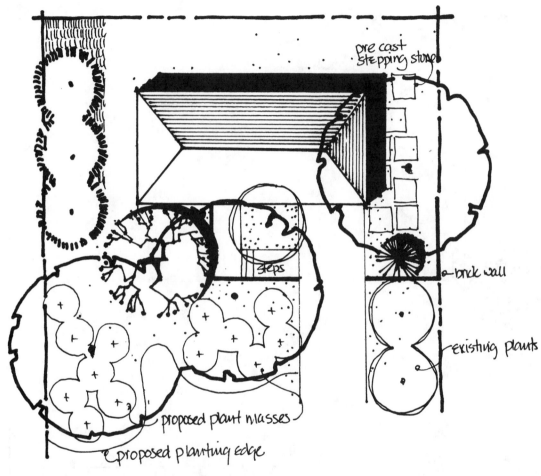

FIGURE 4-17

Site plan presentations. Note that heavier lines define primary drawing elements, and finer lines are used to add textures and to outline secondary plan components. In concept, a plan can be drawn with a light ground plane and dark outline of canopy elements or dark ground plane and light canopy. In an actual residential plan, as seen in Figure 4-18b, the value contrast between ground surfacings, plantings, and the shadows provides a realistic representation of what the actual site area looks like. (Designer: T. G. Kramer)

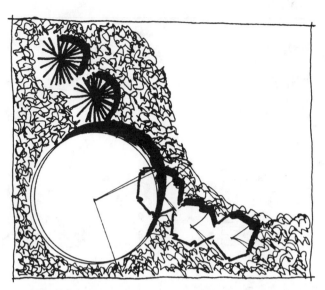

FIGURE 4-18(a)

Simple value contrast illustrations. (Designer: T. G. Kramer)

FIGURE 4-18(b)

Value contrast site plan. (Designer: P. Stinchcomb)

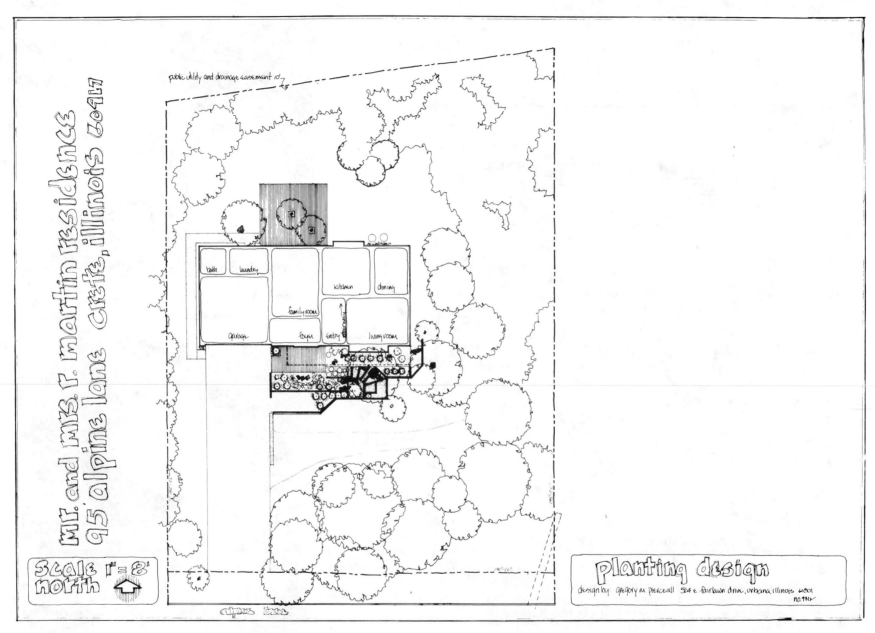

Mr. and Mrs. P. martin residence
95 alpine lane crete, illinois 60417

public utility and drainage easement 10'

bath | laundry

kitchen | dining

family room

garage | foyer | entry | living room

scale north 1"=8'

planting design
design by gregory M. pierceall 524 e. fairlawn drive, urbana, illinois 61801
no.9312

FIGURE 4-19(a)

*This site plan uses little line weight variation and no shadows, resulting in
a flat-looking plan. (Designer: Gregory M. Pierceall)*

planting plan for
mr and mrs
robert martin residence
95 alpine drive, crete, illinois
scale 1"=8   north >

designed by
g.m.pierceall

FIGURE 4-19(b)

This site plan of the same site in Figure 4-19a uses a wider range of line weights, shadows, and more detailed graphic symbols, which provides a more realistic-looking proposal. While this plan and the previous one are of the same site, it should be noted that the more detailed plan takes more drafting time to achieve its results. (Designer: Gregory M. Pierceall)

savings are probably the main advantages of freehand drafting. Freehand graphics also result in a format that is more informal than other drafted presentation styles. It is also less time consuming and can be used if the project is only to communicate the design concepts in a presentation drawing. Figure 4-20 compares the drafted and freehand techniques for the same plan.

SYMBOLS

Symbols are like abbreviations and are used to represent what the proposed elements in a composition will look like before the project is actually developed in plan, section, elevation, and perspective presentations. Graphic styles and techniques should represent the "essence" of what is being symbolized and should read using value contrast. Care should be taken to be consistent with symbols throughout a project, especially when multiple drawings are used. To illustrate existing information and proposed ideas, landscape designers use combinations of line, form, textures, and shading as symbols. These symbols more accurately represent plant materials and surfaces than simple lines, forms, and textures. Remember that they *represent* surfaces, textures, forms of plants, and construction materials; they may not duplicate the actual forms these design elements take. Landscape design symbols are found throughout the text. (See Chapter 6 for specific examples of design symbols.)

PRESENTATION MEDIA

After original drawings are completed and blackline ozalid prints are made, color can be added to enhance the line, textures, shadows, and shading techniques used in drafting the drawing. Blackline prints are usually used for rendering; blueline prints are not as easy to render because of the blue color. Blueprints are usually made for construction drawings. The addition of color can be provided through a variety of media including markers, colored pencils, pastel chalks, or their combinations.

Markers

Colored markers are primary rendering media because of the range of colors, neatness, and boldness of the presentation. Colored markers are produced in a variety of tips including a wide tip, pointed nib, and fine point. *Wide-tip markers* include a soft, felt-tip approx-

imately 1/8″ wide and 1/4″ in length. The widest edge is used to render large areas while the 1/8″ edge provides a narrower line of color. The *pointed nib* has a conelike tip that produces a bold yet finer line than the narrow edge of a wide-tipped marker. The *fine-point* marker has a sharp point that produces a thin, constant line similar to an ink pen. Markers are generally selected because they are easy to work with, dry fast, and are convenient. Markers are expensive and do take practice before they can be used with any proficiency. Seeing markers demonstrated is often the best way to gain the knowledge needed to use them skillfully. However, there are two inexpensive books available on marker techniques: *Landscape Painting with Markers* by Harry Borgman and *Sketching with Markers* by T. C. Wang. Both references cover the equipment, techniques, and products involving markers. A more expensive and comprehensive reference, which includes a discussion of markers and colored pencils, is *Color Drawing* by Michael Doyle.

Colored Pencils and Chalks

Colored pencils are available in a wide range of colors and are neat and convenient. They can be used effectively over markers to add details and/or textures to otherwise flat-looking drawings. However, they are more pastel and, if used alone, do not read well when drawings must be presented to large groups.

Chalk, while offering similar coloring, are often pale and messier than pencils or markers, and a fixative must be applied to hold colors from smearing. While an entire drawing may not be done in chalk, such elements as sky and water may be done more effectively in chalk than other media.

The addition of color enhances the realism of a proposal and helps homeowners better visualize the ideas. Color, like line weight, is layered in a hierarchy relative to the drawing's value contrasts. Rendering all ground plane elements and allowing the lines of canopy elements to "read" through is one presentation option. This technique makes it easy to perceive the various layers of plants and features proposed. Another technique to consider is rendering the canopy elements and thus covering over components under this "overstory" layer. This method provides a realistic plan view yet often eliminates many of the underlying details.

When selecting colors for a presentation, realism is not the sole criteria. Value contrasts provided in a drawing are also important to define the various areas within the proposal. Depth in a drawing may be created by having a light ground plane and dark canopy or

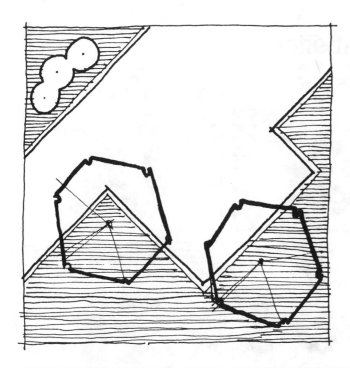

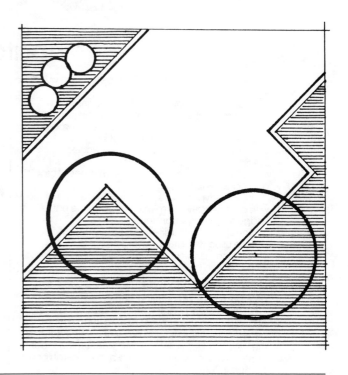

FIGURE 4-20

Drafting styles. Both freehand and drafted drawings are first laid out in pencil or non-print lead using a straight-edge and scale. The difference is that the drafted drawing is finalized using a straight-edge and circle template while the freehand does not. (Designer: T. G. Kramer)

a dark ground and lighter canopy. When selecting colors just as project format, consider the client and presentation uses. For example, selecting a purple ground plane with orange and green trees may have high contrast and readability yet may not be realistic enough to present to a "traditionally" minded client. The best means to gain skill and proficiency in color presentations is through experimentation and practice. Explore the resources, techniques, and references available and try duplicating illustrations as a means to develop your own techniques and style.

Pressure-Sensitive Media

Other media that can be used to save time and create striking presentations are press-on lettering, symbols, and textures. These *press-on* or *pressure-sensitive* materials are used in the production of drawings before prints are made. Many commercial brands of pre-printed, stick-on type graphics are available and appropriate for a range of drawing situations. Note that these press-on media should not be used as a crutch for individual design skills. Effective use re-

quires an understanding of their advantage as a time-saver and not as a substitute for composition presentation skills. While providing a time savings, these materials are expensive for everyday use. Figures 4-21a and 4-21b show examples of the diversity and availability of press-on media.

SUMMARY

The styles or techniques used in graphic communications should express ideas clearly, for whomever they are intended, be realistic enough to produce within the time available for their presentation, and relate to the project needs. Early in the design process, ideas and drawings should be loose and free to provide for maximum creativity and generation of ideas, not graphic perfection. As ideas are reviewed and selected, they should be refined as necessary for presentation and installation. A basic weakness of beginning designers is the desire for finished drawings early rather than at the end of the design process.

Zipatone Dry Transfer Lettering

Zipatone offers well over 250 typefaces in our dry transfer lettering range.

A distortion proof carrier sheet means that a maximum number of characters can be printed close together on each sheet and that it remains workable right down to the last letter.

Carefully researched letter frequencies insure the minimum of wastage.

The ink is pliable, resists abrasion, doesn't crack and adheres to most surfaces.

Intricate typefaces such as A.K.I. Lines are printed with a clear carrier film which enables the entire image to be easily transferred.

The dry transfer adhesive is heat resistant and can be used for diazo copying.

Zipatone dry transfer is packaged in clear bags for protection and storage.

HOW TO ORDER ZIPATONE DRY TRANSFER LETTERING

In this catalog each typeface is shown in every available size. The number printed in bold type beneath the sample is the order number. It denotes the style number, point size and whether the sheet contains capitals or lower case and numerals or a complete font.

Package size 8-1/2" x 11" (21.6cm x 27.9cm-2 sheets) Available in black only except style 505 Manuscript Gothic, 609 Engravers Old English which are also available in gold and style 55 Helvetica Medium which is also available in white.

1. Draw a baseline with a Blue-Zip pen, remove the backing sheet and position the first letter using the guide lines located at the beginning and end of each row of type.

2. Holding the sheet firmly in position, shade lightly over the entire letter with a Zipatone burnisher.

3. When the letter appears completely gray, it has been transferred. Carefully lift away the carrier sheet and repeat process until the complete word or phrase has been set.

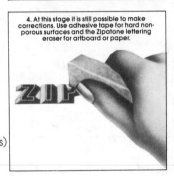

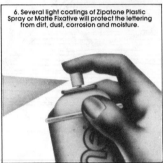

4. At this stage it is still possible to make corrections. Use adhesive tape for hard non-porous surfaces and the Zipatone lettering eraser for artboard or paper.

5. Place the backing sheet over the lettering, hold in position and burnish firmly and thoroughly for perfect adhesion. Carefully erase the baseline with Blue-Zip Eradicator.

6. Several light coatings of Zipatone Plastic Spray or Matte Fixative will protect the lettering from dirt, dust, corrosion and moisture.

CATALOG PAGE

DRY TRANSFER

FIGURE 4-21(a)

Pressure-Sensitive Media. While the examples shown include only lettering and textures, many more types and brands of "press-on" media are available. (Courtesy of Zip-A-Tone Corp.)

Black only

464 465 466 269 461 790 275

78 79 77 262 371 306 274

423 446 447 263 264 341 352

365 366 265 266 281 617 629

623 608 612 267 566 647 665

268 467 273 669 652 785 786

FIGURE 4-21(b)

When detailed patterns are necessary in the development of a proposal, pressure sensitive materials provide a time savings.

For any designer, presentation of ideas on paper is a learning process. Through awareness of examples and illustrations available, one learns to think and communicate graphically. The best means to gain graphic skills and develop self-confidence is to become technically proficient with paper, pens, pencils, and the other equipment and materials used in graphic communications. As you observe new techniques or ideas, try to employ them when appropriate. This practice of observation and application of ideas or techniques improves and sharpens your skills and gives you the background needed for further presentations.

Collecting graphic ideas, composition methods, and techniques in a notebook or file can be of valuable service in stimulating ideas for future projects. Collected graphics can include images from newspapers, magazines, advertisements, or design project work. They will serve as a reference for lettering, lines, symbols, forms, textures, colors, and combinations (Figure 4-22). Collected graphics also give you individual examples of composition. Additional practice in design and graphics can be achieved by tracing objects from a variety of sources and "creating" new compositions, exercising your composition thought process. Figure 4-23 shows an example of tracing elements from two sketches to make a third drawing. Models also can be used to communicate design ideas. Figure 4-24 shows the difference between a sketch and a model, and Figures 4-25 and 4-26 show study and presentation models.

Graphic communication requires an understanding of the vocabulary and applications available to the designer. Graphic proficiency is as good as the designer's use of the skills and techniques available to him or her to express ideas for specific design situations. Much of graphics is trial and error, thus learning often results from your successes and failures. Observe, collect, compose, and practice—these are the guidelines to success and proficiency in graphic communications.

FIGURE 4-22(a)

Collected Graphics. Graphic ideas can be collected from newspapers, magazines, and advertisements. Graphic techniques and styles can be used to develop drawings and sketches, as shown in examples (b) and (c). While these examples are readily available, they should be used as a guide, not as a means of directly tracing proposals.

FIGURE 4-22(b)

Ideas for human figures, plant materials and sheet composition can be gained by observing advertisements and collecting them for future reference.

FIGURE 4-22(c)

In this ad showing the influence of seasonal change, graphic techniques can
be gained and applied relative to showing landscapes in various seasons.

(a)

FIGURE 4-23

Collected Sketches. Part of the process of proposing a design is the selection of graphic techniques to represent ideas. In the three sketches shown, the designer has taken two sketching ideas (a) and (b) and developed a third (sketch c). Tracing provides an opportunity to become comfortable with a pen and style already developed. (Designers: S. M. Halberg/Gregory M. Pierceall)

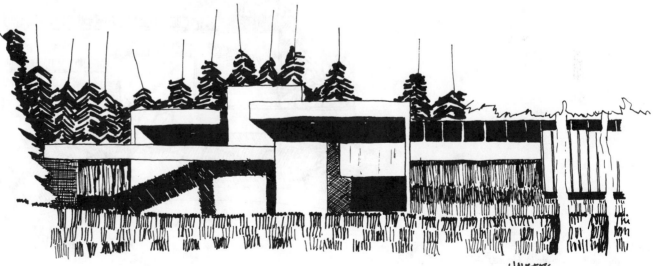

(b)

(c)

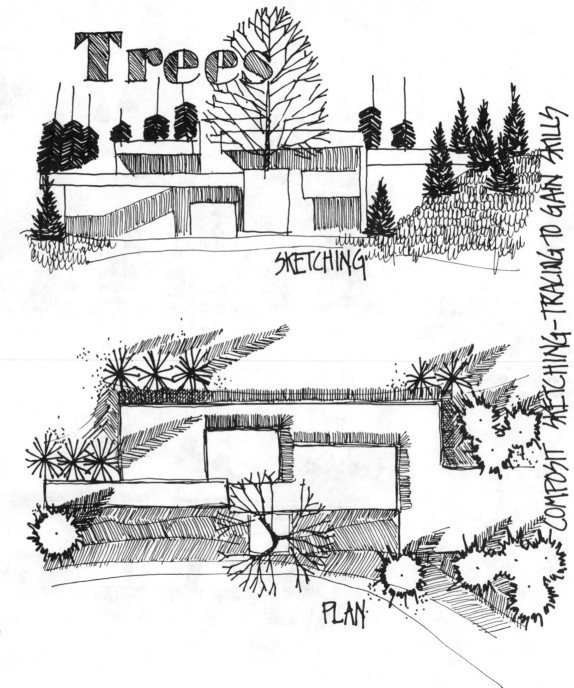

Trees

SKETCHING

COMPOSIT SKETCHING-TRACING TO GAIN SKILLS

PLAN

FIGURE 4-23(c)
From the sketches seen in Figures 4-23(a) and (b), a third sketch and plan were developed.

FIGURE 4-24

Sketch and Model. A model is a three-dimensional representation of a proposal. When a model is used, a layperson can easily relate to and understand a proposal. However, models are time consuming and expensive to construct, and thus not commonly used in residential scale landscape design. The model shown is part of the design package shown in Figures 4-14, 4-15, and 4-16. (Designer: Gregory M. Pierceall)

FIGURE 4-25

Study Model. While presentation models are not often used in residential site proposals, a simple study model may be. Study models are valuable tools and easily constructed. They help beginning designers evaluate spaces and proposals.

FIGURE 4-26

Presentation Models. In contrast to the simplicity of construction and detail of a study model, a presentation model is quite detailed and elaborate. Presentation models such as this may be used as a promotional and advertising tool to sell homes. Total site models help give new homeowners an idea of what newly developed sites can look like. (Courtesy of Kansas State University)

REFERENCES AND READINGS

A. General Graphics

Hanks and Belliston. *Draw! A Visual Approach to Thinking, Learning, and Communicating.* Los Altos, CA: William Kaufmann, 1977.

Hartman, R. *Graphics for Designers.* Ames, IA: Iowa State University Press, 1976.

Lin, Mike. *Economy of Graphics.* Washington, D.C.: ASLA, 1979.

Lockard, W. K. *Design Drawing Experiences.* Tucson, AZ: Pepper Publishing, 1979.

Zipatone. *Zipatone Catalog.* Elk Grove Village, IL: Zipatone Corp., 1982.

B. Line Drawings

Van Dyke, Scott. *From Line to Design.* West Lafayette, IN: PDA Publishers, 1982.

Walker, T. D. *Plan Graphics.* West Lafayette, IN: PDA Publishers, 1975.

—————. *Perspective Sketches.* West Lafayette, IN: PDA Publishers, 1975.

Wang, Thomas C. *Pencil Sketches.* New York: Van Nostrand Reinhold Co., 1977.

—————. *Plan and Section Drawing.* New York: Van Nostrand Reinhold Co., 1979.

—————. *Sketching with Markers.* New York: Van Nostrand Reinhold Co., 1981.

C. Drafting

Ball, John E. *Architectural Drafting.* Reston, VA: Reston Publishing Co., 1981.

Ching, F. *Architectural Graphics.* New York: Van Nostrand Reinhold Co., 1975.

D. Rendering

Borgman, Harvey. *Landscape Painting with Markers.* New York: Watson-Guptill Publications, 1977.

Doyle, Mike. *Color Drawing.* New York: Van Nostrand Reinhold Co., 1981.

Oles, P. Stevenson. *Architectural Illustration.* New York: Van Nostrand Reinhold Co., 1979.

Wang, Thomas C. *Sketching with Markers.* New York: Van Nostrand Reinhold Co., 1981.

*D*esign composition and presentation

As a means of presenting ideas before they are constructed, designers use graphics and various other presentation methods. Graphics are used to illustrate the intended proposals and are used in conjunction with written text and/or verbal dialogue to explain what the graphics may not portray. Models, three-dimensional media, present scaled representations of design ideas. In developments for residential design, models have limited uses because of the time and expense involved. As a landscape designer, graphics are the primary presentation method used to communicate proposals for residential landscape designs.

DRAWINGS COMPONENTS

The fundamental components found in any presentation drawing include sheet borders, a title block, the plan or drawing area, and support information such as legends, labels, leaders, scale, orientation, and notes. The effectiveness of any sheet is in the information presented, its organization and composition. The initial step in composing a sheet is to select a drawing surface that is appropriate for the medium to be used; for example, toothed paper for pencil and smooth paper for ink. The next step is to select a paper size that is in proportion to the size of the drawing to be developed, sheet sizes appropriate for the project's demands, and equivalent to duplication papers available. Standard ozalid print papers include $8\frac{1}{2}'' \times 11''$, $11'' \times 17''$, $12'' \times 18''$, $16'' \times 18''$, $17'' \times 22''$, $18'' \times 24''$, $21'' \times 30''$, $24'' \times 36''$ for individual sheets, or rolls $30''$ or $36''$ wide and almost any length. The final sheet size should provide adequate space for the drawing area and support information. Thus it is best to have a little larger sheet and cut it down than a sheet that is too small. The drawing area should be aligned to permit space for labels, leaders, and notes. Areas for a legend and for title block information should be secondary in their location on the sheet. The title block, plan, legend, notes, and sketches, if any, should be composed in a unified manner rather than scattered on the sheet. Figure 5-1a shows an example of sheet composition that could be improved, and Figure 5-1b shows an example of a well-developed sheet.

If more than one sheet is required for a project, a "base sheet" can be drawn as an original for sepias for the multiple sheets and additions. Use of sepias for information found on more than one sheet provides a time savings and ensures consistency of information. (The use of sepias for multiple sheet presentations is illustrated in Chapter 3, Figure 3-23.)

Title Blocks

Title blocks normally include project and sheet information which is supportive to the drawings. Permanent project data that belongs on all sheets includes the project title, project owner and address, project designer, date, and project numbers. Information that may vary with each sheet is the sheet title, such as the site survey or master plan, and site details. The sheet graphic and written scale and orientation also are relatively consistent pieces of information. A title block is most often located on the bottom edge or right-hand edges of the sheet. The top and left-hand edges of sheets are normally binding edge options. The title block is a continuous block of information and proportionate to the sheet and/or drawing sizes. Figure 5-2 includes options for title block locations and composition.

Within the title block related pieces of information should be organized together. For example, the project title, sheet title, and client/owner information should be grouped together as these pieces of information are related. The project title and sheet title should be more predominant since they relate to the project drawing more than the other pieces of information. The project owner, client/owner, and address are secondary to the sheet and project titles, yet should be located in the same area within the title block. Composition of other pieces of important data, such as the designer's name, project number, and date as well as the sheet number, scale, and orientation is by priorities of the listings and the amount of space available after the project and sheet titles and client information have been organized. Figure 5-3 shows examples of information within a title block.

Borders

Borders are used on a sheet as a frame for information. When developing multiple sheet presentations, the binding edge (top or left sides) will have a wider border than the other edges. Border line sizes depend on the sheet's size and should be proportionate to the other sheet information. After the sheet has its border and title blocks have been defined, the drawing area can be organized.

While in drafting sequence the borders and title block are drawn before the actual drawing, the size and configuration of the anticipated drawing is considered before borders and title block are finalized.

Labels and Leaders

Design support information includes labels, leaders, notes, legends, and titles used to explain information that cannot be fully conveyed graphically. Labels and notes are written descriptions which identify plan components, materials, or details. A leader is used to connect the label to the specific element that it describes. In laying out labels and leaders, try to place them as close as possible to the objects they describe. Labels placed too far away from objects and having long leaders can become confusing and create clutter. Notes are normally used to describe the characteristics or function of an area or elements on the proposal or to present information that cannot be drawn. Figure 5-4 shows examples of sheet support information.

Lettering

Lettering is a major information and design consideration in the organization and composition of any proposal. Lettering is used principally where graphics or symbols alone cannot explain the information. In a presentation, the lettering and the information

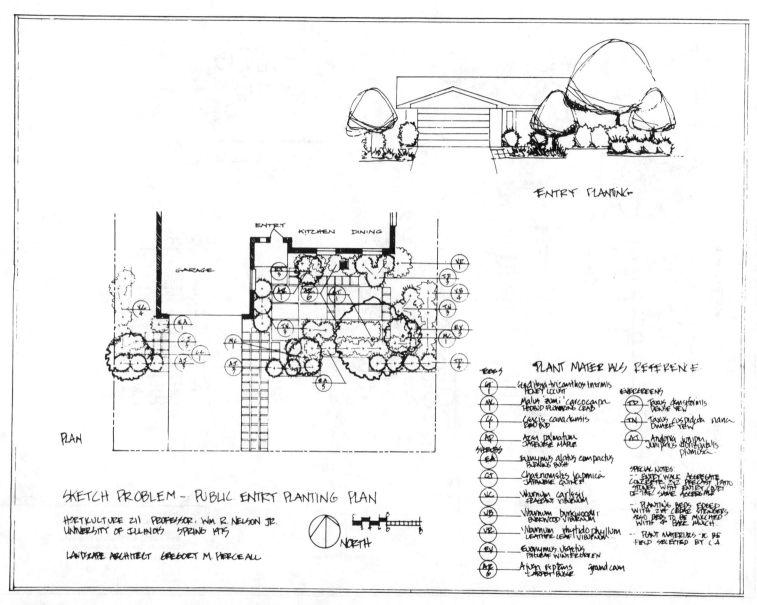

ENTRY PLANTING

PLAN

PLANT MATERIALS REFERENCE

TREES
- GT · Gleditsia tricanthos Inermis · HONEY LOCUST
- ML · Malus 'zumi' carcocarpa · REDBUD FLOWERING CRAB
- CC · Cercis canadensis · REDBUD
- AP · Acer palmatum · JAPANESE MAPLE

SHRUBS
- EA · Euonymus alatus compactus · BURNING BUSH
- CJ · Chaenomeles japonica · JAPANESE QUINCE
- VC · Viburnum carlesii · FRAGRANT VIBURNUM
- VB · Viburnum burkwoodii · BURKWOOD VIBURNUM
- VR · Viburnum rhytidophyllum · LEATHER LEAF VIBURNUM
- EV · Euonymus vegetus · BIGLEAF WINTERCREEPER
- AR · Ajuga reptans · CARPET BUGLE · ground cover

EVERGREENS
- TD · Taxus densiformis · DENSE YEW
- TN · Taxus cuspidata nana · DWARF YEW
- AJ · Andorra juniper · Juniperus horizontalis plumosa

SPECIAL NOTES:
- ENTRY WALK AGGREGATE CONCRETE 2×2 PRECAST PATIO STONES WITH ENTRY COURT OF THE SAME AGGREGATE
- PLANTING BEDS EDGED WITH 2" CEDAR STRANDERS ALSO BEDS TO BE MULCHED WITH 4" BARK MULCH
- PLANT MATERIALS TO BE FIELD SELECTED BY LA

SKETCH PROBLEM - PUBLIC ENTRY PLANTING PLAN

HORTICULTURE 211 PROFESSOR: WM. R. NELSON JR.
UNIVERSITY OF ILLINOIS SPRING 1975

LANDSCAPE ARCHITECT GREGORY M. PIERCEALL

NORTH

FIGURE 5-1(a)

The organization of sheet information within a design proposal is often called sheet composition. In this site plan, all the information is accurate yet misaligned on the sheet. Shifting the entry elevation so that it is aligned with the site plan and moving the plant reference so that it lines up with the site plan would help this sheet composition greatly. (Designer: Gregory M. Pierceall)

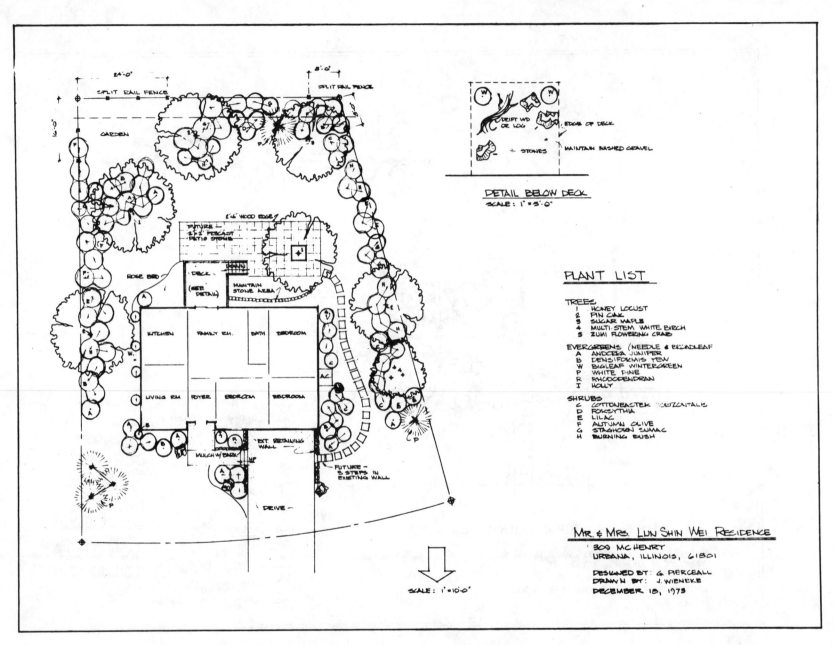

FIGURE 5-1(b)

This is a better example of sheet composition. (Designers: Gregory M. Pierceall and J. Wieneke)

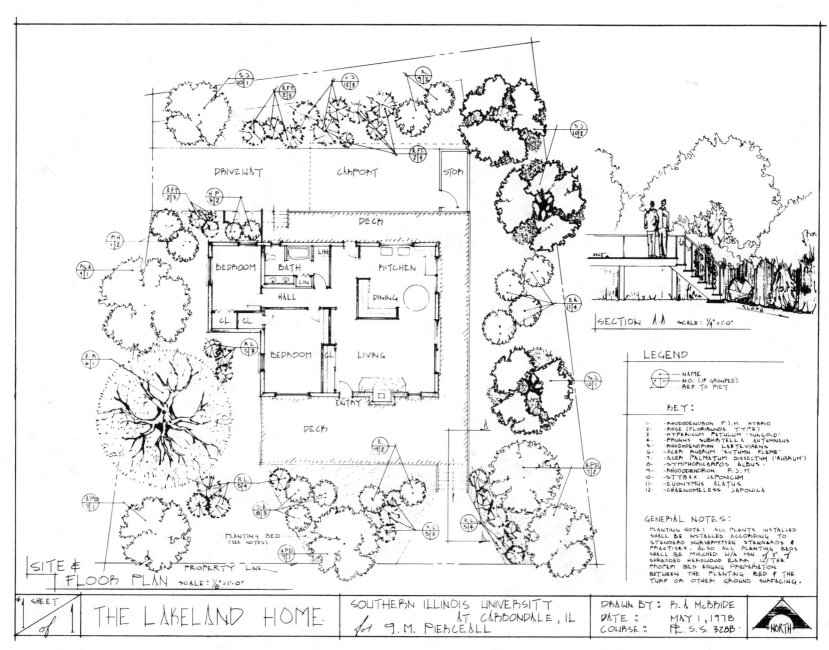

SITE & FLOOR PLAN SCALE: 1/8" = 1'-0"

SECTION A-A SCALE: 1/4" = 1'-0"

LEGEND

⊕ — NAME
   — NO. (IF GROUPED)
   — REF. TO KEY

KEY:

1- RHODODENDRON P.J.M. HYBRID
2- ROSE (FLORIBUNDA TYPE)
3- HYPERICUM PATULUM 'SUNGOLD'
4- PRUNUS SUBHIRTELLA AUTUMNALIS
5- RHODODENDRON LAETEVIRENS
6- ACER RUBRUM 'AUTUMN FLAME'
7- ACER PALMATUM DISSECTUM ('RUBRUM')
8- SYMPHORICARPOS ALBUS
9- RHODODENDRON P.J.M.
10- STYRAX JAPONICUM
11- EUONYMUS ALATUS
12- CHAENOMELESS JAPONICA

GENERAL NOTES:

PLANTING NOTE: ALL PLANTS INSTALLED SHALL BE INSTALLED ACCORDING TO STANDARD NURSERYMAN STANDARDS & PRACTISES. ALSO ALL PLANTING BEDS SHALL BE MULCHED W/A MIN. OF 3" SHREDDED HARDWOOD BARK. W/THE PROPER BED EDGING PREPARATION BETWEEN THE PLANTING BED & THE TURF OR OTHER GROUND SURFACING.

| SHEET 1 of 1 | THE LAKELAND HOME | SOUTHERN ILLINOIS UNIVERSITY AT CARBONDALE, IL for J. M. PIERCEALL | DRAWN BY: R. A McBRIDE DATE: MAY 1, 1978 COURSE: PL. S. S. 328B | NORTH |

FIGURE 5-2(a)

Title block. Title block locations can be included at the bottom or right-hand edge of a sheet as shown or developed as part of a specific area within the sheet as seen in Figure 5-2b. (Designer: R. McBride)

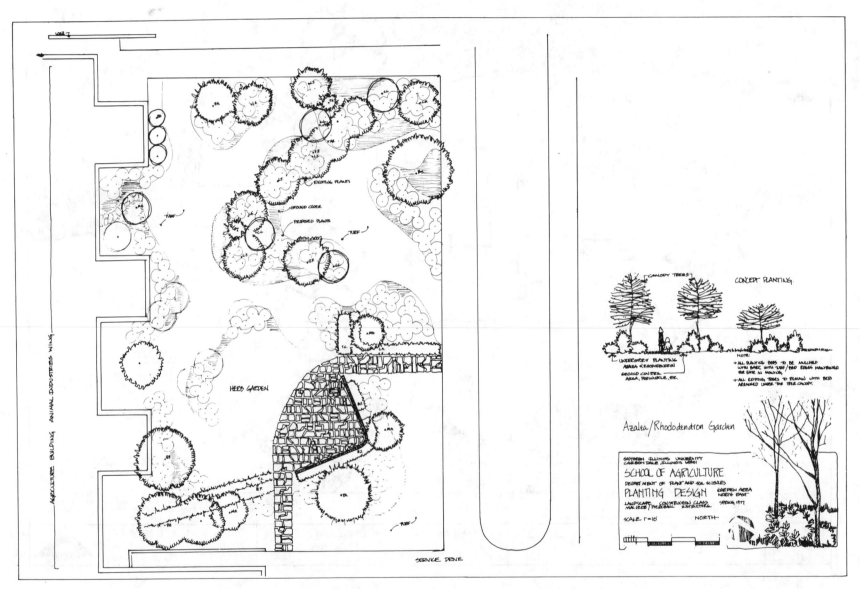

FIGURE 5-2(b)
Title block variation. (Designer: Gregory M. Pierceall)

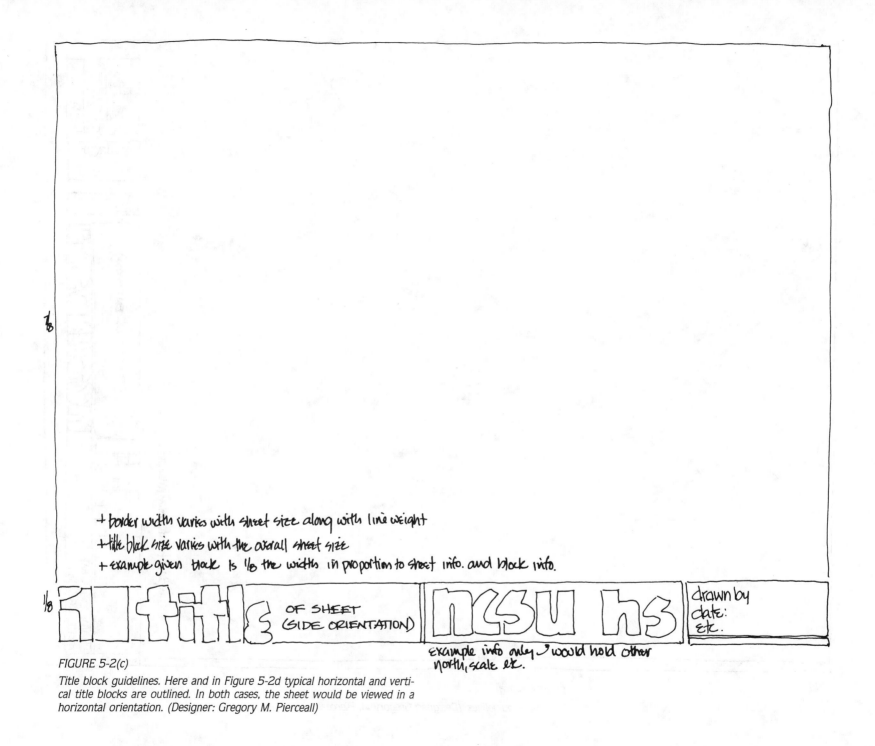

+ border width varies with sheet size along with line weight

+ title block size varies with the overall sheet size

+ example given block is ⅛ the widths in proportion to sheet info. and block info.

⅛ | **title** OF SHEET (SIDE ORIENTATION) | **ncsu hs** | drawn by date: etc.

example info only ⌐ would hold other north, scale etc.

FIGURE 5-2(c)

Title block guidelines. Here and in Figure 5-2d typical horizontal and vertical title blocks are outlined. In both cases, the sheet would be viewed in a horizontal orientation. (Designer: Gregory M. Pierceall)

FIGURE 5-2(d)
Title block guidelines. (Designer: Gregory M. Pierceall)

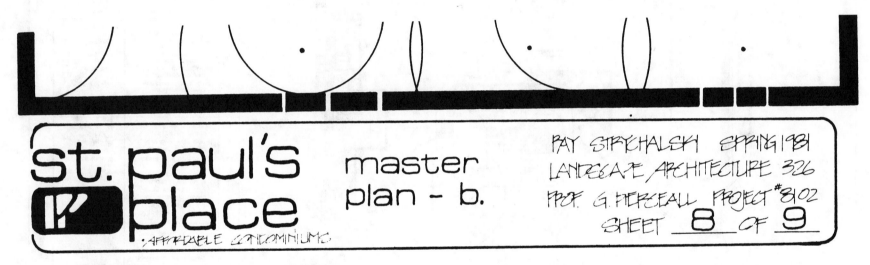

FIGURE 5-3

Title block information. Typical title block information includes the project title, sheet title, client and designer information. A project number, date, logo, and sheet notation may also be included. (Designer: Raymond Paul Strychalski)

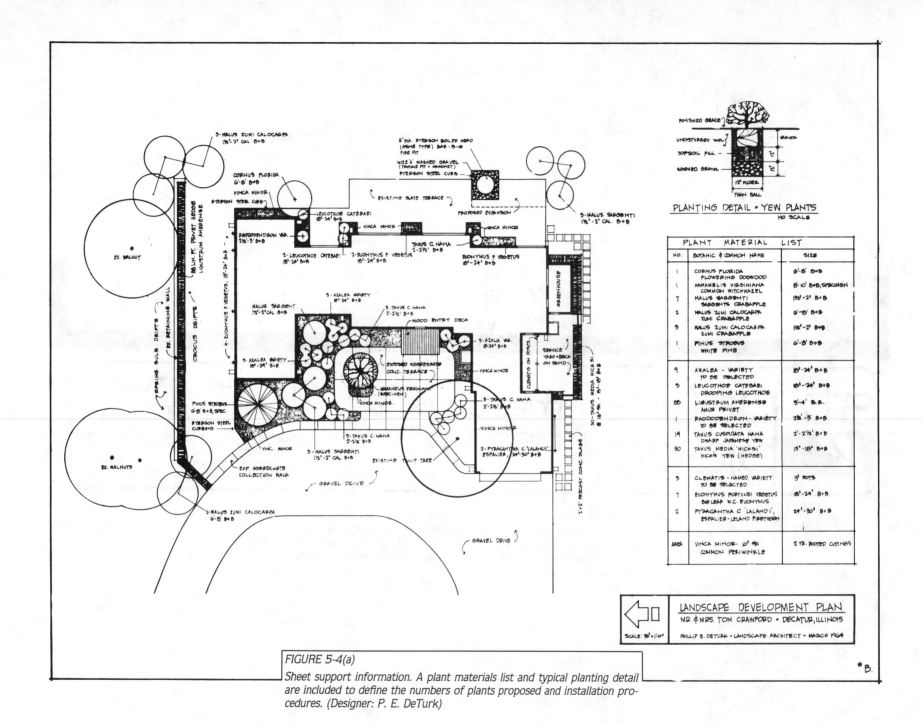

FIGURE 5-4(a)

Sheet support information. A plant materials list and typical planting detail are included to define the numbers of plants proposed and installation procedures. (Designer: P. E. DeTurk)

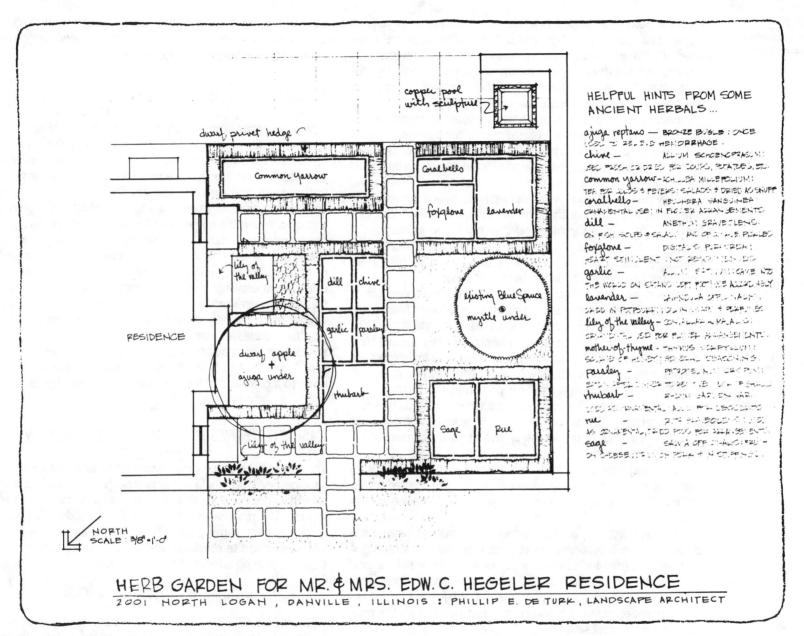

FIGURE 5-4(b)

Notes are used as support information to explain the character of the proposed herbs. (Designer: P. E. DeTurk)

conveyed become a compositional element that must be organized, just as title blocks, drawings, and support information are organized. Consistent, neat, and organized lettering complements a drawing, whereas inconsistent, messy, or haphazard lettering distracts from the overall appearance of the presentation. Lettering, like graphics, requires practice to gain proficiency and skill. Being observant, tracing, and collecting lettering types are means to gain confidence and experience in lettering and its composition.

The key to good lettering is (1) legibility and (2) consistency. That is, lettering must be readable and should have consistent style, height, and weight. The lettering style selected should be simple and relatively easy to produce. A detailed lettering style is not only time consuming, but may distract from the primary drawing focus. Lettering height or size should be selected relative to its purpose. If lettering is for a project title, its size should be relatively large. Major project titles can be in the range of ½″ to 1″, while labels, notes, and so forth can be in the ⅛″ to ¼″ range.

Overall lettering heights are kept consistent through the use of guidelines. *Guidelines* are usually defined by light pencil lines or the use of graph paper under a drawing to maintain lettering heights, spacing, and widths. After a lettering height has been selected for a particular area in a drawing, a cross-bar line is also included where all horizontal portion of letters will cross. Letters such as A, B, E, F, G, H, P, R, and X all have a cross-bar portion that should be consistent within a drawing. The spacing of this cross-bar affects the character of lettering. If the overall height of a letter is divided, the cross-bar can occur in the middle or two-thirds the distance above the base of the letter.

Individual letters should be spaced relative to the words they represent rather than evenly spaced. When reading, we see words, not individual letters; thus, organize and compose lettering accordingly.

Freehand lettering is an important skill to develop because it is quick once one is proficient and it gives character to a drawing. A proficiency in freehand lettering helps one learn the skill of compositing letters into words. This skill of composition is critical when hand lettering or when using preprinted lettering or mechanical lettering sets. See Figure 5-5 for examples of lettering and its composition within proposals.

Scales

Both written and graphic scales are necessary as part of a drawing's support information. A graphic scale indicates the scale of a drawing, and remains consistent even when photographically reduced, or used when an actual scale is unavailable. Examples of graphic and written scales are shown in Figure 5-6.

PRESENTING A DESIGN PROPOSAL

Design proposals often include more than one sheet to completely document and express design ideas and construction details. Residential site planning packages can include the following information: a site survey and analysis, site schematics, a site master plan, illustrative details and sketches. The amount of information presented depends on the client's needs and budget limitations relative to the cost of design. If the homeowner has only enough resources for the development of a master plan, then the survey, analysis, and design details may be verbal or occur on the same sheet in the presentation of concepts. After the design proposal is presented and reviewed, construction drawings may or may not be developed depending on the phasing and installation sequences selected by the homeowner. In addition to the design and/or construction drawings, a title page may be included to reference the project and to list the various sheets that comprise the package. The following case study along with Figures 5-7 to 5-18 shows the development of a presentation given to a client and includes an example of sheet layout.

CASE STUDY: RESIDENTIAL PLANTING DESIGN

The residential planting design proposal to be explained is a design package developed for a homeowner. The client desired a master plan that they could install at a pace relative to their needs and resources. The proposal is for an established residence with existing ornamental and native plants. Included is an inventory and analysis of the existing site conditions and an overall site planting plan, including a phasing schedule for plant installation.

Residential Planting Plan Proposal

DESIGN OBJECTIVES. Due to the existing floor plan of the residence and site orientation and window locations, little opportunity for solar gain to interior spaces was possible. The primary climate control design objectives were to buffer winter winds from the north and west and to shade the west face of the house from hot summer sun. Other design objectives were to functionally and aes-

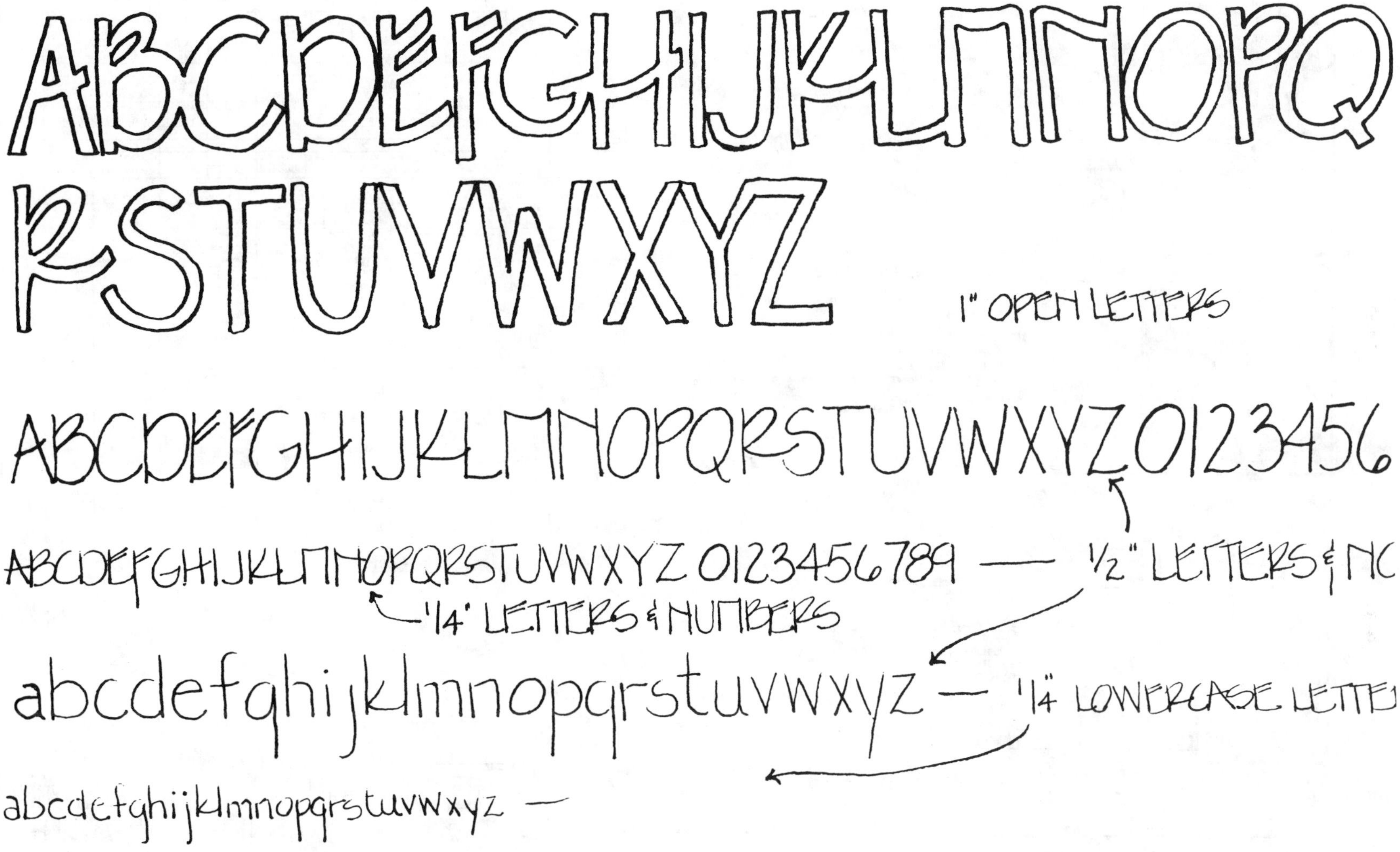

ABCDEFGHIJKLMNOPQRSTUVWXYZ

1" OPEN LETTERS

ABCDEFGHIJKLMNOPQRSTUVWXYZ 0123456

ABCDEFGHIJKLMNOPQRSTUVWXYZ 0123456789 — ½" LETTERS & NC

¼" LETTERS & NUMBERS

abcdefghijklmnopqrstuvwxyz — ¼" LOWERCASE LETTERS

abcdefghijklmnopqrstuvwxyz —

FIGURE 5-5(a)

Lettering. Legibility and consistency are the keys to good lettering. In this example the open lettering is achieved by first using a marker on a scrap sheet of paper, then tracing the outline of the letters onto the final sheet. (Designer: Lynn Marie Campbell)

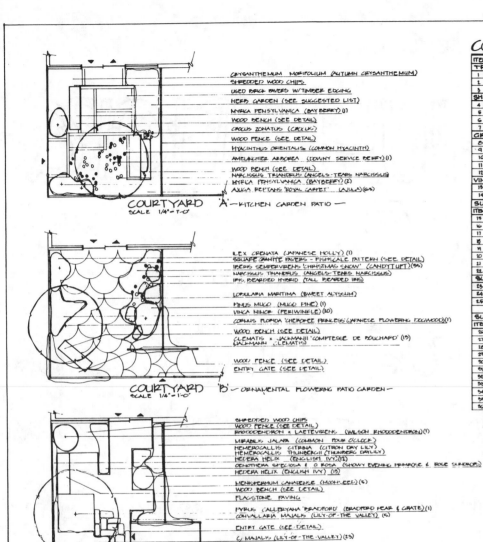

COURTYARD 'A' — KITCHEN GARDEN PATIO —
SCALE 1/4"=1'-0"

- CHRYSANTHEMUM MORIFOLIUM (AUTUMN CHRYSANTHEMUM)
- SHREDDED WOOD CHIPS
- USED BRICK PAVERS W/ TIMBER EDGING
- HERB GARDEN (SEE SUGGESTED LIST)
- MYRICA PENSYLVANICA (BAYBERRY) (1)
- WOOD BENCH (SEE DETAIL)
- CROCUS ZONATUS (CROCUS)
- WOOD FENCE (SEE DETAIL)
- HYACINTHUS ORIENTALIS (COMMON HYACINTH)
- AMELANCHIER ARBOREA (DOWNY SERVICE BERRY) (1)
- WOOD BENCH (SEE DETAIL)
- NARCISSUS TRIANDRUS (ANGELS-TEARS NARCISSUS)
- MYRICA PENSYLVANICA (BAYBERRY) (2)
- AJUGA REPTANS 'ROYAL CARPET' (AJUGA) (65)

COURTYARD 'B' — ORNAMENTAL FLOWERING PATIO GARDEN —
SCALE 1/4"=1'-0"

- ILEX CRENATA (JAPANESE HOLLY) (1)
- SQUARE GRANITE PAVERS - FISHSCALE PATTERN (SEE DETAIL)
- IBERIS SEMPERVIRENS 'CHRISTMAS SNOW' (CANDYTUFT) (35)
- NARCISSUS TRIANDRUS (ANGELS-TEARS NARCISSUS)
- IRIS, BEARDED HYBRID (TALL BEARDED IRIS)
- LOBULARIA MARITIMA (SWEET ALYSSUM)
- PINUS MUGO (MUGO PINE) (1)
- VINCA MINOR (PERIWINKLE) (20)
- CORNUS FLORIDA 'CHEROKEE PRINCESS' (JAPANESE FLOWERING DOGWOOD) (1)
- WOOD BENCH (SEE DETAIL)
- CLEMATIS x JACKMANII 'COMPTESSE DE BOUCHARD' (13) (JACKMANN CLEMATIS)
- WOOD FENCE (SEE DETAIL)
- ENTRY GATE (SEE DETAIL)

COURTYARD 'C' — SEMI-FORMAL EVENING GARDEN —
SCALE 1/4"=1'-0"

- SHREDDED WOOD CHIPS
- WOOD FENCE (SEE DETAIL)
- RHODODENDRON x LAETEVIRENS (WILSON RHODODENDRON) (1)
- MIRABILIS JALAPA (COMMON FOUR O'CLOCK)
- HEMEROCALLIS CITRINA (CITRON DAY LILY)
- HEMEROCALLIS THUNBERGII (THUNBERG DAYLILY)
- HEDERA HELIX (ENGLISH IVY) (12)
- OENOTHERA SPECIOSA & O. ROSA (SHOWY EVENING PRIMROSE & ROSE SUNDROPS)
- HEDERA HELIX (ENGLISH IVY) (15)
- MENISPERMUM CANADENSE (MOONSEED) (5)
- WOOD BENCH (SEE DETAIL)
- FLAGSTONE PAVING
- PYRUS CALLERYANA 'BRADFORD' (BRADFORD PEAR & CRATE) (1)
- CONVALLARIA MAJALIS (LILY-OF-THE-VALLEY) (5)
- ENTRY GATE (SEE DETAIL)
- C/ MAJALIS (LILY-OF-THE-VALLEY) (25)

COURTYARD PLANTING SCHEDULE

ITEM	QUANTITY	BOTANICAL NAME	COMMON NAME	SIZE	SPACING	CONDIT.	REMARKS
TREES							
1	1	AMELANCHIER ARBOREA	DOWNY SERVICEBERRY	4-5'	A.S.	B&B	MULTI-STEMMED, WH FLWRS MID APRIL, RED BERRIES JUNE
2	1	CORNUS FLORIDA	JAPANESE FLWR. DOGWOOD	5-6'	A.S.	B&B	SPECIMEN, PINK FLWRS-MAY
3	1	PYRUS CALLERYANA 'BRADFORD'	BRADFORD PEAR	6-8	A.S.	B&B	WH FLWRS-APRIL
SHRUBS							
4	1	PINUS MUGO	MUGO PINE	18-24"	A.S.	B&B	LOW, EVERGREEN
5	1	ILEX CRENATA	JAPANESE HOLLY	12-15"	A.S.	GAL	EVERGREEN
6	3	MYRICA PENSYLVANICA	BAYBERRY	12-18"	A.S.	GAL	BORDER, SEMI-EVERGRN
7	1	RHODO x LAETEVIRENS	WILSON RHODENDRONS	9-12"	A.S.	GAL	EVERGRN, PINK FL MATJUNE
GROUNDCOVERS							
8	65	AJUGA REPTANS	AJUGA (CARPET BUGLE)	4-6'	12"O.C.	MARKET PAK	PURPLE SPIKES MAY & JUNE
9	25	HEDERA HELIX	ENGLISH IVY	4-6'	12"O.C.	MP	MICROCLIMATE → EVERGRN
10	35	IBERIS SEMPERVIRENS	CANDYTUFT	4-6'	15"O.C.	MP	EVGRN, WH FL APRIL & OCT
11	28	CONVALLARIA MAJALIS	LILY-OF-THE-VALLEY	2-4"	6"O.C.	MP	WH FL MAT, FRAGRANT
12	20	VINCA MINOR	PERIWINKLE	4-6'	12"O.C.	MP	BLUE FL MAR - APR
VINES							
13	13	CLEMATIS x JACKMANII	JACKMAN CLEMATIS	AVAILABLE	24"O.C.	PP	5-6" FLR SATINY ROSE JUNE-OCT
14	5	MENISPERMUM CANADENSE	MOON SEED	AVAILABLE	24"O.C.	PP	NIGHT BLOOMING

ITEM	QUANTITY	BOTANICAL NAME	COMMON NAME	COLOR	SEASON	HEIGHT
SUGGESTED PERENNIALS						
15	OPTIONAL	IRIS, BEARDED HYBRID	TALL BEARDED IRIS	VARIES	SPRING	3'
16		NARCISSUS TRIANDRUS	ANGELS-TEARS NARCISSUS	WHITE	SPRING	1'
17		HYACINTHUS ORIENTALIS	COMMON HYACINTH	PURPLE	SPRING	8"
18		CROCUS ZONATUS	CROCUS	PURPLE	SPRING	4'
19		LOBULARIA MARITIMA	SWEET ALYSSUM	WHITE	SUMM/FALL	12"
20		HEMEROCALLIS CITRINA	CITRON DAYLILY	YELLOW (LIGHT)	SUMMER	4'
21		HEMEROCALLIS THUNBERGII	THUNBERG DAYLILY	YELLOW (LEMON)	SUMMER	3'
22		CHRYSANTHEMUM MORIFOLIUM	AUTUMN CHRYSANTHEMUM	VARIES	FALL	2'
SUGGESTED ANNUALS						
23	OPTIONAL	OENOTHERA SPECIOSA	SHOWY EVENING PRIMROSE	WHITE	E SUMMER	18'
24		OENOTHERA ROSA	ROSE SUNDROPS	ROSE-OPEN@NIGHT	SUMMER	2'
25		MIRABILIS JALAPA	COMMON FOUR O'CLOCK	VARIES	SUMMER	2-3'

ITEM	QUANTITY	BOTANICAL NAME	COMMON NAME	USE	SEASON	HEIGHT
SUGGESTED KITCHEN GARDEN HERBS AND PLANTS						
26	OPTIONAL	ALLIUM SCHOENOPRASUM	CHIVE	SOUPS, SALADS, EGGS	SUMMER	10"
27		OCIMUM SPECIES	SWEET BASIL	MEATS, SOUPS, POULTRY	SUMMER	2'
28		PETROSELINUM CRISPUM	PARSELY	EGGS, FISH SALADS	SUMMER	8"
29		MENTHA SPECIES	SPEARMINT	BEVERAGES, SALADS	SUMMER	2'
30		NEPETA CATARIA	CATNIP	COLD REMEDY, CATS	SUMMER	3'
31		THYMUS VULGARIS	THYME	CHEESE, MEATS, SALAD	SUMMER	12"
32			LETTUCE			
33			ONIONS			
34			RADISHES			
35			TOMATOES			
36		GYPSOPHILA PANICULATA	BABY'S BREATH	CUT & DRY FLOWRS	SUMM/FALL	3'

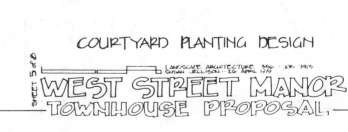

COURTYARD PLANTING DESIGN

LANDSCAPE ARCHITECTURE 356 - JOB 1913
SUSAN JELLISON - 26 APRIL 1979

WEST STREET MANOR
TOWNHOUSE PROPOSAL

SHEET 5 OF 8

FIGURE 5-5(b)

Lettering on a drawing. Besides practicing lettering for style, legibility, and consistency, it is important to remember that we read words, not letters. Thus lettering should be composed as words, not individual, evenly spaced elements. (Designer: Susan Jellison)

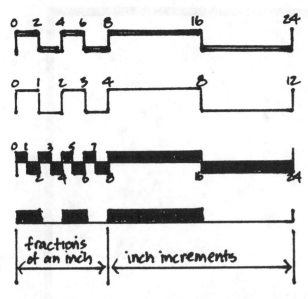

FIGURE 5-6

Graphic scales. (Designer: Gregory M. Pierceall)

thetically develop the site setting as an extension of indoor activities and to be more responsive to client needs. Specific design considerations include the adding of a mix of woody and herbaceous plantings, ground covers, yet a blending of turf to relate to adjoining homes and to provide seasonal interest.

THE PROPOSAL. The title sheet (Sheet 1, Figure 5-7) includes a sketch of the entry as proposed, the schedule of sheets, and the title block. These are the primary components of information on this introductory sheet. Figure 5-8 shows the initial title block and sheet that was drafted as the basis for all the remaining sheets in the package. Sepias were used to save time in developing this repeated information. The sheet title, scale, sheet number, and orientation have been left off the original as this information would change throughout the proposal's progression and would be added to sepia drawings. Figure 5-9 shows the preliminary survey information that was drafted before the analysis information was added to a sepia. The site survey and analysis are shown in Figure 5-10 (Sheet 2 of 10).

The master plan (Sheet 3 of 10, Figure 5-11) shows the overall site proposal. All plantings and design features are conceptual at this stage. Plant and construction material symbols are general, defining deciduous versus evergreen materials. At this stage plant sizes, in-

cluding ground covers and small or large trees, emphasize their function and visual character rather than specific material selections. All proposed plantings have a + for their center locations and are graphically more detailed than the existing plants. This graphic technique is used to highlight the proposed plantings rather than existing plants. The legend area included in the lower right-hand corner not only shows the symbols in plan view but in elevation as a means of communicating the three-dimensional aspects of the proposal and site.

Figure 5-12 is an enlargement of the entry area to show the details of specific species and options for construction materials. This enlargement area gives the client a focus area to concentrate on in the installation process. The enlargement areas were selected because the actual site is physically broken into and perceived as three distinct areas: the entry, the side yard, and the rear yard. Figure 5-13, the western elevation which includes the entry, was drawn with bare deciduous trees and shrubs such that rendering could be used to show the client the seasonal variations of the proposal. These renderings have not been included. They were developed, however, by rendering four separate blackline prints for presentation. Figures 5-14 and 5-15 (Sheets 6 and 7) are details of the south side yard of the site and the rear yard including northern portions of the house. Figure 5-16 (Sheet 8) shows simple sketches of "image areas" within the south and rear yard portions of the proposal. Figures 5-17 and 5-18 (Sheets 9 and 10) are the phasing sheets. They show the site divided in half for ease in the recommended phasing. Each sheet indicates through rendered plans the phasing to consider. Plant schedules are included to indicate the plant types, installation sizes, and growth characteristics to consider. Plant schedules can also identify the plant's landscape effect and any notes relevant to the plant's culture. Planning and design for the proposal were developed in the winter; thus, during the presentation of the package, the designer brought a bouquet of many of the plants proposed to help visualize their winter character. This is a good idea if the opportunity presents itself. Always try to bring live samples or at least photos of proposed plants. This technique helps not only to explain an individual plant but the design and composition of plants in the proposal. Figure 5-19 compares the before and present character of the entry, the west elevation of the site. The present installation has included only plantings. As the project continues, further design details will be developed relative to the construction features to be included such as the playspace in the rear yard area and other structural aspects.

1 TITLE & SCHEDULE OF SHEETS
2 SITE SURVEY & ANALYSIS
3 MASTER PLAN CONCEPT
4 ENTRY ENLARGEMENT
5 ENTRY SKETCH
6 SIDE YARD ENLARGEMENT
7 REAR YARD ENLARGEMENT
8 SIDE & REAR SKETCHES
9 ENTRY PHASING & PLANT SCHEDULE
10 REAR PHASING & PLANT SCHEDULE

RESIDENTIAL MASTER PLAN DEVELOPMENT
DR.&MRS.R.BLOCH   LAZY LANE LAFAYETTE,INDIANA
TITLE & SCHEDULE OF SHEETS
LANDSCAPE ARCHITECT:GREGORY M.PIERCEALL   129 N GRANT W.LAFAYETTE ,INDIANA
NORTH   SHEET 1 OF 10

FIGURE 5-7

Residential design package, Figures 5-7 through 5-18 (originals 18" × 24"). Title sheet. (Designer: Gregory M. Pierceall)

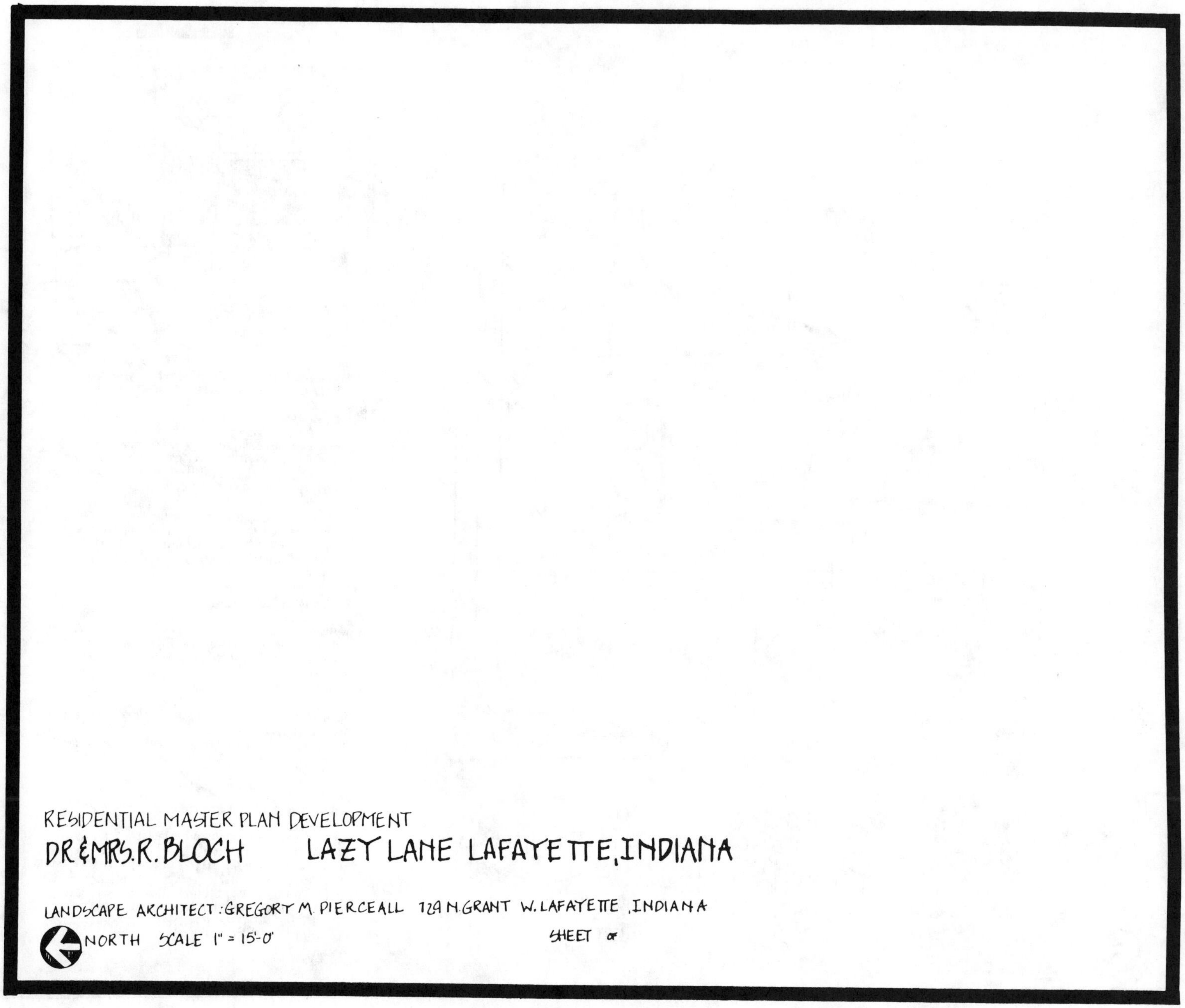

RESIDENTIAL MASTER PLAN DEVELOPMENT
DR & MRS. R. BLOCH   LAZY LANE LAFAYETTE, INDIANA

LANDSCAPE ARCHITECT: GREGORY M. PIERCEALL   729 N. GRANT W. LAFAYETTE, INDIANA
NORTH   SCALE 1" = 15'-0"   SHEET OF

FIGURE 5-8
Base sepia. (Designer: Gregory M. Pierceall)

113

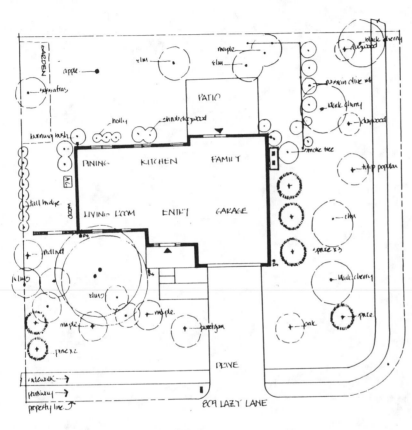

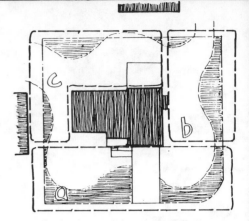

SITE CONCEPT DEVELOPMENT · BLOCH
809 LAZY LANE, LAFAYETTE, INDIANA

(a) entry zone / public area

- western exposure, entry needs protection from hot summer sun yet allow south to SW breezes in
- entry needs protection from harsh northern winter winds, yet open and inviting to guests
- front entry (west elevation) is the primary entry and most visible. existing planting trees started a naturalistic scheme which should be developed into a entry sequence with seasonal interest

(b) side yard / public area

- southern exposure, existing plants provide enclosure and shade thus reducing cooling needs as they mature. additional canopy trees are needed to replace mature species ... allow for breeze access to rear patio area
- this area is a transition area between the entry and rear yard, it is viewed as a part of the entry yet functions to screen and buffer the patio from cul-de-sac traffic.

(c) rear yard / outdoor living area

- eastern exposure, morning sun pocket for patio shaded in the afternoon ... due to cul-de-sac this area needs privacy and screening from adjoining residents to the east. views should be created off family room, kitchen and dining room to extend these interior views out into the landscape ... possible wildlife plantings may be used for seasonal interest

RESIDENTIAL MASTER PLAN DEVELOPMENT
DR. & MRS R. BLOCH   LAZY LANE LAFAYETTE, INDIANA
SITE SURVEY and ANALYSIS
LANDSCAPE ARCHITECT: GREGORY M PIERCEALL 721 N.GRANT W. LAFAYETTE, INDIANA
NORTH SCALE 1"=15'-0"   SHEET   OF

FIGURE 5-9

Survey/analysis base sepia. (Designer: Gregory M. Pierceall)

114

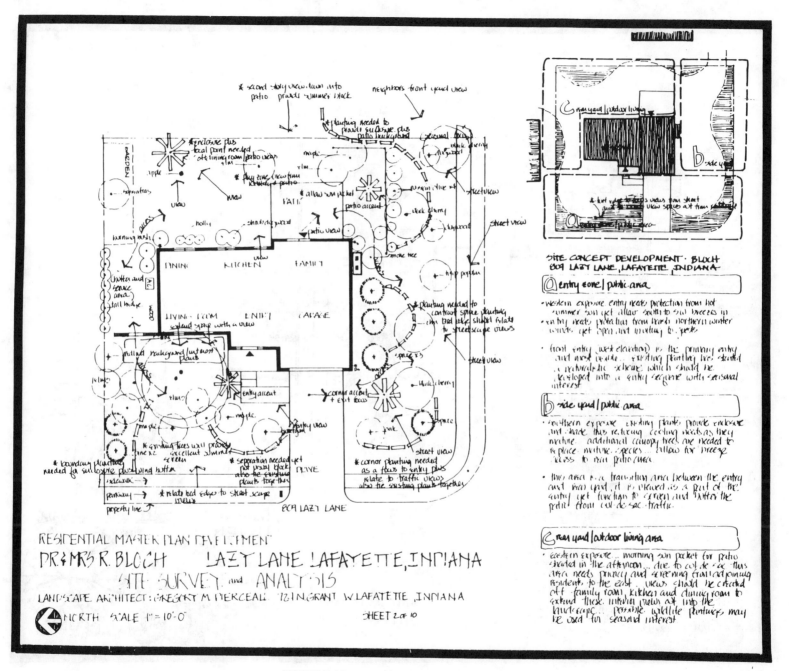

FIGURE 5-10

Survey/analysis. (Designer: Gregory M. Pierceall)

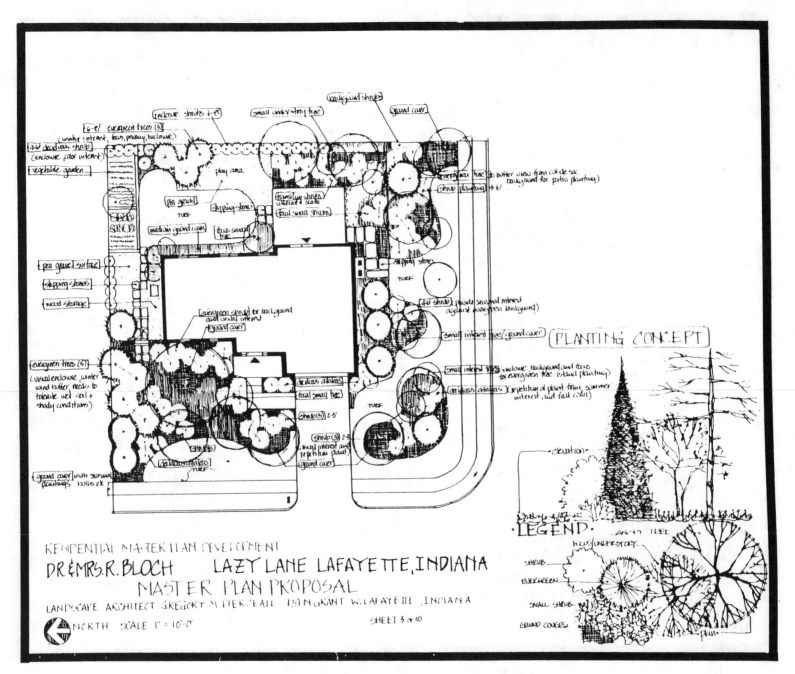

FIGURE 5-11

Master plan. (Designer: Gregory M. Pierceall)

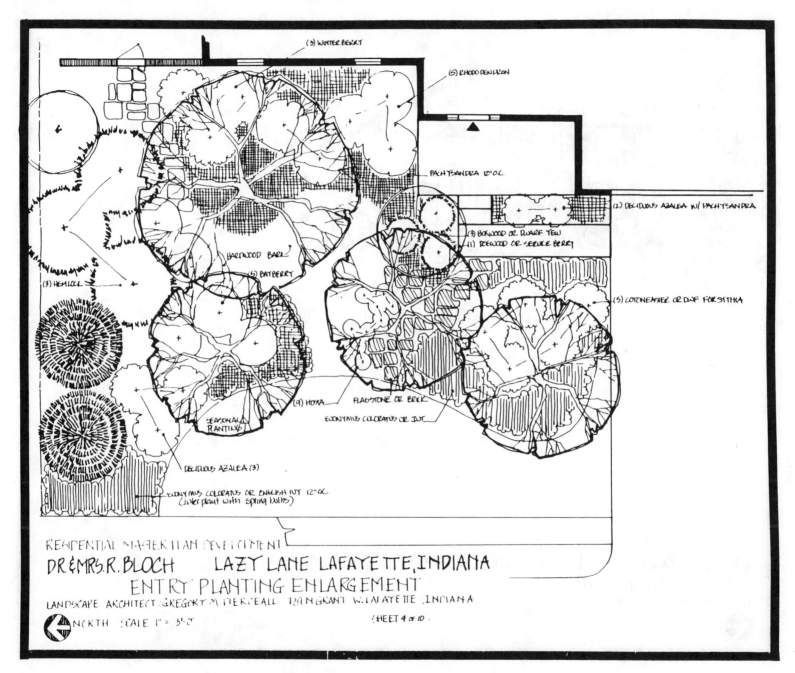

(3) WINTERBERRY

(5) RHODODENDRON

PACHYSANDRA 12" O.C.

(2) DECIDUOUS AZALEA W/ PACHYSANDRA

(3) BOXWOOD OR DWARF YEW

(1) DOGWOOD OR SERVICE BERRY

HARDWOOD BARK

(5) COTONEASTER OR DWF FORSYTHIA

(3) HEMLOCK

(5) BAYBERRY

(9) HOSTA

FLAGSTONE OR BRICK

EUONYMUS COLORATUS OR IVY

SEASONAL PLANTING

DECIDUOUS AZALEA (3)

EUONYMUS COLORATUS OR ENGLISH IVY 12" O.C.
(interplant with spring bulbs)

RESIDENTIAL MASTER PLAN DEVELOPMENT
DR. & MRS. R. BLOCH   LAZY LANE LAFAYETTE, INDIANA
ENTRY PLANTING ENLARGEMENT
LANDSCAPE ARCHITECT GREGORY M. PIERCEALL   129 N GRANT W. LAFAYETTE, INDIANA
NORTH SCALE 1" = 3'-0"   SHEET 4 OF 10

FIGURE 5-12
Entry enlargement. (Designer: Gregory M. Pierceall)

117

the entry proposal - west elevation

RESIDENTIAL MASTER PLAN DEVELOPMENT
DR & MRS. R. BLOCH   LAZY LANE LAFAYETTE, INDIANA
       ENTRY PROPOSAL SKETCH
LANDSCAPE ARCHITECT GREGORY M. PIERCEALL 729 N GRANT W. LAFAYETTE, INDIANA

NORTH   SHEET 5 OF 10

FIGURE 5-13
Entry sketch. (Designer: Gregory M. Pierceall)

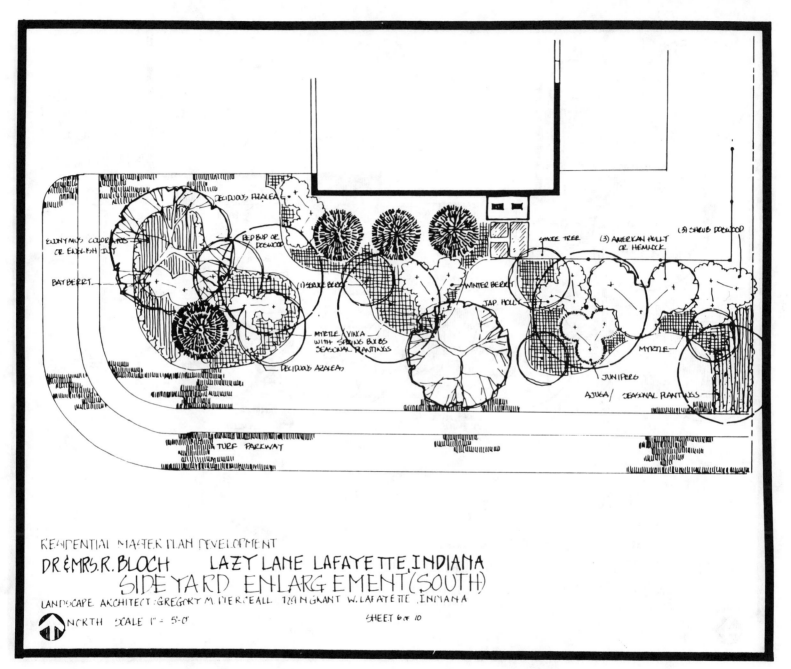

FIGURE 5-14
Side yard enlargement. (Designer: Gregory M. Pierceall)

119

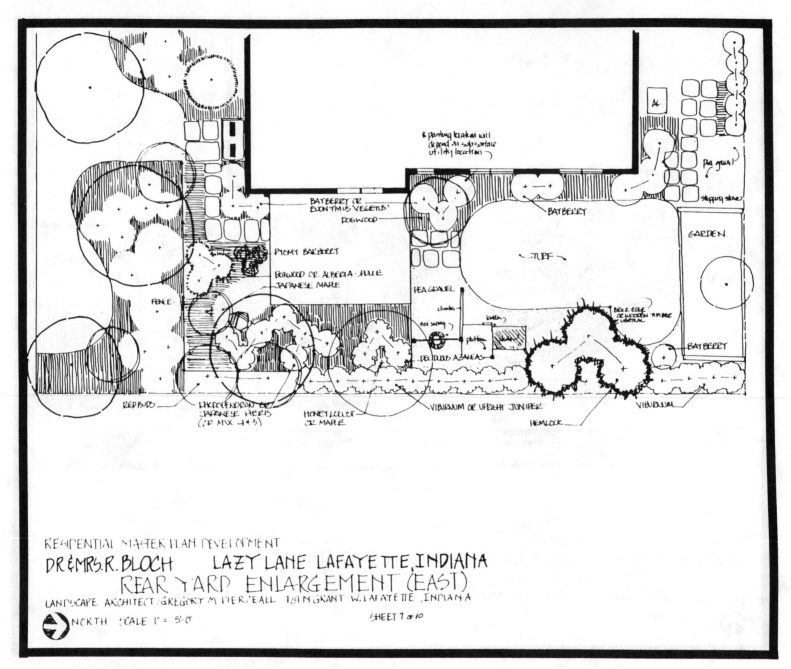

FIGURE 5-15
Rear yard enlargement. (Designer: Gregory M. Pierceall)

FIGURE 5-16
Side and rear yard sketches. (Designer: Gregory M. Pierceall)

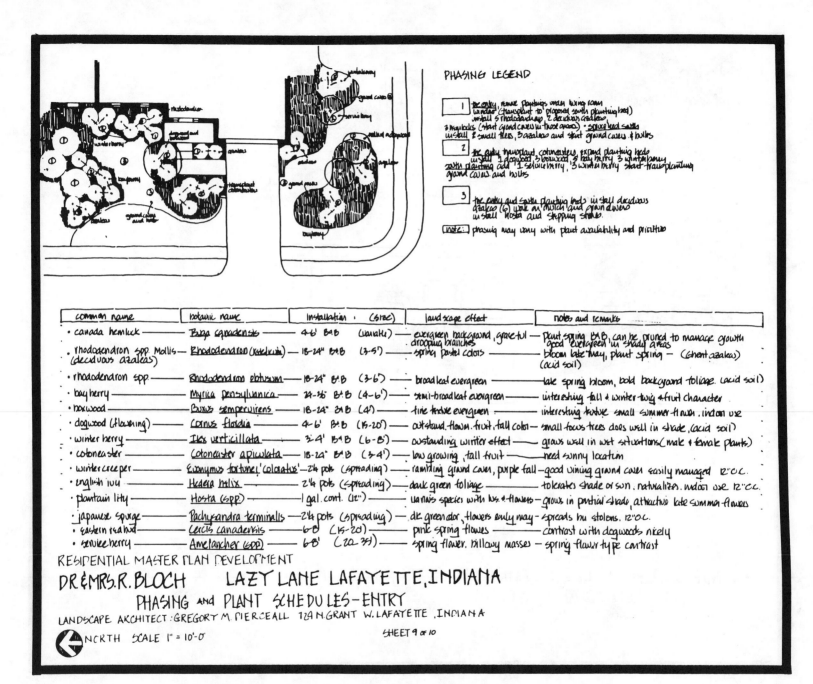

FIGURE 5-17

Plant schedule front. (Designer: Gregory M. Pierceall)

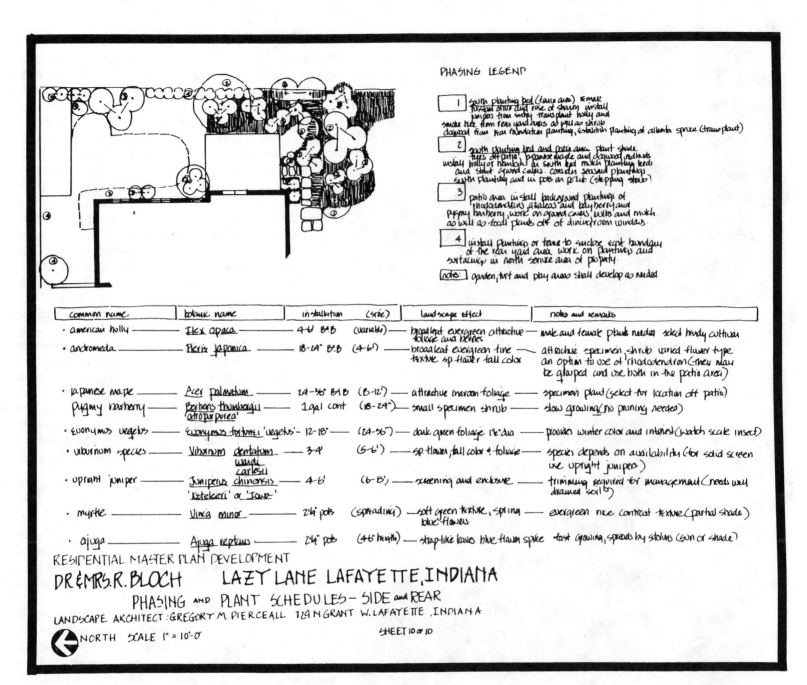

PHASING LEGEND

1 — south planting bed (fence area) remove russian olive and rose of sharon install junipers from entry transplant holly and smoke tree from rear yard areas as well as shrub dogwood from rear foundation planting, establish planting of alberta spruce (transplant)

2 — south planting bed and patio area plant shade trees off patio, Japanese maple and dogwood redbud install holly or hemlock at south bed mulch planting beds and start ground covers. consider seasonal plantings south planting and in pots on patio (stepping stone)

3 — patio area install background plantings of rhododendrons, azaleas and bayberry and pygmy barberry, work on ground covers, bulbs and mulch. as well as focal plants off of dining room window.

4 — install plantings or fence to enclose east boundary of the rear yard area work on plantings and surfacing in north service area of property.

note: garden, turf and play areas shall develop as needed.

common name	botanic name	installation	(size)	landscape effect	notes and remarks
• american holly	Ilex opaca	4-6' B+B	(variable)	broadleaf evergreen attractive foliage and berries	male and female plants needed select hardy cultivar
• andromeda	Pieris japonica	18-24" B+B	(4-6')	broadleaf evergreen fine texture sp. flower fall color	attractive specimen shrub varied flower type an option to use of rhododendron (they may be grouped and use both in the patio area)
• japanese maple	Acer palmatum	24-36" B+B	(8-12')	attractive maroon foliage	specimen plant (select for location off patio)
pygmy barberry	Berberis thunbergii 'atropurpurea'	1 gal cont	(18-24")	small specimen shrub	slow growing (no pruning needed)
• euonymus vegetus	Euonymus fortunei 'vegetus'	12-18"	(24-36")	dark green foliage 1"+ dia	provides winter color and interest (watch scale insect)
• viburnum species	Viburnum dentatum and/or carlesii	3-4'	(5-6')	sp. flower, fall color & foliage	species depends on availability (for solid screen use upright junipers)
• upright juniper	Juniperus chinensis 'Ketelceri' or 'Iowa'	4-6'	(6-8')	screening and enclosure	trimming required for management (needs well drained soil)
• myrtle	Vinca minor	2½" pots	(spreading)	soft green texture, spring blue flowers	evergreen nice contrast texture (partial shade)
• ajuga	Ajuga reptans	2½" pots	(4-6" height)	strap-like leaves blue flower spike	fast growing, spreads by stolons (sun or shade)

RESIDENTIAL MASTER PLAN DEVELOPMENT

DR. & MRS. R. BLOCH   LAZY LANE LAFAYETTE, INDIANA

PHASING and PLANT SCHEDULES – SIDE and REAR

LANDSCAPE ARCHITECT: GREGORY M. PIERCEALL 129 N GRANT W. LAFAYETTE, INDIANA

NORTH SCALE 1" = 10'-0"   SHEET 10 of 10

FIGURE 5-18

Plant schedule rear. (Designer: Gregory M. Pierceall)

FIGURE 5-19(a)

Entry before landscape planting. (Photo by Gregory M. Pierceall)

FIGURE 5-19(b)

Entry after landscape planting. (Photo by Gregory M. Pierceall)

Project Review

The example shown is an actual proposal submitted to a client as a site planting plan. The package's sheet size is 18″ × 24″, with the final copies duplicated on blackline ozalid print paper. The sheet size used is comfortable relative to the project scale, the information included, and for physical handling by the clients. On Sheet 1, the title sheet, the top, bottom, and right-hand edges have a ½″ border. The left-hand edge has a 1″ border as a binding edge. The title block information is organzied without an edge defining its limits to allow flexibility of sheet information. The schedule of sheets is placed high enough on the sheet to allow additional sheet titles to be included as revisions occur and/or construction details are finalized. The sketch is located at the right edge so as to visually lead the reader to Sheet 2 of the package, the survey and analysis sheet.

On the survey and analysis sheet, the larger plan area has specific notes relative to specific site areas. The reduced site plan in the upper right-hand corner is a concept diagram with descriptive notes below for explanations. Included are descriptions of three perceived site areas, the entry, garage side, and the rear yard.

The master plan proposal (Sheet 3 of 10) uses the same sepia base as identified in Figure 5-9 before the analysis, notes, and concept diagram were added. The existing plants to be removed were erased from the back of the sepia and the new proposal was added on the top side of the sheet. When getting sepias to add and delete information, a *reverse sepia* allows a separation between information added and removed. From this master plan development, enlargement drawings and sketches were drafted on sepias of the blank sheet and basic title block (Figure 5-7).

After all ten sheets were finalized, three sets of ozalid blacklines were duplicated. One set was rendered—color added with markers for presentation to the clients. In addition, one unrendered set for "outdoor use" was also given to the clients. This set of drawings could then be used outdoors by a contractor or homeowner when laying out the proposal on site. The remaining printed set was retained by the designer for a record of the presentation in addition to the originals.

In making design proposals remember that lettering and presentation styles develop over a period of years and often become a trademark of an individual designer. Also, the length and intensity of a design proposal is dependent on the design problem, client needs, and budget limitations established by the client for design proposal.

SINGLE SHEET PLANTING PROPOSALS

In contrast to the complete package just presented, design proposals can be shorter in length using an abbreviated format yet include similar information. The basic information should communicate what is proposed yet be illustrated in a much more "bare bones" manner regarding graphics, notes, details and sheet presentation. Figures 5-20 and 5-21 show a project site of similar size to the previous example but produced with a minimal design budget. A shortcut used was to eliminate the graphic production of a title sheet and survey and analysis, making the master plan the first sheet in the presentation. On this sheet plants to be removed are identified through notes. Only plants to remain and proposed plantings are presented. The graphic style used for symbols and sheet borders is more simplified and thus saves time. Phasing was included by using an ozalid print of the master plan sheet, then adding color to indicate the phasing schedule. The third sheet in the proposal is a sketch of the entry elevation and a plan to conceptualize the playspace area's development. While the playspace enlargement plan does not relate to the entry, it was more efficient to include it here and to reduce the number of sheets in the presentation. Overall, the project information communicates the plantings and constructed features yet is compactly presented. This format requires much more explanation as to how the design evolved and instructions for future design direction. Make sure when you contract to do a project that the design budget is sufficient to develop the design to the extent and detail expected by the client and that it can be implemented. If the budget and expectations do not match, explain to the client what can be provided within the limits defined. The purpose of a design proposal is to communicate information, not to produce drawings that are useless.

LANDSCAPE CONSTRUCTION DOCUMENTS

At the residential scale of landscape design, landscape construction may also be included or required in conjunction with plantings to complete a site's development. Landscape construction includes the design of a site's topography, including working with a site's landforms or grading—the altering of the site surface. Grading is done primarily to provide surface drainage and to create areas for activities. Landscape construction also includes the design of site structures such as pavements, ramps, steps, fences, walls, screens, decks, seating, and lighting. In practice, the areas of landscape grading and site structures are handled by a landscape architect rather than landscape designer due to professional liabilities and the restrictions of local legislation. Landscape construction documents are shown in Figure 5-22.

SMALL SCALE DESIGN PRESENTATIONS

If the scale and intensity of design services require the production of many proposals a day, an alternative to the development of an original drawing and blueprint copies may be a preprinted design form. The basic concept is to have a preprinted sheet that includes the basic title block information, borders, and scale reference to develop quick yet professional looking proposals. An easy sheet size to use is $11'' \times 17''$, which equals two $8\frac{1}{2}'' \times 11''$ sheets. Advantages of this sheet size are that it can be halved and easily stored by clients or designers and it is easy to use in the field. Also, copies can be made for the designer's use while originals go to the clients. A preprinted grid or indication of inch subdivisions helps align and scale proposals on the sheet. A colored sheet that relates to the company's logo is helpful. The colored sheet also provides a visible background when black and/or colors are added showing the proposal. Markers can be used to easily define canopy trees in one shade of green, ornamental trees in a contrasting color, and shrubs and other plants in another. Edges can then be added to the colored symbols to define canopy versus ground plane elements and to indicate trunk locations. With practice, designs can even be developed on site or generated in the office, be consistent and professional in format, and yet be cost-effective for the scale and demands of a project (Figure 5-23).

In practice, on-site conceptualization of ideas for small scale design projects are valuable both to the client and the designer. For the client, there is an immediate translation of ideas to the specific site situation. To the designer this sequence of inventory, analysis and development of preliminary ideas is in essence the first step of design process. On-site planning is a method of communications in which the designer defines and interprets what the site conditions are in combination with the clients requests. These rough sketches in plan and elevation then are used as the basis for further design and refinement.

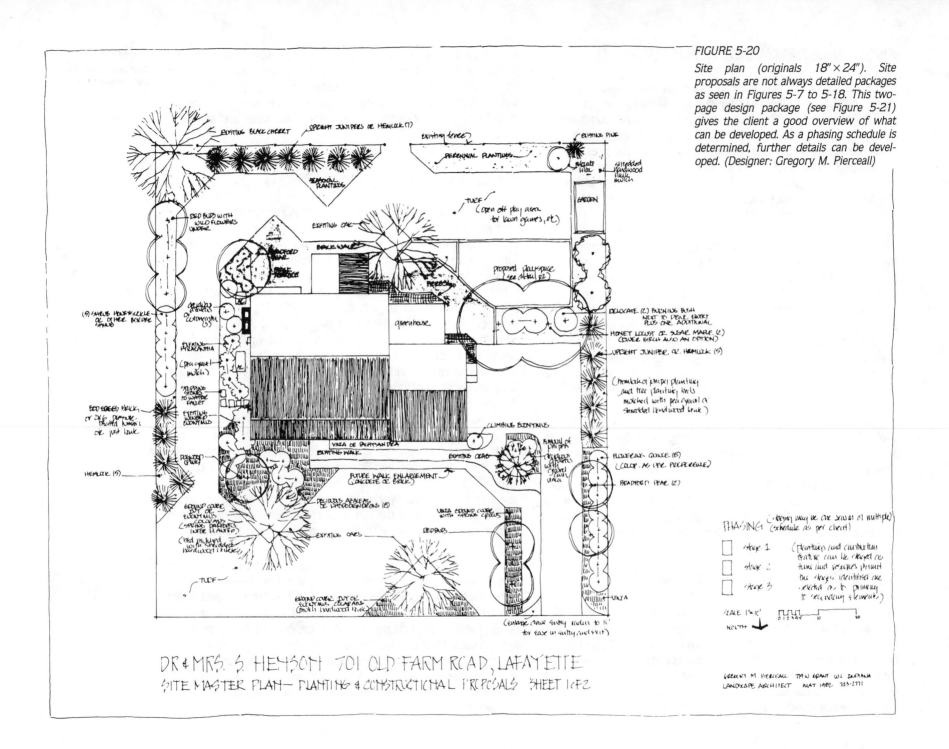

FIGURE 5-20

Site plan (originals 18" × 24"). Site proposals are not always detailed packages as seen in Figures 5-7 to 5-18. This two-page design package (see Figure 5-21) gives the client a good overview of what can be developed. As a phasing schedule is determined, further details can be developed. (Designer: Gregory M. Pierceall)

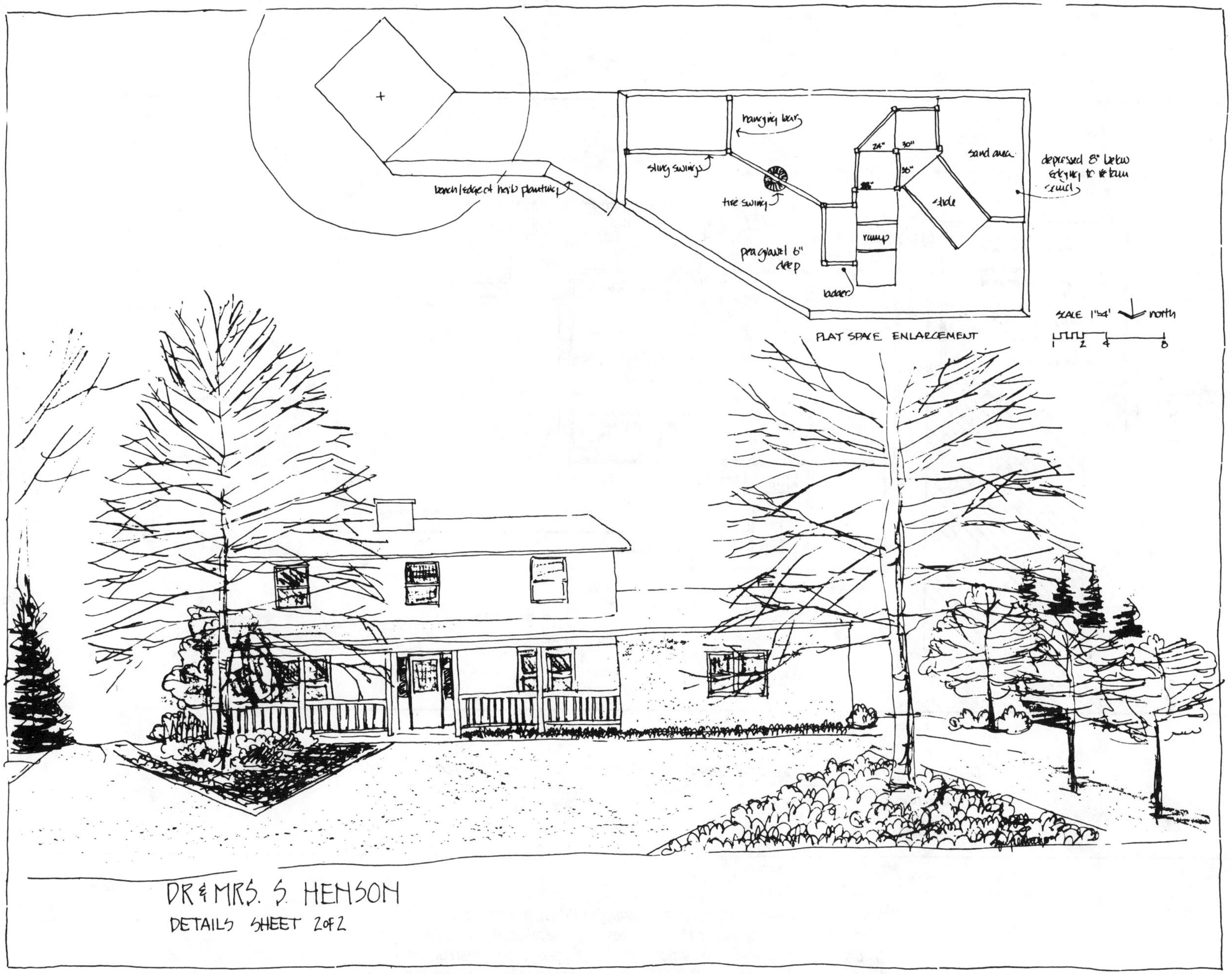

hanging bars
sling swings
bench/edge of herb planting
tire swing
24"
30"
36"
sand area
depressed 8" below edging to retain sand
slide
ramp
pea gravel 6" deep
ladder
SCALE 1"=4'
north
1 2 4 8
PLAT SPACE ENLARGEMENT
DR & MRS. S. HENSON
DETAILS SHEET 2 of 2

FIGURE 5-21
Elevation details. (Designer: Gregory M. Pierceall)

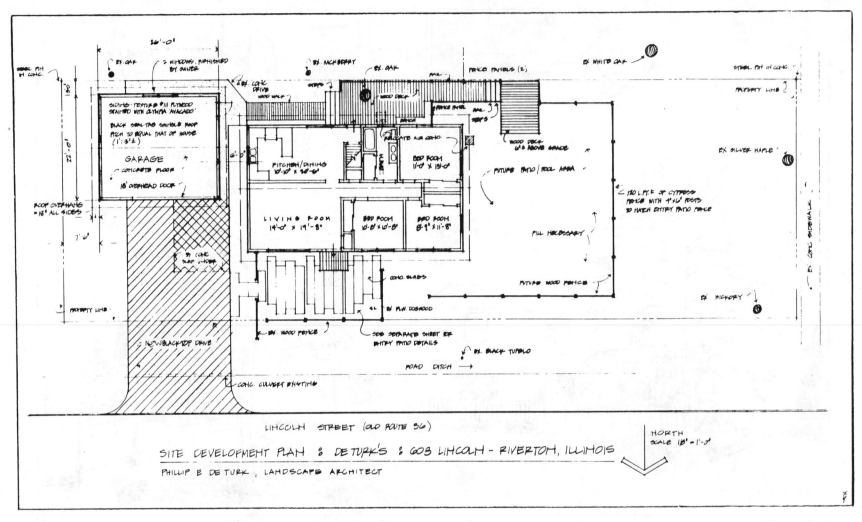

FIGURE 5-22(a)

Site development construction drawings. When a project is to be implemented by someone other than the designer, detailed drawings are required to provide adequate information for the project to be constructed. As seen here and in Figures 5-22b and 5-22c, a master plan was developed with two additional sheets to show the exact details and dimensions of what was to be constructed. (Designer: P. E. DeTurk)

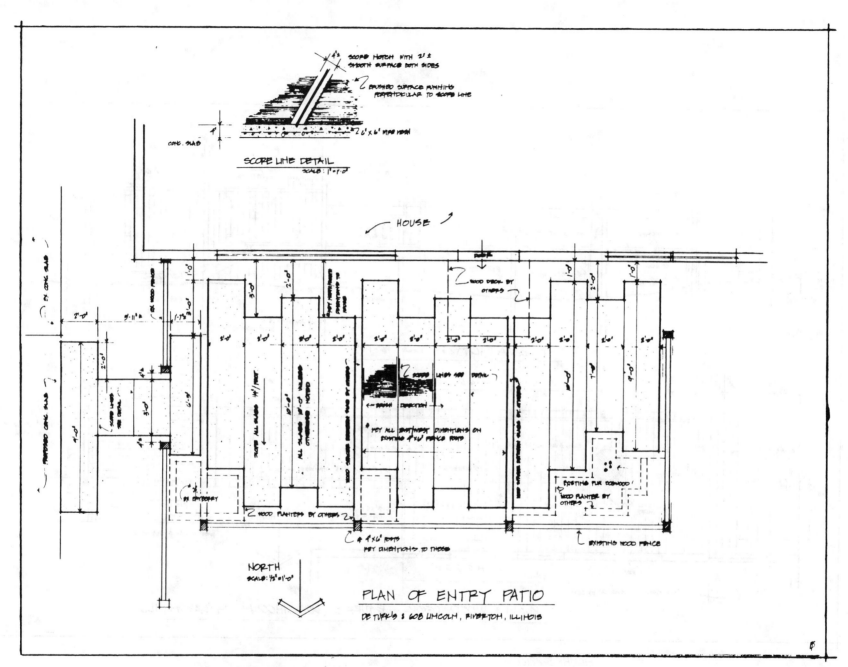

SCORE LINE DETAIL
SCALE: 1"=1'-0"

HOUSE

PLAN OF ENTRY PATIO
DE TURK'S & 608 LINCOLN, RIVERTON, ILLINOIS

NORTH
SCALE: ½"=1'-0"

FIGURE 5-22(b)
The plan represents an enlargement area from the overall site plan seen in
Figure 5-22(a).

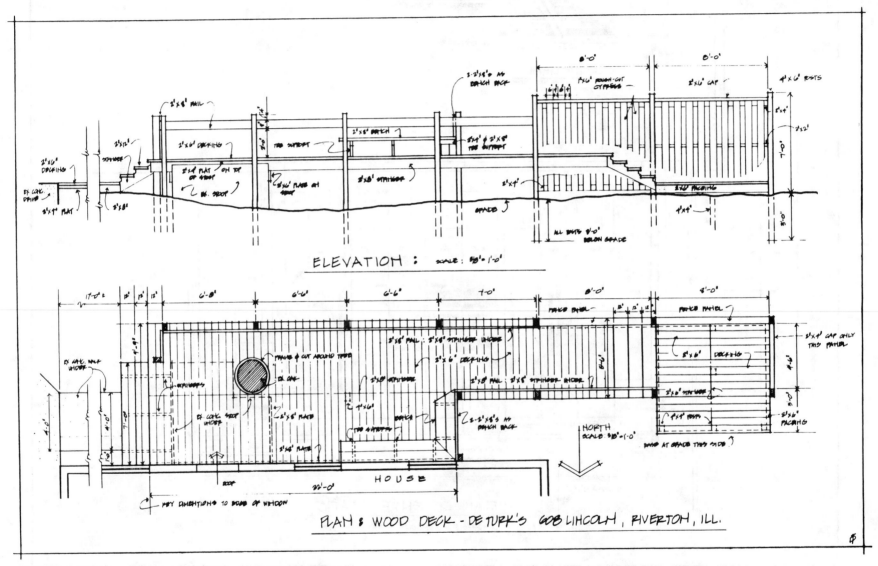

ELEVATION : SCALE: 3/8" = 1'-0"

PLAN : WOOD DECK - DE TURK'S 608 LINCOLN, RIVERTON, ILL.

FIGURE 5-22(c)
This plan and elevation are enlargement details expanded from the plan Figure 5-22(a).

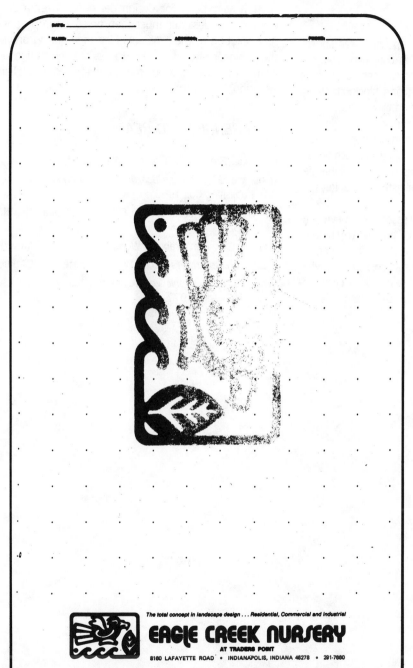

FIGURE 5-23

This preprinted design sheet (original size 11" × 17") was developed to provide a consistent format for on-site design. The small size permits demonstration of ideas immediately. Copies can easily be made using carbon paper. (Courtesy of Eagle Creek Nursery, Indianapolis, IN)

SUMMARY

Graphic presentation of design ideas requires an understanding of the basic components of a drawing and sheet in conjunction with a drafting and design process. Drawing and sheet composition include selection and development of a sheet, border, title block, drawing, labels, and leaders, etc., for a specific project and client.

Presentation styles vary. Specific design formats or styles are often characteristics of an individual designer and develop as trademarks as distinctive as handwriting. Symbols, rendering techniques, and lettering composition are often expressions of an individual designer's preference. Legibility, clarity, and consistency are keys to good graphic presentations.

While graphic skills, techniques, and processes have been emphasized in this chapter, designers also need to be able to communicate through verbal presentations and writing skills. During an initial meeting with a client, designers have to be able to explain what services can be provided, ask questions, and respond to client inquiries. After the client meeting, the designer must record this discussion as a basis for design decisions. After a design proposal is drafted, the designer must then present the proposal to the client. As a solution to the problems identified during previous discussions, the designer should be able to restate the design problem and explain how the drafted solution satisfies the client's needs and situation.

REFERENCES AND READINGS

Lin, Mike. *Economy of Graphics.* Washington, D.C.: ASLA, 1979.

Robinette, Gary. *Off the Board/Into the Ground.* Dubuque, IA: Kendall/Hunt Publishing Co., 1968.

Van Dyke, Scott. *From Line to Design.* West Lafayette, IN: PDA Publishers, 1982.

Walker, T. D. *Plan Graphics.* West Lafayette, IN: PDA Publishers, 1975.

———. *Perspective Sketches.* West Lafayette, IN: PDA Publishers, 1975.

White, E. T. *A Graphic Vocabulary for Architecture.* Tucson, AZ: Architectural Media, 1972.

*L*andscape symbols

In the processes of planning and design, drawings, sketches, and illustrations are used to conceptualize and visualize information relative to site development. In site survey drawings, symbols are used to represent existing site conditions, a site's surroundings, local climatic influences, and pedestrian and vehicular movement. Site master plans use symbols to define both existing and proposed elements to be included in a site's development.

As described in Chapter 4, value contrast should be included in all drawings, and this too influences the landscape symbols used. Figure 6-1 illustrates the use of symbols to show value contrast. The first example (Figure 6-1a) uses simple lines for symbols. Tall plants are represented by heavy lines and low ground plane elements are shown with fine lines. The second example (Figure 6-1b) shows another residential proposal using a similar line hierarchy, but here proposed plants and construction materials are defined by finer lines and more detail. The third example (Figure 6-1c) shows an intensely delineated proposal using detailed lines for the ground

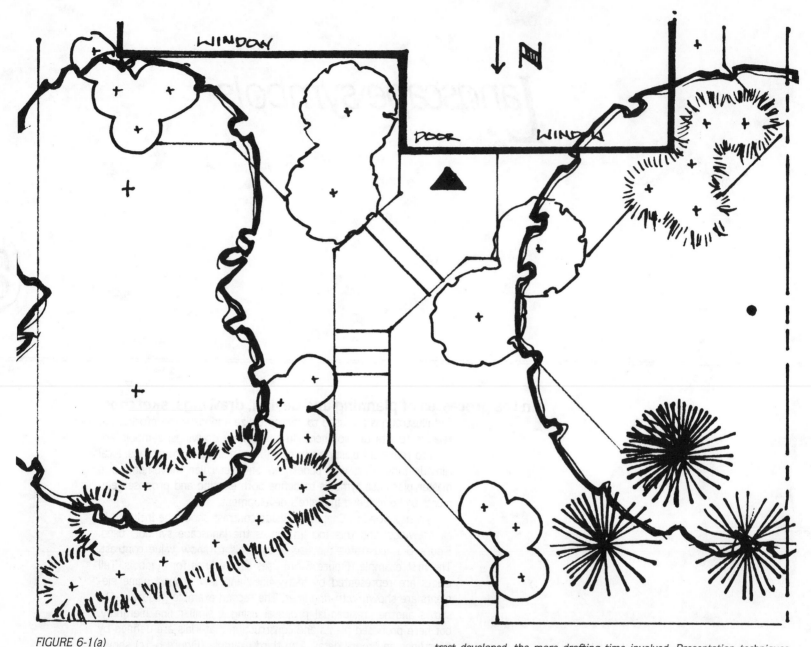

FIGURE 6-1(a)

Site plan. Here and in the site plans that follow a variety of line weights, line hierarchy, and value contrasts are shown. Note that the more value contrast developed, the more drafting time involved. Presentation techniques should always be selected relative to the project's time frame and client's needs. (Designer: M. Powers)

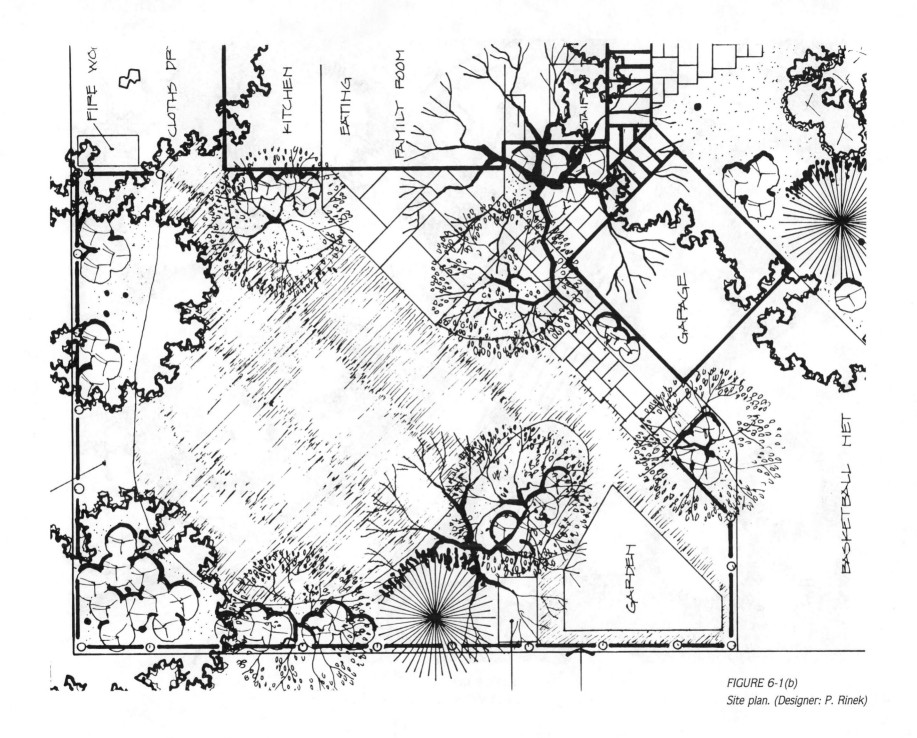

FIGURE 6-1(b)
Site plan. (Designer: P. Rinek)

135

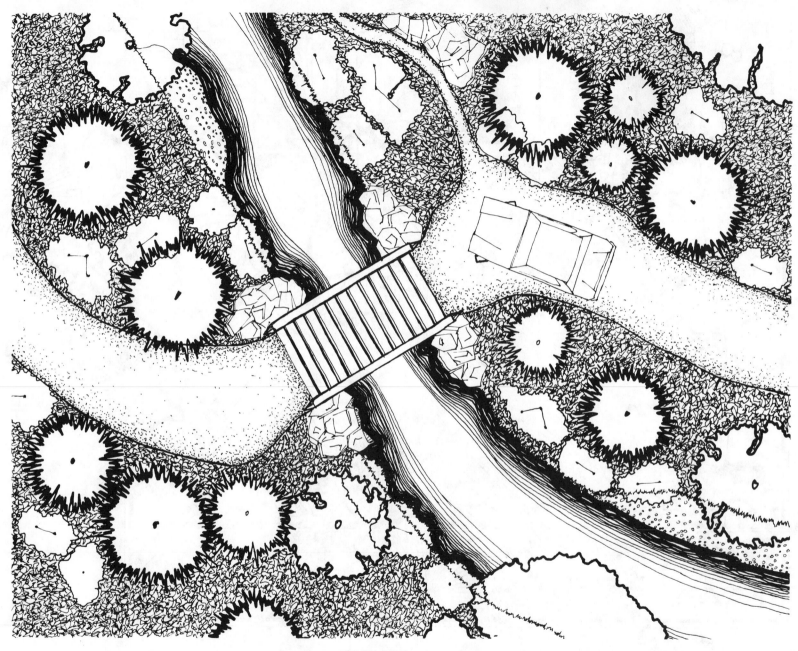

FIGURE 6-1(c)
Site plan. (Designer: D. Staley)

plane elements and bolder outlines for the taller elements in the composition. Each of these examples is an acceptable method of presenting proposals. However, there is a wide difference between the actual drawing time required for the first and third examples. The selection of techniques is dependent on your individual skills, drafting speed, and the project's need for detail or simplicity. Remember, the more detailed the symbol and plan presentation, the more time it takes to present.

Individual symbols and their compositions should relate to the need for simplicity or complexity in the proposal. Symbols represent plant or construction materials, their sizes, shapes, textures, and details. Figure 6-2 shows some typical examples of the way in which plants and construction materials are symbolized in a plan presentation. When reviewing these examples, be aware of the differences between deciduous and evergreen symbols. These two major types of symbols are needed in all plans. Different symbols are also used to distinguish needleleaf and broadleaf evergreens. Use of symbols is only as limited as the minds of designers and the material opportunities to be represented.

When starting to develop a landscape design proposal, a portion of your time is in design development and the remainder is spent trying to decide how to communicate your ideas. As a reference and as a means of stimulating your imagination, examples of plan, section, elevation, and perspective drawings are included in this part of the text. Review the individual symbols or symbol combinations that are present in these examples. If you use the symbols shown here or draw your own, make sure the particular symbol is representative of what you want to illustrate and that it is scaled properly. One common error in developing symbols is to draw them too small or too large for what they are to represent.

As a rule of thumb, you may want to present any plant that will grow and reach a mature size within five years at ⅔ or ¾ the mature size anticipated (Figure 6-3). Ground covers, herbaceous plants, and shrubs would fall into this category. Also make sure to note in the drawing that the plants are drawn at this size. When drawing ground cover or shrub masses, lightly pencil in the anticipated area, then define the mass's edge with a heavier pencil or ink line. Individual plant centers should then be indicated within the planting mass. If planting masses are drawn showing individual plants, the overlapping of edges often clutters the drawing and distracts from the sheet (Figure 6-4). Plant scaling errors are one of the biggest problems for beginning designers.

When presenting trees, a rule of thumb may be to draw them ½ to ¾ their mature spread. Larger trees that take time to mature and to create the desired effect may be planted closer together. In this way they will fulfill their function sooner than mature plants. Depending on how much detail is necessary to show plantings and/or construction features that are proposed under deciduous trees, either open or branched tree symbols may be used. Open tree symbols provide no line conflicts when used over understory elements. Branched symbols, on the other hand, can obscure proposed elements on the ground. For evergreen trees, open or solid symbols can be used, but again the choice depends on the amount of detail necessary to represent ground elements (Figure 6-5).

In an elevation view, plants and materials should be drawn in the same style as is used for the closely related plan view. Figure 6-6 shows some simple examples of plan and elevation symbols.

In both plan and sketching presentations of landscape plants and construction materials, remember that the symbols only represent the actual forms, textures, and lines of the elements. After having outlined the plan, elevation, or sketch forms of elements, add detail to these by selecting a line weight and type that is representative enough to communicate the materials' texture and essence. Graphic presentation like handwriting requires a rhythm and flow to be consistent and effective. Why not use some of the writing or lettering "strokes" you have already mastered as a means of developing abstract textures and forms? Figure 6-7 shows some examples of plant forms developed by using abstractions of the strokes used in writing particular alphabet letters. If you'd like to try the technique, sketch out in pencil the outline of a tree, shrub, or ground cover in plan or elevation. Then use a letter from your name as the basis of the "texture" you develop. Try not to be precise in the letter formation as quick and often incomplete strokes help characterize the forms.

The following graphics are divided into plan view examples, section examples, elevation, perspective and sketching examples. Some of the them are full scale while others have been reduced. Please be aware of the scale if transposing any of the examples in projects you may develop. The sketching examples have been included to illustrate freehand and drafted styles used in the presentation of design proposals. Sketching techniques are important tools in the development of survey information and in the preliminary stages of design. If you sketch out your ideas early in the design process, you can better visualize the proposal at the end of the design process.

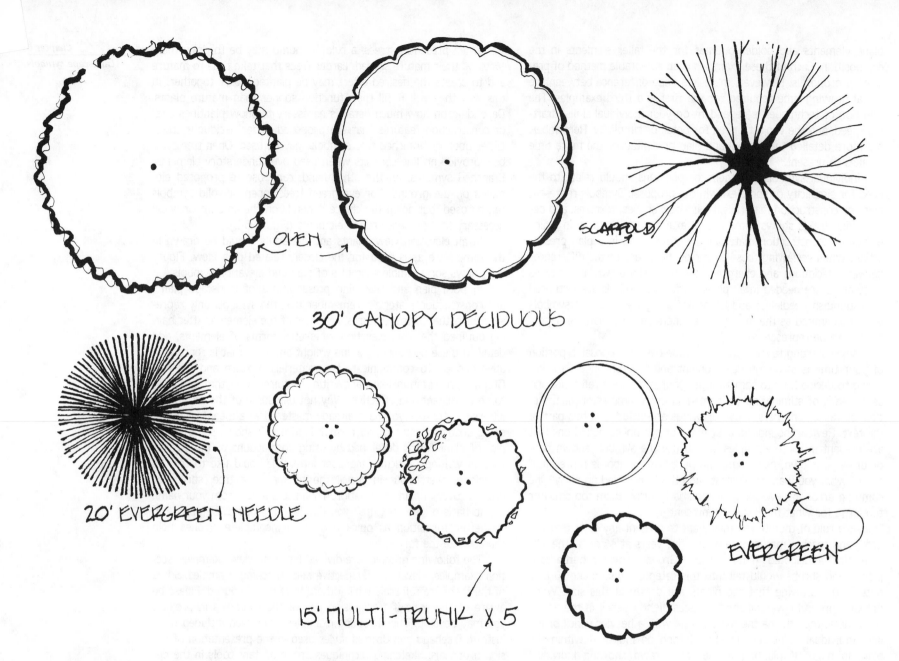

30' CANOPY DECIDUOUS

OPEN

SCAFFOLD

20' EVERGREEN NEEDLE

15' MULTI-TRUNK X 5

EVERGREEN

FIGURE 6-2(a)
Landscape plants and material symbols. (Designer: Lynn Marie Campbell)

8' DEC. SHRUB x 5

3' DEC. SHRUBS x 5

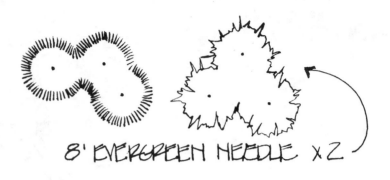

8' EVERGREEN NEEDLE x 2

3' EVRGRN, NEEDLE & B·LEAF

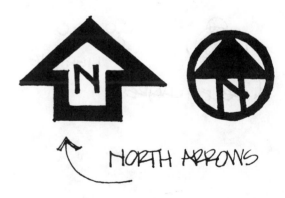

NORTH ARROWS

FIGURE 6-2(b)
Landscape plants and material symbols. (Designer: Lynn Marie Campbell)

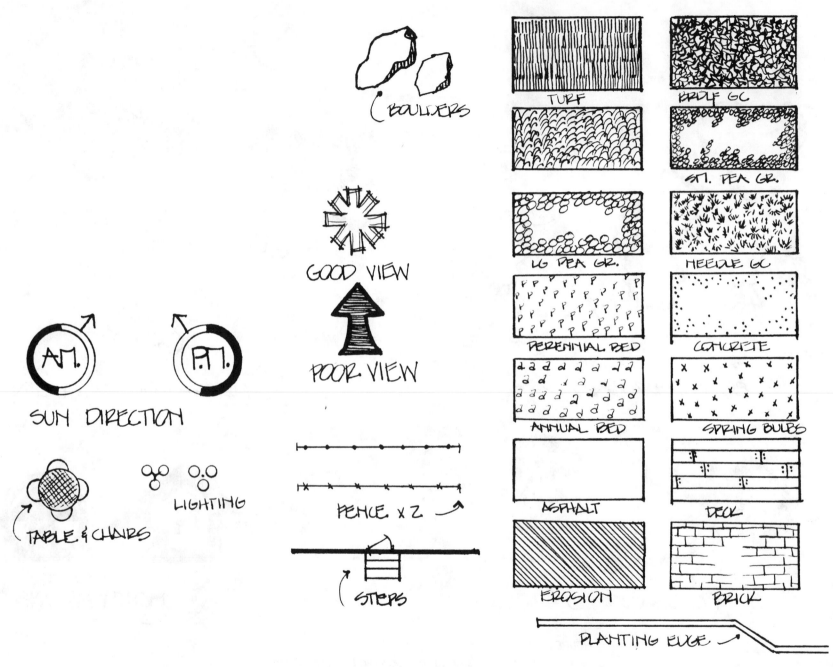

SUN DIRECTION

TABLE & CHAIRS

LIGHTING

BOULDERS

GOOD VIEW

POOR VIEW

FENCE x 2

STEPS

TURF

BRDLE GC

ST. PEA GR.

LG PEA GR.

NEEDLE GC

PERENNIAL BED

CONCRETE

ANNUAL BED

SPRING BULBS

ASPHALT

DECK

EROSION

BRICK

PLANTING EDGE

FIGURE 6-2(c)

Landscape plants and material symbols. (Designer: Lynn Marie Campbell)

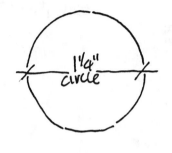

1¼"
circle

at 1/8 scale, a shrub or small tree 10' across

the actual mature spread may be larger
but it is drawn 2/3 or 3/4 size to provide
a more finished looking design when installed
this is the mass planting concept.

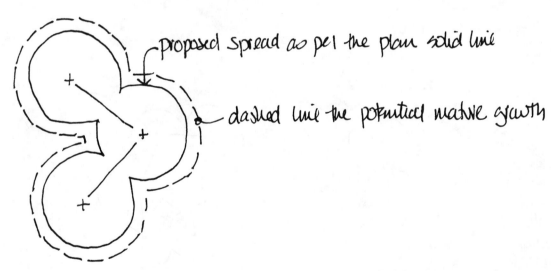

proposed spread as per the plan solid line

dashed line the potential mature growth

FIGURE 6-3
Scaling plant in plan presentations. (Designer: Gregory M. Pierceall)

141

ground cover plantings
and small shrubs

1' spreading plants
drawn individually
verses a mass
which is cleaner and
simpler

cluttered graphics

open mass cleaner
organization.

2' spreading plants
spacing can be as
indicated as per
the center location
or a note: 2' O.C.
meaning 2' on center

scale 1" = 8'

verses

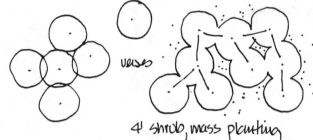

4' shrub, mass planting

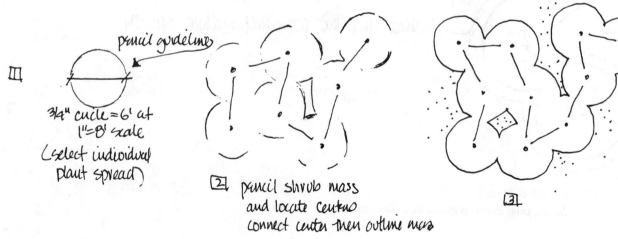

pencil guideline

III

3/4" circle = 6' at
1" = 8' scale
(select individual
plant spread)

[2] pencil shrub mass
and locate centers
connect center then outline mass

[3]

FIGURE 6-4
Drawing plant masses in plan presentations.
(Designer: Gregory M. Pierceall)

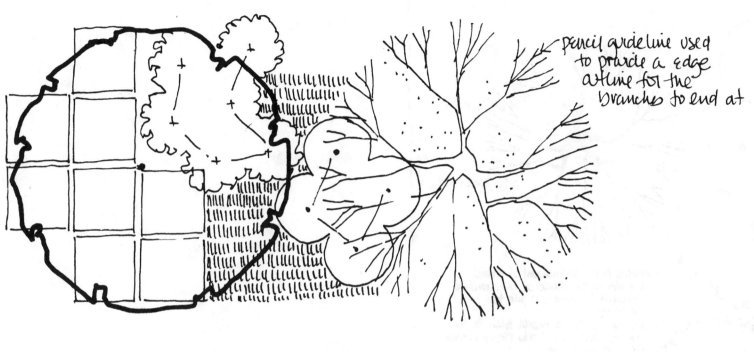

pencil guideline used
to provide a edge
outline for the
branches to end at

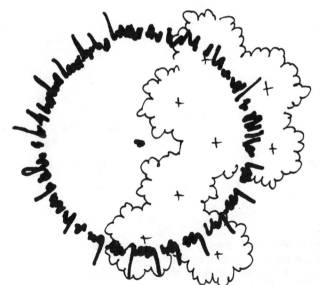

FIGURE 6-5

Symbol overlapping in plan presentations. When drawing a landscape plan, larger canopy elements often overlap smaller understory plantings and constructed features. While laying out a proposal, be aware of these situations and select symbols that most clearly present the various layers of the design. (Designer: Gregory M. Pierceall)

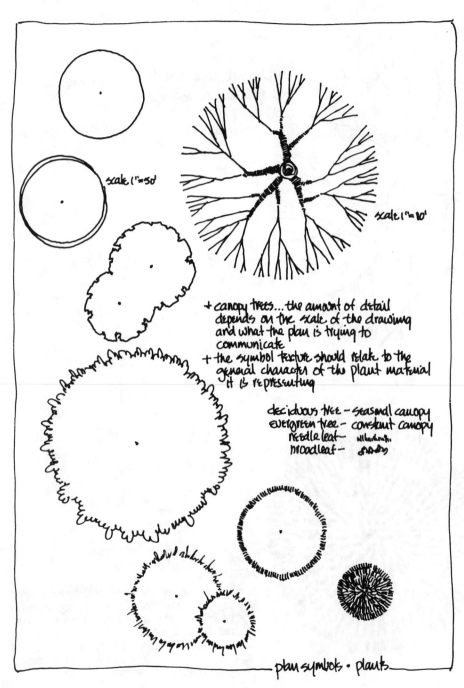

scale 1"=50'

scale 1"=10'

+ canopy trees...the amount of detail
depends on the scale of the drawing
and what the plan is trying to
communicate
+ the symbol texture should relate to the
general character of the plant material
it is representing

deciduous tree – seasonal canopy
evergreen tree – constant canopy
needle leaf –
broadleaf –

plan symbols · plants

FIGURE 6-6(a)

Plan/elevation symbols. When drawing symbols in plan view, make sure to use the same graphic style when showing the same plant in an elevation. Also see Figure 6-6(b) and (c). (Designer: Gregory M. Pierceall)

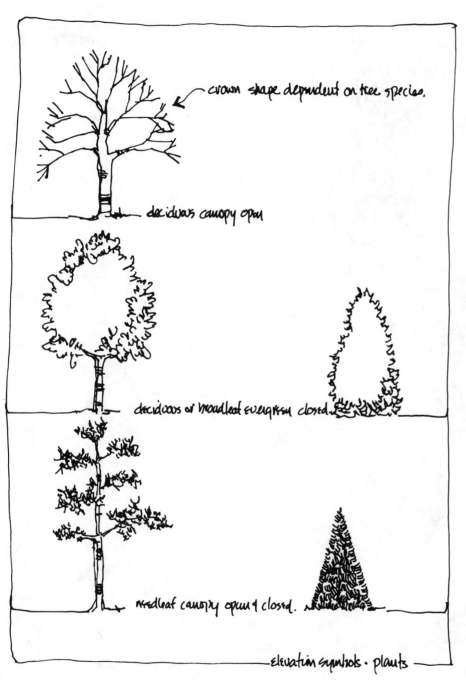

crown shape dependent on tree species.

deciduous canopy open

deciduous or broadleaf evergreen closed.

needleaf canopy open & closed.

— elevation symbols · plants —

FIGURE 6-6(b)
Plan/elevation example.

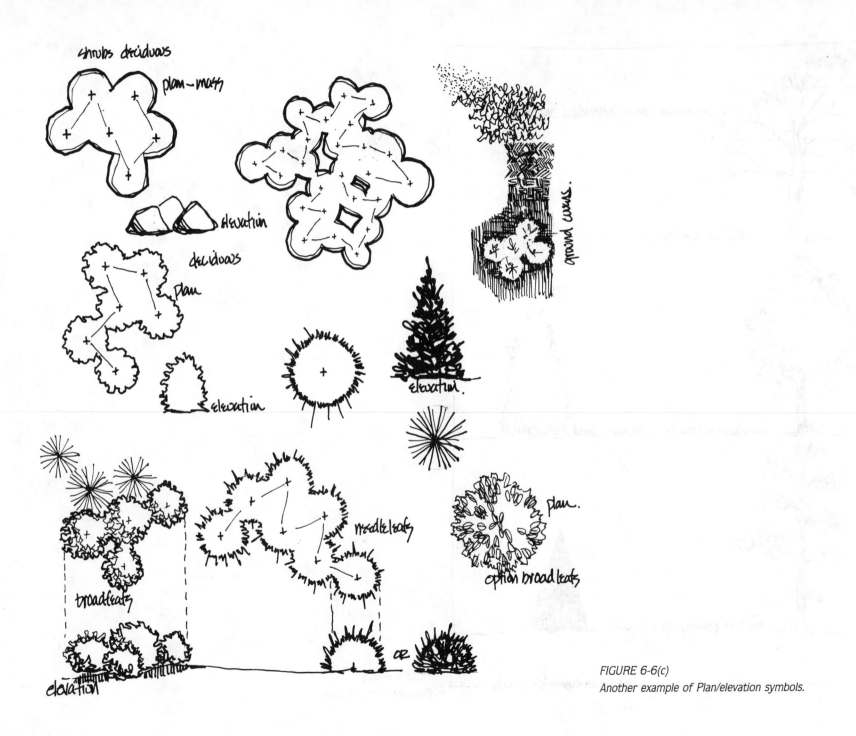

shrubs deciduous

plan – mass

elevation

deciduous

Plan

elevation

ground covers.

elevation

elevation.

broadleafs

broadleafs

needleleafs

elevation

OR

plan.

option broadleafs

FIGURE 6-6(c)
Another example of Plan/elevation symbols.

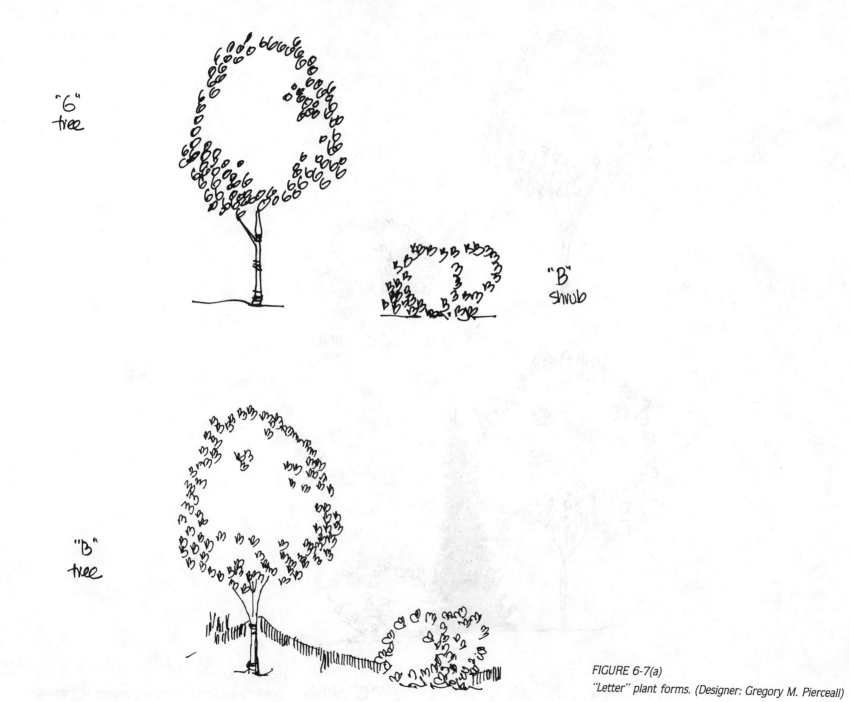

"6"
tree

"B"
shrub

"B"
tree

FIGURE 6-7(a)
"Letter" plant forms. (Designer: Gregory M. Pierceall)

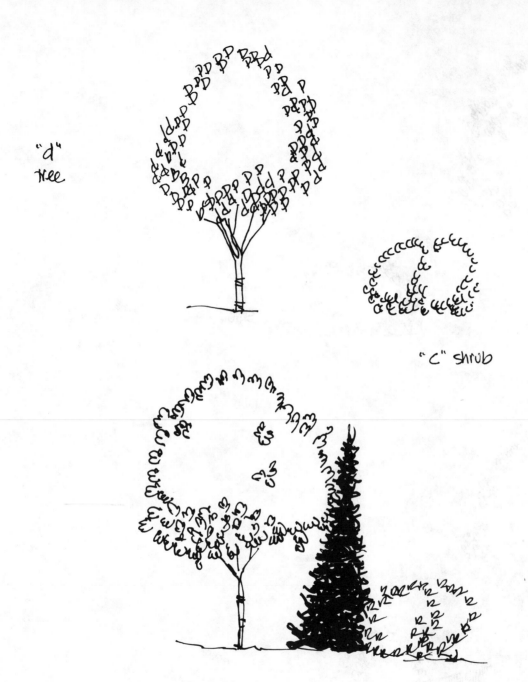

"d"
tree

"c" shrub

"R" shrub

FIGURE 6-7(b)
"Letter" plant forms. (Designer: Gregory M. Pierceall)

PLAN VIEW EXAMPLES

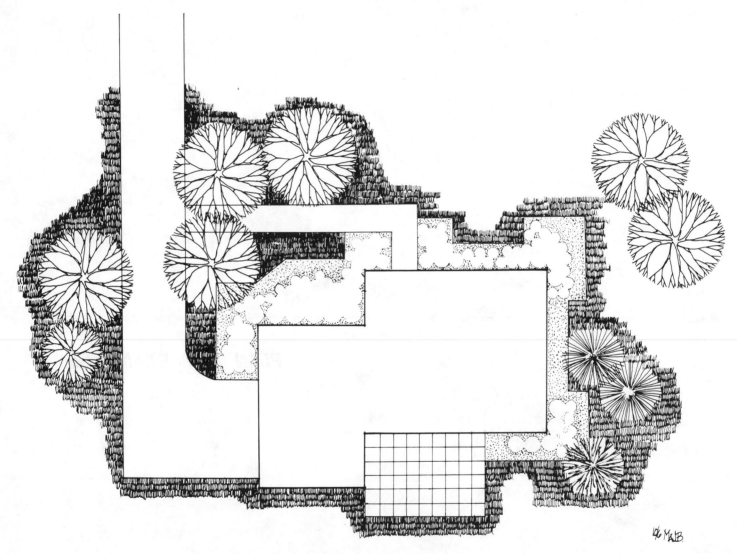

PLAN VIEW EXAMPLE 1
Dark ground plan/light canopy site plan. (Designer: M. Bedolli)

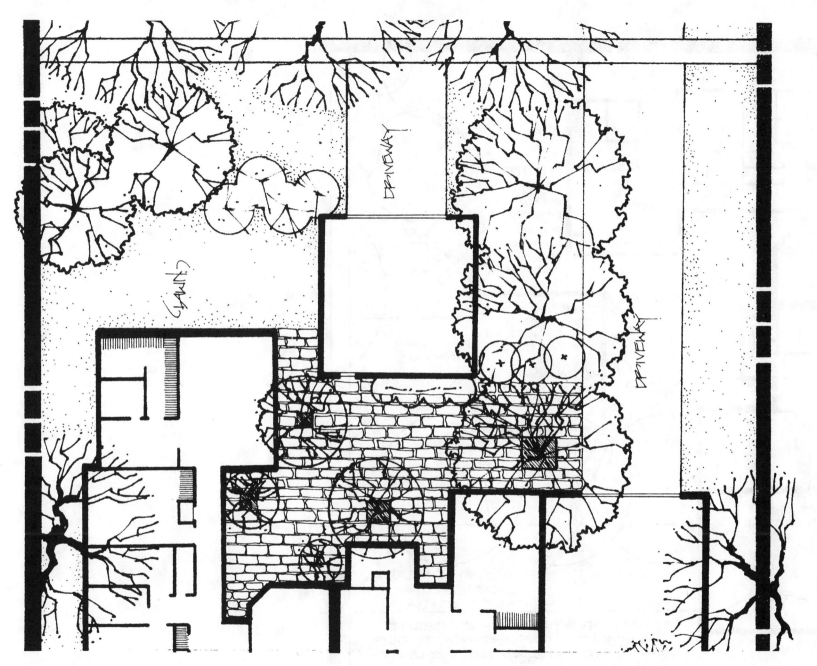

PLAN VIEW EXAMPLE 2(a)
Illustrated site plan. (Designer: Raymond Paul Strychalski)

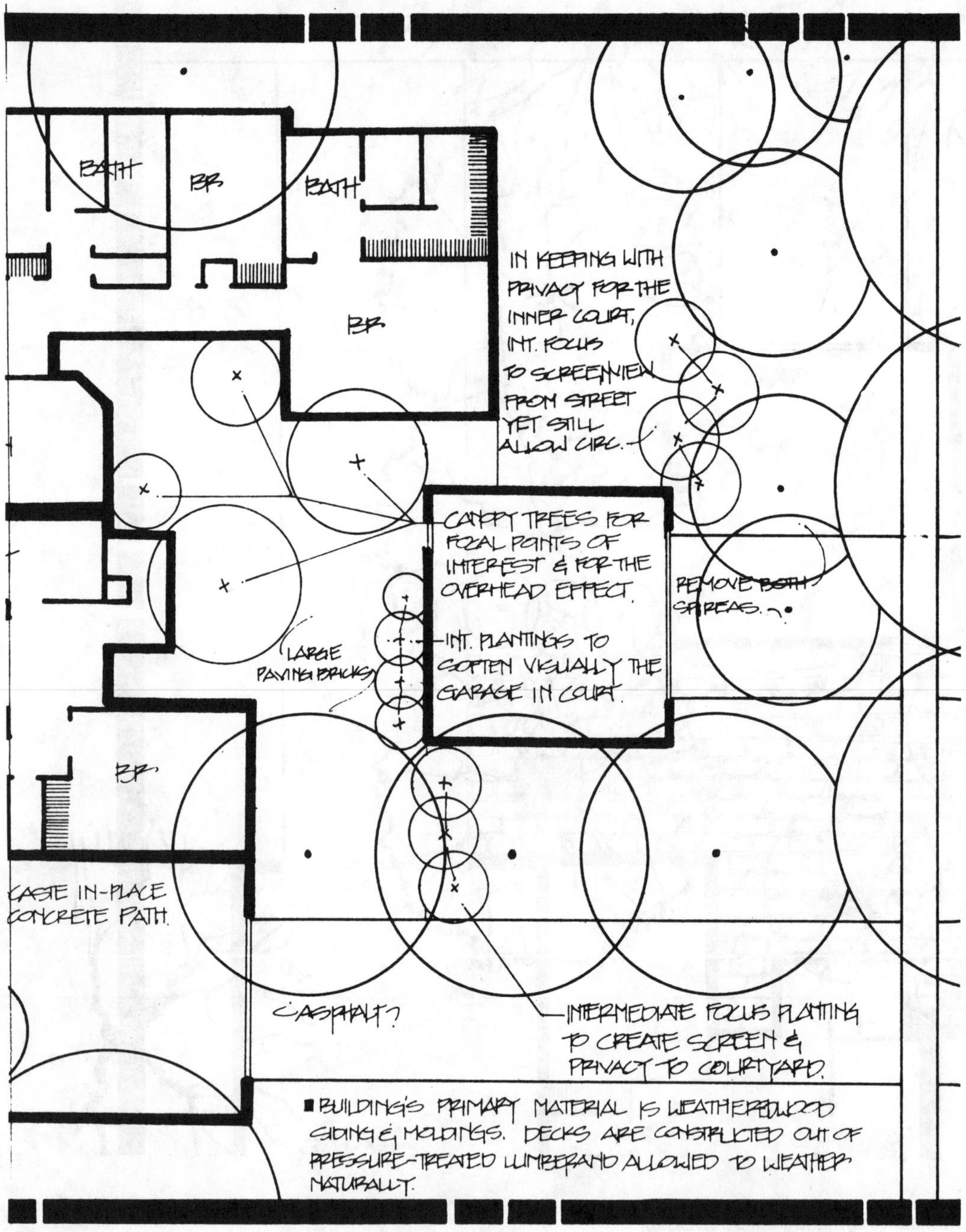
BATH
BR
BATH
BR
IN KEEPING WITH PRIVACY FOR THE INNER COURT, INT. FOCUS TO SCREEN VIEW FROM STREET YET STILL ALLOW CIRC.
CANOPY TREES FOR FOCAL POINTS OF INTEREST & FOR THE OVERHEAD EFFECT.
REMOVE BOTH SPIREAS.
INT. PLANTINGS TO SOFTEN VISUALLY THE GARAGE IN COURT.
LARGE PAVING BRICKS
BR
CASTE IN-PLACE CONCRETE PATH.
ASPHALT?
INTERMEDIATE FOCUS PLANTING TO CREATE SCREEN & PRIVACY TO COURTYARD.
BUILDING'S PRIMARY MATERIAL IS WEATHERED WOOD SIDING & MOLDINGS. DECKS ARE CONSTRUCTED OUT OF PRESSURE-TREATED LUMBER AND ALLOWED TO WEATHER NATURALLY.

PLAN VIEW EXAMPLE 2(b)
Plant selection site plan. (Designer: Raymond Paul Strychalski)

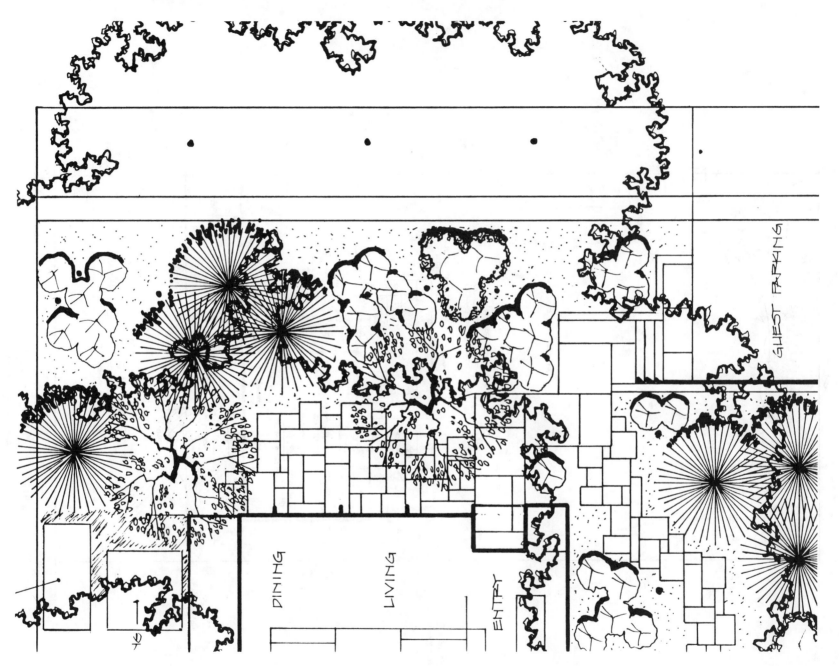

GUEST PARKING

DINING

LIVING

ENTRY

PLAN VIEW EXAMPLE 3
Illustrated site plan, detailed canopy, simple ground plane. (Designer: R. Rinek)

153

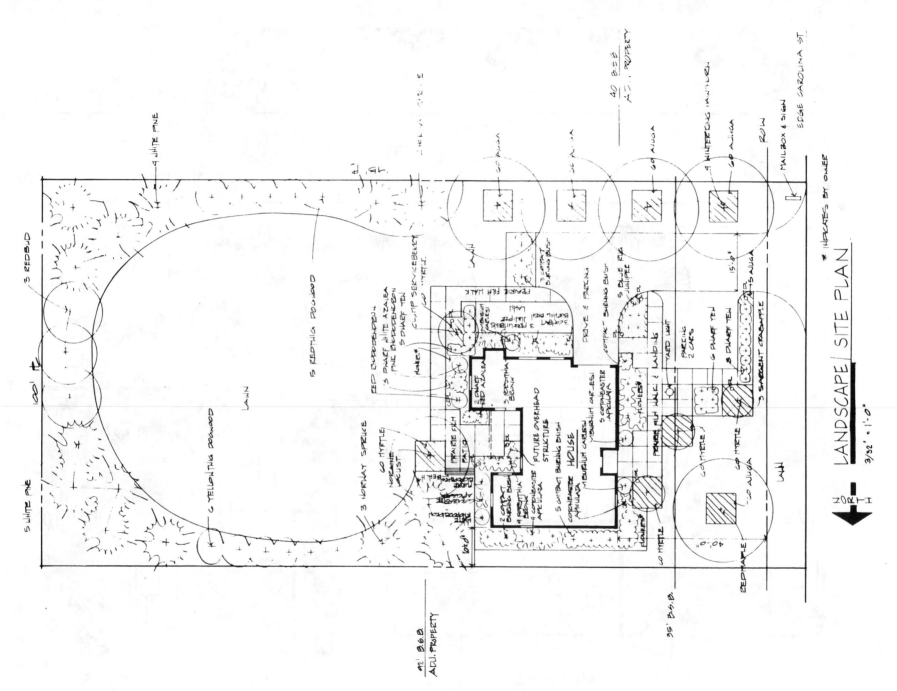

LANDSCAPE / SITE PLAN

3/32" = 1'-0"

* INDICATES BY OWNER

PLAN VIEW EXAMPLE 4
Total site plan, simple line presentation. (Designer: J. Baird)

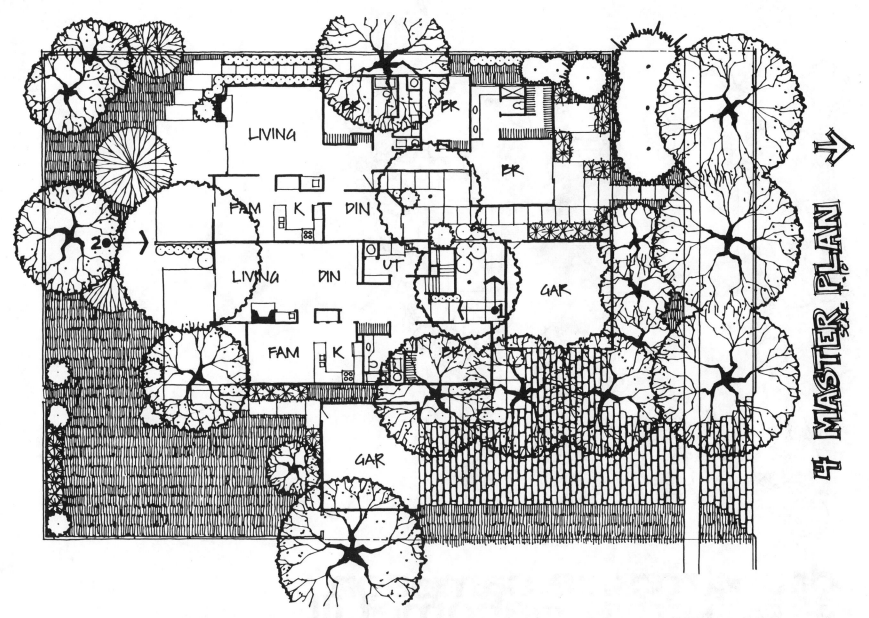

LIVING

BR

BR

FAM   K   DIN

2

LIVING   DIN   UT

GAR

FAM   K

BR

GAR

↙ MASTER PLAN
SCALE 1/8" = 1'-0"

PLAN VIEW EXAMPLE 5
Detailed duplex site plan, dark ground/light canopy. (Designer: D. Staley)

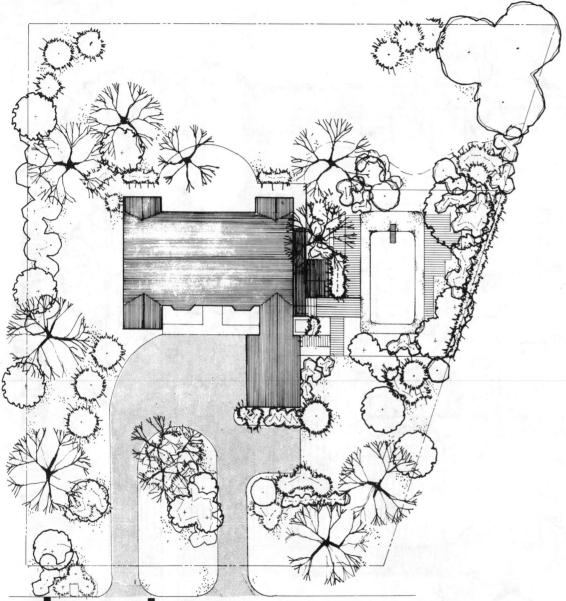

dr. and mrs. r.e. sampson
33 golf drive mahomet, ill.
design by pk associates landscape architects

no. 7410

156

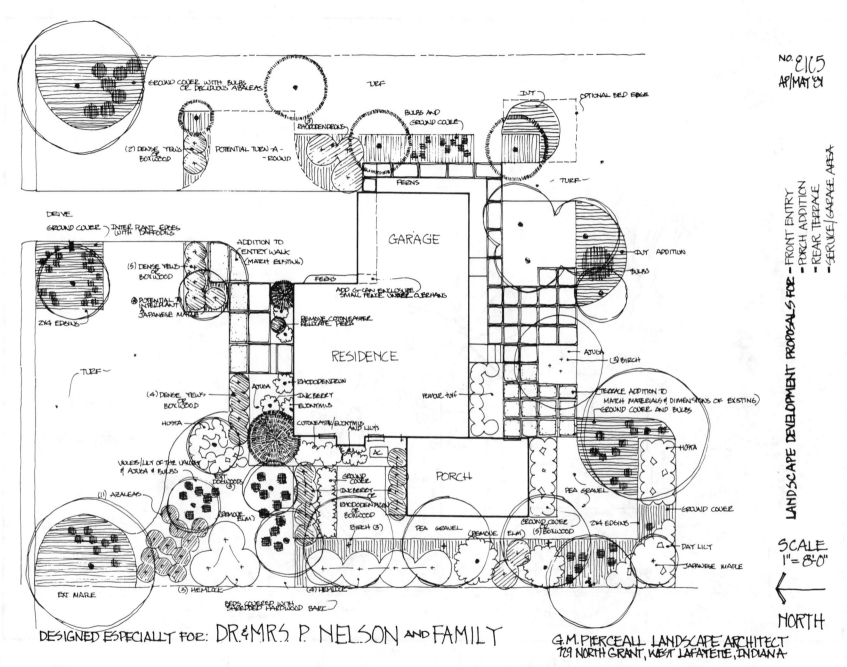

NO. 8105
AP/MAT '84

GROUND COVER WITH BULBS OR DECIDUOUS AZALEAS

TURF

IVY

OPTIONAL BED EDGE

RHODODENDRONS

BULBS AND GROUND COVER

(2) DENSE YEWS OR BOXWOOD

POTENTIAL TURN-A-ROUND

FERNS

TURF

DRIVE

GROUND COVER

INTER PLANT EDGES WITH DAFFODILS

GARAGE

IVY ADDITION

BULBS

ADDITION TO ENTRY WALK (MATCH EXISTING)

(5) DENSE YEWS OR BOXWOOD

FERNS

ADD SCREEN ENCLOSURE SMALL FENCE UNDER OVERHANG

2X4 EDGING

POTENTIAL TO INTERPLANT JAPANESE MAPLE

REMOVE COTONEASTER RELOCATE PIERIS

RESIDENCE

AJUGA

(3) BIRCH

TURF

(4) DENSE YEWS OR BOXWOOD

AJUGA

RHODODENDRON

INKBERRY EUONYMUS

REMOVE TURF

TERRACE ADDITION TO MATCH MATERIALS & DIMENSIONS OF EXISTING) GROUND COVER AND BULBS

HOSTA

COTONEASTER/EUONYMUS AND LILYS

HOSTA

VIOLETS/LILY OF THE VALLEY & AJUGA & BULBS

AC

PORCH

PEA GRAVEL

EXT DOGWOODS (3)

GROUND COVER INKBERRY OR RHODODENDRON OR BOXWOOD

GROUND COVER

(11) AZALEAS

BIRCH (3)

GROUND COVER (5) BOXWOOD

2X4 EDGING

REMOVE ELM

PEA GRAVEL

REMOVE ELM

DAY LILY

EXT MAPLE

(3) HEMLOCK

(4) HEMLOCK

BEDS COVERED WITH SHREDDED HARDWOOD BARK

JAPANESE MAPLE

SCALE 1"= 8'-0"

NORTH

DESIGNED ESPECIALLY FOR: DR. & MRS. P. NELSON AND FAMILY

G.M. PIERCEALL LANDSCAPE ARCHITECT
729 NORTH GRANT, WEST LAFAYETTE, INDIANA

PLAN VIEW EXAMPLE 7
Freehand drafted residential site plan. (Designer: Gregory M. Pierceall)

157

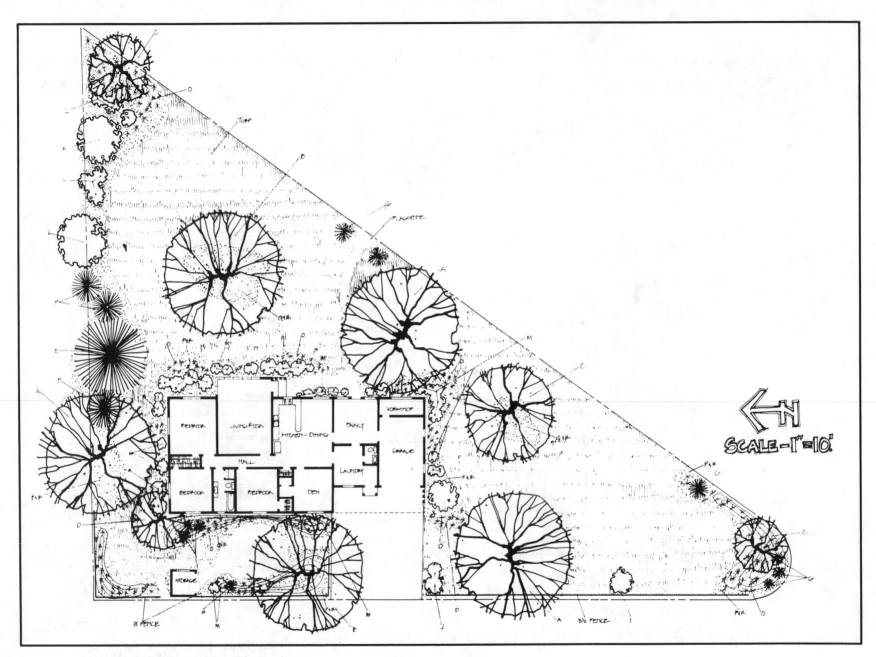

PLAN VIEW EXAMPLE 8
Freehand drafted residential site plan. (Designer: L. Neumann)

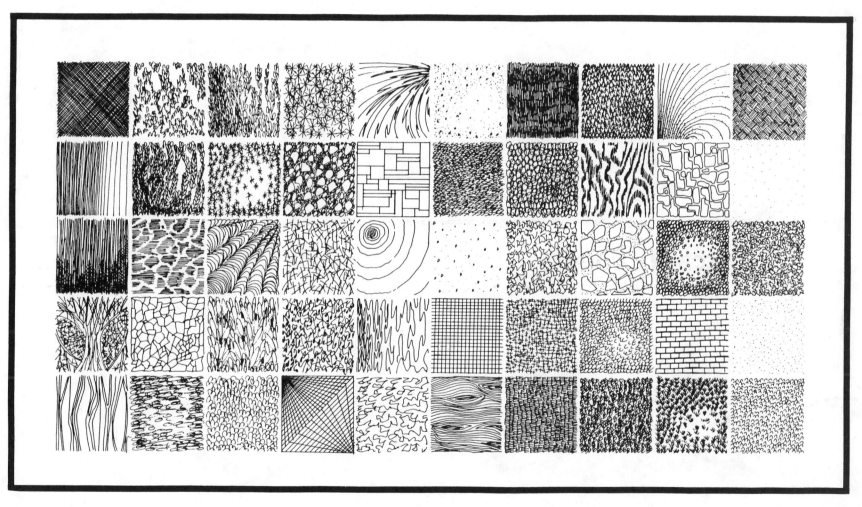

PLAN VIEW EXAMPLE 9
Sample plan view textures. (Designer: J. Lane)

SECTION EXAMPLES

WEST—EAST SECTION/ELEVATION

North.

SECTION EXAMPLE 1
Residential section/elevation. (Designer: Gregory M. Pierceall)

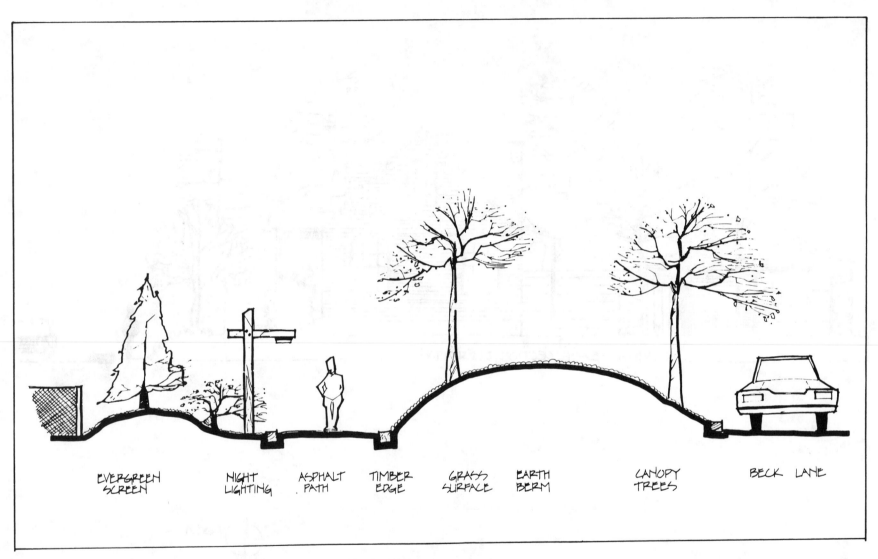

EVERGREEN SCREEN   NIGHT LIGHTING   ASPHALT PATH   TIMBER EDGE   GRASS SURFACE   EARTH BERM   CANOPY TREES   BECK LANE

SECTION EXAMPLE 2
Streetscape section. (Designer: T. G. Kramer)

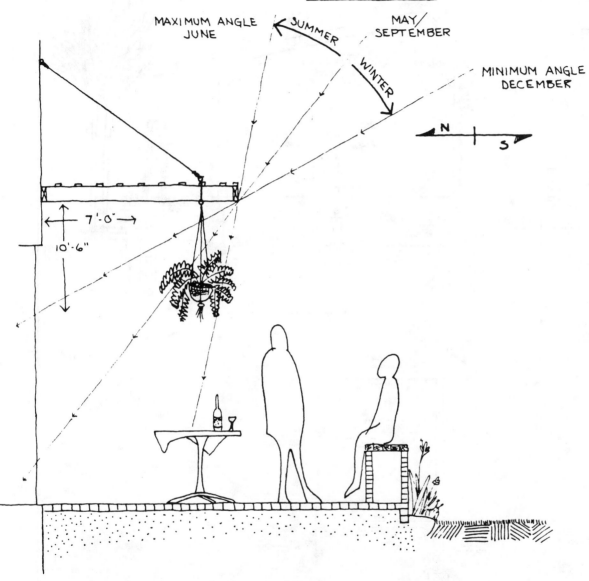

SOLAR DIAGRAM

MAXIMUM ANGLE
JUNE

SUMMER

MAY/
SEPTEMBER

WINTER

MINIMUM ANGLE
DECEMBER

N
S

7'-0"

10'-6"

CROSS SECTION OF PATIO AND LATH SUNSHADE
(NOT TO SCALE)

SECTION EXAMPLE 3
Residential lattice section. (also see elevation example 2) (Designer: J. D. Tarbox)

163

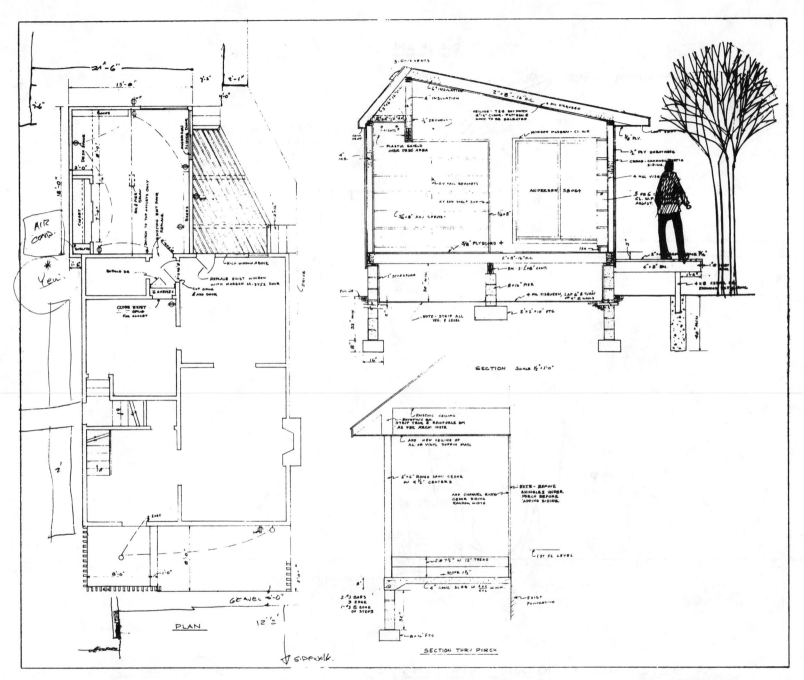

SECTION EXAMPLE 4
Residential architectural section. (Designer: R. Link, Architect)

ELEVATION EXAMPLES

LOOKING SOUTH

LOOKING WEST

1 ENTRY COURT : DUPLEX IDENTIFICATION
SCALE 1" = 5'-0"

2 DECK DETAIL (LOOKING NORTH)
SCALE 1" = 5'-0"

ELEVATION EXAMPLE 1
Duplex elevations reference to Plan View Example 5. (Designer: D. Staley)

5 SITE DETAILS
SCALE 1" = 5'-0"

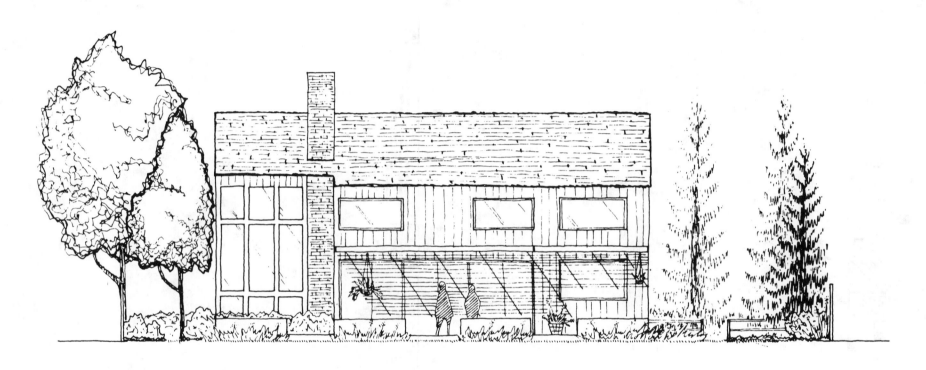

REAR ELEVATION

ELEVATION EXAMPLE 2
Residential elevation reference to Section Example 3. (Designer: J. D. Tarbox)

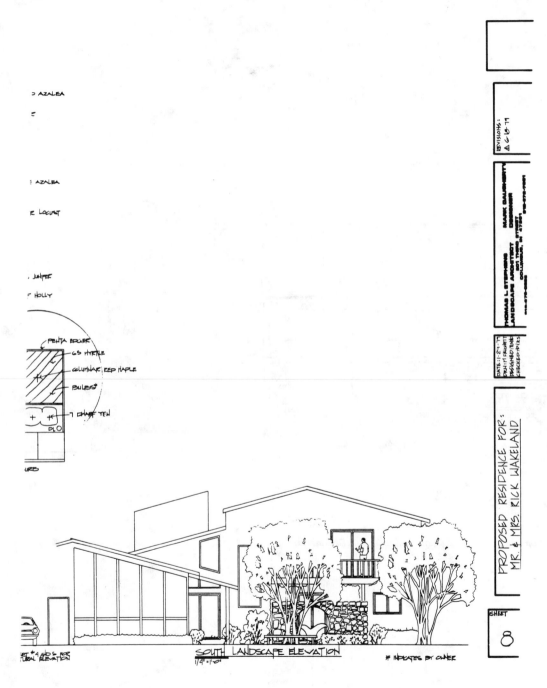

SOUTH LANDSCAPE ELEVATION
1/4" = 1'-0"

* INDICATES BY OWNER

PROPOSED RESIDENCE FOR:
MR. & MRS. RICK WAKELAND

SHEET 8

ELEVATION EXAMPLE 3
Residential elevation (drafted style). (Designer: J. Baird)

south

ELEVATION EXAMPLE 4
Duplex elevation (simplicity). (Designer: Raymond Paul Strychalski)

ELEVATION

ELEVATION EXAMPLE 5
Residential elevation (note window treatment). (Designer: P. Rinek)

PERSPECTIVE EXAMPLES

PERSPECTIVE EXAMPLE 1
Technical residential perspective. (Designer: K. Johnson)

PERSPECTIVE EXAMPLE 2
Technical residential perspective. (Designer: Raymond Paul Strychalski)

ENTRY

PERSPECTIVE EXAMPLE 3
Freehand residential perspective. (Designer: R. Rinek)

Residence Entry Court

PERSPECTIVE EXAMPLE 4
Freehand residential entry. (Designer: Gregory M. Pierceall)

SKETCHING EXAMPLES

SKETCHING EXAMPLE 1
Residential entry planting. (Designer: Gregory M. Pierceall)

SKETCH NO. 1

SKETCH 2

SKETCH 3

4

5

6

SKETCH 9

SKETCH 10

SKETCHING EXAMPLE 2
"10 minute" freehand sketches from viewing slides. (Designer: Raymond Paul Strychalski)

178

GREEK REVIVAL STYLE

402 5TH ST.   LAFAYETTE, INDIANA

SKETCHING EXAMPLE 3
Architectural sketch. (Designer: D. Krall)

SKETCHING EXAMPLE 4
Architectural sketch. Ink and water color. (Designer: L. Neumann)

SKETCHING EXAMPLE 5
Architectural sketch. Ink and water color. (Designer: L. Neumann)

tract 1 , the public boat dock looking northwest

2/11

SKETCHING EXAMPLE 6
Simple line sketch traced from slide. (Designer: Gregory M. Pierceall)

SUMMARY

Designing solely in plan view even though this is the primary presentation mode limits a designer's view and opportunity to understand a design project space fully. Sketching while designing in plan provides a broader perspective and understanding of existing conditions and proposals developed. Please review these examples and practice your graphic techniques by tracing and composing from these illustrations.

REFERENCES AND READINGS

Letraset. *Graphic Art Materials Reference*. Paramus, NJ: Letraset Corp., 1981.

Lin, Mike. *Economy of Graphics*. Washington, D.C.: ASLA, 1979.

Walker, T. D. *Plan Graphics*. West Lafayette, IN: PDA Publishers, 1975.

———. *Perspective Sketches II*. West Lafayette, IN: PDA Publishers, 1975.

Zipatone. *Zipatone Catalog*. Elk Grove Village, IL: Zipatone Corp., 1982.

*R*esidential landscape design portfolio

As a graphic reference and to illustrate the diversity of design situations and design presentations possible, examples of practitioner and student designs are included in this portfolio section.

PORTFOLIO SECTION ONE/DESIGN PROPOSALS

Section One shows examples of design presentations ranging from single-sheet design proposals for an entry, patio, or pool area to complete design packages including master plan proposals for site plantings and landscape construction. Residential feasibility studies, which focus on the design procedures and considerations used when siting a new structure on an undeveloped property, are also included in this section. Lastly, some residential construction drawings are included to complete the range of potential design documents that may be developed for residential properties. Each drawing has a notation as to its original size and its intended use.

PORTFOLIO SECTION ONE:

DESIGN PROPOSALS

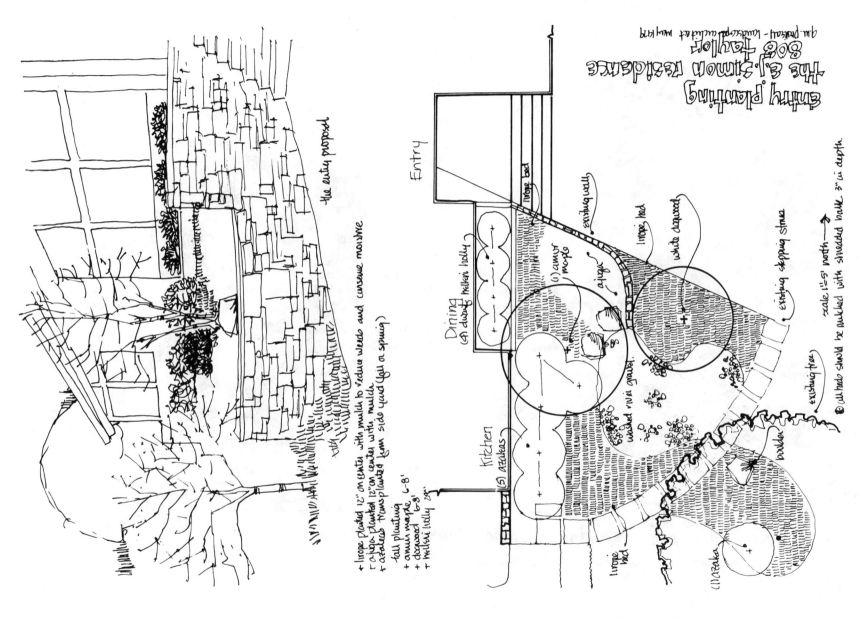

+ liriope planted 12" on centers with mulch to reduce weeds and conserve moisture
  ┌ ajuga planted 12" on centers with mulch.
+ azaleas transplanted from side yard (fall or spring)

tall planting
  + amur maple, 6-8'
  + dogwood, 6-8'
  + helleri holly 23"

the entry proposal

Entry

entry planting
the E.J. Simon residence
Bob Taylor
Jim Prentice – landscape architect, Novi 1978

Entry

liriope bed
existing wall
liriope bed
white dogwood

(7) dwarf helleri holly

Dining
(7) dwarf helleri holly

Kitchen
(5) azaleas

(1) amur maple

ajuga

washed river gravel.

existing stepping stones

(all beds should be mulched with shredded bark 3" in depth.

scale 1"=5' north →

existing tree

boulder

liriope bed

azalea

Entry plan and sketch, original 11" × 17". (Designer: Gregory M. Pierceall)

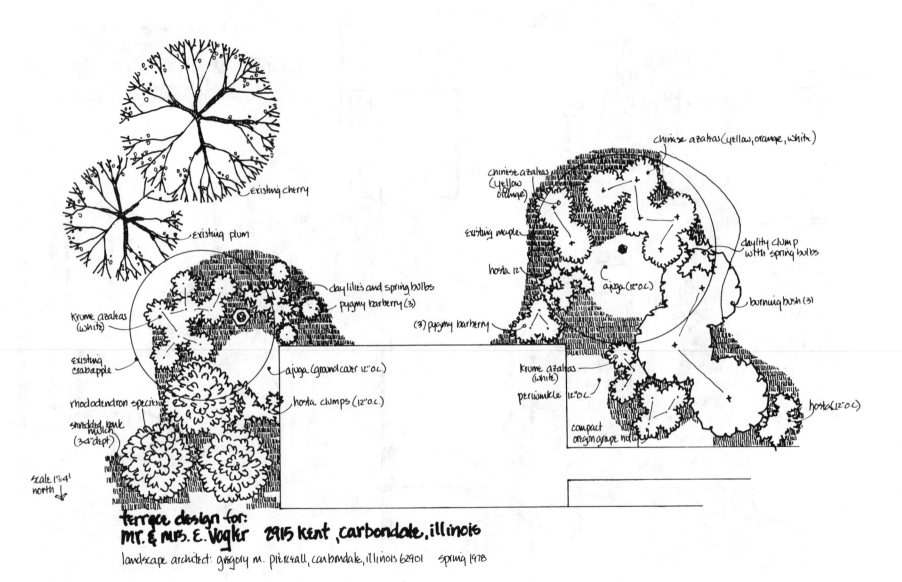

existing cherry

existing plum

chinese azaleas (yellow, orange, white)

chinese azaleas (yellow, orange)

existing maple

hosta 12"

ajuga (12" o.c.)

daylily clump with spring bulbs

day lilies and spring bulbs
pygmy barberry (3)

burning bush (3)

krume azaleas (white)

(3) pygmy barberry

existing crabapple

ajuga (ground cover 12" o.c.)

krume azaleas (white)

rhododendron species

hosta clumps (12" o.c.)

periwinkle 12" o.c.

hosta (12" o.c.)

shredded bark mulch (3-4" dept)

compact oregon grape holly

scale 1"=4'
north

terrace design for:
mr. & mrs. E. Vogler   2915 kent, carbondale, illinois

landscape architect: gregory m. pierceall, carbondale, illinois 62901   spring 1978

Patio area planting, original 11" × 17". (Designer: Gregory M. Pierceall)

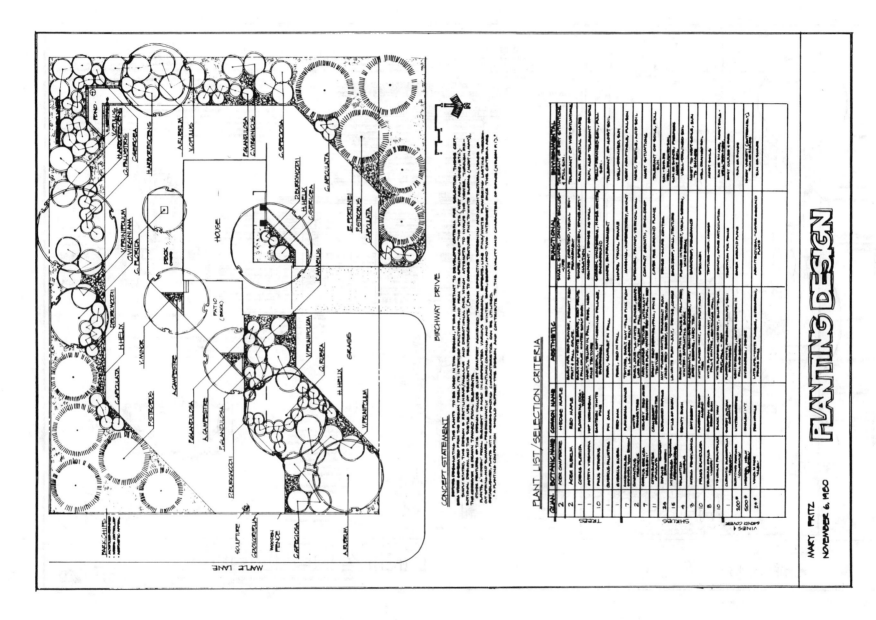

Residential planting design, original 24" × 36". (Designer: M. Fritz)

189

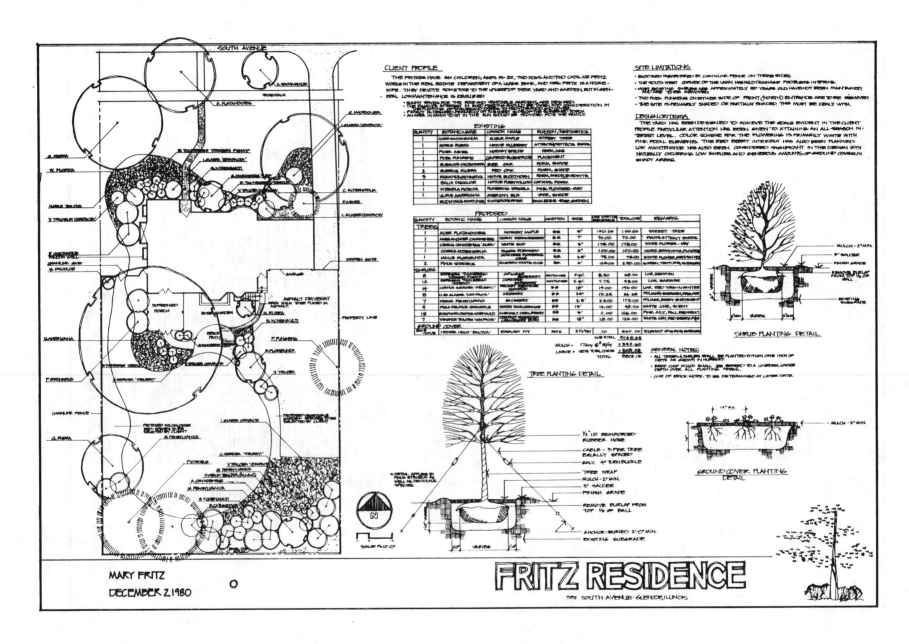

Residential planting design, original 24" × 36". (Designer: M. Fritz)

190

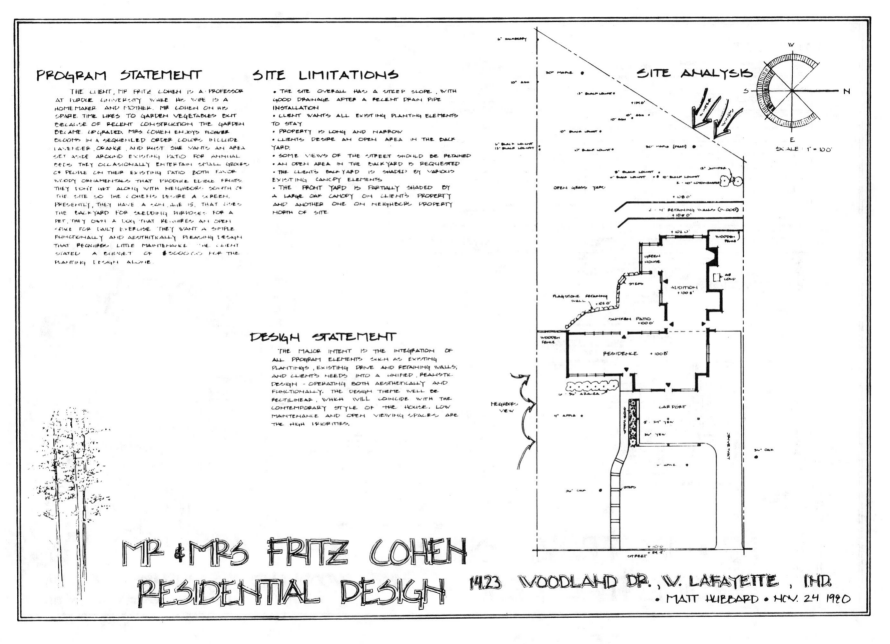

Residential planting inventory, original 24" × 36". (Designer: Matt Hubbard)

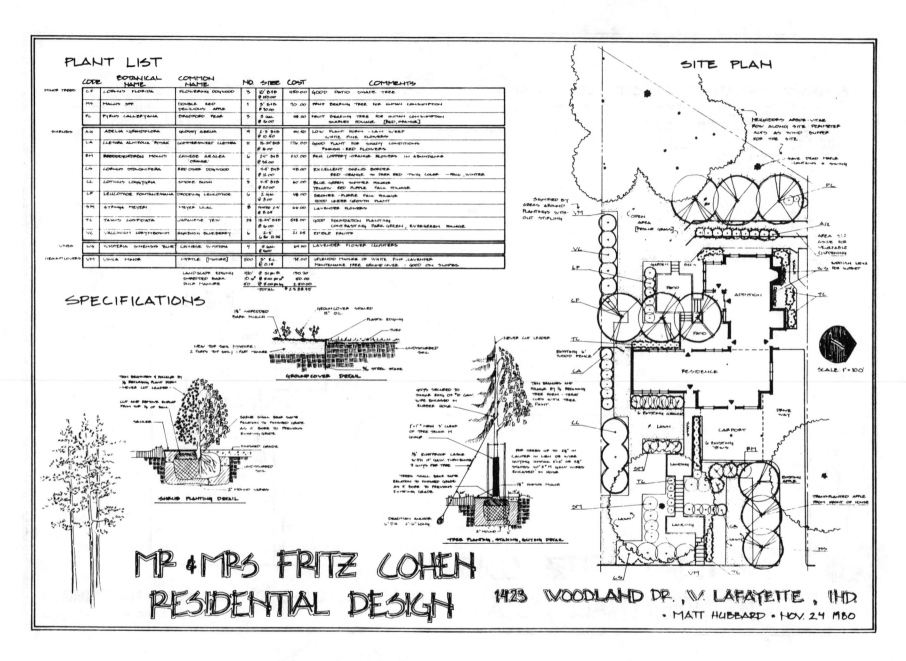

Residential planting proposal, original 24" × 36". (Designer: Matt Hubbard)

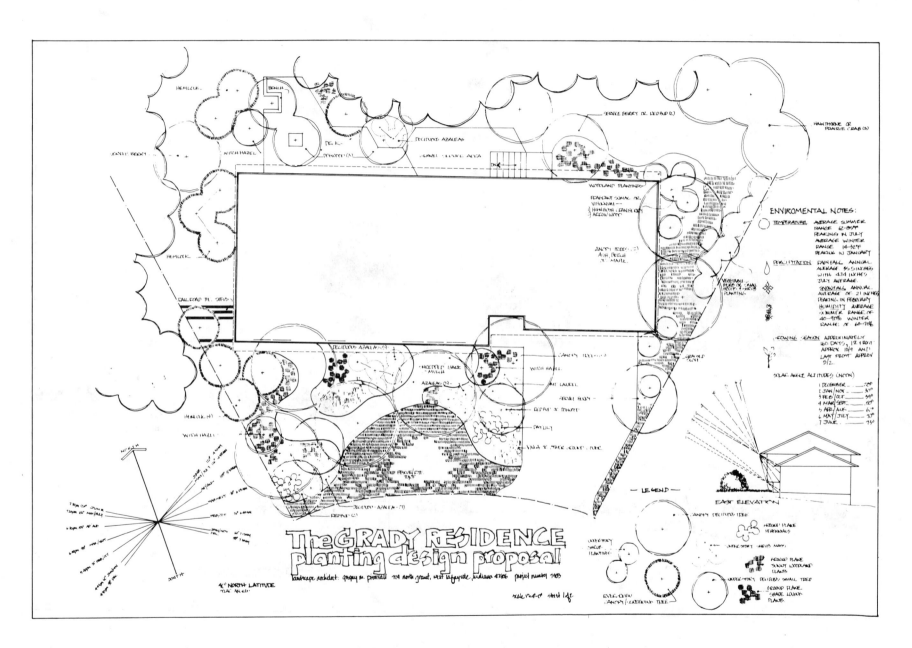

Residential planting design, original 18" × 24". (Designer: Gregory M. Pierceall)

193

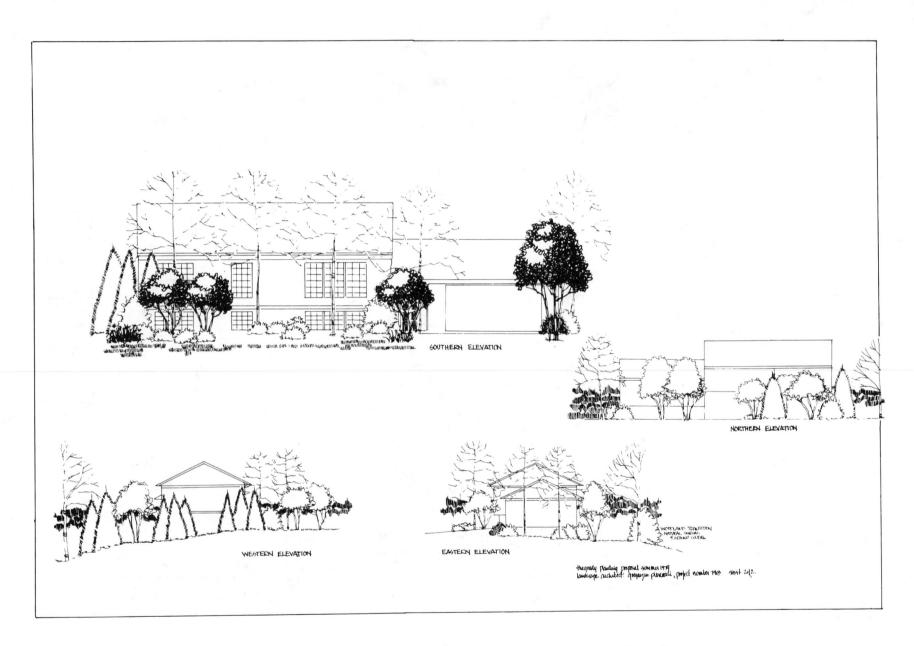

SOUTHERN ELEVATION

NORTHERN ELEVATION

WESTERN ELEVATION

EASTERN ELEVATION

Residential planting design elevations, original 18" × 24". (Designer: Gregory M. Pierceall)

Duplex site planning and development package, individual sheet originals, 11″ × 17″. Title sheet and site analysis. (Designer: M. Fritz)

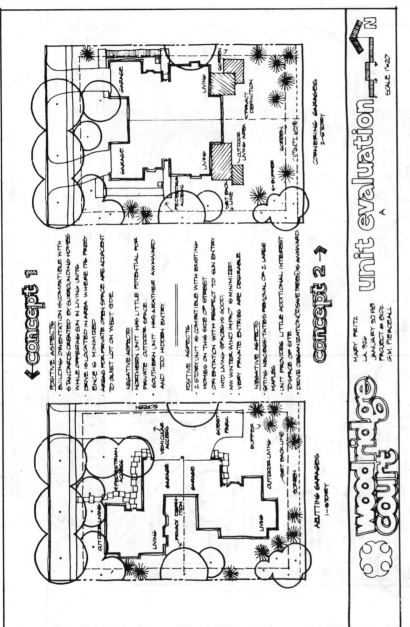

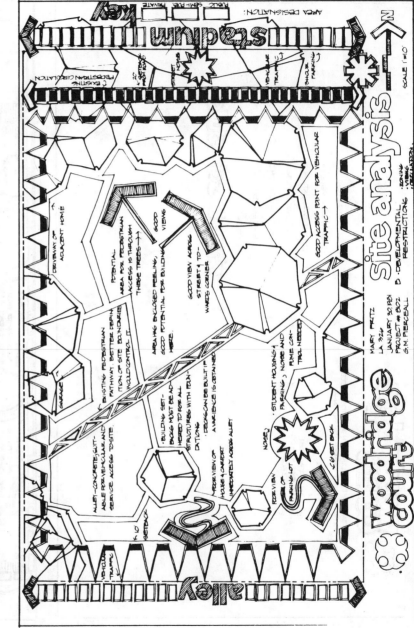

Analysis and concepts. (Designer: M. Fritz)

196

Master plan and details. (Designer: M. Fritz)

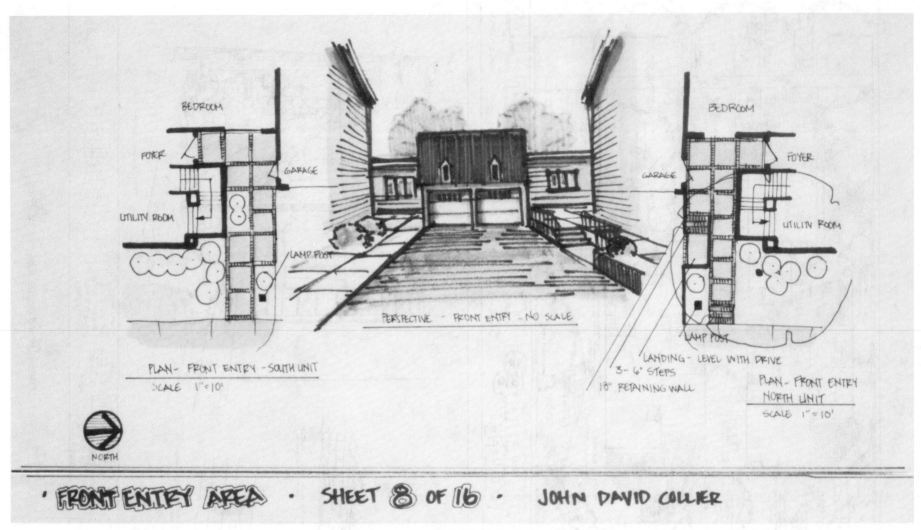

BEDROOM

FOYER

UTILITY ROOM

GARAGE

LAMP POST

PLAN - FRONT ENTRY - SOUTH UNIT
SCALE 1"=10'

NORTH

PERSPECTIVE - FRONT ENTRY - NO SCALE

BEDROOM

GARAGE

FOYER

UTILITY ROOM

LAMP POST

LANDING - LEVEL WITH DRIVE
3 - 6" STEPS
18" RETAINING WALL

PLAN - FRONT ENTRY
NORTH UNIT
SCALE 1"=10'

· FRONT ENTRY AREA · SHEET 8 OF 16 · JOHN DAVID COLLIER

Duplex site design details, original 11" × 14". (Designer: J. D. Collier)

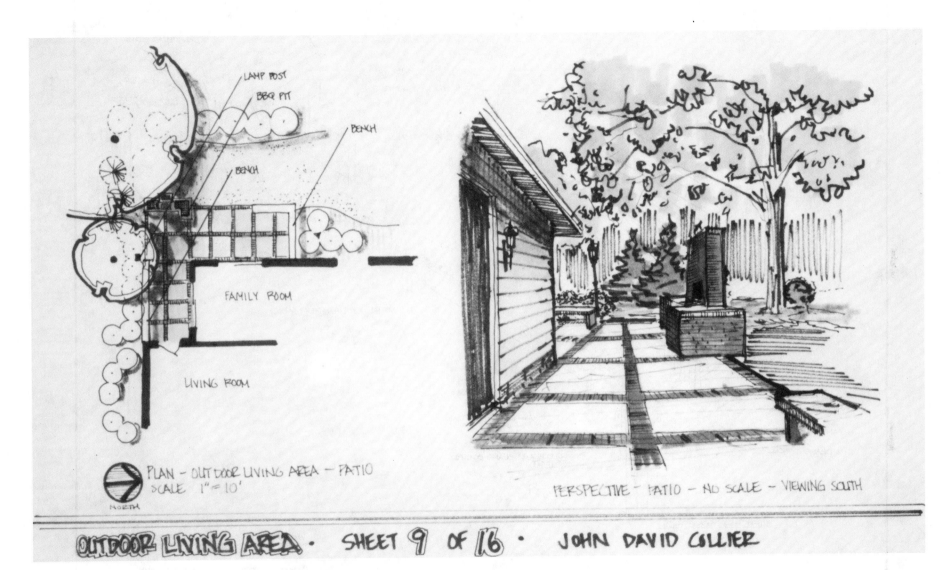

LAMP POST

BBQ PIT

BENCH

BENCH

FAMILY ROOM

LIVING ROOM

PLAN - OUTDOOR LIVING AREA - PATIO
SCALE 1" = 10'

NORTH

PERSPECTIVE - PATIO - NO SCALE - VIEWING SOUTH

OUTDOOR LIVING AREA · SHEET 9 OF 16 · JOHN DAVID COLLIER

Duplex site design details, original 11" × 14". (Designer: J. D. Collier)

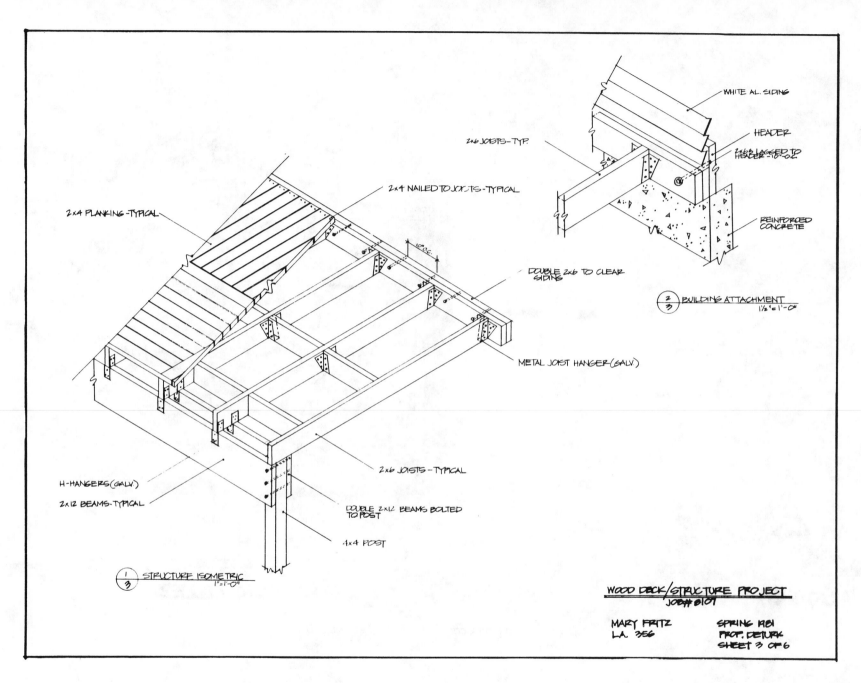

2x4 PLANKING - TYPICAL

2x4 NAILED TO JOISTS - TYPICAL

2x6 JOISTS - TYP.

DOUBLE 2x6 TO CLEAR
SIDING

METAL JOIST HANGER (GALV.)

2x6 JOISTS - TYPICAL

H-HANGERS (GALV)

2x12 BEAMS - TYPICAL

DOUBLE 2x12 BEAMS BOLTED
TO POST

4x4 POST

10" O.C.

① STRUCTURE ISOMETRIC
③ 1"=1'-0"

WHITE AL. SIDING

HEADER

2x6's LAGGED TO
HEADER - 18"-O.C.

REINFORCED
CONCRETE

② BUILDING ATTACHMENT
③ 1½"=1'-0"

WOOD DECK/STRUCTURE PROJECT
JOB # 8101

MARY FRITZ   SPRING 1981
L.A. 356   PROF. DETURK
                    SHEET 3 OF 6

Deck construction working drawings, originals 18" × 24". (Designer: M. Fritz)

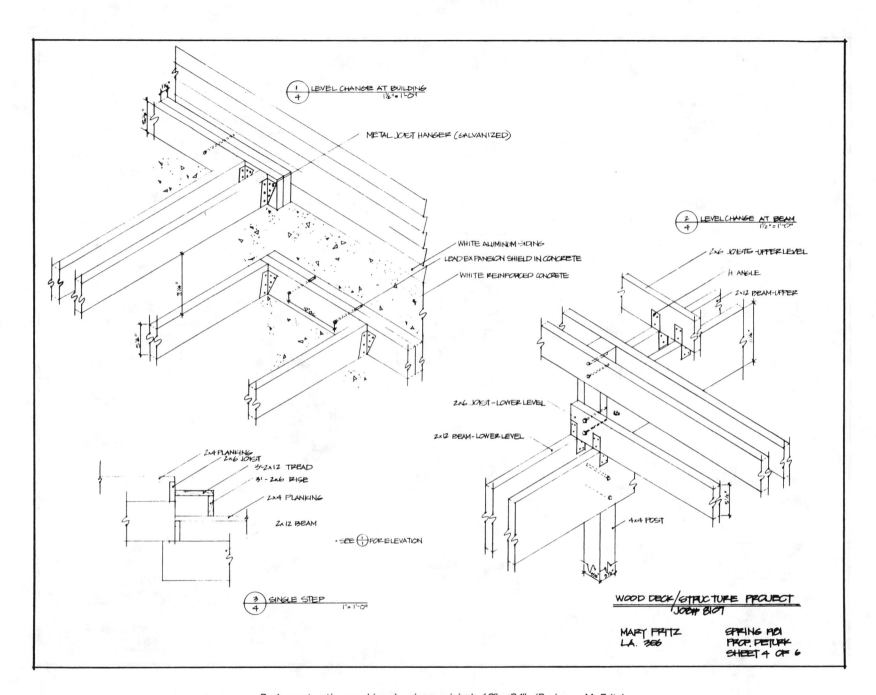

Deck construction working drawings, originals 18″ × 24″. (Designer: M. Fritz)

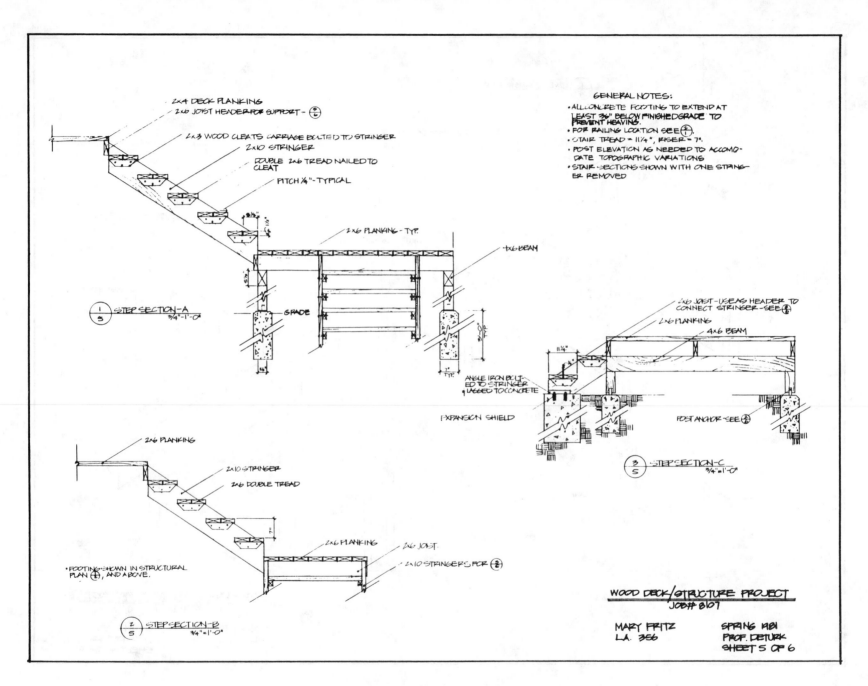

Deck construction working drawings, originals 18" × 24". (Designer: M. Fritz)

Included in this section are examples of sketching and the use of markers in drawings. Eight different residential elevations are shown. The elevations and perspectives were traced from slides projected on a piece of paper. These outlines were then used for planting proposals. The examples illustrate not only how graphics can express plantings and constructed features but how the use of graphics can describe the site and visual character of the locale or region in which it occurs. In reviewing these sketching examples, please be aware that the proposals are examples of sketching techniques used in presenting plantings, not examples of appropriate planting designs.

As a means of practicing design and graphic skills, typical line drawings of residential entry elevations were used as a base in the development of a planting. Each sketch was to include foreground, middleground, and background elements with the main focus the middleground areas. The designers were also encouraged to develop landscapes reflecting various geographic regions and seasons. As you review the examples, the outline sketch is first, then selected student proposals. The sketches originally were $8\frac{1}{2}'' \times 11''$, using marker paper and markers and pen or pentel-type media.

PORTFOLIO SECTION TWO:
RESIDENTIAL ELEVATIONS

RESIDENTIAL ELEVATION 1

RESIDENTIAL ELEVATION EXAMPLE 1 (a)
(Designer: W. Keith Rattay)

RESIDENTIAL ELEVATION EXAMPLE 1 (b)
(Designer: Lynn Campbell)

RESIDENTIAL ELEVATION EXAMPLE 1 (c)
(Designer: John Collier)

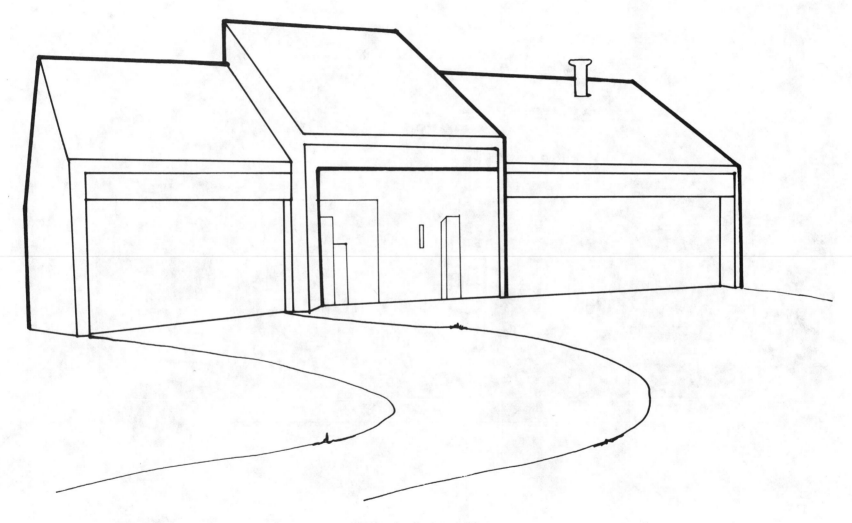

RESIDENTIAL ELEVATION 2

RESIDENTIAL ELEVATION EXAMPLE 2 (a)
(Designer: Lynn Campbell)

RESIDENTIAL ELEVATION EXAMPLE 2 (b)
(Designer: Kim Tarbox)

RESIDENTIAL ELEVATION EXAMPLE 2 (c)
(Designer: Rob Curtis)

RESIDENTIAL ELEVATION EXAMPLE 2 (d)
(Designer: Geoff Roehll)

RESIDENTIAL ELEVATION EXAMPLE 2 (e)
(Designer: Mike Getz)

RESIDENTIAL ELEVATION EXAMPLE 2 (f)
(Designer: Mike Reagan)

RESIDENTIAL ELEVATION 3

RESIDENTIAL ELEVATION EXAMPLE 3 (a)
(Designer: Kim Tarbox)

RESIDENTIAL ELEVATION EXAMPLE 3 (b)
(Designer: John Collier)

RESIDENTIAL ELEVATION 4

RESIDENTIAL ELEVATION EXAMPLE 4 (a)
(Designer: Jan Giese)

RESIDENTIAL ELEVATION EXAMPLE 4 (b)
(Designer: John Lane)

RESIDENTIAL ELEVATION 5

RESIDENTIAL ELEVATION EXAMPLE 5 (a)
(Designer: Beth Wilson)

RESIDENTIAL ELEVATION EXAMPLE 5 (b)
(Designer: Lynn Campbell)

RESIDENTIAL ELEVATION EXAMPLE 5 (c)
(Designer: Mike Powers)

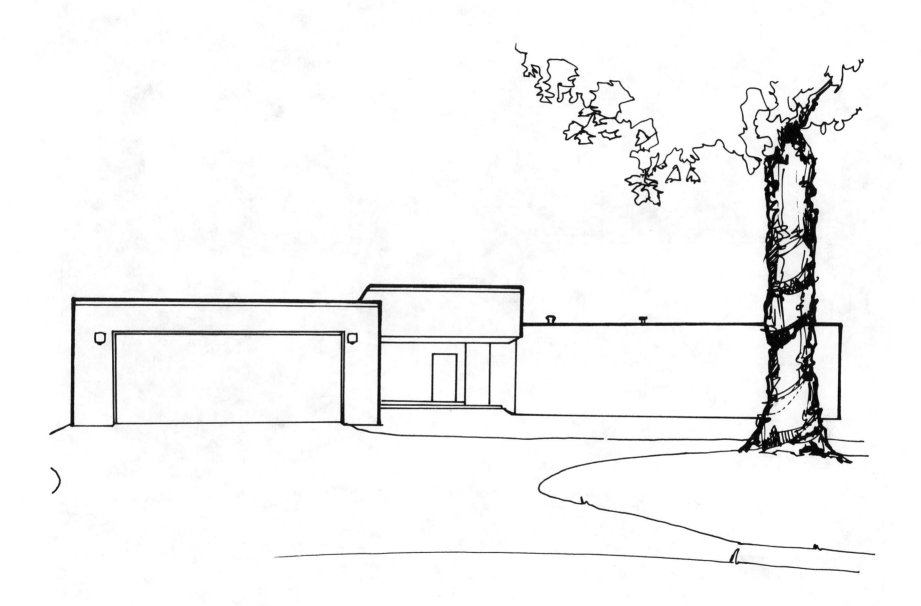

RESIDENTIAL ELEVATION 6

RESIDENTIAL ELEVATION EXAMPLE 6 (a)
(Designer: Kim Tarbox)

RESIDENTIAL ELEVATION EXAMPLE 6 (b)
(Designer: Beth Ann Wilson)

RESIDENTIAL ELEVATION EXAMPLE 6 (c)
(Designer: Jan Giese)

RESIDENTIAL ELEVATION EXAMPLE 6 (d)
(Designer: Lynn Campbell)

RESIDENTIAL ELEVATION EXAMPLE 6 (e)
(Designer: Rob Curtis)

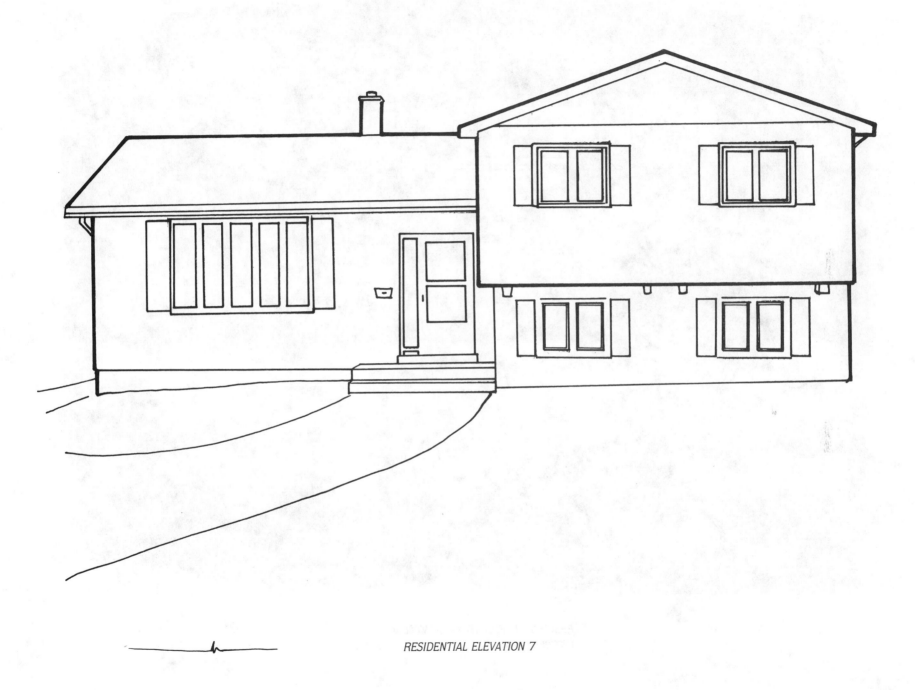

RESIDENTIAL ELEVATION 7

231

RESIDENTIAL ELEVATION EXAMPLE 7 (a)
(Designer: Kim Tarbox)

232

RESIDENTIAL ELEVATION EXAMPLE 7 (b)
(Designer: Lynn Campbell)

RESIDENTIAL ELEVATION EXAMPLE 7 (c)
(Designer: Mike Reagan)

RESIDENTIAL ELEVATION EXAMPLE 7 (d)
(Designer: Jan Giese)

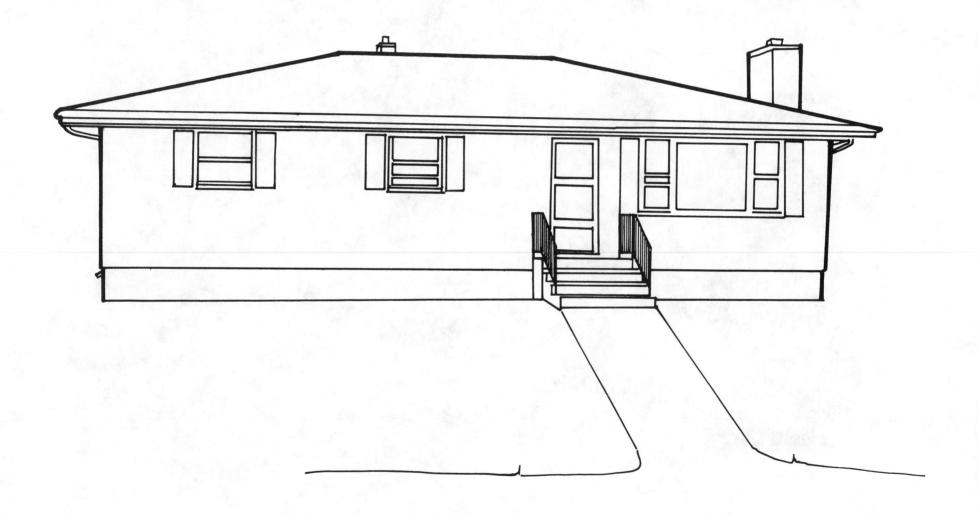

RESIDENTIAL ELEVATION 8

RESIDENTIAL ELEVATION EXAMPLE 8 (a)
(Designer: John Lane)

RESIDENTIAL ELEVATION EXAMPLE 8 (b)
(Designer: Lynn Campbell)

PORTFOLIO SECTION THREE:
PERSPECTIVE INFORMATION

ONE POINT PERSPECTIVE

HORIZON LINE: SET AT ANY DISTANCE ABOVE
GROUND LINE ACCORDING TO VIEW WANTED (BIRD'S-EYE, WORM'S-EYE, ETC.)
IN THIS EXAMPLE, HL WAS SET 55.0' ABOVE G.L.

V.P.   H.L.

PERSPECTIVE: SCALE 1"=20'

D   B   C   G.L.

0 10 20 30 40 50   A   80 90 100 110'

"EYE-BALL" FIRST SQUARE THEN DRAW
DIAGONAL THROUGH SQUARE... ALL OTHER
SQUARES ARE DETERMINED BY THAT
DIAGONAL LINE INTERSECTING VANISHING
LINES.

GROUND LINE (OR MEASURE LINE)
MEASURE ALL HEIGHTS BY SCALE
FROM GL AND PROJECT BACK TO
CORNER OF OBJECT AS SHOWN
BY DASHED LINES ...
(THIS EXAMPLE, SCALE OF 1"=20';
∴ PERSPECTIVE SCALE = 1"=20') ...

110' 100 90 80 70 60 50 40 30 20 10 0

0 10 20 30 40 50 60 70 80 90 100 110'

D C B A

PLAN & ELEVATION: SCALE 1"=40'

1) GRID THE PLAN AT A CONVENIENT SCALE (THIS EXAMPLE, 10' GRID @ 1"=40' SCALE)
2) DRAW GROUND LINE AND SCALE PLAN WIDTH ALONG IT AT CONVENIENT SCALE
3) SET HORIZON LINE AND V.P. ACCORDING TO PERSPECTIVE VIEW DESIRED
4) "EYE-BALL" FIRST PERSPECTIVE GRID SQUARE; OTHERS BY DIAGONAL CUTTING VANISHING LINES
5) TRANSFER PLAN TO PERSPECTIVE GRID; SCALE HEIGHTS AT GL AND VANISH TO OBJECTS TO FINISH

PERSPECTIVE INFORMATION EXAMPLE 1

*The principles of a one-point perspective are shown through this simple
example. (Designer P. E. Deturk)*

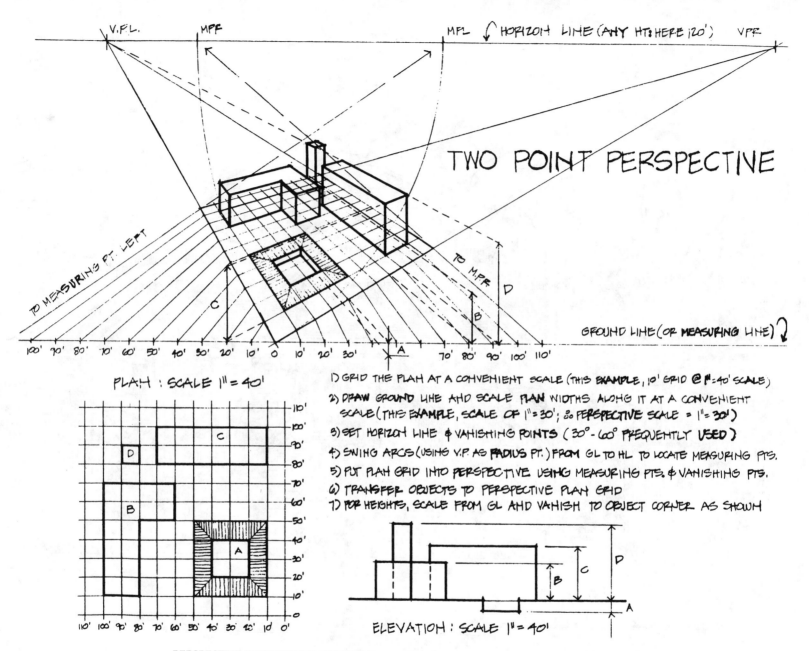

TWO POINT PERSPECTIVE

V.P.L.   MPF   MPL ↱ HORIZON LINE (ANY HT; HERE 120')   VPR

TO MEASURING PT. LEFT

TO M.P.F.

GROUND LINE (OR MEASURING LINE) ↷

100' 90' 80' 70' 60' 50' 40' 30' 20' 10' 0 10' 20' 30'   A   70' 80' 90' 100' 110'

PLAN : SCALE 1" = 40'

1) GRID THE PLAN AT A CONVENIENT SCALE (THIS EXAMPLE, 10' GRID @ 1"=40' SCALE)

2) DRAW GROUND LINE AND SCALE PLAN WIDTHS ALONG IT AT A CONVENIENT SCALE (THIS EXAMPLE, SCALE OF 1"=30'; SO PERSPECTIVE SCALE = 1"=30')

3) SET HORIZON LINE & VANISHING POINTS (30°-60° FREQUENTLY USED)

4) SWING ARCS (USING V.P. AS RADIUS PT.) FROM GL TO HL TO LOCATE MEASURING PTS.

5) PUT PLAN GRID INTO PERSPECTIVE USING MEASURING PTS. & VANISHING PTS.

6) TRANSFER OBJECTS TO PERSPECTIVE PLAN GRID

7) FOR HEIGHTS, SCALE FROM GL AND VANISH TO OBJECT CORNER AS SHOWN

110' 100' 90' 80' 70' 60' 50' 40' 30' 20' 10' 0'

10' 100' 90' 80' 70' 60' 50' 40' 30' 20' 10' 0'

ELEVATION : SCALE 1" = 40'

PERSPECTIVE INFORMATION EXAMPLE 2

In comparison with example 1, this perspective utilizes two vanishing points. Note the difference in the amounts of information shown between these examples. (Designer P. E. Deturk)

241

PERSPECTIVE INFORMATION EXAMPLE 3

While this sketch is not a technical drawing, the principles shown in example 1 still apply.
(Designer Gregory M. Pierceall)

PLANNING AND DESIGN IDEAS

THREE

*R*esidential planning and design processes

Useful and attractive residential site developments including plant and construction materials are a result of planning and design accomplished through a partnership between a homeowner and designer. The designer, trained in planning and design, inventories and evaluates the site, in terms of on- and off-site conditions and client expectations and priorities. *On-site conditions* that are inventoried include the site's shape and surface configuration, existing vegetation, and surface drainage. The building or buildings' location, doors, windows, walls, fences, walks, drive, and utilities are also defined. In conjunction with these physical characteristics of the site and structure, the architectural type, style, color, materials, and details are noted.

Off-site conditions that influence a site's use and design include climatic influences of sun, winds, adjoining residences or land uses, and pedestrian and vehicular access to the site. After this and other relevant information are collected, the survey components are evaluated in terms of the client's needs, priorities, and preferences. To determine what the client sees when viewing the site, a dialogue between the designer and client is required. During this interview, the designer tries, through the use of selected questions, to determine the client's immediate and long-term needs with respect to the site, specific design elements desired, and expectations from the proposal to be developed. A group of design questions can be found in Appendix 3.

In the planning and design processes, the homeowner provides the designer with his or her needs, priorities, and preferences. The best environment to discuss the landscape and to define needs, priorities, and preferences is outdoors (Figure 8-1).

Homeowners are often not familiar with the design process or design considerations. Landscape design often becomes something magical, and clients may make designers guess their needs and expectations so as not to "limit" the designer's creativity. Since landscape site design is site specific and for a particular client, the design proposal can be only as realistic and relevant as is the information offered. One requirement of any initial client/designer discussion is to explain what landscape design is and is not and exactly what services can be expected. Much of the landscape design process is first understanding it as a designer and then communicating this information to a client.

A landscape designer's professional responsibilities lie in the evaluation of the site and its surroundings and development of a site proposal that is functional, attractive, and relates to the site conditions and clients' needs. Enhancing client awareness of the benefits and opportunities available in site development is often the hardest part of the design process.

The designer most likely is contacted by the prospective clients. Before the time of the visit, it is important to understand how and why the clients contacted you. Are they being referred by an existing design client? Have they seen your work? Did they find your name in the phone book? Understanding how they have come to call on you for services can help determine the type of information you will need and the amount of detail and explanation required. If the prospective clients have seen your work and/or know other clients, they may be aware of what you provide and the quality of your work. If you are talking with clients unfamiliar with your work, explain and show examples of completed work and/or refer the clients to others who can be used as references. This initial meeting is important in establishing yourself as a professional and defining the project, product expected, and terms. At this stage you would then explain planning and design as related to site development.

There are two distinct aspects of the design process: (1) planning and (2) design. *Planning* is a process of anticipating or formulating future needs, activities and developments. The definition of *site planning* which most accurately describes the design process involved in landscape development is as follows: A design process which explores relationships between buildings, vehicular and pedestrian circulation, ground forms, vegetation, and site use in order to produce an aesthetic and functional development (HRI 1971). In residential landscape design, planning objectives may include proposal of plantings and construction features for aesthetics, energy conservation, or to provide a barrier-free site for handicapped persons. While planning is a mental process trying to imply what may occur, it is directed by specific objectives defined by the client and designer.

The term *design* may be defined as (1) to plan, (2) make preliminary sketches, (3) to form in the mind, (4) propose (Webster Dictionary, 1974). Design, when discussed in relation to a landscape, is the selection of components, materials, and plants and their combinations as solutions to limited and well-defined site problems (Laurie, 1975). The common landscape components that are designed include landforms, vegetation, water, pavements, and site structures (Booth, 1979). While these elements may be included in any site development, the design of landforms, specifically grading and drainage, water, pavements such as drives and parking lots, and walls, bridges, decks, shelters, etc., as site structures may by law be limited to a landscape architect rather than a landscape designer. Some states do have registration of landscape architects which defines the types of services and projects that they can be involved with. See Appendix 2 for states requiring registration and/or certification of landscape architects.

PLANNING CONSIDERATIONS

Since the conditions that influence residential landscape design are climate, the particular site and its surroundings, and client needs, these are the basic site planning considerations used in the development of site proposals (Figure 8-2). Landscape designers need to understand the regional landscape character, its landforms, vegetation, and climatic conditions to adequately propose site designs. Understanding regional conditions that affect the site, such as climate, temperature, prevailing winds, and solar orientation, helps designers in the planning process. Regional information is then interpreted to

FIGURE 8-1

An on-site visit with the client and designer is usually the first step in the design process. While "walking" the site, the client and designer can discuss existing conditions and development needs. (Designer: Gregory M. Pierceall)

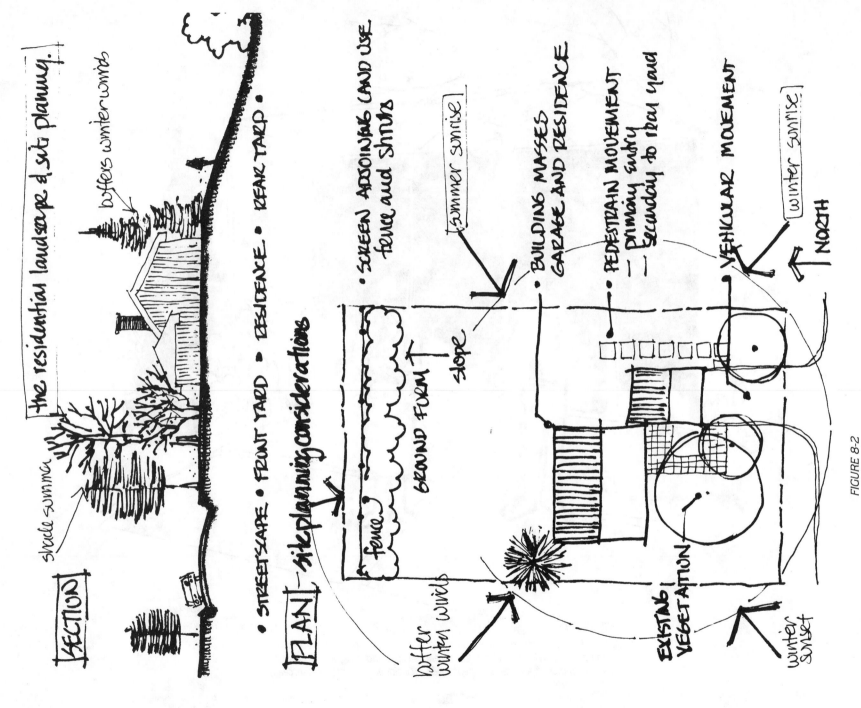

the residential landscape & site planning.

SECTION

- shade summer
- buffers winter winds

- STREETSCAPE • FRONT YARD • RESIDENCE • REAR YARD •

PLAN – site planning considerations

- SCREEN ADJOINING LAND USE fence and shrubs

- SUMMER SUNRISE

- BUILDING MASSES GARAGE AND RESIDENCE

- PEDESTRIAN MOVEMENT — Primary entry — Secondary to rear yard

- VEHICULAR MOVEMENT

- WINTER SUNRISE

NORTH

GROUND FORM

slope

fence

buffer winter winds

EXISTING VEGETATION

winter sunset

FIGURE 8-2
Site planning considerations. (Designer: Gregory M. Pierceall)

248

see how the site specific conditions may be modified. Figure 8-3 is a conceptual diagram of regional to site area conditions that influence site planning decisions.

Basic regional landscape and local climate data needed include a map of the physiographic or plant growth regions which identifies landform and vegetation characteristics and a hardiness map which indicates the minimum temperature extremes (Figure 8-4). Local rainfall and precipitation, minimum and maximum temperature variations, and prevailing winds are all influences that will affect landscape use by residents and also plant hardiness. After an understanding of the locale, the designer can better interpret the neighborhood and site specific variations of the local climate, also called microclimate. *Microclimate* not only influences plant growth, but may influence the use of interior and exterior spaces exposed to sun and winds. These two climatic influences, sun and wind, affect personal comfort, the use of outdoor spaces, and the energy resources needed to heat and cool interior spaces. See Figure 8-5 for an interpretation of site microclimate and the resulting design proposal.

CLIMATIC INFLUENCES

Solar Radiation

The sun takes a regular, cyclic path through the sky. Through an understanding of its movement we can better anticipate the location for shade trees or for shaded areas created by landscape structures. In general terms, the sun rises in the east and sets in the west. However, there are some variations in this cycle east to west and differences in the sun's height in the sky which relate to the latitude of the site and the season. For example, the summer sun in the more temperate regions of the U.S. rises early in the northeastern sky and sets late in the northwestern sky. In its summer cycle, the sun is high overhead and produces shadows almost directly beneath trees and plantings. The winter sun in comparison rises in the southeast and sets in the southwest. Due to the rotation of the earth on its axis, the rays of the sun strike the earth's surface at more acute angles resulting in long shadows during the winter.

In a site analysis, solar angle information is used to locate features and outdoor uses/functions and to determine the resultant sun or shade patterns. As a residence or other site feature is established in the landscape, the sun and shadow patterns are altered. Each el-

evation of the house has a different orientation, thus a different interface to heat, light, and shadows. Site orientation not only influences exterior areas, but the amounts of light and heat penetrating into interior living spaces.

With the sun's patterns so regular and predictable, designers should realize that they have the opportunity in landscape development to modify this influence. Modifying both exterior and interior spaces with respect to the amounts of heat, light, and shade that result is a design opportunity to consider. Each wall of a residence has a different exposure to the sun, thus outdoor use and plant establishment should reflect these differences (Figure 8-6). The north wall receives light both early and late in the day in the summer. In winter it does not usually receive direct sun and thus is cooler in winter than south-facing walls. East and west walls receive similar amounts of sunlight, but the western wall is hotter because it has had more time to warm up and the sun is hotter in the afternoon. The south wall is the hottest face of the house when it receives full sun. It is also the hottest in the winter. In the summer the west wall is hottest because it is exposed to the hotter, more direct rays of the afternoon sun. It is the buildup of heat from late morning to late afternoon that causes the west side of the house to be the hottest. To modify the heating influence of the summer sun the southeast to northwest areas of the site are critical. Depending on the site situation and client needs, plantings and/or constructed features may be used to provide shade. Shade for the house interior spaces and outdoor activities is important in summer, but options for solar gain during colder times of the year should also be considered.

In addition to the shade provided by trees, summer breezes, further cool exterior spaces and influence a resident's cooling needs inside. See Figure 8-7 for a site specific illustration of microclimate and design considerations.

Winds

Winds are more of a problem in site development as they are not as predictable as the sun. Since the north side of a structure is normally colder in temperate zones because there is no direct solar gain in winter, the presence of prevailing winds acts to cool the site and residence even more. To modify the effects of winter winds, fewer windows and a doorway opening to the north is helpful. Evergreen windbreaks also help modify the cold effects of wind by buffering wind direction and creating "dead air" space between the plantings and residence.

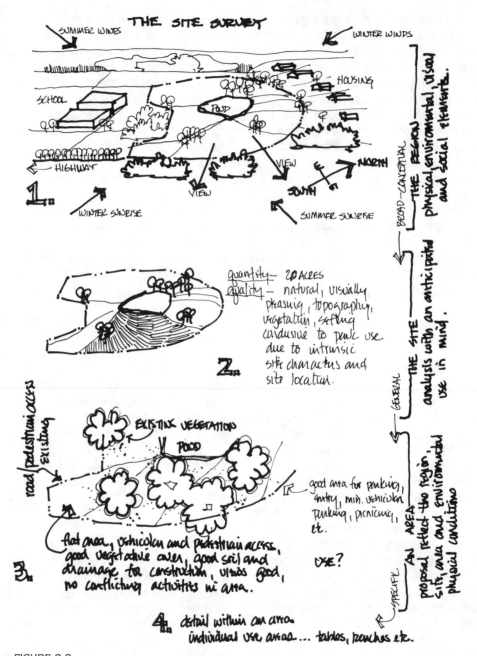

THE SITE SURVEY

SUMMER WINDS

WINTER WINDS

HOUSING

SCHOOL

POND

VIEW

HIGHWAY

NORTH

SOUTH

VIEW

1.

WINTER SUNRISE

SUMMER SUNRISE

BROAD-CONCEPTUAL — THE REGION physical, environmental, visual and social elements.

quantity — 20 ACRES
quality — natural, visually pleasing, topography, vegetation, setting conducive to park use due to intrinsic site character and site location.

2.

GENERAL — THE SITE analysis with an anticipated use in mind.

road/pedestrian access
existing

EXISTING VEGETATION

POND

good area for parking, entry, min. vehicular parking, picnicing, etc.

flat area, vehicular and pedestrian access, good vegetative cover, good soil and drainage for construction, views good, no conflicting activities in area.

USE?

3.

SPECIFIC — AN AREA proposal reflect the region, site, area and environmental physical conditions.

4. detail within an area individual use areas ... tables, benches etc.

FIGURE 8-3

Regional to site specific influences that affect site development. (Designer: Gregory M. Pierceall)

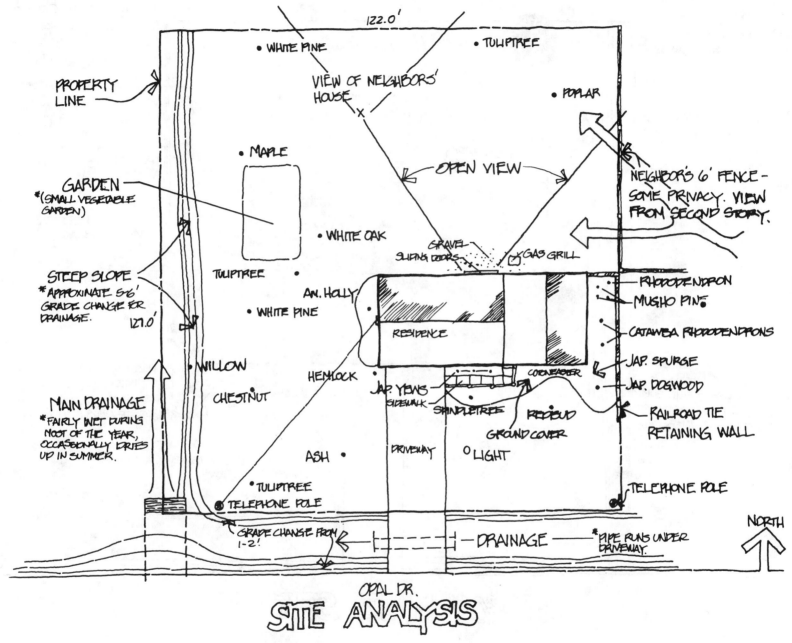

122.0'

• WHITE PINE   • TULIPTREE

VIEW OF NEIGHBORS' HOUSE   • POPLAR

PROPERTY LINE

• MAPLE

OPEN VIEW

GARDEN
*(SMALL VEGETABLE GARDEN)

NEIGHBOR'S 6' FENCE - SOME PRIVACY. VIEW FROM SECOND STORY.

• WHITE OAK

GRAVEL
SLIDING DOORS   GAS GRILL

TULIPTREE   •

STEEP SLOPE
*APPROXIMATE 5-6' GRADE CHANGE FOR DRAINAGE.

127.0'

AN. HOLLY

RHODODENDRON
MUGHO PINE•

• WHITE PINE

RESIDENCE

CATAWBA RHODODENDRONS

JAP. SPURGE

WILLOW

HEMLOCK

COTONEASTER

JAP. YEWS
SIDEWALK

JAP. DOGWOOD

CHESTNUT

SPINDLETREE

MAIN DRAINAGE
*FAIRLY WET DURING MOST OF THE YEAR, OCCASIONALLY DRIES UP IN SUMMER.

REDBUD

GROUND COVER

RAILROAD TIE RETAINING WALL

ASH   •

DRIVEWAY   ○ LIGHT

• TULIPTREE

TELEPHONE POLE

TELEPHONE POLE

GRADE CHANGE FROM 1-2'

DRAINAGE   *PIPE RUNS UNDER DRIVEWAY.

NORTH

OPAL DR.
SITE ANALYSIS

FIGURE 8-4
Site inventory/analysis. (Designer: Raymond Paul Strychalski)

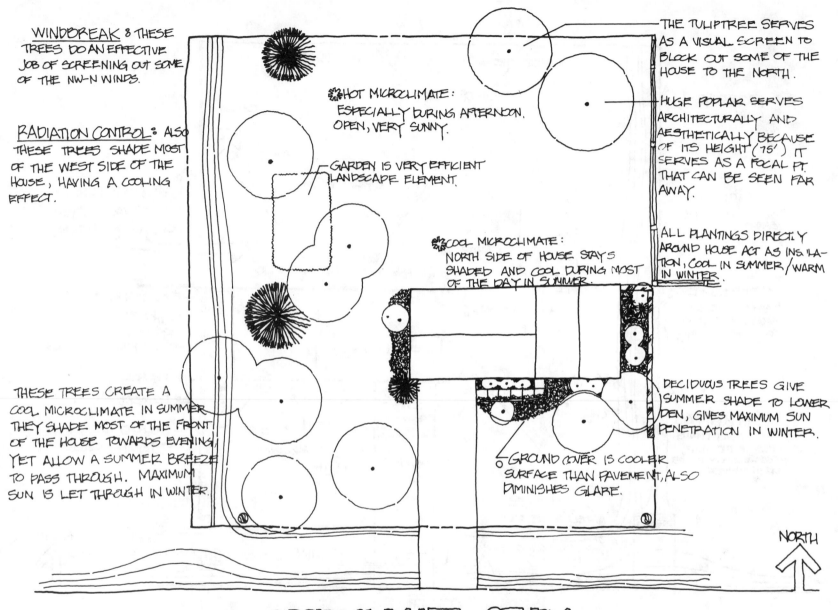

WINDBREAK: THESE TREES DO AN EFFECTIVE JOB OF SCREENING OUT SOME OF THE NW-N WINDS.

RADIATION CONTROL: ALSO THESE TREES SHADE MOST OF THE WEST SIDE OF THE HOUSE, HAVING A COOLING EFFECT.

HOT MICROCLIMATE: ESPECIALLY DURING AFTERNOON. OPEN, VERY SUNNY.

GARDEN IS VERY EFFICIENT LANDSCAPE ELEMENT.

COOL MICROCLIMATE: NORTH SIDE OF HOUSE STAYS SHADED AND COOL DURING MOST OF THE DAY IN SUMMER.

THE TULIPTREE SERVES AS A VISUAL SCREEN TO BLOCK OUT SOME OF THE HOUSE TO THE NORTH.

HUGE POPLAR SERVES ARCHITECTURALLY AND AESTHETICALLY BECAUSE OF ITS HEIGHT (75') IT SERVES AS A FOCAL PT. THAT CAN BE SEEN FAR AWAY.

ALL PLANTINGS DIRECTLY AROUND HOUSE ACT AS INSULATION, COOL IN SUMMER/WARM IN WINTER.

THESE TREES CREATE A COOL MICROCLIMATE IN SUMMER THEY SHADE MOST OF THE FRONT OF THE HOUSE TOWARDS EVENING, YET ALLOW A SUMMER BREEZE TO PASS THROUGH. MAXIMUM SUN IS LET THROUGH IN WINTER.

GROUND COVER IS COOLER SURFACE THAN PAVEMENT, ALSO DIMINISHES GLARE.

DECIDUOUS TREES GIVE SUMMER SHADE TO LOWER DEN, GIVES MAXIMUM SUN PENETRATION IN WINTER.

NORTH

MICROCLIMATE STUDY

FIGURE 8-5(a)

Site microclimate evaluation. (Designer: Raymond Paul Strychalski)

Program Statement

THE CLIENTS, MR & MRS RAYMOND STRYCHALSKI, LIVE AT 20325 OPAL DR., SOUTH BEND, IN. THEY HAVE 3 CHILDREN, ALL OLDER. ONLY ONE LIVES AT HOME – JUST FOR THE SUMMERS WHILE ATTENDING COLLEGE. THEIR HOME IS FAIRLY NEW, AND THEY HAVE LIVED THERE ONLY 3 YEARS. THE PREVIOUS OWNERS HAD THE EAST & SOUTH SIDES LANDSCAPED BEFORE DECIDING ON MOVING.

THE CLIENTS, WHO ARE IN THEIR EARLY 50's, ENJOY WORKING ON THE YARD AND WOULD LIKE THE REST OF THE HOUSE (WEST & NORTH SIDES) LANDSCAPED. AS PART OF AN EARLIER JOB I DESIGNED AND BUILT A WOOD DECK AS PHASE I OF THE OVERALL LANDSCAPE DESIGN. THE CLIENT WOULD NOW LIKE, IN EITHER 1 OR 2 PHASES, A PLANTING DESIGN TO ACCOMMODATE THIS EARLIER PHASE AND TO ADD TO THE OVERALL BEAUTY AND VALUE OF THEIR HOME.

Site Limitations

THE SITE IS 121' × 146' AND IS BOUND ON THE WEST BY A RAVINE APPROXIMATELY 6-8' DEEP AND 15-20' ACROSS, OTHERWISE THE TOPOGRAPHY IS VERY FLAT – EVERYTHING SLOPES AWAY FROM THE HOUSE.

THE EXISTING PLANT MATERIALS, THOUGH OF A GOOD VARIETY ARE STILL YOUNG AND NEED SOME TIME TO MATURE, ESPECIALLY FOR THE CANOPY TREES. ALSO, ON THE WEST SIDE OF THE SITE, EXISTS THE CLIENTS GARDEN (15'×30') WHICH THEY PLANT EVERY YEAR AND MUST BE TAKEN INTO ACCOUNT.

Design Objectives

DUE TO THE PREVIOUS LANDSCAPING DONE ON THE EAST & NORTH SIDES, ONE OBJECTIVE WOULD BE TO RELATE ANY FURTHER DESIGN TO THE EXISTING AND CARRY ON OR RELATE THE PLANT SPECIES USED IN THE NEW DESIGN TO THOSE OF THE EXISTING DESIGN. THE DESIGN SHOULD REQUIRE AS LITTLE MAINTENANCE AS POSSIBLE BUT KEEP IN MIND CLIENT'S LIKING TO WORK OUTDOORS ON THE YARD.

BECAUSE OF THE ADDED DECK, THERE IS NEED FOR CIRCULATION FROM DRIVEWAY TO DECK AREA, AROUND WEST SIDE OF GARAGE. AN INFORMAL BRICK PATH WOULD SATISFY THE CLIENT'S CRITERIA. ALSO IN THE DESIGN, THE USE OF SUBTLE GRADE CHANGES THROUGH BERMS, TO BREAK-UP THE MONOTONY OF THE FLAT TOPOGRAPHY. THE PLANTINGS SHOULD ADD TO THE PRIVACY OF THE DECK AND AT THE SAME TIME ENHANCE IT, WHILE ALSO GIVING MORE PROTECTION FROM COLD NORTH WINTER WINDS, WHICH DIRECTLY HITS THE DOUBLE SLIDING GLASS DOORS.

SCIENTIFIC	COMMON	QUANTITY	SIZE	CONDITION	COST UNIT	TOTAL
BETULA NIGRA	RIVER BIRCH	FOUR	6'	2 STEM · B/B	$120°°	$480°°
PINUS STROBUS	EASTERN WHITE PINE	THREE	5'	B/B	$147°°	$570°°
QUERCUS RUBRA	RED OAK	TWO	12'	B/B	$140°°	$280°°
MYRICA PENNSYLVANICA	BAYBERRY	FIVE	2-2½'	B/B	$50°°	$250°°
PINUS MUGO	MUGHO PINE	SIX	2'	B/B	$60°°	$360°°
SPIRAEA BUMALDA	ANTHONY WATERER SPIREA	TWELVE	18"-24"	B/B	$18°°	$216°°
HEDERA HELIX	ENGLISH IVY	120	3" POTS	POTS	$80	$192°°
PACHYSANDRA TERMINALIS	JAPANESE SPURGE	250	—	FLATS	5°	$125°°
					TOTAL	$2513°°

MATERIALS	QUANTITY		
PEAT MOSS	12 BAGS	$1°°	$11°°
WOOD CHIPS	8 BAGS	$6.50	$52
		GRAND TOTAL	$2715°°

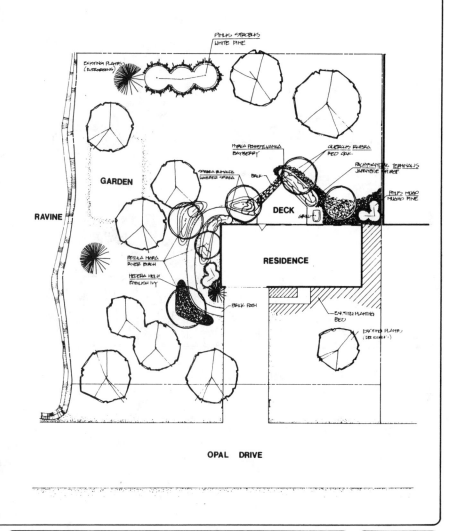

PINUS STROBUS
WHITE PINE

EXISTING PLANTS
(EVERGREENS)

GARDEN

MYRICA PENNSYLVANICA
BAYBERRY

QUERCUS RUBRA
RED OAK

SPIRAEA BUMALDA
ANTHONY WATERER SPIREA

BRICK

PACHYSANDRA TERMINALIS
JAPANESE SPURGE

RAVINE

DECK

PINUS MUGO
MUGHO PINE

OPAL

BETULA NIGRA
RIVER BIRCH

RESIDENCE

HEDERA HELIX
ENGLISH IVY

BRICK PATH

EXISTING PLANTING
BED

EXISTING PLANTS
(DECIDUOUS)

OPAL DRIVE

STRYCHALSKI RESIDENCE

Ray Strychalski   **December 2, 1980**   **north**

FIGURE 8-5(b)

Site master plan. (Designer: Raymond Paul Strychalski)

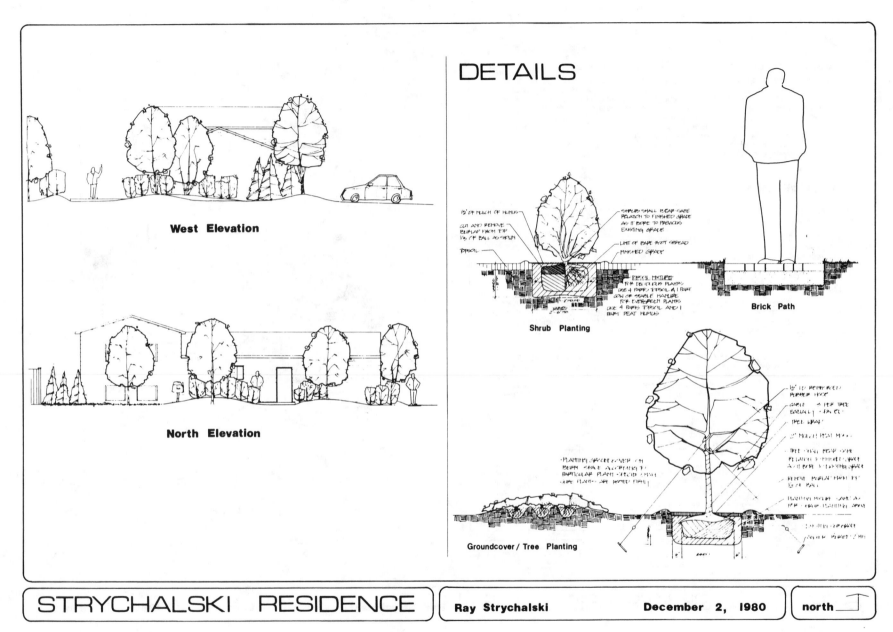

West Elevation

North Elevation

DETAILS

Shrub Planting

Brick Path

Groundcover / Tree Planting

STRYCHALSKI RESIDENCE

Ray Strychalski   **December 2, 1980**

north

FIGURE 8-5(c)

Site details. (Designer: Raymond Paul Strychalski)

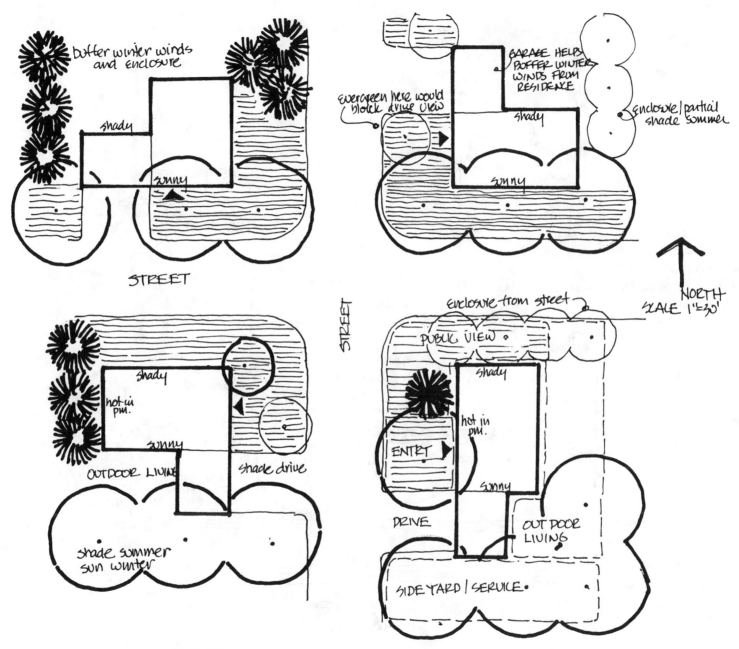

FIGURE 8-6
Planting proposals relative to site/building orientations. (Designer: Gregory M. Pierceall)

255

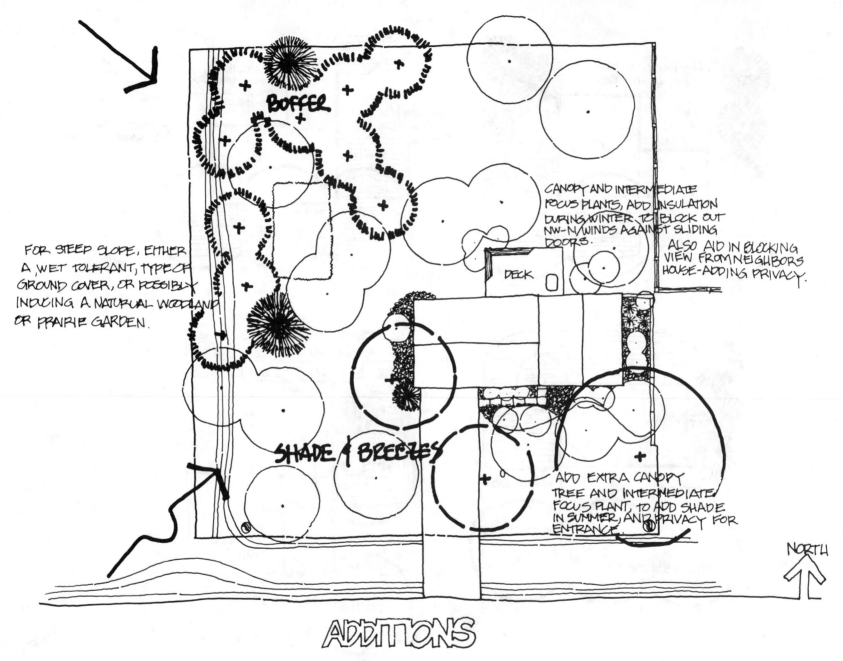

BUFFER

FOR STEEP SLOPE, EITHER A ,WET TOLERANT, TYPE OF GROUND COVER, OR POSSIBLY INDUCING A NATURAL WOODLAND OR PRAIRIE GARDEN.

CANOPY AND INTERMEDIATE FOCUS PLANTS, ADD INSULATION DURING WINTER. TO BLOCK OUT NW-N WINDS AGAINST SLIDING DOORS.

ALSO AID IN BLOCKING VIEW FROM NEIGHBORS HOUSE-ADDING PRIVACY.

DECK

SHADE & BREEZES

ADD EXTRA CANOPY TREE AND INTERMEDIATE FOCUS PLANT, TO ADD SHADE IN SUMMER, AND PRIVACY FOR ENTRANCE.

NORTH

ADDITIONS

FIGURE 8-7
Site planting to modify microclimate influences. (Designer: Raymond Paul Strychalski)

Summer breezes from the south and southwest in the temperate zone are cooling and should be utilized in site design as a method of modifying temperatures. Other climatic influences that affect site use are snow, daily temperature variations, and reflected heat or heat absorbed from surfaces within the site or residence. If further information is desired concerning the climate control aspects of planting and construction features in site design, read *Plants, People, and Environmental Quality*, by G. Robinette, 1972, and *Landscape Design That Saves Energy*, by Anne S. Moffat and Mark Schiler, 1981.

FUNCTIONAL USES OF PLANTS

Residential planting design should help provide a more functional and aesthetically pleasing home setting and should evolve using site planning objectives. Some of these objectives are to provide shade, buffer winter winds, encourage summer breezes, provide enclosure areas for privacy, and to use accents for enhancing the beauty of the site. For example, appropriately located deciduous trees provide shade from summer sun yet allow winter sun to warm interior spaces. Coniferous plants buffer cold winter winds and also can create air pockets which may further insulate interiors from cold winds. Before exact plant selections are made, an understanding of how plants function to modify microclimate and their visual effects is needed (Figure 8-8).

The functional aspects of plants in our contemporary landscape are discussed in *Plants, People, and Environmental Quality* (1972) by G. Robinette. In this work Robinette observes that plants have always been considered aesthetic due to the visual appearance of twigs, leaves, flowers, and fruit. However, architectural, engineering, or climatic control uses for plants are often dismissed because plants are living and growing things, and they change with time. Through growth and response to cultural and environmental conditions, they become excitement elements for use in site design.

According to Robinette, when plants are used as structural elements to create floors, walls, and/or ceilings, they are providing *architectural uses* in the landscape. Proper plant selection should consider heights and densities that provide privacy and screening, and a focus of views within or beyond a site's limits (Figure 8-9). *Engineering uses* of plants and plantings include traffic control, reduction of erosion, glare, and noises, and cooling of air immediately under trees (Figure 8-10). Plants that modify a site's microclimate,

that is, climate near the ground, function as *climate controls*. Reducing the intensity of, or redirecting, winds, cooling spaces with reduction of surface temperatures, and controlling snow drifting are all climate control functions of plants (Figure 8-11). *Aesthetic functions* of plants include selection and placement of plants relative to their inherent design elements of line, form, texture, and color. Appropriate placement and selection may provide enframement, pattern, background, or sculptural accents within a landscape design (Figure 8-12).

MULTIPURPOSE PLANT SELECTION

Determination of a plant's size, type, and location should reinforce the site scheme and functional needs of the anticipated site activities as determined by the design program and site analysis. With these four functional plant areas identified, designers should remember one plant can provide more than one function if properly selected and placed relative to site conditions and needs. A tree can provide shade for a patio area as well as create a ceiling for the space and be visually appealing due to the color of leaves, flowers, or fruits, thus providing architectural, engineering, and aesthetic functions (Figure 8-13). For an example of a residential planting plan with plant functions identified, see Figure 8-14.

The selection and location of plants in the landscape should reinforce desired site activities, provide functional benefits, and increase the physical and visual enjoyment of the property. During the initial stages of design, plants should be considered by size, form, and function, rather than by specific species. Look at the size of plants in relation to the size of a person and the spaces they encompass and define. Canopy, intermediate focus, and ground plane are basic size categories of plants relative to the spaces defined and in scale with people within the spaces (Figure 8-15). *Canopy trees*, for example, provide enclosure or a ceiling for the space. The ceiling or enclosure may be solid, open, or a combination. When selecting canopy trees, they should relate to the site in which they are to be used. Smaller sites will need smaller maturing species, while larger maturing species should be used for large sites. A sycamore selected as enclosure for a large site is appropriate yet not for a smaller site where a dogwood would be in proper scale.

Intermediate focus plants are small trees and large shrubs that are at eye level and fit within the cultural and physical limits defined by the canopy. Intermediate focus plants function to provide wall-

background and buffer winter winds
focal point enclosure
scale and enclosure
shade and foreground for framing
NORTH

FIGURE 8-8

Functional and aesthetic uses of plants in a residential proposal. (Designer: Gregory M. Pierceall)

FIGURE 8-9(a)
An interior space defined by architectural components. (Designer: Gregory M. Pierceall)

FIGURE 8-9(b)

An exterior space defined by plant materials. (Designer: Gregory M. Pierceall)

FIGURE 8-10

Engineering uses of plants—shade for cooling, ground covers for erosion control, and evergreen plantings to reduce streetscape noise. (Designer: Gregory M. Pierceall)

modifies winds

low branched shrub
collect snow

FIGURE 8-11

Climate control functions may vary from redirecting winds and snow to reduced ground level temperatures through plant evaporation. (Designer: Gregory M. Pierceall)

FIGURE 8-12

Aesthetic uses of plants—foreground, background, and accents. (Designer: Gregory M. Pierceall)

FIGURE 8-13

Plants should be selected to serve many functions. The need for shade, enclosure, seasonal interest, and cooling can easily be satisfied with the selection of a tree. (Designer: Gregory M. Pierceall)

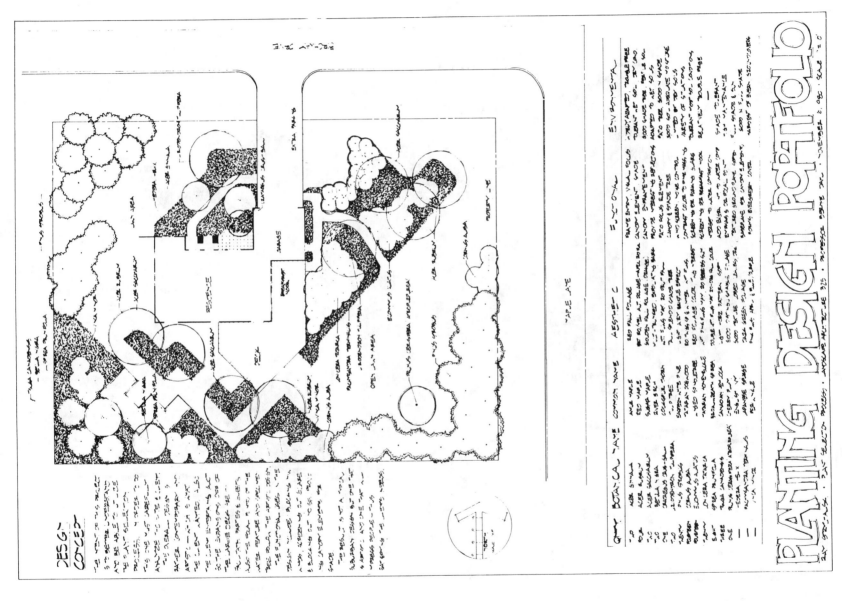

FIGURE 8-14
The residential planting plan shown illustrates the plant functions anticipated
by the designer for this site situation. (Designer: Raymond Paul Strychalski)

265

FIGURE 8-15

Canopy, intermediate focus, and ground plane plantings. (Designer: Gregory M. Pierceall)

like enclosure, more intimate scale, and visual interest in their over-all forms, leaf textures, and colors of leaves, flowers, branches, or fruits. These plants are most likely multitrunked, and there are many more specimens to choose from.

The last category, *ground plane plants*, are used to define ground areas. In size they are waist high and below. These plants may physically or visually define spaces depending on their height and may also provide visual interest. They may be used to reinforce the intermediate focus and canopy plantings by defining the ground area below them. They can also help to unify plantings in a space just as a rug unifies the furnishings in a room. Ground plane plantings in combination with other ground surfaces and pavements define spaces and activities. In selecting ground plane plantings consider durability, function, maintenance, and the desired visual effect.

When choosing plants from these three categories remember that size is relative. Plants must be appropriate to the site or space in which they are to be used. In a small courtyard, a small tree, say a dogwood, may define the canopy and small shrubs and ground covers may be used to define the sides and floor. In another site situation, a large shade tree may be needed as a canopy with a range of other plantings used for enclosure, floors, and definition of spaces.

Landscape plantings and construction features are the basic design components used to develop and detail a site. Site landscape development provides an extension of interior activities outdoors and modification of climatic influences for optimal use. The proper plantings or construction elements for a proposal are based on a site survey and analysis of existing conditions, environmental influences, and direct needs. Often in site design, due to space limits, cultural conditions, or the intensity of use, construction components rather than plantings are used to provide for the functions of shade, privacy, surfacings, and so forth. Landscape construction includes pavements, walks, steps, decks, walls, overhead structures, such as lattice or lighting, and other accessories. Landscape design is the selection of plants, construction materials, or a combination of the two as solutions to limited, site design problems (Laurie, 1975). See Figure 8-16.

Durability and cost are also considerations in selecting any constructed elements or plantings to be used to develop the exterior of a living space. Selection and definition of plant and construction materials are made after use areas have been defined, functional requirements listed, and relative forms, shapes, and sizes outlined. Landscape design, while developed using plants and construction materials, is made into functional and aesthetic compositions through the use of a design process.

THE DESIGN PROCESS, SITE PLANNING, AND LANDSCAPE DESIGN

Landscape design is a problem-solving process that strives to develop functional yet attractive site spaces through the coordination of planting, constructed site features, and design considerations. Landscape design deals with existing and proposed site conditions, including topography, vegetation, pavements, plantings, and site structures such as ramps, steps, walls, fences, lighting, and seating. In conjunction with these physical elements, landscape design proposals should consider the site's surroundings, which affect access patterns as well as the visual relationships within and beyond the site's limits. A site's microclimate and macroclimate are also important factors to consider. They dictate the amount of sun that the site receives and account for daily variations in temperature, wind direction and intensity. With these functional considerations and design concepts in mind, the designer must inventory, evaluate, and interpret all these project concerns. The final solution developed attempts to coordinate the site, environment, and uses into a compatible composition that is functional and attractive.

The process of landscape design uses guidelines rather than rules in the development of a design solution. (In design disciplines such as landscape architecture, architecture, and interior design there are numerous "design processes.") Design process is used to guide and direct designers towards functional and aesthetic solutions as well as alternatives to specific design problems. It is important to remember that the application of the process varies depending on the design situation. Basic to any design process is a systematic approach that identifies and defines problems, outlines data collection procedures, evaluates information, and utilizes existing and proposed concerns to develop design alternatives.

The concepts of site planning and landscape design individually relate to stages of landscape architectural "design process." The site planning process identifies, defines, evaluates, and combines existing and proposed site and program components into a generalized or "schematic" solution. During this schematic stage of development, adjustments and modifications are made between the site conditions and proposed uses to achieve some compatibility. In this generalized functional scheme, site and use areas and interrelationships are de-

FIGURE 8-16

Landscape design, plantings, and constructed site features such as walls, steps, lighting, and fences. (Designer: Gregory M. Pierceall)

fined as diagrammatic spaces. From these basic areas and interrelationships come selection of forms, materials, and detailing that relates to site, client and surrounding conditions. Without the early schematic developments to identify the various site areas and use and/or circulation interrelationships to maintain, the proposing of plantings and construction would not provide a totally functional or attractive proposal. Both planning and design considerations are needed to conceptualize and detail any landscape design.

An example of one design process is identified in the following paragraphs. This example is written in general terms in order to communicate the concepts and steps of design processes. Application of this design process to a specific case study in landscape design is found in Part Four, Chapters 10, 11, 12, and 13.

RESIDENTIAL LANDSCAPE DESIGN PROCESS

The residential landscape design process is a systematic approach to the planning and design of a landscape (Figure 8-17). To start, a situation or problem is given as a focus for the process. As an example, the problem could be the development of an entry space for a residential property, including both plantings and constructed features. Another problem could be to site a new residence on a site to maximize the desirable yet minimize the adverse climatic influences of the region.

The Problem

As an introduction to the process of design, an existing site including the purposes for which it will be used (modified) are the basic parts of most design problems in landscape design. A survey of existing conditions is developed, called a site survey or site inventory, in conjunction with a listing of client's needs, called a program. After a listing is established concerning the site, use, and client needs, the process focus shifts to details and interrelationships between these project elements.

Phase One

STEP ONE: PROGRAM ESTABLISHMENT. A list of objectives and project elements must be defined before an actual proposal is developed. These elements concerning the site, use and user are often called *program requirements*. They may be suggested by the designer or identified by the client.

Objectives are established to describe the character and quality of the areas within the site to be developed. Typical objectives concern visual, convenience, safety, security, opportunity for change, image and flexibility. Other considerations such as budget, maintenance, legal restrictions, priorities, responsibilities, and historical data are also included in the program and used throughout the design process.

Typical program objectives for an entry design proposal may be as follows:

1. Create a sense of separation between the entry and the street.

2. Propose plants that provide shade to the south and western residence elevations in order to reduce cooling demands in summer.

3. Provide an opportunity for summer breezes to circulate yet buffer winter winds.

4. Select plant materials that provide seasonal interest.

5. Propose planting and constructed features that can be implemented by the clients.

STEP TWO: PROGRAM RESEARCH. After all the basic design objectives have been defined, all the design program elements must be thoroughly understood. Of particular importance are the homeowner's requirements and whatever they translate into in terms of minimum and maximum size, types of areas, numbers, linkage, and so forth. In this research effort, one always considers the three umbrella considerations of image, function, aesthetics and structure or constructibility.

From the list of program requirements established by the client and designer in Step One for a typical entryway, research would define the following relative to the general objectives:

1. Is "separation" as defined to be physical, visual, or both? In regards to shade what is the entry's orientation?

2. In what areas should shade trees be planted to provide shade in summer? Where exactly and at what time of day is shade desired? What site limitations such as underground utilities will affect shade tree locations? If shade is provided, how will other plantings be affected? As an example, if sun loving plants exist will the shade be too much?

3. What are the predominant wind directions in summer and winter? How will breezes infiltrate into the house or influence outdoor areas? Where are outdoor use areas that might benefit

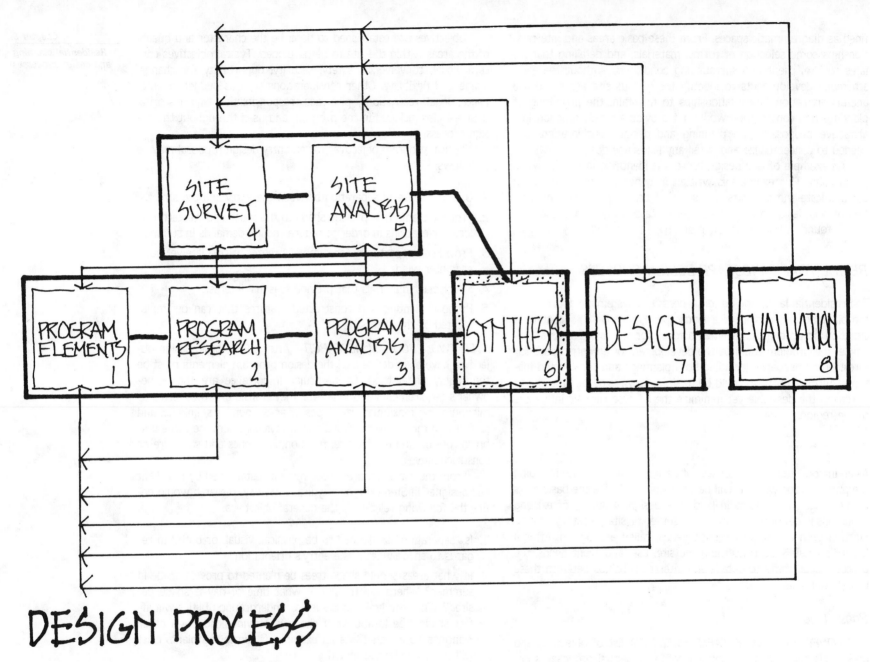

DESIGN PROCESS

FIGURE 8-17
The design process. (Designer: Gregory M. Pierceall)

from breezes? Are there site or adjoining conditions that may block or influence breezes such as neighboring homes (fences, walls, topography)?

4. What exactly is meant by *seasonal interest?* What plant opportunities are available? Leaves, flowers, fruit, bark? Are deciduous, evergreen, or both to be used?

5. What skills or capabilities do the clients have with respect to planting and construction?

STEP THREE: PROGRAM ANALYSIS. The various design requirements are grouped so that compatible elements, functions and influences are brought together.

This analysis and combination of program elements can be called a functional diagram. In the entry example mentioned the ideal relationships between program elements are defined. In this simple design situation the functional diagram can be drawn directly over the base survey. In more complex design situations, functional diagrams may be developed separately then later applied to the base plan.

A compatibility matrix (and/or a bubble diagram) may be employed to express graphically the many relationships which usually become too complex to store in one's head. Based on these interrelationships, an abstract plan is developed. The concepts developed and communicated through this general plan show the arrangement of the design parts and/or functions to be introduced into the landscape. When considering these elements independent of the site this step is begun without scale. As a final scheme develops, scale is then included to determine the relative size and shapes the various interrelated parts will take.

Phase Two

STEP FOUR: THE SITE SURVEY. As an independent step (parallel to Steps One, Two, Three) a site survey is developed. This survey gathers together natural, cultural, and perceptual information about the site, its surroundings and climatic influences that may affect the landscape design that is to be developed. In the entryway design example all existing site residence and surrounding features are noted. Also building set-backs, easements, and other restrictions are noted.

STEP FIVE: THE SITE ANALYSIS. The survey information is analyzed to determine inherent opportunities and limitations for the site functions anticipated. This is accomplished by the use of graphics, diagrams, tone, color, or pattern on top of the survey or on an

additional site map. The analysis may be set up to determine how the site can best serve the intended use(s) or how the site should be used based on its inherent qualities. With the inventory of existing conditions the design evaluates the situation relative to the desired changes. In the entryway program, locations may have been identified to plant shade trees. Here an assessment is needed such that no underground utilities are in that same area, etc. This same process would review the existing conditions versus the other program elements.

Phase Three

STEP SIX: SYNTHESIS. This is the critical "putting it all together" stage. A plan starts to appear when the program concepts (functional diagrams) are superimposed over the site analysis map using an overlay process. Revisions of scale, the aligning of spaces, stretching, warping, raising, and lowering of design program elements occur to relate to site specific situations. At this synthesis stage it is often helpful to project existing edges that are inherent to the project. The corners of buildings, windows, doors and other fixed features help establish edges and spaces for development of program requirements.

Although some site or schematic compromise may be necessary to develop site alternatives, the plan should exhibit a "fine fit" between the site analysis and program. Care should be taken not to sacrifice client priorities and the schematic relationships established in the earlier stages of planning.

A great deal of adjustment and refinement are usually required to achieve this fine fit. Although adjustments have been made with regard to function, visual image, and structure throughout the process, continued refinement now insures that the project is realistic and can be constructed in accordance with the three umbrella considerations—function, aesthetics, and constructibility.

Phase Four

STEP SEVEN: PROBLEM SOLUTION COMMUNICATION. The plan or problem solution selected now must be communicated. The client must be able to understand the proposal, and the drawings/documents that provide information necessary for construction must be produced. Items such as master plans, grading plans, planting plans, construction details, specifications, models, and detailing through sketches would be undertaken at this time. Some of these drawings/documents may be drawn up during the master plan development or after review and construction are considered. It should be also mentioned that the type of drawings and services provided may be regulated by local registration laws relative to the designer's status as a landscape architect, landscape designer, etc. Please review the registration information in Chapter 2.

Phase Five

STEP EIGHT: EVALUATION. The last step, which in one sense could be considered the beginning, is the evaluation of the master plan and design solution. No one evaluation technique can be defined that adapts to every project. However, at least two points should be considered in an evaluation:

1. The degree to which the stated objectives were met in the design developed.
2. The validity of the objectives as determined by the user and site situations.

Design changes considered after evaluation may be used in the project development. Also, the knowledge gained through this evaluation can be applied to subsequent projects. Through post-design review of any project or design, one better learns the design process and better understands what decisions must be made to achieve functional and aesthetic design proposals.

Design Process: Summary

The process presented reads as if one were to follow a step-by-step path in one direction—forward, yet at any point in the process it is usually necessary to circle back and reevaluate, reexamine, or gather more information. The design process then is a cyclic sequence of definition, analysis, concepts and details working towards a unified and functional proposal.

DESIGN DOCUMENTS

As mentioned in the seventh step of the design process presentation of ideas, concepts, and planning for site plantings and landscape construction normally includes plans, drawings, sketches, or other graphics. These presentation media are used to detail and communicate information that cannot be written in words. Graphics and drawings, while being representations of a site, its spaces, and proposed ideas are pictorial in the sense that designers and clients use

them as an expression of the essence and character of existing conditions and proposed changes.

As ideas are formalized and finished presentation drawings are completed, the sketches and drafts of plans, elevations, and perspectives become design documents. Design documents then can be categorized into two groups, presentation drawings and construction or working drawings. *Presentation drawings* include graphics used to communicate an analysis of a site's conditions, conceptual ideas, or illustrative master plans. In each of these cases, the drawings are used to present ideas. *Construction or working drawings* are used to actually build the project and thus are exactly scaled with directions and instructions for development. These design documents are called "working" because they often change when on-site decisions are made during construction.

In the average situation, the scope and scale of a residential planting proposal may not require working drawings. The important point to be made is that drawings produced to propose ideas should be complete enough for someone other than the designer to understand and implement. When drafting design drawings, make sure to provide adequate labels, directions, and instructions so that the completed proposal results in the quality you as designer had envisioned.

Design documents used in preliminary design stages include a plat of survey or the legal description of a site (Figure 8-18). If a plot plan or plat of survey is not available or if it is drawn at a scale too small to use as a base map for the design, the designer may have to generate another survey prior to any graphic presentation of ideas and/or design (Figure 8-19). Rough site survey, site analysis, and preliminary design ideas are sketched out prior to any formal or final presentation being developed. After the designer has a good understanding of the given site elements, surrounding influences, and client's design needs, then design solutions and selection of presentation formats can proceed. Figures 8-20 and 8-21 are alternative proposals for the site described in Figure 8-19.

Graphic presentation of design documents may be detailed or simple in the techniques and information included. Presentation of information and the methods used should relate to the scale of project and the audience or client for which the project is being developed. In the case of a homeowner installing his own landscape, more descriptive information may be needed to adequately install and achieve the design character intended. In the case of a large, contracted project, many different professionals may be involved in an installation, thus a varied format may be required to communicate the design proposal. Figure 8-22 shows a more detailed plan

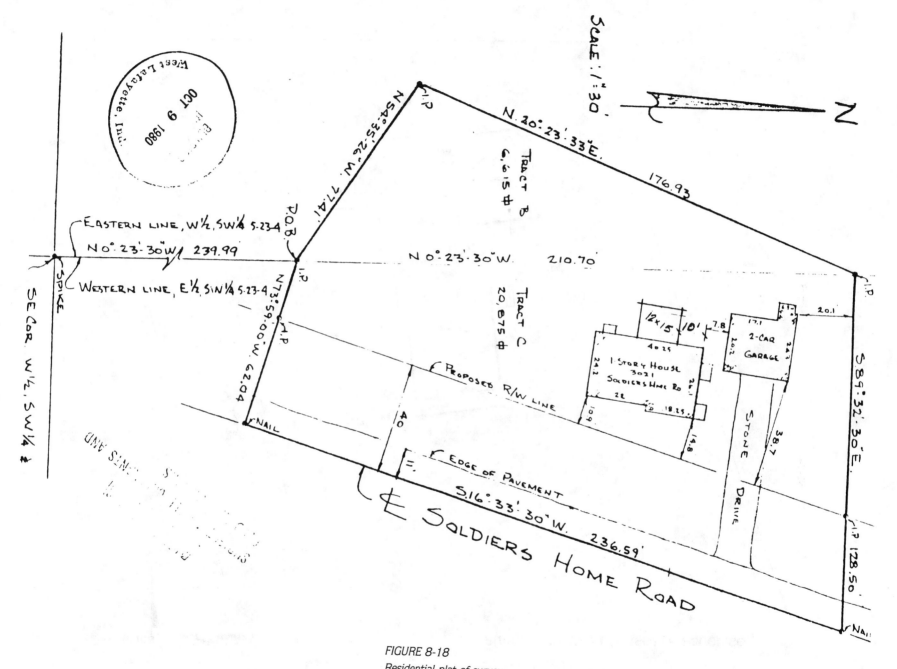

FIGURE 8-18
Residential plat of survey.

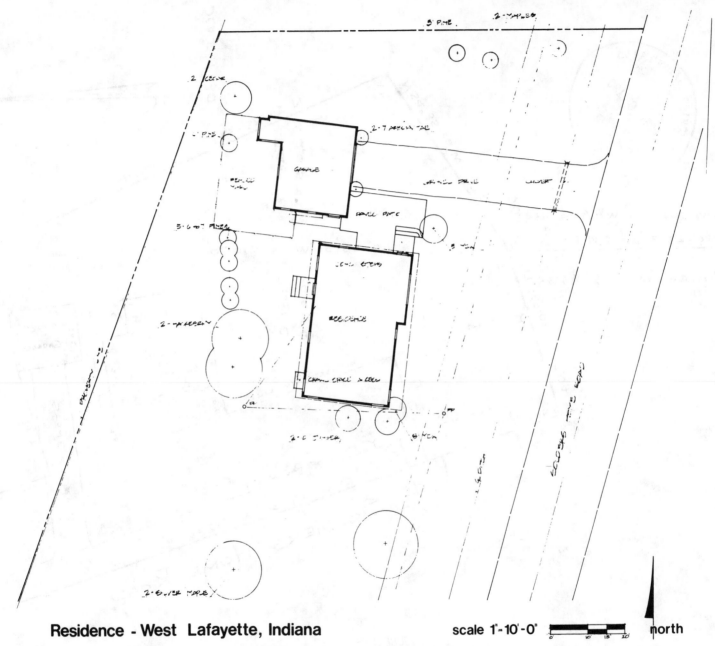

Residence - West Lafayette, Indiana   scale 1"-10'-0"   north

FIGURE 8-19

Residential site base plan. (Designer: Ada Niedenthal)

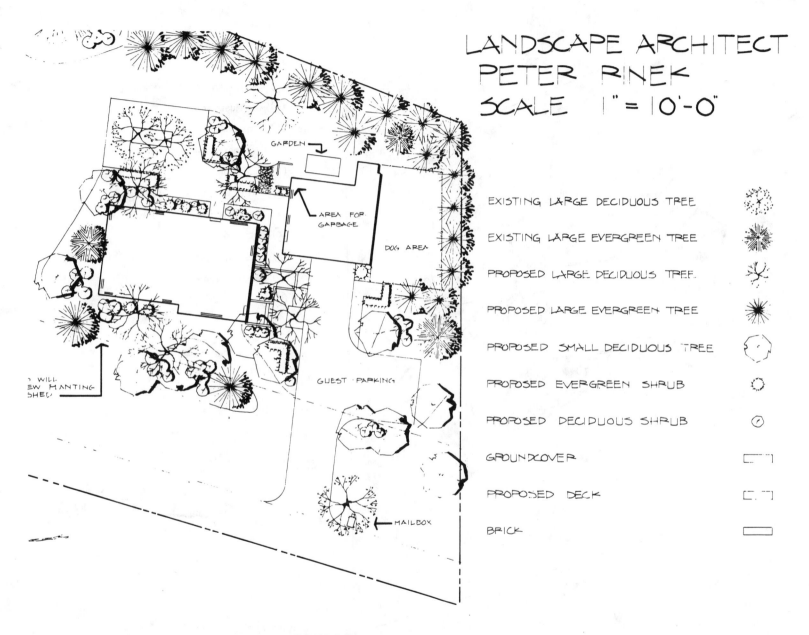

LANDSCAPE ARCHITECT
PETER RINEK
SCALE 1"=10'-0"

GARDEN

AREA FOR GARBAGE

DOG AREA

WILL
EW PLANTING
SHED

GUEST PARKING

MAILBOX

EXISTING LARGE DECIDUOUS TREE

EXISTING LARGE EVERGREEN TREE

PROPOSED LARGE DECIDUOUS TREE

PROPOSED LARGE EVERGREEN TREE

PROPOSED SMALL DECIDUOUS TREE

PROPOSED EVERGREEN SHRUB

PROPOSED DECIDUOUS SHRUB

GROUNDCOVER

PROPOSED DECK

BRICK

FIGURE 8-20
Residential site design proposal. (Designer: P. Rinek)

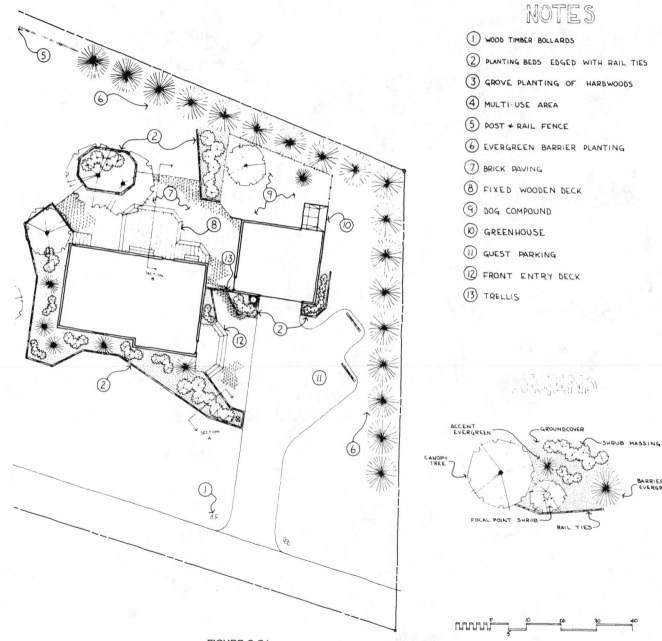

NOTES

1. WOOD TIMBER BOLLARDS
2. PLANTING BEDS EDGED WITH RAIL TIES
3. GROVE PLANTING OF HARDWOODS
4. MULTI-USE AREA
5. POST & RAIL FENCE
6. EVERGREEN BARRIER PLANTING
7. BRICK PAVING
8. FIXED WOODEN DECK
9. DOG COMPOUND
10. GREENHOUSE
11. GUEST PARKING
12. FRONT ENTRY DECK
13. TRELLIS

LEGEND

ACCENT EVERGREEN
GROUNDCOVER
SHRUB MASSING
CANOPY TREE
BARRIER EVERGREEN
FOCAL POINT SHRUB
RAIL TIES

SECTION B
SECTION A

FIGURE 8-21
Residential site design proposal. (Designer: Kim Tarbox)

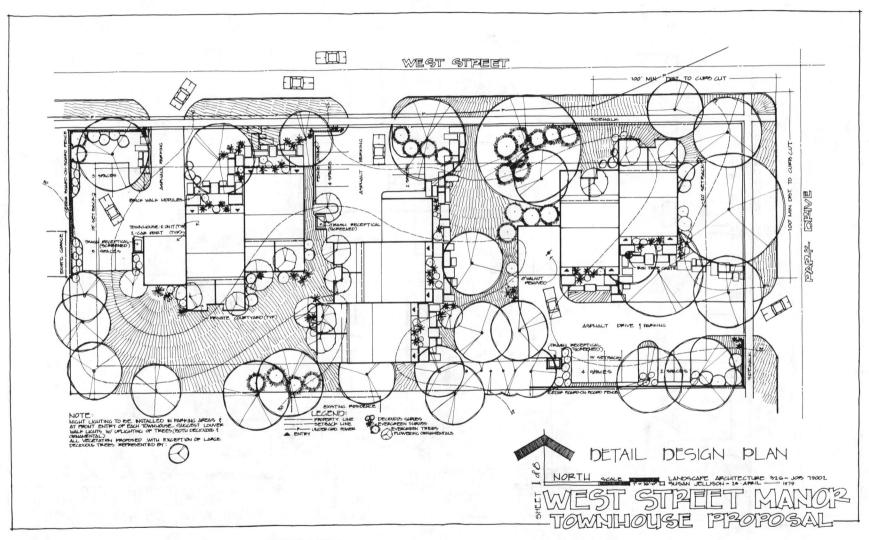

FIGURE 8-22(a)

A multi-family residential site proposal showing the basic building, parking
and circulation locations. (Designer: Susan Jellison)

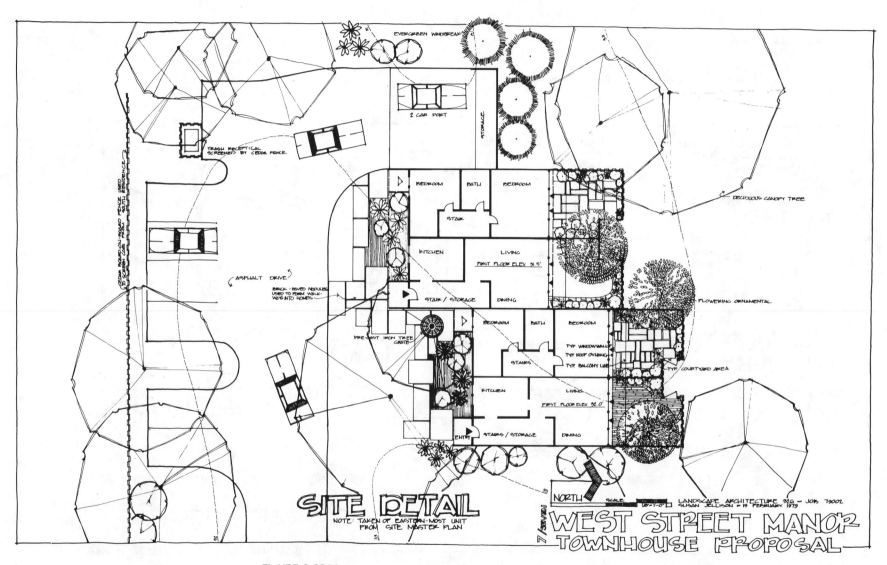

FIGURE 8-22(b)

An enlargement from the overall site proposal showing individual units lay-out including plantings and constructed features. (Designer: Susan Jellison)

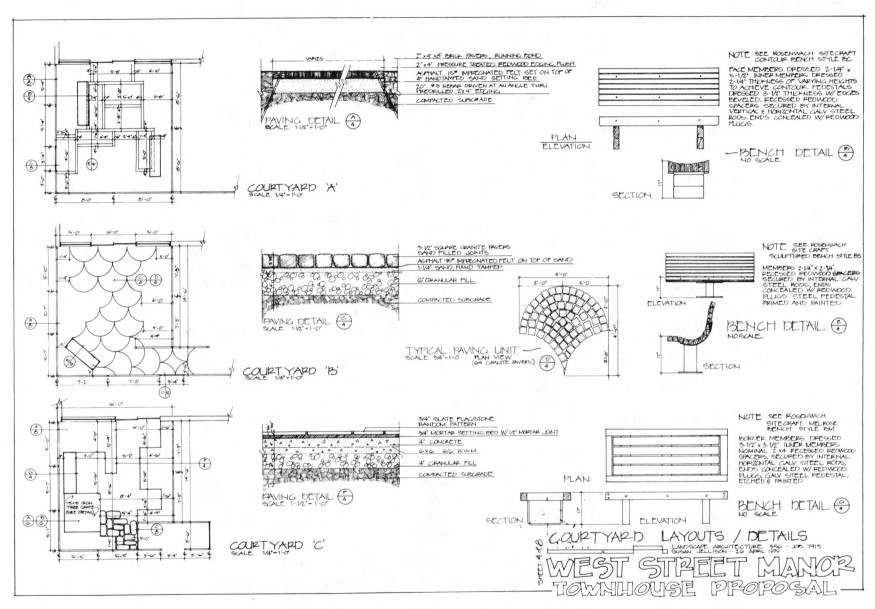

FIGURE 8-22(c)

Layout and details of constructed features for the courtyard spaces. (Designer: Susan Jellison)

for the site design proposal. For a project to be implemented basic concepts need to be identified with written information as further explanation for a homeowner or contractor to install it. Typical working drawing packages include information such as layout plans, grading plans, planting plans, and construction drawings in addition to details of pavements, steps, walls, fences, and any other constructed features.

Planning, design, and implementation start with the ground forms, including grading and drainage, then proceed to the development of ground plane surfacings, paving, walks, walls, and plantings which enclose and further define site spaces. In the pre-planning the designer has evaluated the existing site conditions, the environmental influences, client needs and activities, then has used planning and design principles to propose a "total" design composition for function and beauty. Final proposals should include the combination of land forms, light construction, and plantings. Descriptions of typical design documents are as follows:

Master plans show the development of a comprehensive proposal. Landscape planting and construction proposals are included in conjunction with all existing site features to remain. This plan may also be called a *site plan. Planting plans*, probably the most commonly recognized landscape design drawing, locate and identify all plant materials to be proposed and any existing on-site plantings to be preserved or removed. *Grading plans* show existing and proposed landform elements and elevations. They are used to determine appropriate landform levels for buildings, roads, retaining walls, steps, ramps, and planting beds and surface drainage prior to development. Topographic plans and grading plans also provide information used in determining existing surface drainage patterns as a basis for planting and constructed site developments. *Layout plans* are specific working drawings that accurately identify by specific measurements and dimensions the location of existing and proposed buildings, walls, walks, roads, parking areas, and planting areas. This drawing (or drawings) may include the entire property or it may be an enlargement of specific areas within a master plan. Lastly, *construction details* are drawings of plans, sections, and elevations concerning individual elements of the site or master plan. Elements such as walks, walls, drains, paving, and fences may be included. (See Figure 8-22 for a residential design construction package.) As can be seen from these brief descriptions and illustrations,

a residential landscape design proposal can entail much more than a single sheet planting plan.

SUMMARY

Residential landscape design is a professional design area that strives to create functional and aesthetic settings for homes, homeowners, and related site uses and activities. Landscape designers need to develop an understanding of the functional considerations relative to site development. As design professionals, landscape designers need both technical skills of delineation and design and construction backgrounds to relay their specific concepts and ideas as communicated through the use of the design process. The previous sections have acknowledged the need for, and technical use of, graphic skills in the site planning/landscape design process. For the design professional, graphics are a means of proposing concepts, ideas, and philosophies to clients relative to site specific situations. Landscape designers also need an understanding of planning and design to communicate with other design professionals—landscape architects, land surveyors, and engineers—and with clients.

REFERENCES AND READINGS

Energy Conservation

Moffat, A. S. and Schiler, *Landscape Design That Saves Energy.* Wm. Morrow, 1981.

Robinette, Gary O. *Landscape Planning for Energy Conservation.* Reston, VA: Environmental Design Press, 1977.

Design Process

Booth, Norman K. *Basic Elements of Landscape Architectural Design.* New York: Elsevier Publishing Company, 1983.

Laurie, Michael. *An Introduction to Landscape Architecture.* New York: Elsevier Publishing Company, 1975.

Lynch, Kevin. *Site Planning.* Cambridge, Mass.: MIT Press, 1972.

Smyser, Carol. *Natures Design.* Emmaus, PA: Rodale Press, 1982.

Wilson, Dan A., Wilson, Thomas S., and Tlusly, Wayne G., *Planning and Designing Your Home Landscape,* Madison, WI: Univ. of Wisconsin Extension, 1981.

Design principles and elements

Successful **design, communication, and development of** landscape design proposals include the application of the principles and elements of design. The principles and elements of design are generally accepted design concepts applied in the development of a planned and visually attractive composition. In architecture, interior design, and landscape design, compositions are three-dimensional in that the spaces developed are visual and functional as people use and live within these "compositions." Photography and graphic design disciplines use the same principles and elements of design yet the compositions are two-dimensional. The disciplines of photography and graphic design are often used to express a space's design.

When a design proposal or actual design project looks attractive, it is not an accidental occurrence—it most likely is an anticipated and planned effect created by application of the principles and elements of design. Landscape design as a "design discipline" includes design composition in the site design, presentation, and installation of a "total" site proposal. Site design and composition involve a layering of information and ideas. From the base map showing existing conditions comes an evaluation of what is at hand. Combined with the basic given information, the client's program needs directing the composition towards appropriate changes to satisfy functional requirements. After the site is defined as to use areas, the design of these areas occurs. While working on paper, it is important to remember that the plan represents actual site areas and spaces. As seen in Figure 9-1, plan composition represents a site that not only has length and width but the dimension of height.

Landscape design, like other design areas including architecture and interior design, should consider the axiom of "form follows function" in the creation of attractive yet useful three-dimensional spaces. The aesthetic and functional development of a site design first considers the use and the uses that should be accommodated through design rather than development of a single planting or construction composition within a site space. In the development of design compositions, the graphic skills and format used to communicate the proposal are also important in that they represent the "on-site" details to be installed. Both the presentation and design concepts should strive to achieve a total function and aesthetic site solution through the use of the principles and elements of design.

PRINCIPLES AND ELEMENTS OF DESIGN

The *principles of design* are the foundations and considerations for composition in all design areas. These principles of composition found in art and design are applied in landscape design and include scale, proportion, order, unity, emphasis, repetition, rhythm, and balance. Landscape composition can be thought of as the arrangement of plantings and constructed features to form a unified, harmonious development. In residential landscape design, a blending between the residence and site is needed. Landscape composition considers both the project's visual and physical relationships in its development. The most important visual aspect in landscape design is scale.

Scale

Scale is the relative size of an object or space compared to other objects or spaces within a single composition. One basis for determining an appropriate scale is the human body, or the numbers of people or activities to be provided within a space. In Figure 9-2 the vertical element shown is a graphic example of how scale is determined by a comparison of adjoining elements if no written information is available as to size. In each comparison, the vertical is seen in relation to the adjoining elements.

In landscape design, the size of a site should determine the scale of activities and what size design elements will be included. Plants and constructed features should be selected relative to the scale of the site, the size of the residence, and resulting site space. Selection of site elements including plantings and constructed elements should also consider the site's enclosure relative to its surroundings, existing plantings, fences, other structures. In the small site and residence situation shown in Figure 9-3, the plantings have grown beyond the limits of what is in scale. The existing 30' vertical plants are out of scale with the size of the site, which is 60' wide, and with the residence, which is 30' across. The size and shape of these existing plants are so overpowering that the entry is dwarfed and is made to seem smaller than it really is. Properly scaled and designed planting for this same entry can be seen in Figure 9-6.

In properties having smaller spaces, design proposals should utilize appropriately scaled plantings and constructed elements. Selection of dwarf or smaller plants and built-in or designed site furnishings can help provide attractive site areas which are functional and efficient for the space available. Installation of trees with potential "forest" proportions can be a frustrating experience in small properties. As larger species mature, they overwhelm the space and outgrow the site by extending beyond the property's bounds.

In settings where outdoor spaces are more expansive, larger maturing plants and more varied and movable site furnishings can be used. Site design should strive to achieve a solution that provides physical and visual scale through an understanding of a space, its uses, the users it is to serve. Figure 9-4 shows an example of scale in a residential neighborhood. The plantings shown in plan and elevation are drawn as to mature sizes and shapes. While the plants may not represent an optimal planting design, the plants are in scale with the respective homes.

Proportion

Directly related to scale is the concept of proportion. *Proportion* is a comparison of compositional components to each other. The relative sizes of elements or the amount of a color in a composition can be examples of proportion. In residential design, proportion can relate to the size relationships among the residence, its surroundings,

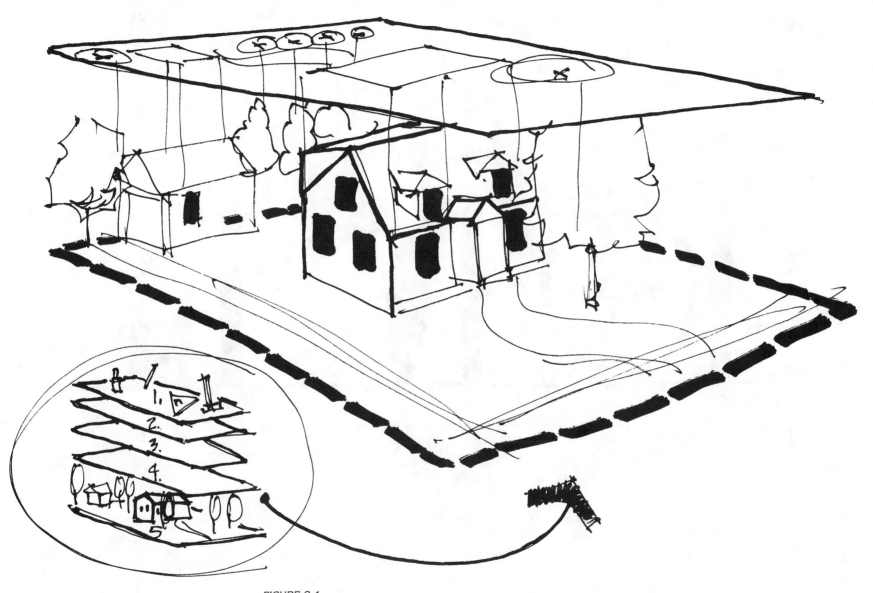

FIGURE 9-1

Scaled drawings of a residential site not only make the design of specific areas easier, but provide a total overview of the site. (Designer: Gregory M. Pierceall)

FIGURE 9-2

In the drawing of plans and the actual site spaces created, the "human" element is a measure of scale. (Designer: Gregory M. Pierceall)

FIGURE 9-3

A line drawing of an actual residential entry that has been allowed to be-come overgrown. (Designer: Gregory M. Pierceall)

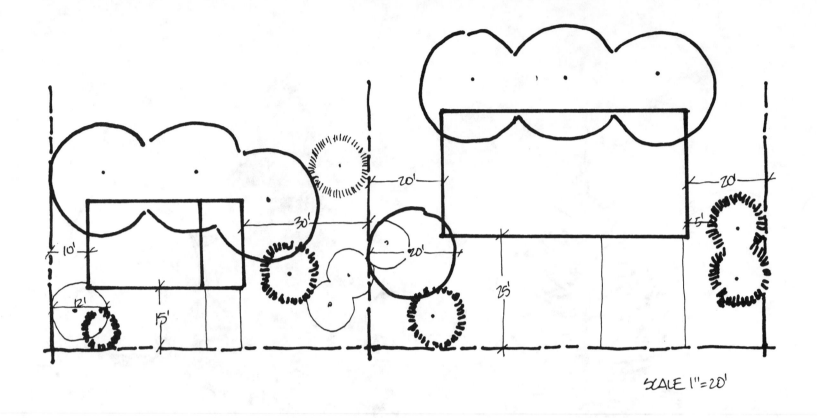

SCALE 1"=20'

FIGURE 9-4

While the site and residence play an important role in the selection and scale of plants, an awareness of the neighborhood and adjoining plantings also influence plant selection and installation. (Designer: Gregory M. Pierceall)

or site areas. In Figures 9-5a and 9-5b the proportion of numbers and sizes of plants to the elevation of the residence and entry space is awkward. In both sketches the plants are seen in comparison to the vertical dimension of the elevation and the horizontal dimension of property's width in the foreground. In Figure 9-5a, while the four smaller plants are in scale with the elevation, the proportion of planting relative to the entry from the steps to door is lacking. In Figure 9-5b, the proportion of the plants shown relative to the height of the elevation is equal to the eave line, thus visually reinforcing this strong edge rather than softening it. A better solution using these same plants would be to shift them beyond the edges of the house and to incorporate a small tree that is two-thirds the height of the house at one edge and facer plants at the other. A better proportioned design is created, and the emphasis of the planting is more visually attractive (see Figures 9-5c and 9-5d for alternatives).

When trying to select proper proportions relative to size within landscape design proposals, remember physical sizes used in exterior design have larger proportions than do interior spaces. In reference to constructed features, exterior steps and edges are exaggerated to accommodate varying degrees of use and climatic influences such as snow and ice. In regards to color proportions, use of accents and contrasts relative to the simplicity or complexity of the residence and site construction are possibilities (Figure 9-6).

Order

The *principle of order* is a visual and emotional reaction to the overall organization and structure of edges, lines, and forms in a design. To evaluate order, one may ask, "Do the planting and constructional parts of the composition seem to fit together logically and relate to the site, its surrounding, and the residence?" When evaluating an existing site design or design proposal, try to determine if an overall theme or scheme has been developed. (See Figures 9-7a and 9-7b for a comparison of order between two site plans of the same residence.) The design scheme or theme may be relative to the line or forms established as you look at ground forms and edges. Straight lines, rectangular, diagonal, or curved lines can be themes to develop in the design proposals. (Figures 9-8 a, b, c, and d show preliminary sketches for an entry using varied themes.) Proposals that develop a design theme through line need to include the inherent line in the house edges, property configuration, sight lines, views inside and out, and circulation ways.

Since site designs are composed of many different spaces and edges including the building, walks, walls, planting beds, a sense of order is needed so that the site spaces created are unified and no single area stands out. Ground plane elements, including ground covers, pavements, planting beds, and mold, are most visually predominant in reference to line and the perceived order. Thus planning should start at the ground plane, and continue with design components above this level of development.

Unity

Unity, closely related to order, is the harmonious relationship among elements or characteristics in a design. Unity is a perceived feeling of the visual quality of a design considering forms, texture, color. Unity is more specifically the coordination of design elements appropriate for a specific area and use rather than a perception of the overall line and composition. In design proposals including many subspaces, unity within a defined area can be achieved by separating spaces using transition zones between diversely different site spaces. Unity provides an integration of details and reduces the number of competing components, thus creating a feeling of completeness between the parts. (Figure 9-9 compares cluttered and unified designs.)

Dominance

Within a composition, one or more elements, due to size, shape, texture, or location, may have *dominance* or *emphasis*. Structures, sculpture, fountains, or specimen plant materials can be dominant site elements. They can be made to dominate by contrasting them to their surroundings using varied backgrounds, of secondary importance.

Dominance is used in composition to show the importance of an element or to create interest. When trying to determine what should have emphasis or be dominant within a residential design, the first step is to visually evaluate the site. When arriving at a design site for the first time, visually critique the entry area as to existing focal points or the need for an emphasis in the space. Often the focus of the entry area between a residence and the street is the front door because this is the primary access way for guests. The designer should also determine the primary and secondary vantage points towards the focus of the front door in developing or evaluating the emphasis of the area. In the case of an entry, the pri-

FIGURE 9-5(a)

This example of proportion and that shown in Figure 9-5(b) are poor. Figure 9-5(c) and 9-5(d) are better designs. Correct (a) and (b) by using more porportioned plantings and compositions. (Designer: Gregory M. Pierceall)

FIGURE 9-5(b)
A poor example of proportion.

FIGURE 9-5(c)

While using the same foundation plantings as in Figure 9-5(a) this proposal has better composition through the addition of foreground trees.

FIGURE 9-5(d)

While similar plants are used from Figure 9-5(b) these plantings are placed better and are better proportioned.

FIGURE 9-6

While color is not communicated in this black and white illustration, value changes can be noticed in the composition. The large tree to the left is tied to the right side of the composition through the two smaller trees of similar value. The shrub massing (texture or color) left is then repeated in the foreground ground cover. As an additional contrast, the middleground ground cover provides an accent and complement. (Designer: Gregory M. Pierceall)

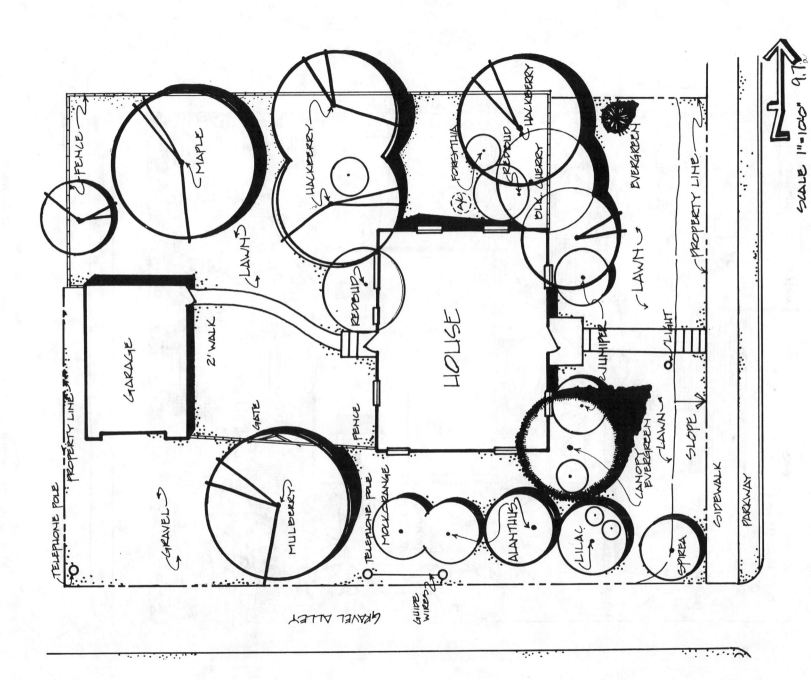

FIGURE 9-7(a)

Order in a composition is the development of a basic skeleton of lines within the total. Shown here is a collection of unrelated elements.

SCALE 1"=100'

293

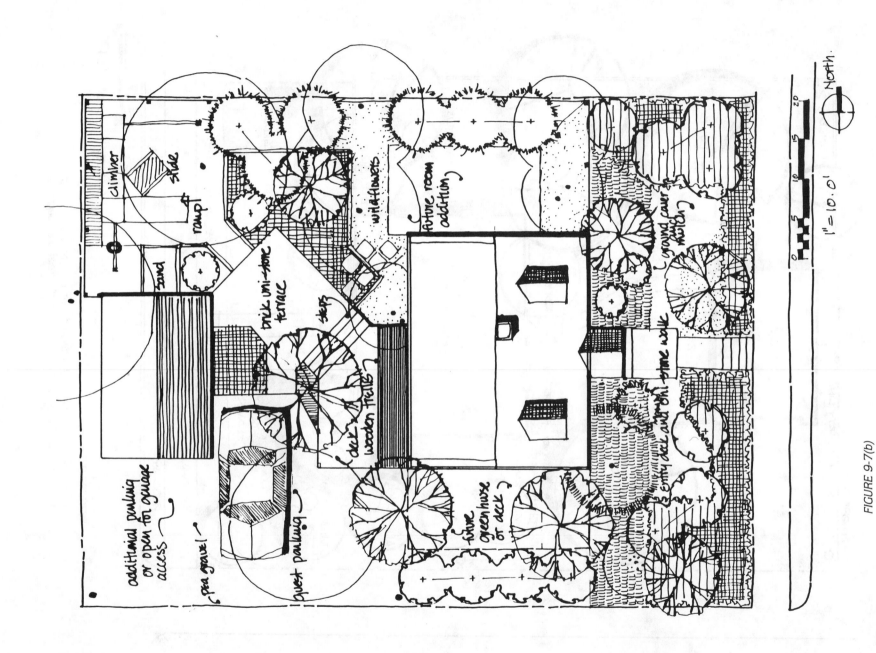

climber

slide

ramp

sand

additional parking
or open for garage
access

pea gravel

guest parking

brick uni-stone
terrace

steps

deck &
wooden trellis

wildflowers

future room
addition

future
greenhouse or deck

ground cover w/mulch

entry deck and brick stone walk

0 5 10 15 20

1" = 10.0'

North.

FIGURE 9-7(b)

A design proposal, this example projects a line scheme developed by edges and views related to the site and activities. (Designer: Gregory M. Pierceall)

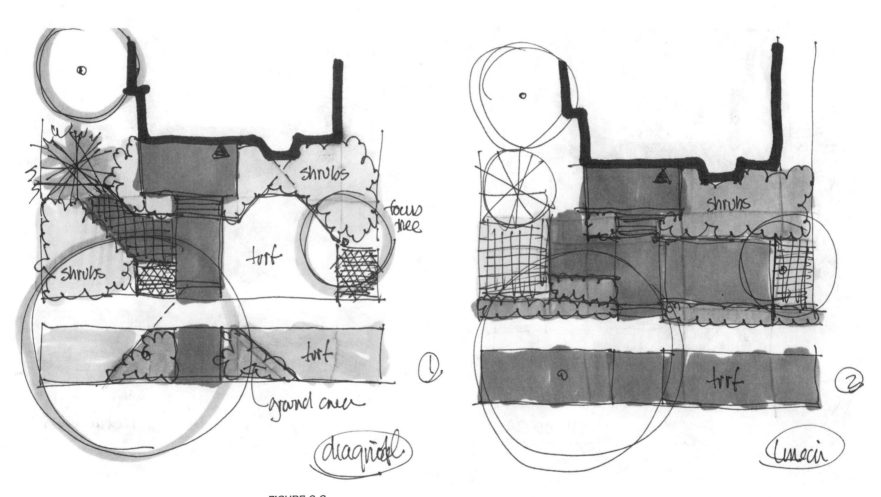

FIGURE 9-8

The preliminary sketch and those following are informal concept designs. Early in the design process ideas are sketched freely to develop options for later review. In this entry proposal, each sketch represents use of various lines and schemes as a basis for discussion and refinement towards a finished proposal. (Designer: Gregory M. Pierceall) (continued)

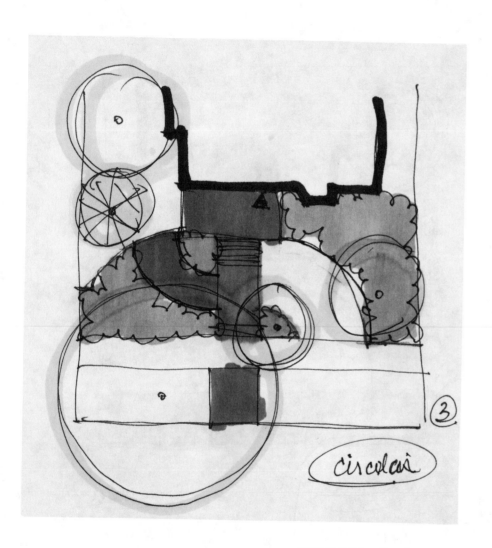

circular ③

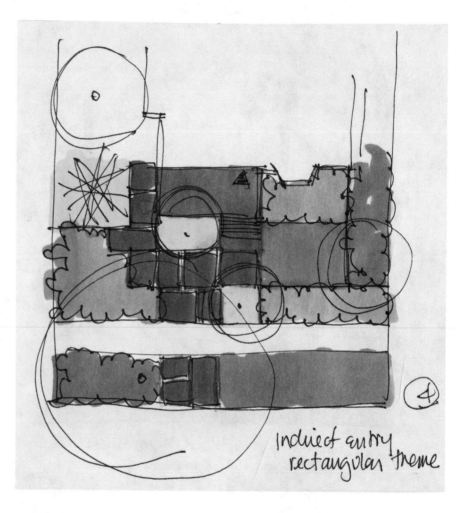

indirect entry
rectangular theme ④

FIGURE 9-8 (continued)

As seen in the design concepts found on the preceding page and in the ones above, the purpose of the informal sketches are to quickly develop varied design composition for review, then to select a scheme for detailing and refinement.

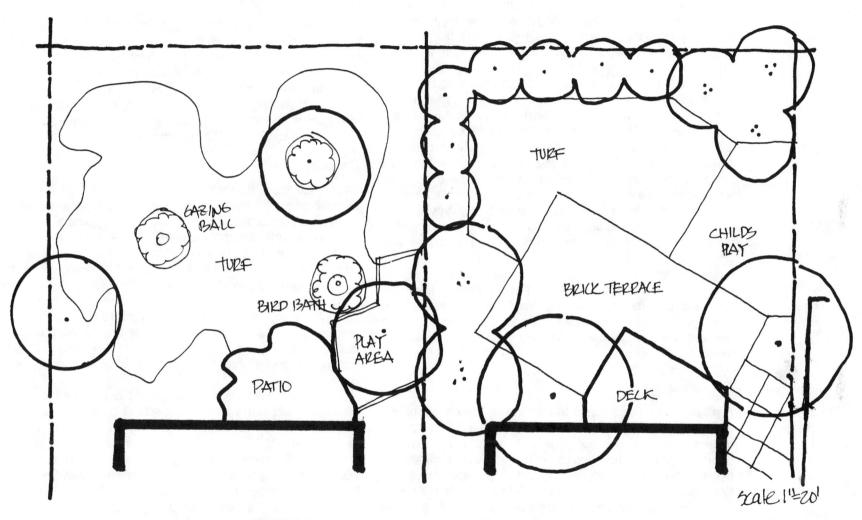

Labels within figure: GAZING BALL, TURF, BIRD BATH, PLAY AREA, PATIO, TURF, CHILDS PLAY, BRICK TERRACE, DELK

scale 1"=20'

FIGURE 9-9

In the adjoining rear yards, one designer has developed independent areas within the site (left). The other has used the same components yet developed them into a unified composition (right). The simplicity of line and repetition of angles help create this unified feeling. (Designer: Gregory M. Pierceall)

mary focus towards the door is probably the main route the resident and guests would use to get to the house. When developing a proposal for an entry space, caution should be taken that the plantings and constructed features do not dominate the composition and distract from the primary focus, the residence. If an entry proposal were to include a front door as the primary access and focal point and a mature oak which was dominant due to size, both of these very dominant elements should be developed into a unified composition.

Figure 9-10 is an example of a composition having two dominant elements and that have been combined into a unified scheme. The existing oak to the left of the sketch is dominant due to its size and location near to the street. The entry is the focus of attention and is given emphasis by the roof detailing over the door. The designer in this proposal has developed a shrub and small tree mass to the foreground at the right side of the sketch. While this planting is smaller than the oak, use of broadleaf evergreens and a flowering tree helps pull a viewer's attention toward the opposite side of the yard. The evergreen character provides year-round visual color and the tree seasonal interest with flowers and fruit. While the foreground planting mass visually balances the oak, the evergreen shrubs are repeated next to the entry to tie this area visually together with the foreground planting. This repetition of forms and color helps pull one's eye toward the front door. With the proposed plantings more detailed in respect to leaves, flowers, and so on, the oak, while dominant in size, is secondary to the plantings and entry focus.

Repetition

Repetition is a technique used to reinforce an element throughout a composition by repeating it. In a composition using repetition, a more simplified composition results by using fewer elements. Ground covers, mulches, pavings, or other plantings may be repeated within a design to give unity and order. Repetition also establishes an emotional and visual linkage or pattern to the design, creating physical movement within the design. In site design, repetition of recognizable materials such as pavement or constructional features can also tie separated areas such as the entry and outdoor living area together. At a site scale, mulched or planting beds between the fronts of individual properties can be repeated to tie together visually these separated residences. At a neighborhood scale, repeated street tree plantings may help to tie individual sites together. Figure 9-11 identifies the use of smaller tree forms between two adjoining residences as a means of unifying the neighborhood streetscape.

Rhythm

Rhythm is the establishment of a physical and visual pattern of movement in a proposal. Rhythm within a residential scale design may be used to move a visitor to the front door through repeated plants across a straight walk. The visual recall of similar plantings establishes movement up the walk, and the pattern reinforces the sequence of walking. Figure 9-12 shows a good and poor example of the use of rhythm in the repetition of walkways, ground covers and plantings to direct guests up to the entryway.

Balance

Balance, the last of the design principles to be discussed, is the visual equilibrium of elements within a composition. Balance may be achieved through composition of equal numbers, types, or colors of elements on each side of an assumed visual axis. It is called *symmetrical* balance. Unequal elements organized to achieve a visual balance is called *asymmetrical* balance. Due to the tradition and efficiency of geometric lot shapes and often standardized home designs, visual balance is a concept that individuals strive to achieve. Through planting masses in conjunction with the building mass and openings in the elevations, clients often develop symmetrical compositions that are static (Figure 9-13). Balance as a design consideration helps create visual emphasis and physical direction to a site development.

Often, the street, walk, and residence location on the property set up the skeleton that visual balance can be based on in plan view and elevation. The entry walk is often the physical and assumed visual axis from which planting masses are proposed. When identical planted or constructed masses are placed equally on each side of the axis, a formal or symmetrical balance is established. This type planting often is static and problems result if one plant dies. When one mass is balanced by another mass of varying elements but an equality is established, the composition is asymmetrical. In compositions such as this, movement is established making the proposal more lively. Balance is often an individual preference and site specific as to the desire to create an informal setting.

Figure 9-14 shows examples of balance within a residential site plan. In the entry area, the building door and window locations es-

FIGURE 9-10

In this entry situation, the existing tree on the left frames the house and is a dominant design element in conjunction with the doorway. The remaining plants are proposed to create a balanced scheme visually yet allowing the doorway and tree to remain key compositional elements. (Designer: Gregory M. Pierceall)

scale 1"=20'

FIGURE 9-11

Repetition of an element within a site design or at the neighborhood scale is helpful to tie otherwise separated units together. In this illustration, the repeated tree forms, by shape, texture, and color, visually tie the individual sites together. In a residential site, repetition of shape, texture, color, or forms of plants and construction materials helps create a more unified composition. (Designer: Gregory M. Pierceall)

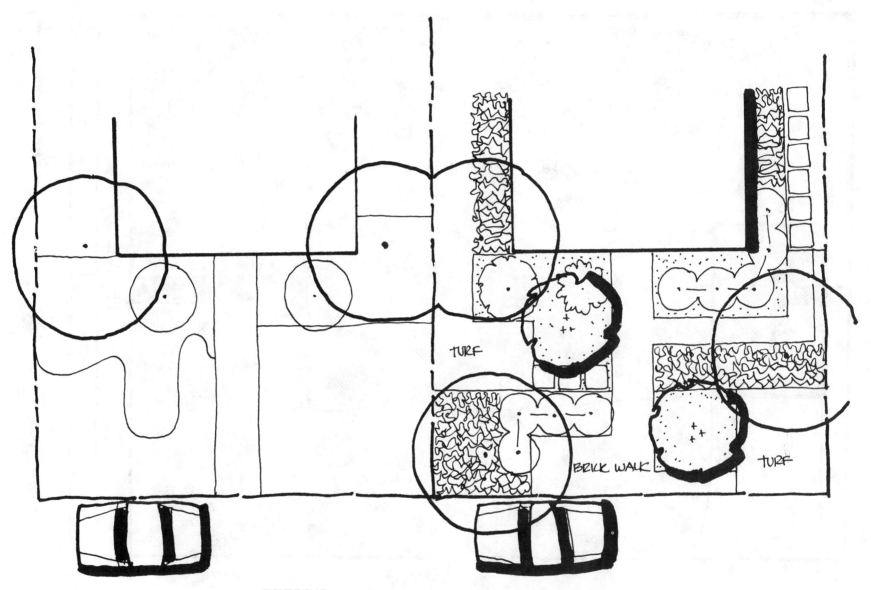

TURF

BRICK WALK

TURF

FIGURE 9-12

Rhythm is a visual and physical feeling created within a composition. No real sense of street versus entry is established in the site at the left while the right site has a sense of arrival and movement from the street to the door. (Designer: Gregory M. Pierceall)

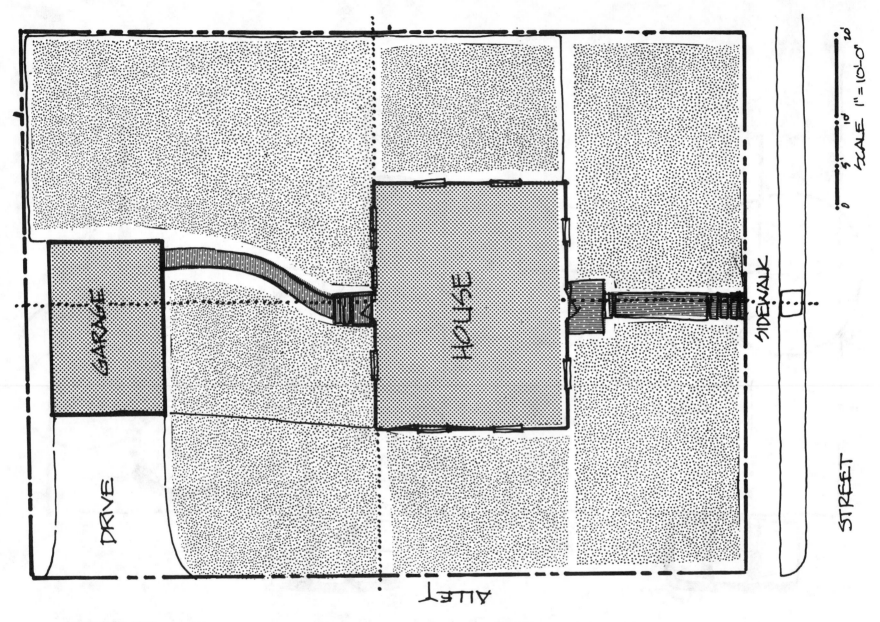

FIGURE 9-13(a)

During the initial inventory of a site, the designer should in plan view evaluate the lines of the house and property relative to physical or visual axes
that are inherent in the composition. Door and window placements often
establish an elevation's symmetry and the related landscape. As ones moves
out and away from man-made features, site design proposals can be less
structured and asymmetrical. (Designer: Gregory M. Pierceall)

FIGURE 9-13(b)

Here and in the following sketches, the entry planting is shown as being symmetrical next to the house, then asymmetrical as we move out to the property's edge. In the rear yard proposal, the lines of the deck run perpendicular to the house which is projecting window and door sight lines out. This is contrasted by the asymmetrical angle of the deck which is introduced to direct a user physically and visually into the rear yard space rather than toward the garage wall. (Designer: Gregory M. Pierceall)

FIGURE 9-13(c)
In the rear yard, the deck's attachment to the house requires a formal, direct relationship. Line variations can then occur beyond this connection related to the design intent.

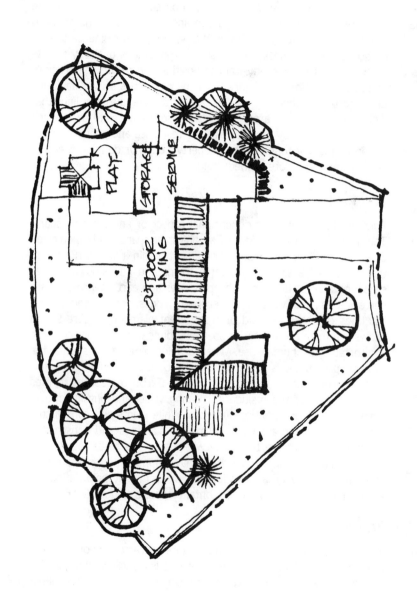

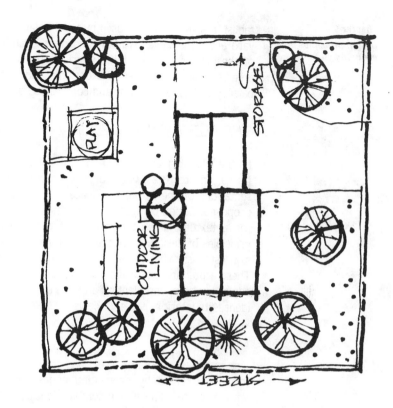

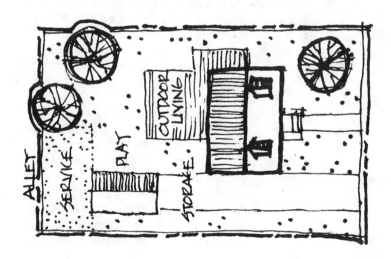

FIGURE 9-14

In residential landscape design proposals, the lot and house shapes should dictate the shape and character of site spaces developed. (Designer: Gregory M. Pierceall)

tablish a symmetrical or asymmetrical balance scheme. In the backyard areas the varied window and door locations and the influence of the property lines establish varied site spaces and asymmetrical areas. In these instances, the designer can emphasize or vary the balance with site plantings and constructed elements proposed.

THE ELEMENTS OF DESIGN

In the planning and design of site solutions, plans include lines, forms, and textures, with color or descriptions of colors as representations of the actual site space and materials both existing and proposed. Design composition includes the *elements of design*—line, form, texture, and color, and their combinations—guided by the principles of design. After the site survey and analysis, stages of design establish what physically and visually is existing and desirable. These acutal and perceived considerations are used to define walks, edges, surfaces, and planting areas as extensions of the site, the residence, its interior uses and views.

Line

Line in a design creates visual and physical movement and defines forms and areas by delineating edges and shapes. Line can be straight or curvilinear or a combination. Line can create feelings of formality when straight and naturalness when curved. Intersecting lines create points of hestitation. In landscape design, line is found in the edge of a planting bed or the alignment of stepping stones. Ground patterns may be established by use of lines projected from the residence. Pavements, pathways, or planting areas may use lines projected from the edges or linkages from the house. Vertical line can be found in the shape or construction materials of the residence, in tree forms, fences, or other existing side enclosure elements.

All materials used in landscape design have inherent line. An understanding of the inherent line quality and combinations associated with a material is an important consideration prior to selection of shapes and materials for a composition. If early in your planning you are alerted that wooden timbers may eventually be the basic construction material for a retaining wall, an understanding of their inherent lines should tell you that tight curves cannot be a realistic design solution if the timbers are to be used horizontally. A design option that would be possible in this situation would include use of

the timbers vertically rather than horizontally to create a curved theme if desired.

Selection of line within a composition should also relate to the shape of the property and residence and the shape of the areas to be developed for activities. Often, the property and residence configuration dictate the lines used in site design. Line is one way to manipulate the visual and physical composition and to provide order to design compositions. In Figure 9-14 the properties shown have distinctive shapes defined by line. In each of the sketches, the lines that define outdoor living areas and other use areas relate to the line that is established by the shape of the residence and property. Repetition of the line found in the property's edge or defining the residence provides a more unified design.

Form

Form is the actual three-dimensional aspect of an object or space. The height, depth, and width of an object or space can be perceived as a solid, hollow, or transparent element within a design (Earle). In the context of a site design, earth forms and buildings "read" as solids; covered structures with open sides and earth depression are perceived as hollows; and the property edges, fences, and border plantings can read as solid or transparent elements. Figure 9-15a shows the form of an interior space. Its dimensions are scaled to be comfortable for human use. When developing exterior spaces, the form a space takes is often determined by the placement of plantings and constructed features. In Figure 9-15b the spaces formed are extensions of the residence, creating visual and physical movement from indoor activities outdoors. While plants and constructed features can define a space's form, the plantings and constructed forms should relate to the space where they are to be located. An upright plant form in a wide space may emphasize openness rather than enclosure, whereas a wide plant or form may help define the space more and establish a horizontal emphasis (Figure 9-16).

Texture

Texture is the visual and/or tactile surface characteristic of an object or element in the landscape. *Visual texture* is a surface configuration that evokes sensations of relief or touch yet may be untouchable. Clouds often give a feeling of being fluffy and soft yet cannot be touched; similarly, one perceives smooth sensations when viewing a distant pool of water. Some plant materials viewed from a distance

FIGURE 9-15(a)

To create a transition between indoor and outdoor spaces, landscape design
proposals should attempt to create outdoor spaces that through plant and
constructed features blend the interior and exterior. (Designer: Gregory M.
Pierceall)

FIGURE 9-15(b)

*In this scene the view from indoors is directed by the overhead lattice and
the garden's enclosure is established partially by the tree canopy and screening evergreens.*

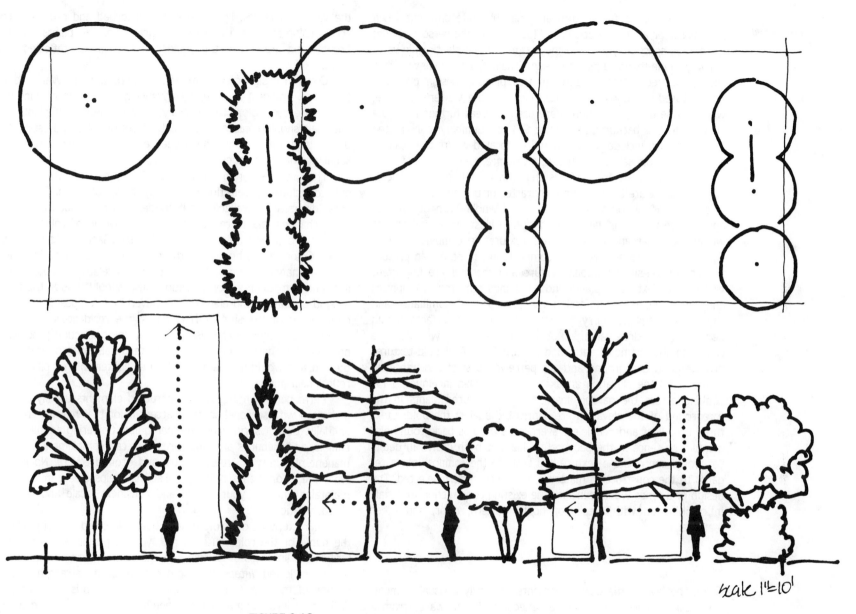

scale 1"=10'

FIGURE 9-16

When plants are used within the spaces defined by a site and residence, new subspaces are created. Plant placement and their forms thus help to subdivide and define the scale and activities that occur within a site. (Designer: Gregory M. Pierceall)

give the illusion of flat texture and may be quite different when seen closer or actually touched. In Figure 9-17a the person viewing the garden space may perceive the textures of the plantings in varying ways. Fine-textured plants recede visually from the viewer while coarse-textured plants advance. In this planting design proposal, fine-textured plantings are located close to the viewer's vantage, while coarse-textured plantings are used in areas further from the view or in the background (Figure 9-17b). Similarly, constructed features which include details should be located where they can be seen in the proposal rather than at a distance.

Tactile textures are surfaces that can be felt or experienced. Texture can relate to the overall character of the object or be specific to individual component parts of the whole. Without textures and surface variations, landscape design in illustrations and on site would seem flat and uninteresting. Textures in combination with light and shadows add depth to compositions. In both plan presentations and on-site situations, texture and shadows are important visual cues. Texture in plants and surfacings can provide emphasis and repetition, thus reinforcing the principles of dominance and rhythm. Remember, highly textured plantings and surfaces should be viewed at a close vantage, not at a distance, since with distance comes an abstracting of detail and texture. Therefore, bold textures provide good background and are perceived best at a distance. In Figure 9-18 the elevation is taken from the plan in Figure 9-17. Looking across the garden space, the fine-textured plants in the foreground of the elevation are contrasted against the bolder textured broadleaf and needleleaf evergreens used as background elements. The fence in the background has not been drawn in detail, yet would contribute a texture and scale to the composition in regards to the construction materials and fence pattern selected. The design of a fence would consider the existing construction materials in combination with details of board pattern, color, and other features.

Color

Color, the last of the design elements, is totally a visual element. Technically, color is an observed reflection of light waves from a surface. As light strikes an opaque surface, some light waves are absorbed and others reflected. This gives an object its color. In Figure 9-19 natural light composed of a spectrum of colors is striking the opaque surfaces of the plants, pavements, and constructed features from a source behind the person in the scene. As the light hits the various surfaces, light waves are absorbed and reflected. The actual color seen, in this case the greens of the plants and the browns and oranges of the boulder and fence, are reflected light waves.

Color in design creates excitement and contrast. Warm colors (reds and oranges) are visually advancing colors, while blues and greens are cool colors that visually recede. Selection of plants and materials should consider the visual effects of color and establish a theme that complements the residence and surroundings with seasonally colorful additions.

The use of color in the residential landscape is often thought only to include the selection of varying shades of green. Due to the great diversity of available plant species and the influences of seasonal changes, plants can express a wide range of color. Leaves, flowers, fruits, and twigs all contribute to a landscape's color and effect. Color should be used with knowledge of a plant's individual seasonal changes and desirable compositions relative to other plantings and components. Considerations also should include the background or foreground elements perceived in a composition. An understanding of the site's surroundings, the residence's color, and regional color themes can also help your color selection process. In hot climates, dark-colored plants or materials absorb heat, thus these plants would not be as practical as lighter colored plants that reflect heat and light.

Permanent plantings and constructed elements usually are coordinated with seasonal spots of accent color that may be changed annually. Use of spring and summer bulbs, flowering annuals, perennials, and biennials are all choices that can complement the permanent plantings of trees, shrubs, and ground covers. No matter what the color theme, select a pallet that helps create interest yet maintains unity in your design and considers locale and regional characteristics.

Characteristics of colors include hue, value, and intensity. *Hue* is the name of the color such as red, yellow, purple, etc. *Value* describes the lightness or darkness of the color, indicating the quality of light reflected. *Intensity* is the degree of purity, strength, or saturation of the hue. A monochromatic composition is one that uses different values and intensities of one hue, or color. Complementary colors are hues that are on opposite sides of the color wheel and are used side by side for emphasis (Figure 9-20). Red next to green or blue next to yellow are complementary colors that have an increased intensity because of the strong contrasts created by their proximity to each other.

FIGURE 9-17(a)

In the perspective sketch of the patio design, the space can seem visually to be shorter by the inclusion of the broadleaf shrubs and canopy trees on each side of the space. The broad leaves of these plants and the influence of their darker color, advance, while finer texture plantings visually recede. (Designer: Gregory M. Pierceall)

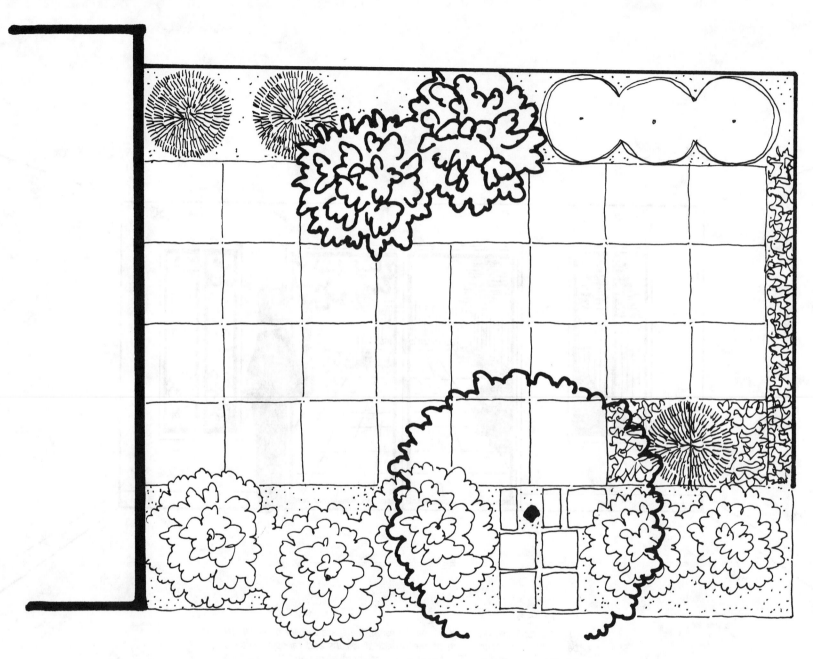

FIGURE 9-17(b)
Plan view of the area seen in Figure 9-17(a).

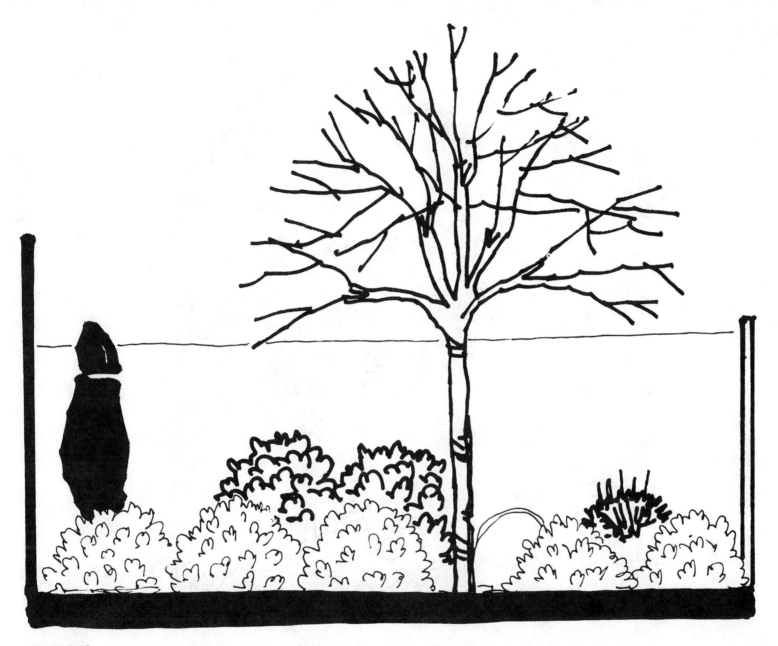

FIGURE 9-18

In the elevation taken from the plan in Figure 9-17a, the contrast between course- and fine-textured plants can be seen. Also notice that the deciduous canopy tree is drawn as it would be seen in the winter with its fine branching character in contrast to its otherwise coarse leaf texture. When using deciduous plant materials, remember that their summer character can be quite different from their winter effect. The overall effect of evergreen plantings, on the other hand, is much more consistent year-round. (Designer: Gregory M. Pierceall)

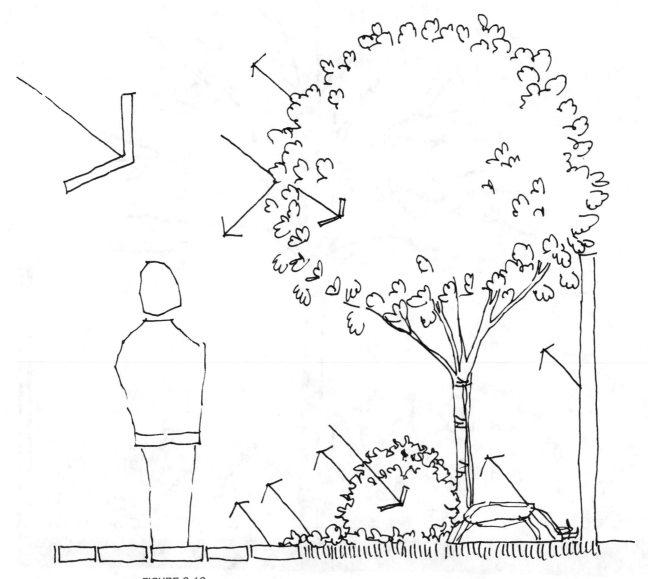

FIGURE 9-19

While color is not shown in this illustration, the actual colors we see are a result of absorbed and reflected light waves. Because naturally occurring light is composed of a spectrum of colors, we actually see the reflected light waves. (Designer: Gregory M. Pierceall)

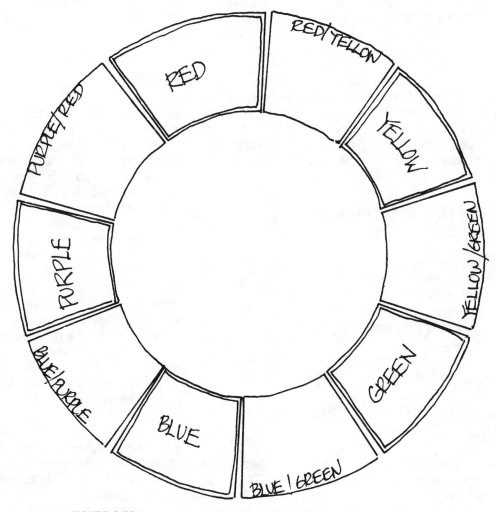

FIGURE 9-20

This simple color wheel shows the basic relationships between primary and secondary colors. Color schemes that use colors that are side by side on the wheel are monochromatic while color selections across from each other are considered complementary. (Designer: Gregory M. Pierceall)

DESIGN DEVELOPMENT

In the *site design* process, planning and design should include consideration of the line, form, texture, and color of plant and construction materials recommended such that they can be used to enhance and unify a proposal. A designed site should express a sense of place, create a feeling of establishment between the site, and the residence, and relate to the region or local influences of design and style in which the project occurs. The selection and coordination of design elements should complement the site situation and consider the visual and physical site relationships among interior spaces, the site, and the surroundings. Planning and design should start with an understanding of the site, the residence, and proposed uses. The designer should appreciate the existing character, condition, and inherent capabilities of the site situation. Then the design principles using the elements of design should define the detailing of planning considerations for site development.

USING DESIGN CONCEPTS IN GRAPHIC PRESENTATIONS

While design considerations help to create a unified site composition the presentation and communication of landscape design apply the principles and elements of design as background for drawing and information composition. Using the characteristics of line, form, texture, and color, existing and proposed plants and construction materials are presented to portray their inherent characteristics. To present the project qualities desired, designers need to understand design elements and the principles used to develop compositions.

DESIGN CONCEPTS INFLUENCE ON-SITE INSTALLATION AND CARE

After the site design has been presented, the actual implementation is the next stage in achieving a "designed landscape." No matter how much time and effort goes into the planning or design of a proposal, if it is not installed or maintained relative to the design qualities desired, the effects can be lost. Design qualities are included in design proposals. A design proposal not only considers the location of a "specimen tree" but the placement positioning in an "ideal" location relative to views and vantages defined by the site or building situation. Pruning as a maintenance method can also ruin an effect that was designed for when an individual tree was selected for its form or character. Sensitivity to design is an important consideration for any landscape industry professional. It is a means to communicate and develop quality landscapes. Remember that it is the "details" that separate designed compositions from just landscapes.

SUMMARY

In the composing of a landscape design proposal, the principles and elements of design are used to give site spaces definition, character and composition. Thus, selecting and combining appropriate lines, forms, textures, and colors are important in creating well-defined and unified compositions. Landscape sites are three-dimensional spaces, thus landscape composition is three-dimensional. Landscape design must consider the ever-changing viewing plane, level changes, and seasonal variations. Landscape designs may be experienced with constantly changing views of foreground, middleground, and background as homeowners or visitors move through the site. The designer can often select the viewing points within a design and create vistas or hesitation points at intersections to relate to a designed view. In the visual and functional design of site spaces, the landscape designer anticipates the most desirable views, vistas, and pathways (Figure 9-21). These provide depth and alignment to the sequence of spaces and elements experienced from within a site and its surroundings (Figure 9-22). Besides the creation and manipulation of the views in the landscape, the daily, seasonal, and growth changes inherent in a landscape development further enhance the dynamics of a landscape design (Figures 9-23 and 9-24).

Landscape design is active, never static. It is a collection of moments, not a singular moment as is captured in a landscape painting or photograph (Figures 9-25 and 9-26).

In the use and appreciation of an established landscape, specific plant and or constructed features are often the components that are most noticed and a focus of attention. The success of a garden or landscape area both physically and visually is usually the result of good planning and design. A planned and designed composition is only the underlying principle used to achieve a useful and pleasing landscape environment.

FIGURE 9-21

The existing sideyard walkway was direct and placed too close to the side of the residence. In the after photo, the walkway alignment was moved away from the residence to allow plantings and a more pleasing walkway sequence. These photos show the impact that line has on a walkway development. (Designer: Gregory M. Pierceall)

FIGURE 9-22

Line can be created in a composition by developing planting beds.

FIGURE 9-23

Deciduous plant forms, shapes, and textures vary with the season. The columnar hornbeam have an open feeling in winter and spring but create a screen during summer.

FIGURE 9-24

While color is inherent in all landscape elements, seasonal color change can be an exciting design consideration. In the photos shown the total charac-teristics of these flowering crabs change dramatically from twig to bud to flower to leaves within their growing season.

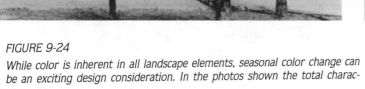

FIGURE 9-25

Symmetrical balance is the theme that has been developed. (a) The formal garden area with sculpture is developed from the axis selected for viewing. (b) The knot garden, while formal, has an informality in the materials included.

FIGURE 9-26

Example of asymmetrical balance. Often, existing trees and site features provide the means of creating an asymmetrical design.

REFERENCES AND READINGS

Carpenter P. L., Walker, T. D., and Lanphear, F. O. *Plants in the Landscape.* San Francisco, CA: W. H. Freeman and Company, 1979.

Nelson, Wm. R. *Planting Design, A Manual of Theory and Practice.* Champaign IL: Stipes Publishing Company, 1979.

Snow, Marc. *Modern American Gardens.* New York: Reinhold Publishing Corporation, 1967.

Walker T. D. *Residential Landscaping I.* West Lafayette IN: PDA Publishers, 1982.

SITE DESIGN CASE STUDIES

FOUR

Residential site development

As one skims through architecture, landscape architecture, interior design, and housing magazines and texts, concepts and illustrations abound concerning the improvements, planning, and design of home environments. As first-time home buyers and existing homeowners look at the housing alternatives available, they realize that the trend is toward living with less space both inside and out. Changing economics, family needs, and use patterns are generating a shift away from larger homes to smaller and more efficient home designs. Inflation and escalating building, financing, and operating expenses all have contributed to the demand for more efficient, smaller new homes and the increased interest in remodeling exisiting homes. Lifestyle changes, including smaller households, two-career families, and now more informal entertaining preferences have also influenced the interest in home designs which are more flexible and serve dual purposes. Formal and informal rooms, such as living rooms and family rooms, are being combined and duplication in room uses is being eliminated. Multipurpose design concepts provide home spaces and landscapes that are functional, efficient, and livable at reduced construction, operation, and maintenance costs. Figure 10-1 shows an example of a multipurpose home interior. The room shown serves as a living/dining area with the interior activities and views extended beyond the space's limits with the inclusion of sliding glass doors on to a deck space.

HOUSING TRENDS AND THE RELATED LANDSCAPES

Multifamily Housing

In contrast to traditional, single-family homes, some homeowners choose new forms of housing such as townhouses, atrium homes, zero-lot-lines, and earth-sheltered homes. These new forms of housing are attempts by the home-building industry to provide efficient yet adequate housing. Often these units are spaced closer together to save land and maintain affordable pricing. In Figure 10-2a, four identical properties have been developed to illustrate how the housing form selected can increase densities. The property in the upper, left-hand corner shows the 200' × 120' lot subdivided to provide building sites for two homes. Each residence has a separate entry drive, door, and front, side, and rear yards. The property located to the lower, left-hand side shows the same 200' × 120' lot developed using the zero-lot-line concept. Four units have been designed with each lot developed such that the building is sited on one edge of the property. In the architectural design, this elevation has no windows and all access and views are oriented toward the open side yard. For each residence separate entries have been provided, and yard space which is private and usable. The advantage of this and the other lotting options illustrated is maximum use of land which is often 20 percent of the cost of a home. This 20 percent figure includes not only the cost of the land but development costs such as grading, roadways, sidewalks, street lights, and utilities. The clustering of units and increased densities reduces individual land and development costs per unit, thus a savings to homeowners.

With reduced sites and increased densities comes a different housing form and variation from the detached, single-family home. The remaining examples illustrate a quad-plex, the upper, right-hand corner, and townhouses in the lower, right-hand corner of Figure 10-2a. Both of these examples are attached housing which describes the construction method of shared, common walls between units. In each case, with increased use of the land, individual outdoor spaces are reduced. In large-scale multifamily developments, common open space is then incorporated to provide areas for larger, group-type activities like baseball or volleyball.

Multifamily housing and new variations in housing design are being discussed to make landscape designers aware of housing trends and the changes to come in landscape design relative to these developments. See Figures 10-2b and 10-2c for a comparison between single-family detached and attached housing variations.

Existing Homes

For other homeowners, the often available smaller, older home in established neighborhoods offers a more livable housing alternative than newer forms of housing. The challenge of retrofitting the interior and exterior of an older home is an exciting endeavor for residents and designers alike. As housing trends reflect increased densities with interiors and sites decreasing in size, site planning and landscape design become more important. Visually and physically, home landscape designs need to be extensions of interior spaces and activities, and relate to surrounding conditions and climatic influences. Smaller interiors can seem larger if windows and site spaces are designed to visually extend views beyond a room's limits. Physical accessibility between interior activity areas and airy garden, patio, or deck spaces can provide both physical and visual relief as extended or "overflow" areas. In Figures 10-3a and 10-3b the living/dining area in the residence is physically and visually expanded by the adjoining deck space. As the need arises, the deck space can function instead of or in addition to the interior space available. The extent to which this indoor/outdoor relationship is developed often depends on the climatic conditions of the locale in which the project occurs or site specific conditions. In warmer parts of the country, outdoor living is possible year around, thus extensive indoor/outdoor use areas may be justified. In more temperate and colder areas, outdoor entertaining is limited to specific seasons. Thus less extensive entertaining areas may be reasonable relative to the time used. Indoor activities in the living, dining, and kitchen areas are easily extended to the outdoors. The lack of exterior space or adverse conditions such as prevailing climatic conditions, mosquito infestations or negative surroundings can affect utility and thus development.

When redesigning existing residential landscapes or development of new sites, a design process including planning and design considerations provides a method to propose functional and aes-

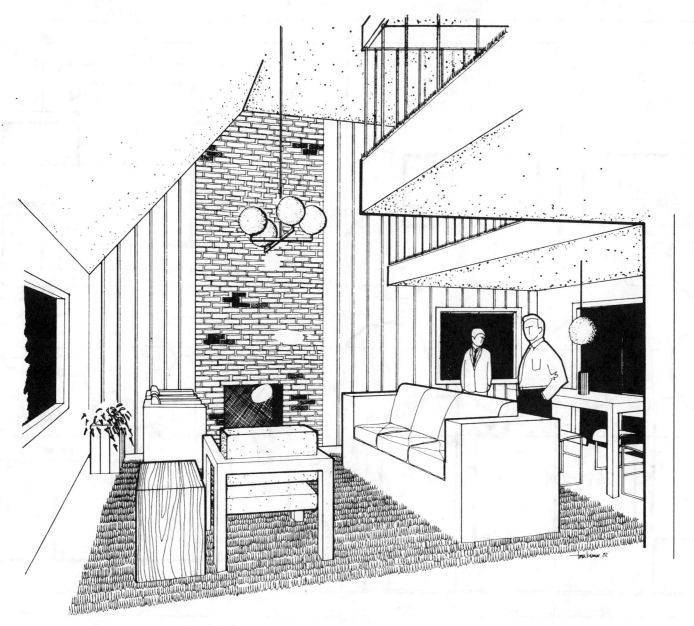

FIGURE 10-1

Just as architects include room arrangements to serve multipurpose activities in their new home designs, landscape designers need to consider the opportunities in proposing site spaces that serve a variety of functions. (Designer: T. G. Kramer)

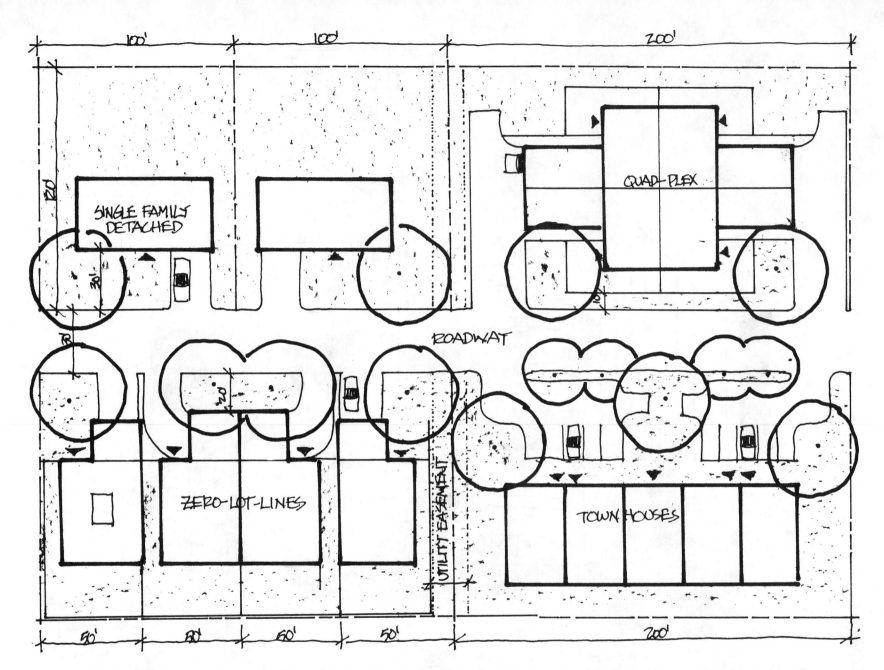

FIGURE 10-2(a)

As land and building costs increase, multifamily housing develops land areas to their maximum while keeping individual unit costs within a reasonable range. While the density of development increases, the related outdoor living space decreases. If housing trends continue, the need for landscape design and services should also increase. (Designer: Gregory M. Pierceall)

(b)

FIGURE 10-2(b)(c)

In the development of residential entry design proposals for multifamily housing, the function and views of two dwelling units rather than one must be considered.

(c)

FIGURE 10-3(a)

In the development of outdoor spaces, the use or activities of interior rooms should influence the exterior's design. As shown here and in Figure 10-3b, the living/dining area is physically and visually extended by the proposal of a deck for seasonal outdoor entertaining. (Designer: T. G. Kramer)

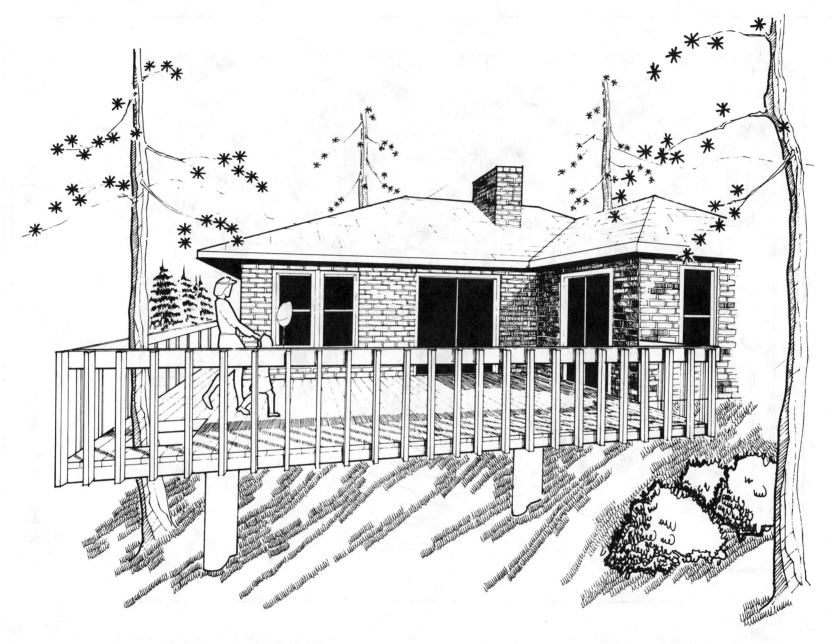

FIGURE 10-3(b)
This deck extends the interior activities both physically and visually outdoors.

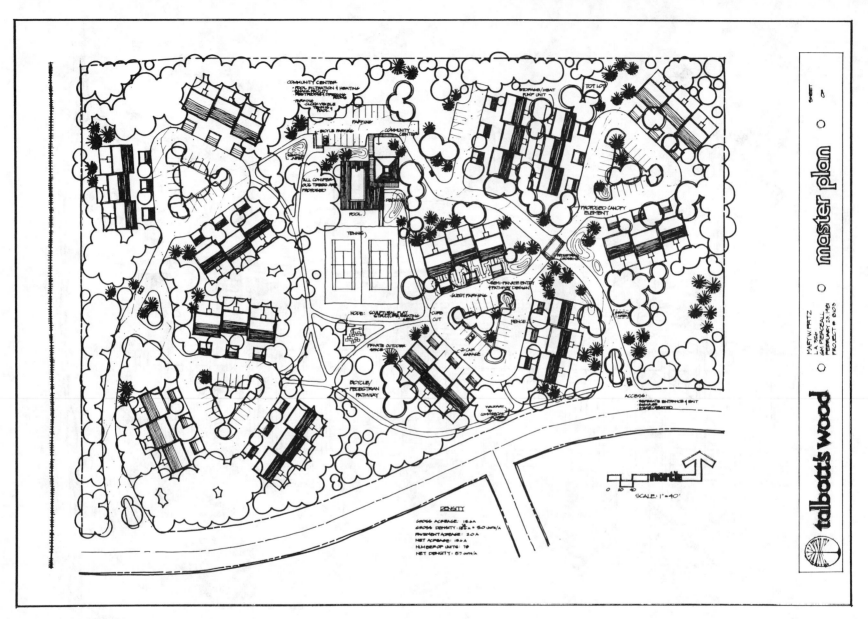

FIGURE 10-4

Multifamily master plan. Here and in the following examples, it can be seen that planning and design is critical in the development of multifamily proposals. As the intensity of development increases, the overall and specific details are needed to make the development functional, efficient, and attractive. The illustrations shown are all design concepts developed before the actual construction drawings. While at this conceptual stage of design, the basic character and details of the housing and site development are defined. (Designer: M. Fritz)

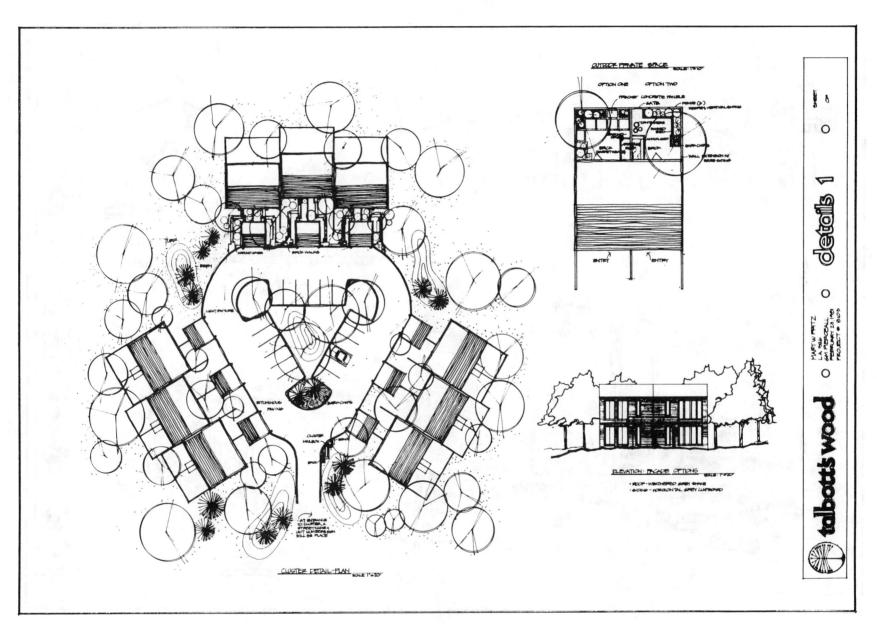

FIGURE 10-5
Multifamily cluster detail. (Designer: M. Fritz)

FIGURE 10-6
Multifamily landscape details. (Designer: M. Fritz)

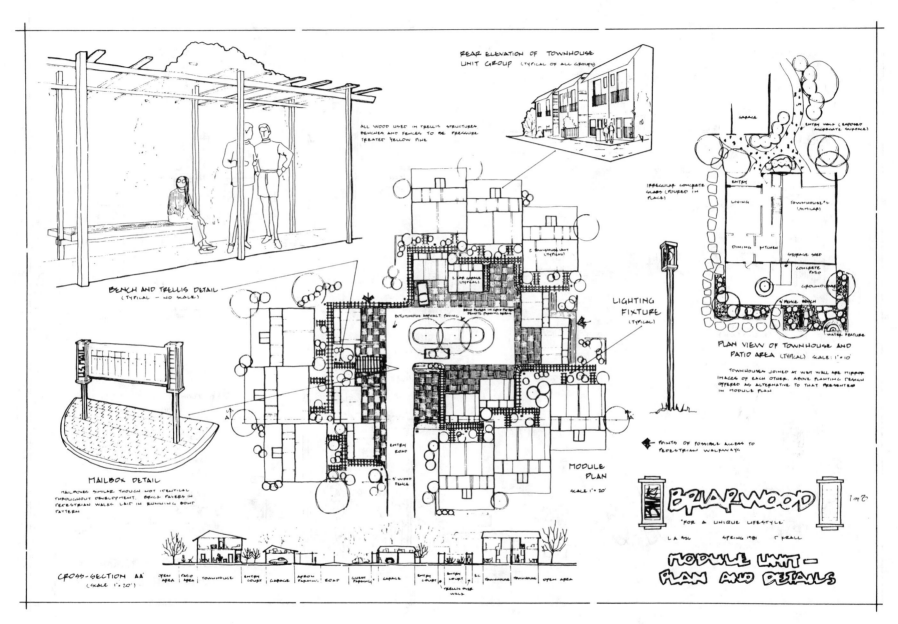

FIGURE 10-7
Multifamily cluster plan and details. (Designer: D. Krall)

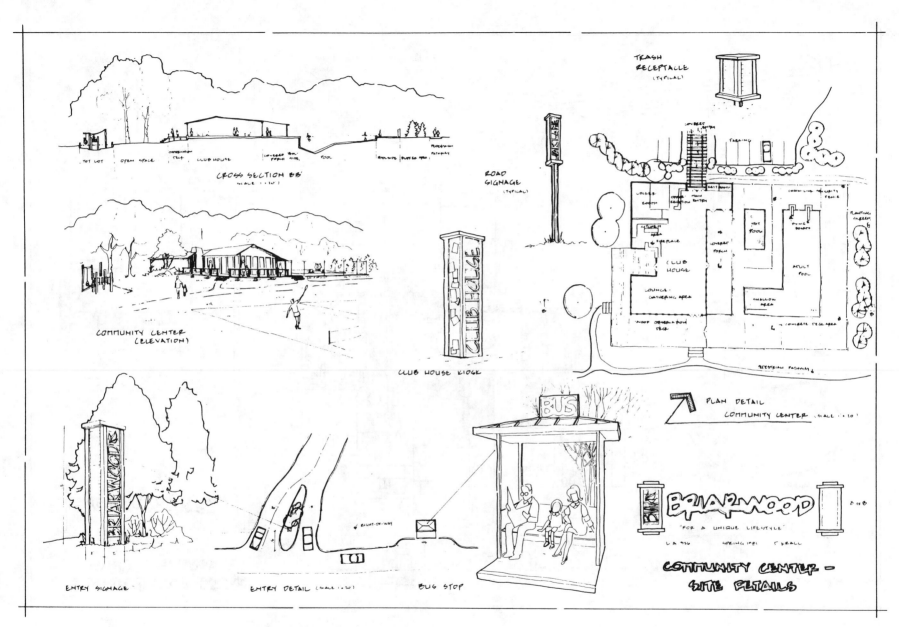

FIGURE 10-8
Multifamily housing development details. (Designer: D. Krall)

thetically pleasing solutions. In residential design situations the planning and design services most requested by homeowners usually relate to site specific areas; for example, the entry, outdoor living or specific garden spaces. Secondary to these specific design requests, master plans may be desired that project or anticipate all the plantings and structural features to be eventually developed. As a design professional, you have an obligation to explain the short- and long-term benefits planning and designing have on specific areas versus the advantages of developing a proposal for the entire site. The short-term benefits, for example, of planning the entire site rather than single areas is (1) overall proposals maximize dollars and human resources; and (2) development towards a final product is more effective and efficient than implementation of unrelated site design pieces. On the other hand, long-term planning and design proposals establish a master plan which provides a phasing plan and a unified property design. The attractiveness and utility of one's residence can then be developed over a period of time toward a final goal. Only when the entire site is considered can the design blend the residence and site into a composition that is functional and aesthetically pleasing.

The specific objectives for a site's design and development are established by the physical and visual aspects of the site and the client's needs and priorities. As existing residential sites are improved and new housing developed, site design proposals will have to be more responsive to the changing context of residential landscapes and client needs. As home interiors and site spaces decrease in size and land and construction costs increase, site planning and landscape development help to maintain privacy and a unit setting. As site developments become more detailed with increased densities and varied uses and landscape design, site planning provides an opportunity to study the feasibility of a proposal before construction and the character of the development to occur.

Figures 10-4 to 10-8 are examples of multifamily proposals, including plans and details. The multifamily feasibility studies are examples of the use of the design process showing how attached housing would fit on this site and how the site spaces could be developed.

SUMMARY

As designers of residential landscapes, awareness of housing trends and the changing needs of residential clients is needed. Economics, lifestyle changes, and smaller households have influenced housing design, and these changes will affect the planning and design of residential sites. As the densities of new housing increase, the demand for better planned and designed sites that provide for privacy, energy efficiency, and effective land use will increase. The best way to prepare for the future and changes in residential landscape design is to develop an understanding of the planning, design, and homeowner needs as a basis for landscape design decisions. As part of the total site design process landscape design establishes the details, forms, and materials used to create exterior environments.

REFERENCES AND READINGS

Carpenter P. L., Walker, T. D., and Lanphear, F. O. *Plants in the Landscape.* San Francisco, CA: W. H. Freeman and Co., 1979.

Clay, Grady. *Landscapes for Living.* New York: McGraw-Hill, 1980.

Laurie, Michael. *An Introduction to Landscape Architecture.* New York, N.Y.: American Elsevier, 1975.

Newton, Norman T. *Design on the Land: The Development of Landscape Architecture.* Cambridge, Mass., Belknop Press of Harvard Univ. Press., 1971.

Residential landscape design

11

The example selected to illustrate the design process of site planning and landscape design is a small site and older home in an established residential neighborhood. If one can say any residential design project is typical or average, it could be in the kinds of considerations and influences that impact the design proposals developed here. Principal site opportunities and limits may involve surrounding land uses, microclimatic considerations of sun and wind, and the site's existing landforms and vegetation. With housing trends moving towards smaller homes and properties, and with increased interest in remodeling existing residential environments, the illustration used is particularly relevant.

Basic considerations used in any residential site design include evaluation of client needs, the residence's location, size in relation to the site and surroundings, and the physical and visual interaction of interior rooms and activities. The residential site is in the Midwest, thus the energy conservation opportunities associated with site development should attempt to maximize winter sun and summer breezes while minimizing summer sun and winter winds. As you follow the design process in the redesign and improvement of this site, note that many of the concepts and concerns are the same as those encountered in evaluating and designing the siting of a new residence and development of a landscape on an undeveloped property. In reviewing the site survey and analysis information, remember these influences vary from site to site and are influenced by a project's immediate surroundings and the geographic region in which a project occurs. The suggested readings at the end of this chapter include information on planning for energy conservation and regional differences in climate that affect site design.

BACKGROUND INFORMATION—CLIENT, SITE, NEEDS

The clients located a house that was in an established neighborhood, near schools, not too big, affordable, and close to work. As can be seen in the "before" photos of the residence, "beauty" or, in this case, "home" is in the eye of the beholder (Figure 11-1). The Cape Cod house, some 45 years old and including 1,200 square feet, was sited on a 5,400 square foot lot (60' × 90'). It was structurally sound and located on a main city street only a few blocks from elementary and high schools and work (Figure 11-2). The house, its

FIGURE 11-1

The "before" character of the residence when purchased by the new homeowner.

size, location, and proximity to community facilities served the clients' needs and lifestyle exactly. However, the clients found it hard to admit that they lived in a house with a "yard" as it existed.

Homes are personal places that reflect the character of their residents. Even though landscapes can be designed through the site planning process, the total house/site environment is not complete until the design and detailing relate to and complement the site's immediate users, the residents. The following is a description of the design and development process used in renovating this existing landscape.

THE REDESIGN AND RENOVATION PROCESS

After settling in during summer, the remainder of the clients' fall and winter was consumed in remodeling the interior of the once-rented house. The impact of the renters had not been felt as much inside as out. The landscape, in great disrepair and neglect, represented plantings conceived some 45 years before. The once "cute" evergreens at the front corners of the house had grown to be monsters in a "green jungle." Besides their overgrown size, one of the evergreen trees had been invaded by a grape vine that jokingly represented a "pyramidal grape." Upon recommendation of a landscape architect and before fall had set in, the "beast" vine was pulled out of the evergreen tree and the skeleton of a Douglas fir remained (Figure 11-3). The following spring the tree and vine remains were cut down to reveal a much improved front yard (Figure 11-4).

As spring began to bloom, the clients found the urge to venture outdoors and discover what was new in their landscape. To their surprise they found spring bulbs and a patch of wildflowers. With the reality of owning a house and site with "great potential," they proceeded to have a site inventory completed to evaluate the existing plantings, surrounding influences, and problems as related to the site's location and conditions and their personal needs. The basic site inventory is shown in Figure 11-5. This plan and the analysis of existing conditions and considerations (Figure 11-6) were the basis for the landscape architect's master plan development. The vegetation indicated on the analysis sheet includes the only plant materials to be kept. Plant condition, function, location, and program needs were the determinants in the evaluation of the existing vegetation. Present needs, future plans, and site potentials were the basic guidelines in the development of the master plan.

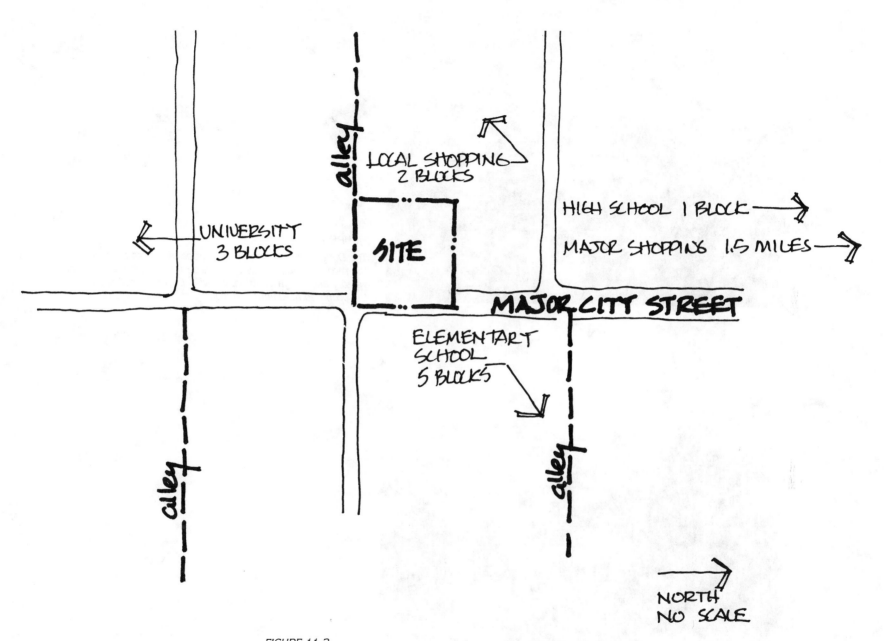

ALLEY

LOCAL SHOPPING
2 BLOCKS

HIGH SCHOOL 1 BLOCK →

UNIVERSITY
3 BLOCKS

SITE

MAJOR SHOPPING 1.5 MILES →

MAJOR CITY STREET

ELEMENTARY
SCHOOL
5 BLOCKS

ALLEY

ALLEY

NORTH
NO SCALE

FIGURE 11-2

Site location plan. While landscape design recommendations are site specific, the designer should understand the surrounding land uses, vehicular circulation, and related influences. (Designer: Gregory M. Pierceall)

FIGURE 11-3

The Douglas fir, covered with a grape vine, was badly damaged and thus the recommendation was easily made for its removal. In a normal site inventory and design situation, it is visually best to define what is existing and the proposed needs prior to making site recommendations.

FIGURE 11-4

It can be seen that the removal of the skeleton of the tree has greatly improved the appearance of this residential situation.

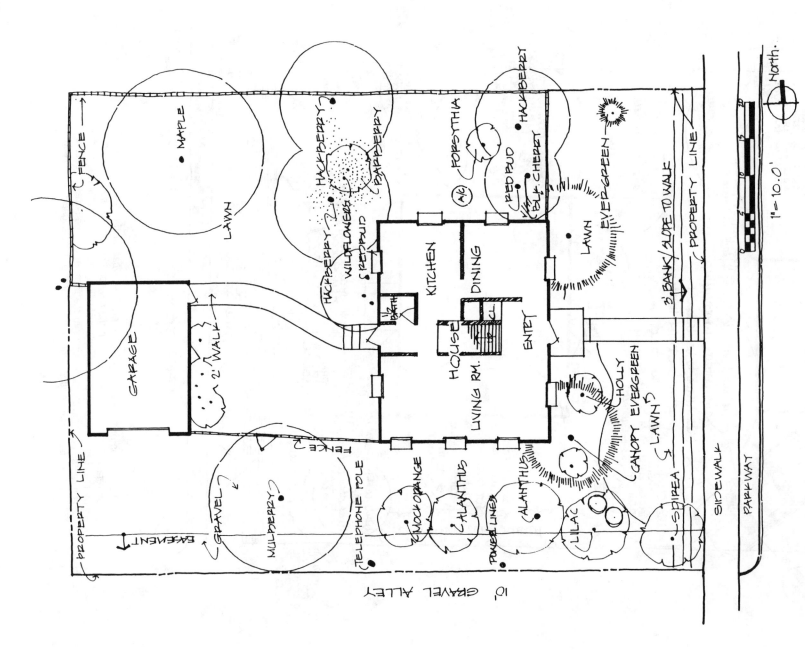

FIGURE 11-5

The purpose of a site inventory or survey is to record and establish all the existing features to be considered in the planning and design of a site. All physical features including below and above ground utilities, services, and site limits such as topography, property lines, set backs, and easements are also included. This is the base information used to develop the final design proposal. (Designer: Gregory M. Pierceall)

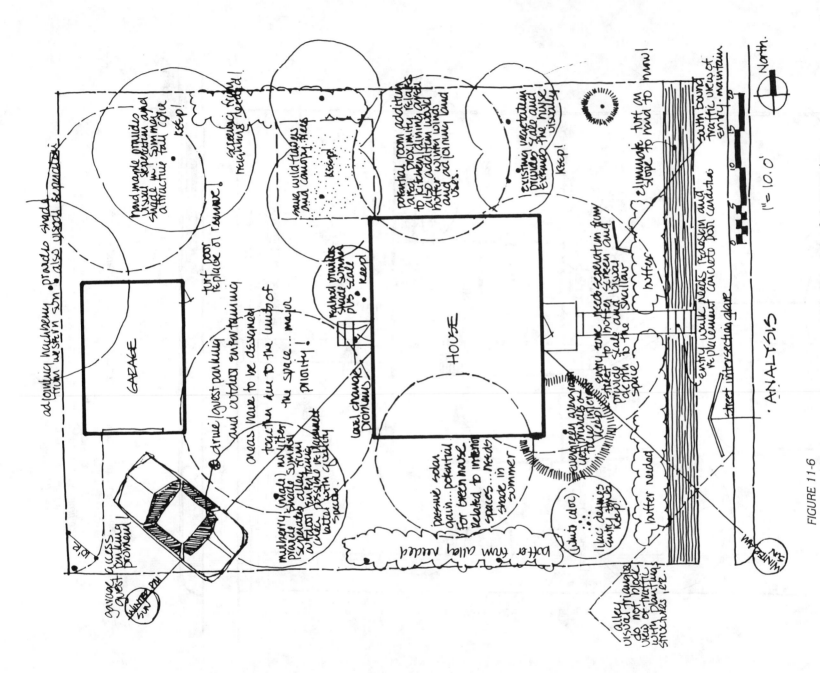

FIGURE 11-6

The function of the site analysis is to establish what existing features are to be retained, removed, or revised in the development of the site as defined by the client's needs and designer's evaluation. While a graphic site analysis is nice, the actual evaluation may be in the form of written notes that serve as guidelines in the development of the master plan. (Designer: Gregory M. Pierceall)

As the landscape architect collected site inventory and analysis data, parallel client information was collected on site design priorities. Desired landscape planting, construction, and specific use areas were also discussed. Consideration was given to both immediate and long-term needs such as room additions and recreation or play areas. Review of the site inventory and analysis plan as well as the clients' design program will help you to understand the preliminary data needed prior to generating design alternatives and site master plans.

THE DESIGN PROGRAM

The basic client program included the following information:

Outdoor Living/Rear Yard Requirements

1. Give priority to the rear yard over the front yard as it would be used immediately by the clients for personal and social activities. Also important to the clients was improved organization of the garage/guest parking areas off the alley, directly related to the garage.

2. Provide an outdoor entertaining area at the same level as the interior floors. The space would have to accommodate groups not to exceed 30 persons. Approximate size would be at least 10' × 20' or 200 sq. ft.

3. Install accent plantings such as ground covers, shrubs, and small trees to complement the established shade trees. Turf was not a main priority as the yard was small and shady which reduced the quality and effectiveness of turf.

4. If possible, block cold winter winds from the north and west. Provide shade for the house and outdoor areas from the south and southwest areas of the site to block hot western sun of summer yet allow the sun warmth in winter months.

5. Allow space for a possible room addition, most likely off the kitchen/dining room areas.

6. Consider a child's play area (future development, no children presently).

Front Entry Requirements

1. Remove the grape vine and resultant dead Douglas fir.

2. Eliminate the turf on the embankment which made mowing difficult.

3. Consider the removal of all turf eventually due to the shady location and long and narrow shape of the front yard which parallels the sidewalk and street.

4. Establish partial visual screens and buffers to separate the street view and noises from the front of the house. Create some foreground for the stark entry yet allow the winter sun to reach active living areas, primarily the living room which has the most window space south to southwest.

5. Develop a planting theme. Include ground covers and small shrubs consistent with sunlight available; also provide seasonal interests such as fall color, spring flower and winter contrasts.

6. Develop a unified site design that repeats the forms and materials established in the rear yard.

In review, the site inventory, analysis, and client program phases of the site planning and landscape design identify and organize what is existing and what is to be designed.

The basic site planning considerations included (1) the microclimatic conditions (seasonal sun and winds), (2) the need for an outdoor space or spaces more integrated physically and visually with interiors, and (3) a phased development to service immediate needs yet working towards a total master plan. After identification of the vegetation that was to remain or be removed, planning focused on the development areas identified in the site analysis (Figure 11-6) and conceptual plan (Figure 11-7). Preliminary design schemes (functional diagrams) were developed for the entire site and then enlargements were used to detail the priority areas; the garage/rear yard area, the entry, and so on. (See Figures 11-8 and 11-9 for these concept sketches.)

To effectively design and develop any aspect of the landscape, the landscape designer must understand the site as a whole. All too often landscape design is approached as the development of single components such as a deck, a bench, a planting bed, where the sum of the parts does not provide a "total composition." Through planning and design, an overall concept and theme is established from which component parts can be selected for installation, thus working towards the completion of a total composition, a *site master plan* (Figure 11-10).

After understanding the program requirements, fixed site elements, priorities, and the site's overall limits and opportunities, the landscape architect or designer next develops design alternatives. At this stage of design, program elements are given site locations, areas, and shapes as related to the site analysis and client's needs.

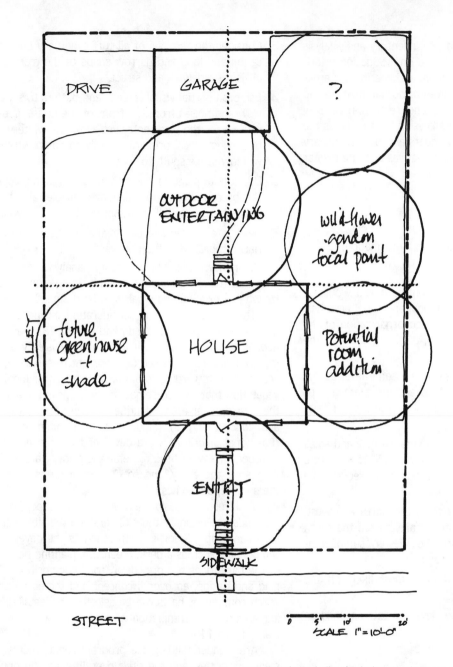

FIGURE 11-7

As a basic guideline to the development of specific areas within a landscape setting, a concept plan may be used. This is a planning tool that establishes the areas where specific design elements are to be located. The site inven-tory analysis and client's design needs serve as the basis for decision making. This drawing is only a planning document and thus is very loose and informal in its presentation. (Designer: Gregory M. Pierceall)

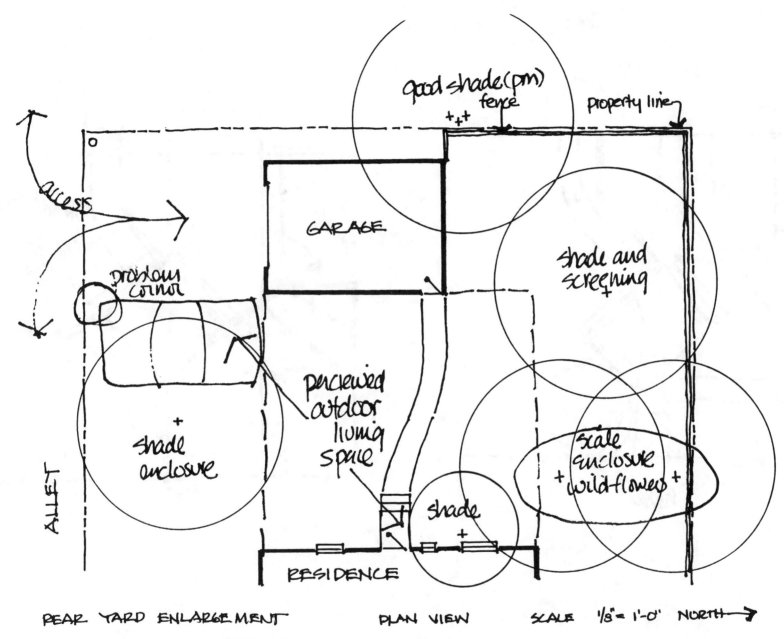

good shade (pm)
fence
property line

GARAGE

shade and
screening

previous
corner

access

ALLEY

shade
enclosure

perceived
outdoor
living
space

shade

scale
enclosure
wildflowers

RESIDENCE

REAR YARD ENLARGEMENT   PLAN VIEW   SCALE ⅛"=1'-0" NORTH →

FIGURE 11-8(a)

Preliminary sketches are then more detailed drawings which follow the development of the concept plan. (Designer: Gregory M. Pierceall)

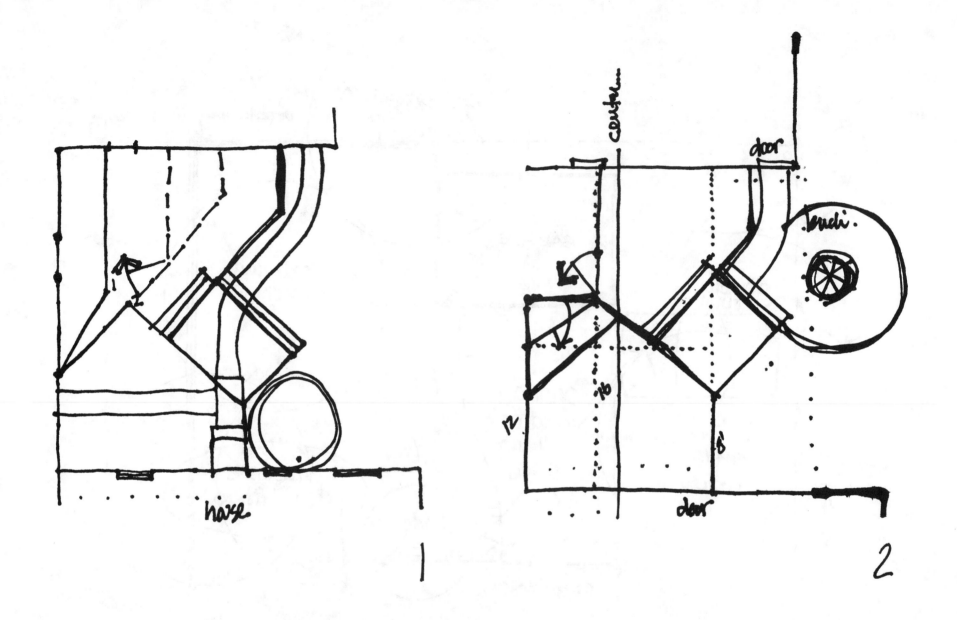

FIGURE 11-8(b)
Preliminary sketches. (Designer: Gregory M. Pierceall)

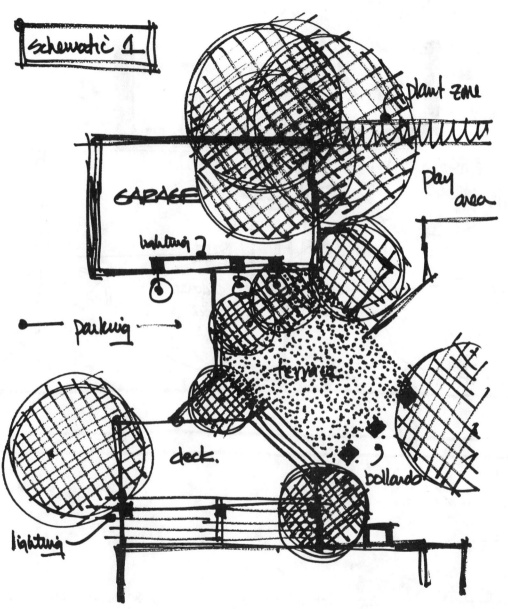

Schematic 1

plant zone

GARAGE

lighting?

play area

parking

terrace

deck.

bollards

lighting

FIGURE 11-8(c)
Preliminary sketches. (Designer: Gregory M. Pierceall)

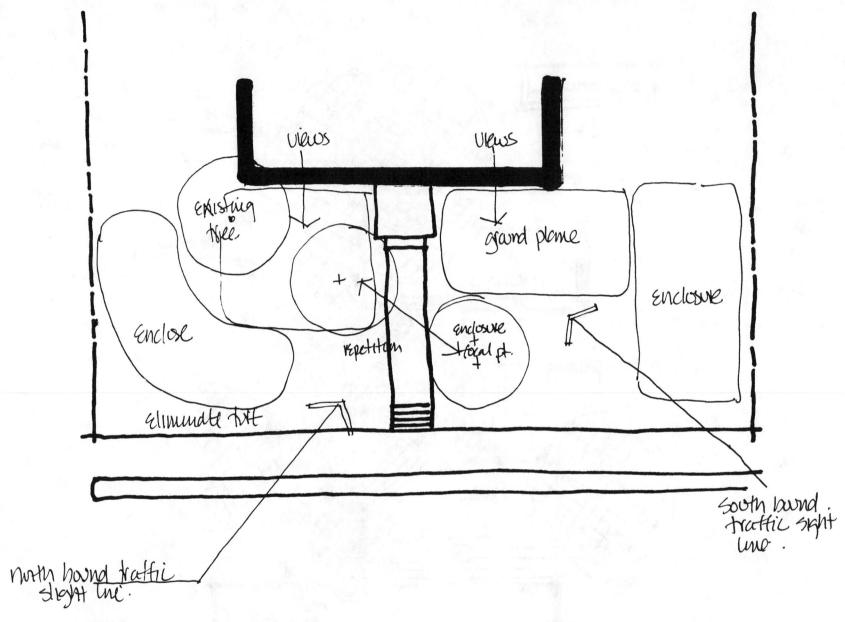

views

views

Existing tree.

grand plane

Enclose

Enclose

repetition

enclosure + focal pt.

enclosure + focal pt.

Enclosure

Eliminate turf

South bound traffic sight line.

North bound traffic sight line.

FIGURE 11-9

After the site has been organized relative to anticipated use areas (the concept plan), each area can then be developed further as to the form, shape, and detail to be included. From the concept to the final master plan stage of refinement, many preliminary sketches are generated using varied line, composition, and material ideas from which an ideal or combination of ideas will be selected. (Designer: Gregory M. Pierceall)

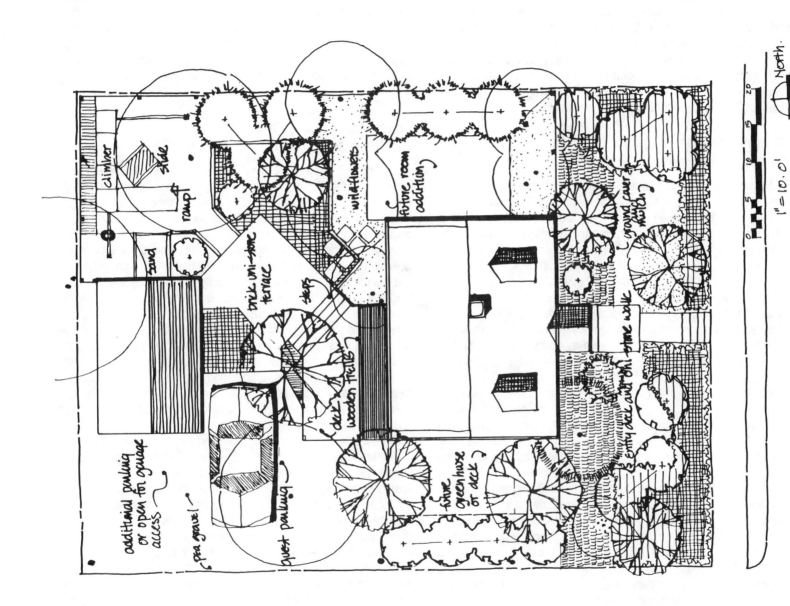

Labels within the plan:
- climber slide
- ramp
- sand
- brick uni-stone terrace
- steps
- deck + wooden trellis
- additional parking or open for garage access
- spa gravel
- guest parking
- future greenhouse or deck
- wildflowers
- future room addition
- ground cover mulch
- only deck and other stone walk

1" = 10.0'

North.

FIGURE 11-10

This final master plan is the result of the early steps of the design process including the inventory, analysis, conceptual plans, and preliminary sketches. It should be noted that a master plan is only as definite as the moment in which it was developed. Often, as time passes, the clients' needs change, thus modification to the master plan is required. (Designer: Gregory M. Pierceall)

The resulting site master plan shows the total site design from which phasing is determined by designer making recommendations reflecting the client's priorities. Figure 11-11 shows a section/elevation of the south edge of the proposed site plan. Before final details and construction begin, local building codes and regulations are checked to determine their effects on the proposed landscape construction and plantings. As a point of reference, these legal concerns should be part of the site inventory and program development to avoid a total revision late in the design process.

Construction Phase One: The Deck and Garage/Parking Area

The first priority for renovation and construction was the site area immediately between the rear of the house, garage and alley. The limited off-street parking, awkward back door steps, and the visually and physically unsuitable area for entertaining prompted the development of a deck and interfacing guest parking area. (See Figures 11-12, 11-13, 11-14, and 11-15.) In the design of this area, the fixed physical elements of the alley access, garage and rear door locations collectively defined the zones the parking and entertaining areas would take. At any design scale and especially when designing small site areas, the designer has to understand the location and interrelationships of fixed elements such as doors, windows, and access prior to designing of any additional site features. In this parking/deck area, the two design elements had to be unified as they would share a common edge, as can be seen in the master plan. Figures 11-12 through 11-15 show that the first construction phase was completed in three days by the client; material costs were $900. The wood deck physically and visually extends the rear yard utility by providing an entertaining area at the same level as interior rooms. The overhead trellis attached to the house provides visual and physical transition, scale for the deck area, and partial shade as it is next to the otherwise strong vertical dimension of the two-story house. Viewed from the back door, the overhead trellis also focuses views downward, away from the otherwise apparent alley power lines. The 2"×2" lattice which composes the trellis provides summer shade and an ideal location for hanging seasonal plants. The wide bench which edges the open side of the deck functions to provide seating and as a railing. The diagonal angle of the wide steps provides visual and physical directional keys toward the main yard space. These wide steps also provide extra seating when needed. The expanded parking area allows a guest to park some-

what parallel to the garage, yet the garage door is accessible. Previous to the redesign, cars had to park perpendicular to the garage door, thus causing conflicts in and out of the garage. The existing trees to the west edge of the property were retained because they provide good summer shade, blocking the hot western sun. Additional plantings were added in the parking area to shade the cars and to provide additional shade for the deck area.

Construction Phase Two: The Terrace and Playspace Construction

As the outdoor deck area developed, the clients found themselves expecting a child, thus changing their next design priorities and directions. Phase two of their master plan was then altered to include development of a paved area off the deck and a playspace. In the original program development for the "rear yard," a child's play area was considered, yet no requirements had been established. Now with a change in design direction, the paved area, playspace, and plantings would have to be visually or physically tied together with the existing deck. In the initial site survey, the existing walk, 18" wide, and rear yard turf were considered inadequate. The walk was too narrow and inconveniently located and the condition of the turf was poor. A paved area was selected as a design component to physically and visually extend the deck out into the yard. In this location it could provide unified circulation from the parking to the deck and garage areas and tie the various site areas together. This central paved terrace could provide a multipurpose, overflow area for the deck, unified circulation, and potential for "wheel toy" uses as the needs of a growing child and family expand.

A brick paving surface for its ease in construction and visual appeal was finally selected and constructed to extend from the deck area out into the yard both physically and visually (Figures 11-16, 11-17 and 11-18). Brick was used to add visual texture, color, and a more human scale. Brick's flexibility was also a consideration in that if an area would have to be dug up to service utilities, it can easily be reinstalled. While providing a multi-purpose space, the brick also replaced poor quality turf and covered the inadequate walk, both of which did not serve the needs of the clients. Overall, the paved brick terrace unifies and provides access to other rear yard elements surrounding its perimeter. The clients installed the terrace in three days at a cost of $350 for materials, which included the interlocking paver and sand base.

WEST–EAST SECTION/ELEVATION

 North.

FIGURE 11-11

The south section/elevation helps the client to understand what the alley
view of the proposal will look like. (Designer: Gregory M. Pierceall)

FIGURE 11-12

Basic construction sequence involved in the installation of the rear yard deck, Phase One. (Before)

FIGURE 11-13

Basic construction sequence involved in the installation of the rear yard deck, Phase One. (During deck construction)

FIGURE 11-14

Basic construction sequence involved in the installation of the rear yard deck, Phase One. (During deck construction)

FIGURE 11-15

Basic construction sequence involved in the installation of the rear yard deck, Phase One. (After)

FIGURE 11-16
Terrace installation, Phase Two, of the rear yard's development. (Before)

FIGURE 11-17
Terrace installation, Phase Two, of the rear yard's development. (Base preparation)

FIGURE 11-18
Terrace installation, Phase Two, of the rear yard's development. (After)

(a)

(b)

FIGURE 11-19

During Phase Two, the playspace area was developed after the terrace was established. The photos show the before and after of the playspace. Note the efficient and safe circulation pattern established between the ramp and slide. For a supervising adult, a child can be easily helped up the ramp and down the slide with minimal running front to back as often occurs in traditional play equipment.

The playspace adjoining the brick terrace area was designed and constructed to provide an opportunity for "on-site" play since "tot lots" were not within a realistic distance from the house for frequent use. Since the early developing years of children are often spent around the home, the design and development of the playspace in the master plan were scaled for the ages ranging from one to six years old. (Figure 11-19 shows what the playspace area looked like before and after.) The playspace area rests in the shade and understory of the existing maple with a surfacing bed of practical and "imaginative" pea gravel. The ramp, platform, and slide organization is such that helpful parents can stand at the center of the action and assist small ones up the ramp and down the slide with minimal movement. The remaining activities include swinging, climbing, and sand play.

The playspace was built by the client using recycled and new lumber materials. The proposal developed by the client took approximately four days to construct costing $400. The cost may seem excessive, yet if you consider the life expectancy of the project (approximately ten years) and the valuable "play" experience it provides, the benefits outweigh the expenditures. The considerations for playspace design are included in the following paragraphs. A conceptual residential playspace design can be seen in Figure 11-20.

In the design of a playspace, the proper ground surfacing material is the primary safety consideration in conjunction with the appropriate selection of play apparatus for a child's capabilities. Selection of play structures and ground surfacings should consider: (1) the ages of the children and their play capacities; (2) the number of children the area is to accommodate; (3) the intensity of the activity in areas where falls may often occur (resilient surfacings should be used to cushion falls from apparatus); (4) maintenance; (5) costs. Before selecting play equipment for a residential space, research and reading are needed to better understand play and play environments. Some helpful hints in regards to play surfacings are as follows:

1. *Pea gravel* is a water-rounded aggregate suitable in most active areas where durability is a prime consideration. It has good surface drainage which is important if the play area is to be used directly after a rain. The sound created by small feet shifting through the gravel also makes it a play element.

   Initially, you may not consider pea gravel as an optimal surfacing; yet the ¼" rounded aggregate is more durable, resilient, cleaner, and safer than bark, sand, or turf. Installation of a depth of 4–6″ provides a stable surface that is easily trained by small feet and adults alike.

2. *Shredded hardwood bark* is a fibrous, natural material which is durable yet requires seasonal reapplications because of natural decay. It is soft and provides visual relief in the area.

3. *Sand* is a durable surface material but is limited in its use, especially when wet. Use sand under portions of climbing apparatus to cushion falls, yet do not totally surround the equipment. This separates access and play after rains. Sand also can be used as a molding element by children as part of their play experience.

4. *Turf* should be avoided as a surface covering if possible. It is appropriate for lawn games; however, it should be eliminated in active play zones because hard playing activity compacts the soil and makes it less resilient in cushioning falls. Also, intense activity makes a good stand of turf impossible and greatly increases turf maintenance.

FIGURE 11–20

In this typical residential yard, the playspace has been located within view of the house. This planning allows easy supervision by parents and a shaded location for outdoor play.

Construction Phase Three:
The Rear Yard Planting Areas

The planting area adjoining the playspace was established in "durable" ground cover. Lirope was chosen for its textural interest and daffodils were interplanted for their spring color. Included also in this focal point area are plantings of hemlocks to serve as background and screening from adjoining neighbors and for the buffering of winter winds. A flowering dogwood for spring color and accent with fall seasonal interest completes this planting area. Parallel to this defined planting bed is the existing wildflower patch, a mass of dogtooth violets, Dutchmans breeches, Solomon seal, wild geranium, and a few bluebells. The remaining space to the north of the house is left fallow as a potential site for a future room addition.

Through the redesign and development of the rear yard, the increased utility and attractiveness has resulted in a more functional space with decreased overall maintenance time. Seasonal maintenance includes raking leaves from the play area to the adjoining planting zones as mulch. Watering, fertilizing, and the average "grooming" are the other maintenance aspects. The time involved in the installation of the rear yard planting beds was approximately 1 to ½ days, at a cost of $250. Included were ground covers, mulch, and shrubs.

Construction Phase Four:
The Entry Planting and Construction

Having established the rear outdoor living areas relative to family needs, design attentions now shifted to the front yard. The primary concern of the front yard was its openness to the street, the uninviting and awkward entry sequence, and the lack of scale and enclosure. From a practical standpoint, the shallow depth of the front yard (20 feet × 60 feet) and turfed slope provided no functional use. The turf was removed in favor of wintergreen euonymus, a broadleaf evergreen ground cover. The slope was then mulched with shredded hardwood bark to conserve moisture and reduce erosion. Since the installation and establishment of the ground cover and mulch, maintenance has been greatly reduced, and visual interest from the street is much improved. To help enclose, screen, buffer, and scale the entry from the street, native redbuds were selected, in addition to sourwoods and yellow birch for varied seasonal interest and contrasts. The remaining Douglas fir at the southeast corner of the house provided shade to the planting area south of the entry. Ivy was planted in this shady site in contrast to the myrtle in the sunnier location north of the entry. For additional seasonal interest and color variations, deciduous azaleas, bayberries, and viburnums were installed. These plants proviced a contrast to the ground cover base plane and complemented the entry sequence (Figure 11-20).

The straight sidewalk alignment was most realistic in the small entry space. In redesign, the concrete walk was resurfaced with brick pavers similar to the rear yard terrace. Brick was selected to unify the total site design. It also provided a more intimate and scaled surface. The awkward entry stoop was covered with a wooden deck which was consistent with the decking materials in the rear yard. Figures 11-21 and 11-22 compare the entry area both before and after redesign. The deck and brick additions have created a more functional, comfortable, and attractive entry for guests. The entry is also more attractive to passersby.

The entry area redevelopment was phased over the span of a year, from fall to fall. The initial work included planting the ground cover on the bank and establishment of small trees to provide foreground, enclosure, and spring interest. The following spring, additional ground covers and shrubs were added to the planting zones for contrast and to provide varied seasonal color. Included were the ivy, myrtle, and rhododendrons. During the summer, the remaining strip of turf on the upper terrace was removed and replaced with shredded bark. The elimination of the turf further reduced maintenance and made the establishing ground cover areas more visually pronounced. The final stage of the entry development involved construction of the entry deck and bricked walk. The total cost of materials over the development period of one year was $1,000. Installation was again completed by the client.

THE LANDSCAPE ENVIRONMENT

To date, the appearance and utility of the site have changed dramatically from the "jungle" beginnings to a unified site design. The existing, mature trees continue to provide scale, background, and shade as new plantings are establishing seasonal contrasts, screening, enclosure, and energy efficiency to the landscape. As the clients reflect on the money and hard work involved in their landscape design and development, they realize that it is these details that make their house a home. The reality of the landscape that has evolved is the result of *their needs* and the *inherent sites limits* and *opportunities*. See Figures 11-23, 11-24, and 11-25. The evaluation of what

1" = 10.0'

North

entry deck and old stone walk   ground cover and mulch

FIGURE 11-21

The entry of this residence has changed dramatically from its "jungle" beginnings (see Figure 11-1). The entry area was developed after the rear yard space in Phase Three of the master plan. The remaining areas to be developed include the spaces immediately north and south of the residence.

FIGURE 11-22

The construction involved in the entry redevelopment included an entry deck, new walk, and steps. The redesign not only made the entry visually more attractive and functional but repeated materials and forms established in the rear yard which helps create a more unified site design.

FIGURE 11-23

One design detail included in the deck development is the overhead lattice. The lattic extends 4' from the house and is 7.5' above the deck surface. This feature helps focus one's view downward when exiting the house. It also scales down the two-story rear elevation. The lattice provides partial shade to interior rooms in summer and a framework for hanging plants.

FIGURE 11-24

Neighbors' view. When developing a residential site, it is important to understand the surrounding activities and views onto the site. During winter the site is open to the neighbors' views yet this same vantage is blocked when the trees are in leaf.

(a)

(b)

FIGURE 11-25

In this residential situation, the site development was an integral part of the total remodeling process. The room addition and new entry walk were designed as a unit rather than as separate architecture and landscape architectural proposals. Photos (a) and (c) are the before images and (b) and (d) are the after photos of the addition and entry sequence. (Photos courtesy of R. Rolley)

(c)

(d)

was existing, their landscape needs, priorities, and surrounding site influences have developed into a designed living environment rather than a collection of unrelated landscape features.

REFERENCES AND READINGS

Clay, Grady. *Landscapes for Living.* New York: McGraw-Hill, 1980.

Hannebaum, Leroy. *Landscape Design: A Practical Approach.* Reston, VA: Reston Publishing Co., 1981.

Landscape Architectural Magazine, 1982, "The Home Landscape." Louisville, KY: Publications Board, ASLA.

Landscape Architectural Magazine, 1981, "The Home Landscape," Louisville, KY: Publications Board, ASLA.

Landscape Architectural Magazine, 1980, "The Home Landscape," Louisville, KY: Publications Board, ASLA.

Moffat, Schiler. *Landscape Design That Saves Energy.* New York: Wm. Morrow & Co., 1981.

Nelson, William R. *Planting Design: A Manual of Theory.* Champaign, IL.: Stipes Publishing Co., 1979.

_____ . *Landscaping Your Home.* Urbana, IL: University of Illinois Extension, 1975.

Readers Digest Association. *Practical Guide to Home Landscaping.* Pleasantville, NY: Readers Digest Association, 1972.

Robinette, G. O. *Landscape Planning for Energy Conservation.* Reston, VA: Environmental Design Press, 1977.

_____ . *Plants/People/and Environmental Quality.* Washington, D.C.: U.S. Department of Publications, 1972.

Smyser, Carol A. *Natures Design.* Emmaus, PA.: Rodale Press Book, 1982.

Walker, T. D. *Residential Landscaping I.*: West Lafayette, IN: PDA Publishers, 1982.

_____ . *Site Design and Construction Detailing.* West Lafayette, IN: PDA Publishers, 1978.

Wilson, Wilson, Ilusty. *Planning and Designing Your Home Landscape.* Madison, WI.: University of Wisconsin Extension, 1981.

Residential site planning

Residential landscape design is diverse in that it may in-volve site improvements such as landscape construction and plant-ings for an established residence or for a new home or siting rec-ommendations for the development of a residence on a selected property. As a landscape designer, use of a design process provides a procedure that applies to a wide range of design situations. In res-idential scale landscape design, or any site development, site plan-ning should be the basis of a functional, useful, and visually attrac-tive proposal.

Site planning has long been accepted by landscape architects and is their primary activity in developing site proposals. Ideally, res-idential site development through the design process allows the client, designer, and contractor an opportunity to determine the structural, physical, and visual relationships between the residence, site, surroundings, and climatic influences before final design and siting decisions are made. Through the design planning process, al-ternatives and options can be tested as to their feasibility and desir-ability. The basic process of site planning attempts to adapt the client's needs and priorities to meet the limits and opportunities of the site and, conversely, to adapt the site to meet the design objectives of the client. As an example of the design process, a residential site planning proposal will be examined. In this feasibility study, the clients wanted to determine if a selected site was realistic for the development of a residence that suited their family needs and lifestyle.

RESIDENTIAL DESIGN PROCESS

This feasibility study was developed by a student in landscape architecture as the final project in an introductory site planning and landscape design course. The objective of this feasibility study is to determine the possible siting of selected residences and specific outdoor family activities on a defined site. In contrast to the landscape design example of Chapter 11, this case study uses the design process to site a new residence and site features. Features to be located include the residence, garage, entry, outdoor living area and service areas in conjunction with landscape construction and plantings. One overall objective is to determine the optimal area for the residence and related use areas on the site. The location of the entry should also reflect the physical and visual interrelationships of the interior and exterior of the residence, the site, and eventual user needs. While reviewing this project, please be aware of the design process, site and client considerations, and graphic presentation used in developing the proposal.

The design process used in development of this package is outlined in Chapter 8. This design process or sequence is comprised of eight steps divided into five basic stages or phases. *Phase One* includes the problem statement and the design program. These identify what function and character the eventual proposal should take. In the example here this phase comprises the first three steps of the design process discussed in Chapter 8. *Phase Two* is defining and evaluating the physical and visual characteristics of the site, surroundings, neighborhood, and the local climatic and regional environmental data. This phase of the design sequence relates to steps four and five of the design process. *Phase Three* is the synthesis of the program and the site analysis information that has been collected. This phase combines Phases One and Two by adapting the design program to meet the site considerations and conversely, adapting the site to meet program objectives. This synthesis or combining of information is step six of the design process. *Phase Four*, which is the master plan stage, represents step seven of the design

process. At this stage of development, the designer gives the use areas and concepts developed in the synthesis stage more definite form and shape and describes materials, textures, and colors. This detailing is the final stage that is reviewed and refined before construction drawings are developed. *Phase Five* of the design sequence is the eighth step of the design process. If program changes occur or other site or design information becomes available, this step of the process allows new information to be added into the design. In the example to be shown, the master plan was evaluated by the clients in terms of the construction opportunities and utility. A few changes did result and are found in the construction package that follows the site planning proposal. The objectives of the proposal were (1) to express one's knowledge and understanding of the design process of site planning and landscape design at a residential scale; (2) to express one's interpretation of a defined design problem; (3) to experience working with a "real world" site and client; and (4) to produce the required graphics to complete a site development proposal. A base survey sheet and a statement of client needs and priorities were given to the student, and from this information the site design proposal and package were developed.

Background Information: The Client

Mr. and Mrs. Robert Moss purchased a home site in an established neighborhood because of its central location to community facilities, school, and employment. (Figure 12-1 is a site location map.) Building a new home in town had the potential advantage of reduced transportation costs resulting from the clients' being able to walk rather than drive to work and school. The Mosses needed an efficient home and landscape that better served their individual family needs. Basic considerations to be included in their new home were more energy efficiency and a strong interaction between indoor and outdoor activities.

The Moss family includes the parents and two children, aged five and seven, and a small dog. Their needs will be changing as the children grow. Initially, an enclosed yard would be needed for the children and dog. A specific activity area for the children would also be desirable. As the children grow and family needs change, the total site could be used for recreation, limited only by the site's size and shape. Generally, the family's needs include flexible site spaces that can provide multiple uses. The following is a list of design programs initially considered and defined by the designer through client interviews. Figure 12-2 is the title sheet developed for the Moss residence.

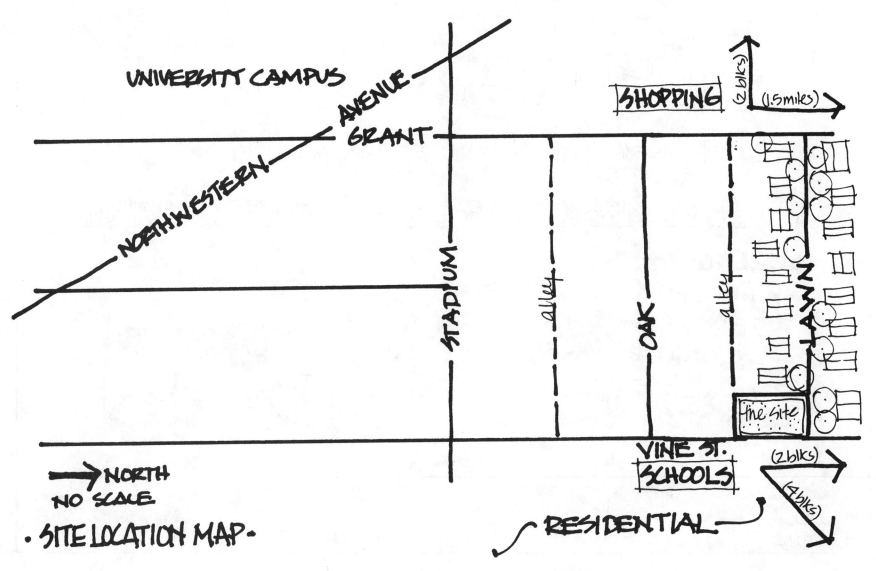

UNIVERSITY CAMPUS

NORTHWESTERN

AVENUE

GRANT

SHOPPING

(2 blks)

(1.5 miles)

STADIUM

alley

OAK

alley

LAWN

the site

NORTH
NO SCALE

• SITE LOCATION MAP •

VINE ST.
SCHOOLS

RESIDENTIAL

(2 blks)

(4 blks)

FIGURE 12-1
Site location map. (Designer: Gregory M. Pierceall)

RESIDENTIAL
LANDSCAPE DESIGN
FOR MR AND MRS R. MOSS—LAWN ST. AT VINE, W.LAF., IN.

SCHEDULE OF SHEETS

1. TITLE SHEET
2. SITE SURVEY & ANALYSIS
3. DESIGN PROGRAM
4. DESIGN SYNTHESIS
5. MASTER PLAN
6. ELEVATIONS/SKETCHES
7. ELEVATIONS/SKETCHES
8. CROSS SECTIONS/DETAILS

LA 216, SEC. 2	RESIDENTIAL SITE PLANNING	MR. & MRS. R. MOSS
PROJECT #8108	AND LANDSCAPE DESIGN	W.LAF., IN. SHEET 1 OF 8
JOHN LANE FALL 1981		TITLE SHEET

FIGURE 12-2
Title sheet, site planning proposal. (Designer: John Lane)

Residential Design Program

General exterior site spaces adjoining a residence:

1. Visual and physical interaction between interior and exterior spaces. Especially consider the interaction between active interior areas such as the living room/dining room, and kitchen. Bedroom and bathroom areas need not have strong indoor/outdoor relationships.

2. Maximize the opportunity for indoor activities outdoors by including areas such as decks, terraces, patios. These outdoor activity areas should be sunny in winter and shady in summer. If possible, site daytime interior activity areas, kitchen, and living areas to maximize the sun in winter.

3. Try to shelter inside and outdoor use areas from the harsh winter winds to reduce their cooling effects, yet allow the possibility for summer breezes to reduce cooling needs in summer.

4. Depending on where the house and related rooms are oriented, attempt to screen undesirable views and develop any promising views or vistas.

5. Evaluate the existing vegetation as to the opportunity to provide shade, enclosure, privacy, as well as for durability and interest in relation to interior and exterior use areas.

Specific site design requirements:

1. On-site parking for two family cars (garage or carport), and two on-site guest parking spaces; these can be included in the drive area adjoining the garage or carport.

2. A portion of the rear yard should be physically enclosed to keep the children and dog from running into the street and traffic. The fencing may be solid or open, using board or wire materials, or possibly a combination of the two with plantings as a visual break.

3. A child's play area approximately 300 square feet within view of the active areas inside the house (kitchen, living/dining) and yard.

4. An informal entertaining area related directly to the active interior living areas. This area would be used two to three times monthly for about 25 to 30 persons maximum. Some permanent seating would be desirable in the form of a planter wall. Also, night lighting and a fire pit would be desirable.

5. A small seating area for family dinners outdoors. This area could be with or adjoining the informal entertaining area. A table and chairs would most likely be used.

6. An open turf area for volleyball, badminton, or running. This area need not be regulation size.

7. Vegetable garden approximately 500 square feet; it should include a compost area for leaves, etc. This use area should be located near the garage for tool storage yet easily accessed from the kitchen if possible.

8. Service area and storage needed; if the proposed home has a fireplace, firewood storage space also needed.

9. Trash can storage near or in garage.

This is the basic needs and priorities list developed by the client. As a site planner, these use areas should be defined in terms of the minimum space needed and the physical or visual relationships between these site components. Figure 12-3 is the design program sheet prepared for the design proposal. In the proposal, the design program relationships were evaluated through the use of a compatibility matrix. Another option in defining program relationships is a *bubble diagram*, often called a *functional diagram*. (Figure 12-4 shows a functional diagram of the matrix analysis.)

Definition and Evaluation

THE SITE. The undeveloped property attracted the clients' attention because it was available in an established neighborhood and had existing vegetation that encompassed the site. Figure 12-5 is the combined site survey and analysis sheet. The site is a rectangle with its longest edge running north/south and its narrowest edge east to west. The site is $170' \times 60'$ and approximately 10,200 square feet. The topography is a gradual slope from north to south with a grade change of 3.5' from north to south property lines. The north edge of the site adjoining the sidewalk is steep and eroding. The lowest point on the site is the southwest corner which probably has seasonal puddling during rainy periods.

In evaluating the site's topography, it is the landform that is the base of the proposal to be developed. The landform shape is such that if a building were located at the upper end of the property, it could include a walk-out basement if desired. In any siting of a residence, the slope changes will have to be taken into consideration to develop safe access and proper surface drainage. Soils are well

PROJECT DEFINITION

MR. AND MRS. R. MOSS HAVE PURCHASED A PROPERTY IN WEST LAFAYETTE TO CONSTRUCT A HOME. ALONG WITH THEIR SITE THEY HAVE PRESENTED EXAMPLES OF THE HOMES IN WHICH THEY ARE INTERESTED. AS A LANDSCAPE ARCHITECT, I AM TO REVIEW ALL ASPECTS OF THE SITE & GENERATE A MASTER PLAN UTILIZING THE MOST DESIREABLE HOME. THE MASTER PLAN SHOULD REFLECT CONDITIONS OF THE SITE, THE NEIGHBORHOOD, AND THE ENVIRONMENT AS WELL AS THE CLIENTS NEEDS. THE SOLUTION TO BE SUBMITTED FOR REVIEW SHOULD BE A SITE PLAN SHOWING EXISTING AND PROPOSED FEATURES OF THE SITE. SUPPORT DOCUMENTS INCLUDING SURVEY, ANALYSIS, SCHEMATICS, ETC. WILL ALSO BE ATTACHED.

PROJECT ANALYSIS

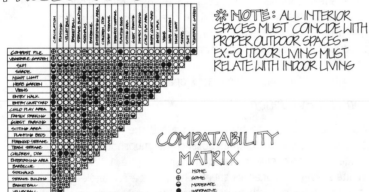

✳ NOTE: ALL INTERIOR SPACES MUST COINCIDE WITH PROPER OUTDOOR SPACES - EX. - OUTDOOR LIVING MUST RELATE WITH INDOOR LIVING

COMPATABILITY MATRIX

○ NONE
⊕ SOME
◍ MODERATE
● IMPERATIVE

DESIGN OBJECTIVE: IS TO CREATE A FUNCTIONAL AND AESTHETICALLY PLEASING LANDSCAPE THAT MEETS CLIENTS NEEDS.

PROJECT RESEARCH

THE SITE IS LOCATED ON VINE STREET JUST OFF LAWN STREET IN WEST LAFAYETTE. THE NEIGHBORHOOD IS RESIDENTIAL, HOUSING PERMANENT RESIDENTS AS WELL AS STUDENTS. THE MOSS'S DESIGN PROGRAM LIST INCLUDES:

- A ENTRY WALK WITH SAFETY AND ACCENT LIGHTING - POSSIBLY AN ENTRY COURTYARD. - VISUAL AND PHYSICAL INTERACTION BETWEEN INTERIOR AND EXTERIOR SPACES. - MAXIMIZE DESIREABLE AND MINIMIZE UNDESIREABLE ENVIRONMENTAL INFLUENCES. - SCREEN ANY BAD VIEWS AND TREAT ANY SITE PROBLEMS OR NUISANCES. - TAKE ADVANTAGE OF ALL GOOD VIEWS; HIGHLIGHT WITH PLANTING ADDITIVES. - PARKING FOR TWO FAMILY CARS. - SMALL SITTING AREA FOR FOUR TO SIX PEOPLE. - AN AREA FOR ENTERTAINING GUESTS. - CHILDS PLAY AREA - 15'X 20'OR 300 ◊. - VIEWS FROM KITCHEN OR REAR OF HOUSE. - AREA OR AREAS OPEN FOR SPORTS. - FLOWER AND PLANTING BEDS. - VEGETABLE GARDEN - 500 ◊. - COMPOST PILE FOR LEAVES (SCREEN). RELATE TO USE AREAS. - STORAGE FOR FIREWOOD. - TRASH STORAGE AREA. - REAR AREA ENCLOSED TO CHILDREN AND DOG - CONSIDER PARTIAL OR TOTAL ENCLOSURE FENCE AND OR PLANTINGS.

PROJECT NOTES

ALL WALKS SHOULD BE 4' WIDE; SHOULD BE A TRANSITION BETWEEN HOUSE AND YARD; ALL PARKING SPACES SHALL BE 10'X 20'; FLOWER & PLANTING BEDS SHALL INCLUDE A 50 ◊ HERB GARDEN; PARKING MUST INCLUDE 2 ON SITE GUEST SPOTS; 15' TURNING RADIUS FOR CARS; FIREWOOD STORAGE SHOULD ALLOW FOR 2 CORDS OF WOOD; TRASH STORAGE AREA SHOULD ALLOW FOR 3 30 GALLON TRASH CANS; BASKETBALL AREA, DRIVE, & GARAGE CAN ALL BE COMBINED.

LA 216, SEC. 2
PROJECT #8108
JOHN LANE FALL 1981

RESIDENTIAL SITE PLANNING AND LANDSCAPE DESIGN

MR. & MRS. R. MOSS
W. LAF. IN. SHEET OF
DESIGN PROGRAM

FIGURE 12-3

The design program describes the basic needs and priorities that have been established by the client and designer. These design elements and information are the basis for evaluation of any site proposal. (Designer: John Lane)

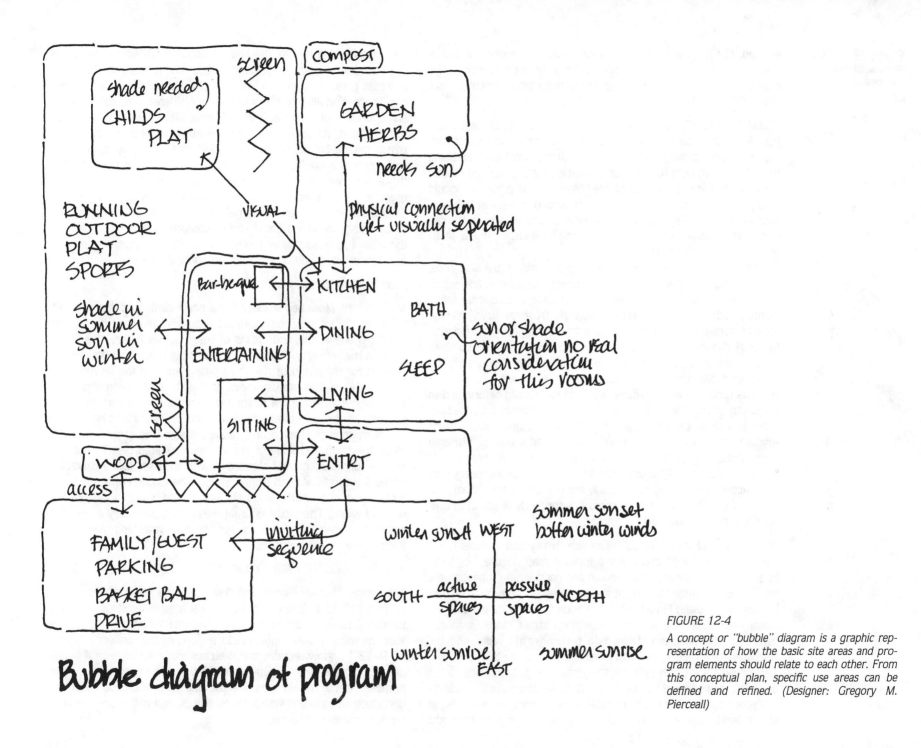

Bubble diagram of program

FIGURE 12-4

A concept or "bubble" diagram is a graphic representation of how the basic site areas and program elements should relate to each other. From this conceptual plan, specific use areas can be defined and refined. (Designer: Gregory M. Pierceall)

367

drained, and no problems are anticipated with regards to construction or plantings. The slight slope to the south would permit solar gain opportunities in the winter for activity areas oriented in a southerly direction.

CLIMATIC INFLUENCES.   The site's location is in the Midwest, thus the climate includes cold winters and hot summers. An understanding of regional climatic data is often a starting point in establishing the type of influence to consider in locating a residence and related outdoor use areas. In the temperate region, design proposals should attempt to maximize the sun in the winter and breezes in the summer while minimizing the winter winds and summer sun. In the site survey and analysis (Figure 12-5), these site specific climatic influences have been evaluated.

Microclimatic influences are also important. At the site scale, microclimate comprises the winds, breezes, sun, and shade which affect the site and its surroundings. This data and regional information, such as average rainfall, snowfall, frostfree days, average days of sunlight, and so forth are used in the planning of a site. Regional climatic information such as this can usually be obtained from a local airport or weather recording service. Site specific climatic variations have to be evaluated at the site itself.

The residence and activities requiring sun should be oriented to the south of the site. Shading devices or trees should be added for summer use where shade is needed. Site activities and interior spaces to the north will be cooler in winter and should be buffered from winter winds. The bedrooms or nondaytime use areas should face the north end of the site because sunlight is not a primary concern. Active living areas such as the living room, dining room, and kitchen if possible should be oriented in a southerly direction to benefit from passive solar gain in winter.

SURROUNDING INFLUENCES.   The site survey and analysis information (Figure 12-5) and the site location map (Figure 12-1) can be helpful in documenting influences and considerations beyond the site's physical limits. Starting at the north end of the site and moving clockwise, using Figure 12-5, the boundaries north and east are minor residential streets with the eastern street more frequently used than the northern. There is a parkway strip separating the sidewalk and property boundary from the street to the north and just a sidewalk's width between the street and property line to the east. The most logical access point off these two streets would be the southeastern corner of the site as its topography is almost at street level. The northern topography is 3.5' higher than the street and would require grading for access and visibility; thus, this is a less desirable access point for autos. The housing to the north and east is far enough away that no physical or visual conflicts occur. There is an alley to the south and a residence close to the western boundary of the site. The 10' wide alley could provide vehicular access if necessary, yet adequate turning radius would require that a garage be set back at least 15' from the alley in order to easily pull in and out. The western boundary has an existing residence sited within 6' of its property line; thus, this area has the greatest potential for physical and visual conflicts when the site is developed. However, an adjustment of window locations or the use of boundary screening could reduce conflicts at this edge. Overall, the adjoining residence and vehicular access opportunities are the only limitations resulting from the surrounding areas.

The Residence and Site Synthesis

Mr. and Mrs. Moss had selected three home plans that they thought would fit the lot size, neighborhood character, and their needs. Figure 12-6 shows the floor plans of these homes before they were sited on the property. Figure 12-7 shows the conceptual designs developed for the siting of the three base plans and the location and scale of the related site use areas. At this stage of design, the client and designer evaluate the limits and opportunities of each proposal in terms of the objectives established and the limitations of the site and surroundings. The second concept design was ranked first because the form and scale of the residence related best to the site and its surroundings and blended in with the established character of the site conditions and neighborhood. The location of active living areas indoors and out also related well to the climatic influences of sun and winds. The actual housing mass being two-story allows adequate development of the site for other activities and uses as defined in the design program.

The Site Master Plan Proposal

The master plan, developed and detailed, is the result of the design process defined by the client, site, and surroundings (Figure 12-8). Climatic influences, the location of active interior spaces and associated site use areas also influenced the siting of the residence. Figure 12-9–12-11 show sections and sketches that may be helpful in understanding the various details identified in the master plan of the proposal. In the master plan, the plantings and landscape construction features including walks, walls, fences, and patios are the now refined shapes and forms.

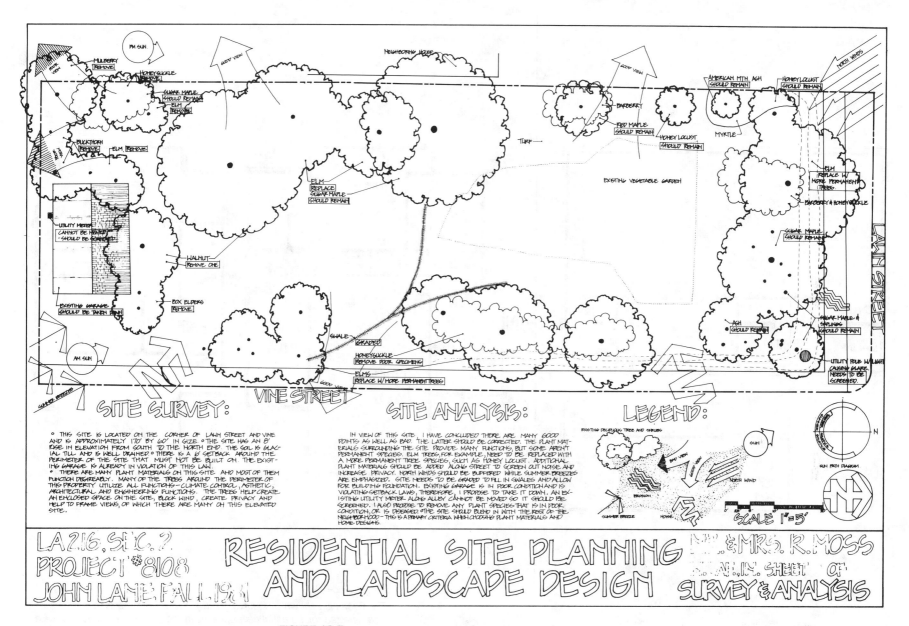

SITE SURVEY:

○ THIS SITE IS LOCATED ON THE CORNER OF LAWN STREET AND VINE AND IS APPROXIMATELY 170' BY 60' IN SIZE. ○THE SITE HAS AN 8' RISE IN ELEVATION FROM SOUTH TO THE NORTH END. THE SOIL IS GLACIAL TILL AND IS WELL DRAINED ○ THERE IS A 6' SETBACK AROUND THE PERIMETER OF THE SITE THAT MUST NOT BE BUILT ON. THE EXISTING GARAGE IS ALREADY IN VIOLATION OF THIS LAW.
○ THERE ARE MANY PLANT MATERIALS ON THIS SITE. AND MOST OF THEM FUNCTION DIFFERENTLY. MANY OF THE TREES AROUND THE PERIMETER OF THIS PROPERTY UTILIZE ALL FUNCTIONS - CLIMATE CONTROL, AESTHETIC, ARCHITECTURAL AND ENGINEERING FUNCTIONS. THE TREES HELP CREATE AN ENCLOSED SPACE ON THE SITE, BLOCK WIND, CREATE PRIVACY AND HELP TO FRAME VIEWS, OF WHICH THERE ARE MANY ON THIS ELEVATED SITE.

SITE ANALYSIS:

IN VIEW OF THIS SITE, I HAVE CONCLUDED THERE ARE MANY GOOD POINTS AS WELL AS BAD. THE LATTER SHOULD BE CORRECTED. THE PLANT MATERIALS SURROUNDING THE SITE PROVIDE MANY FUNCTIONS, BUT SOME AREN'T PERMANENT SPECIES. ELM TREES, FOR EXAMPLE, NEED TO BE REPLACED WITH A MORE PERMANENT TREE SPECIES, SUCH AS HONEY LOCUST. ADDITIONAL PLANT MATERIALS SHOULD BE ADDED ALONG STREET TO SCREEN OUT NOISE AND INCREASE PRIVACY. NORTH WINDS SHOULD BE BUFFERED WHILE SUMMER BREEZES ARE EMPHASIZED. SITE NEEDS TO BE GRADED TO FILL IN SWALES AND ALLOW FOR BUILDING FOUNDATION. EXISTING GARAGE IS IN POOR CONDITION AND IS VIOLATING SETBACK LAWS, THEREFORE, I PROPOSE TO TAKE IT DOWN. AN EXISTING UTILITY METER ALONG ALLEY CANNOT BE MOVED SO IT SHOULD BE SCREENED. I ALSO PROPOSE TO REMOVE ANY PLANT SPECIES THAT IS IN POOR CONDITION, OR IS DISEASED ○THE SITE SHOULD BLEND IN WITH THE REST OF THE NEIGHBORHOOD - THIS IS A PRIMARY CRITERIA WHEN CHOOSING PLANT MATERIALS AND HOME DESIGNS.

LEGEND:

EXISTING DECIDUOUS TREE AND SHRUBS

SUN PATH DIAGRAM

SCALE 1"=5'

LA 216, SEC. 2
PROJECT #8108
JOHN LANE FALL 1981

RESIDENTIAL SITE PLANNING AND LANDSCAPE DESIGN

MR. & MRS. R. MOSS
SHEET OF
SURVEY & ANALYSIS

FIGURE 12-5

The site survey (inventory) and analysis is a graphic record and evaluation of site conditions that will influence the eventual site development proposal. As a project's complexity and scale increase, a ready reference such as this is very helpful. (Designer: John Lane)

369

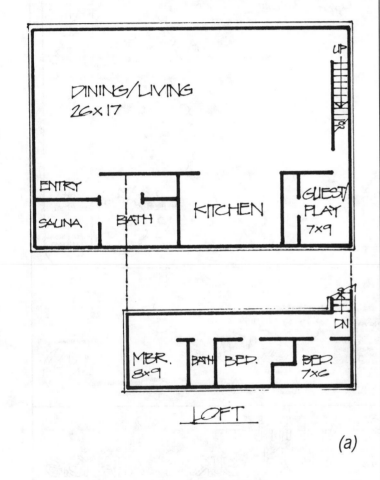

DINING/LIVING
26×17

ENTRY

SAUNA   BATH   KITCHEN   GUEST/
                                    PLAY
                                    7×9

UP

DN

LOFT

MBR.   BATH   BED.   BED.
8×9   7×6

(a)

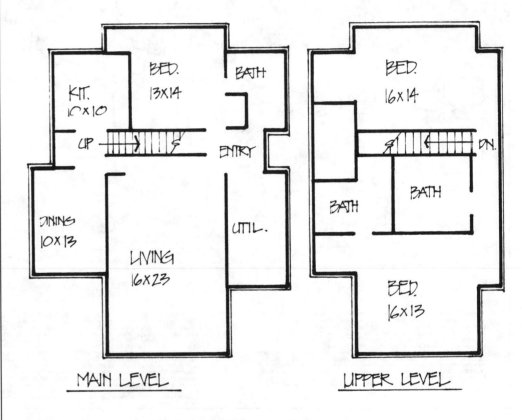

KIT.
10×10   BED.   BATH
              13×14

UP   ENTRY

DINING   UTIL.
10×13

              LIVING
              16×23

MAIN LEVEL

BED.
16×14

DN.

BATH   BATH

BED.
16×13

UPPER LEVEL

(b)

FIGURE 12-6

The floor plan shown in Figures (a), (b), and (c) are the homes the clients have selected for potential development. In the process of developing a feasibility study such as this, the designer may conceptually site each house plan on the property using the design program criteria (Figure 12-3). After a critical review of the options, the best study is selected to be developed into a detailed master plan. (Designer: Raymond Paul Strychalski)

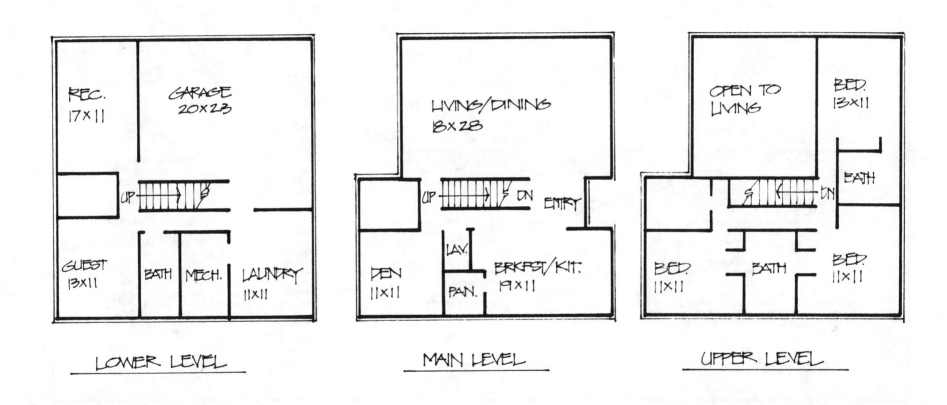

LOWER LEVEL

MAIN LEVEL

UPPER LEVEL

(C)

371

COMPACT SOLAR SALTBOX

TASTE OF TIMELESSNESS

BOXFUL OF LIGHT

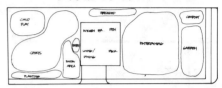

✳ NOTE – THESE THREE HOME DESIGNS WERE CHOSEN BECAUSE OF BASIC SITE FUNCTIONING.

THE COMPACT SOLAR SALTBOX IS AN ENERGY EFFICIENT, VACATION RETREAT-TYPE HOME OF 1,400 SQUARE FEET. THIS HOME DESIGN USES A PASSIVE SOLAR SYSTEM FOR HOME HEATING, THEREFORE REDUCING HEATING BILLS.

THE HOME FITS WELL ON THE SITE, WITH ITS LARGE LIVING AND DINING ROOM WINDOWS OPENING OUT TOWARDS A LARGE EXPANSE OF GROUND DESIGNATED AS THE ENTERTAINING AREA. THE SMALL FLOOR PLAN OF THE HOUSE ALLOWS FOR MUCH OF THE REMAINING AREA TO BE USED FOR SPORTS ACTIVITYS AND PLANTING USES. THE SALTBOX FITS ON THE SITE BUT DOESN'T SEEM TO FIT IN WITH THE NEIGHBORHOOD. THE HOME WAS DESIGNED MORE FOR A VACATION RETREAT INSTEAD OF A PRIMARY LIVING UNIT. THE APPEARANCE OF THE HOME IS APPEALING, BUT NOT OF THE SAME WAY AS SURROUNDING LIVING UNITS. THESE ARE SOME OF THE REASONS WHY THIS HOME WAS NOT CHOSEN.

THE TASTE OF TIMELESSNESS IS A VERY APPEALING HOME IN A MORE SUBTLE WAY THAN THE OTHER HOME DESIGNS CONSIDERED. THE HOME IS NOT PARTICULARLY "FLASHY" DESIGN, AND IT BLENDS IN WELL WITH THE OTHER HOMES IN THE AREA. THE HOUSE DESIGN IS ALSO VERY FUNCTIONAL – IN THAT IT FITS WELL ON THE HOME SITE; THE LIVING AND DINING AREAS FACE SOUTH AND OPEN OUT INTO AN ENCLOSED AREA DESIGNATED AS ENTERTAINING; THE ENTRY FACES TOWARD VINE ST. – THEREFORE MAKING IT ACCESSABLE FROM THE SIDEWALK; AND THE FLOOR PLAN ITSELF IS SMALL ENOUGH THAT THE REMAINDER OF THE SITE CAN BE UTILIZED FOR OTHER ACTIVITYS. THESE ARE SOME OF THE REASONS WHY I HAVE SELECTED THIS HOME FOR USE IN MY DESIGN. THE PRIMARY REASON BEING THE HOME BLENDS IN WELL WITH THE PRESENCE OF THE NEIGHBORHOOD.

THE BOXFUL OF LIGHT IS A VERY CONTEMPORARY AND FUNCTIONAL STRUCTURE. THE HOME IS JUST WHAT THE NAME SAYS – A BOX. HAVING SUCH A SMALL FLOOR PLAN, THE BOX FITS WELL ON SITE – ALLOWING FOR ALL THE DESIRED AREAS OF THE CLIENT. SINCE THE GARAGE IS LOCATED UNDERNEATH THE HOME, THE EXISTING BUILDING CAN BE TORN DOWN AND NOT REBUILT – ALLOWING FOR EXTRA SPACE OR THE EXISTING BUILDING COULD BE USED FOR STORAGE OR TURNED INTO A GREENHOUSE. SINCE THE NORTH SIDE OF THE HOME FEATURES A WALK OUT BASEMENT, AN EXTENSIVE AMOUNT OF EARTH MUST BE EXCAVATED DUE TO THE GRADE RISE ON THE NORTH SIDE OF THE HOUSE. ALSO A RETAINING WALL SHOULD BE BUILT FOR MAXIMUM USE OF THAT AREA AND TO CONTROL DRAINAGE. THESE ARE SOME OF THE REASONS WHY THIS HOUSE WASN'T CHOSEN.

SECOND CHOICE

FIRST CHOICE

THIRD CHOICE

LA 216, SEC. 2
PROJECT #8108
JOHN LANE FALL 1981

RESIDENTIAL SITE PLANNING
AND LANDSCAPE DESIGN

MR. & MRS. R. MOSS
W. LAF., IN. SHEET OF
DESIGN SYNTHESIS

FIGURE 12-7

Conceptual designs. A part of the feasibility study is to site the three selected homes and to define the various program areas established by the client. At this stage of the design process, the client and designer discuss the options and proceed to more refinement and details. (Designer: John Lane)

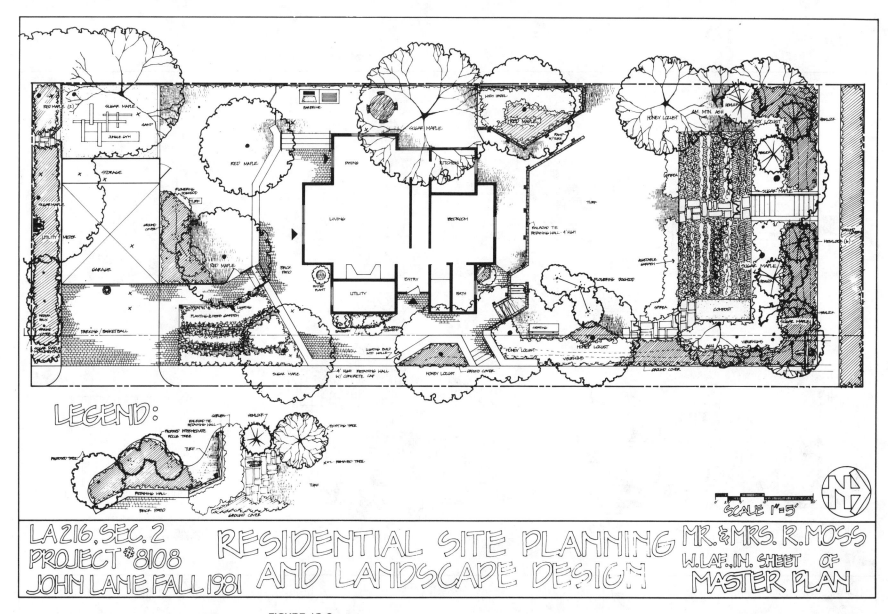

FIGURE 12-8

Site master plan. The final stage of the site planning feasibility study is the generation of an illustrative master plan and support drawings. The basic function of a feasibility study is to determine if a site and a specific program can be developed. This planning is done rather than investing a major portion of funds into construction that may not be realistic. (Designer: John Lane)

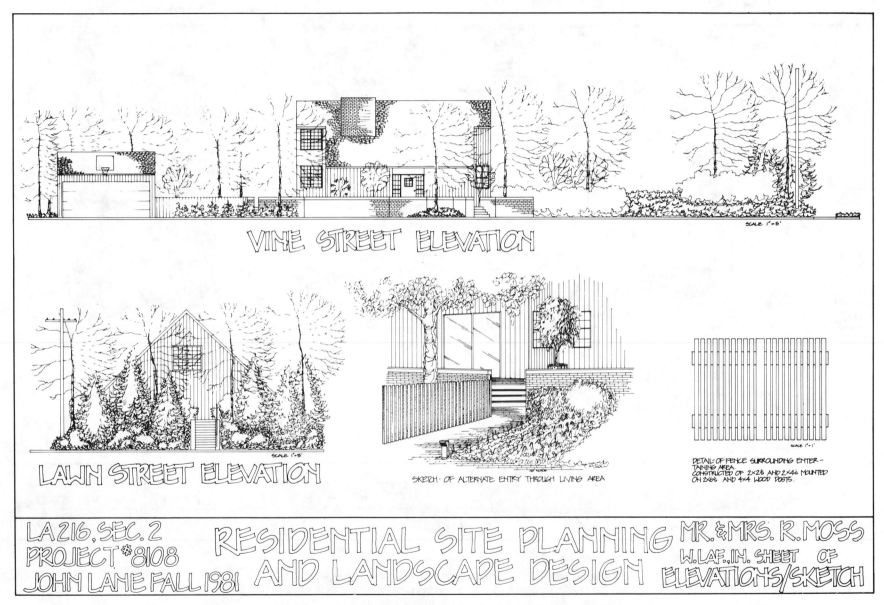

VINE STREET ELEVATION

SCALE 1"=5'

LAWN STREET ELEVATION

SCALE 1"=5'

SKETCH OF ALTERNATE ENTRY THROUGH LIVING AREA

SCALE 1"=1'

DETAIL OF FENCE SURROUNDING ENTER-
TAINING AREA.
CONSTRUCTED OF 2x2'S AND 2x4'S MOUNTED
ON 2x6'S AND 4x4 WOOD POSTS.

LA 216, SEC. 2
PROJECT #8108
JOHN LANE FALL 1981

RESIDENTIAL SITE PLANNING
AND LANDSCAPE DESIGN

MR. & MRS. R. MOSS
W. LAF., IN. SHEET OF
ELEVATIONS/SKETCH

FIGURE 12-9
Elevations/sketches. (Designer: John Lane)

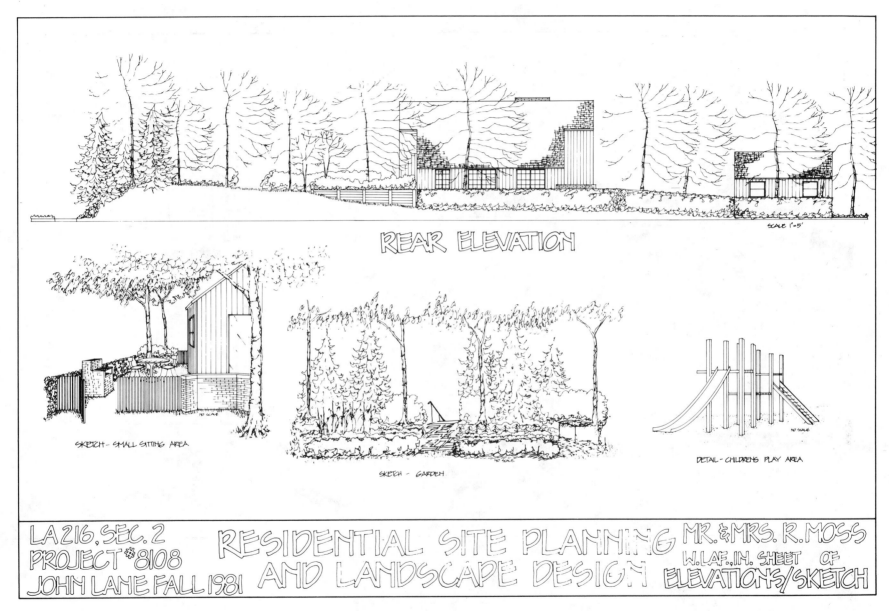

REAR ELEVATION

SCALE 1"=5'

SKETCH - SMALL SITTING AREA

SKETCH - GARDEN

DETAIL - CHILDREN'S PLAY AREA

LA 216, SEC. 2
PROJECT #8108
JOHN LANE FALL 1981

RESIDENTIAL SITE PLANNING
AND LANDSCAPE DESIGN

MR. & MRS. R. MOSS
W. LAF., IN. SHEET OF
ELEVATIONS/SKETCH

FIGURE 12-10
Elevations/sketches. (Designer: John Lane)

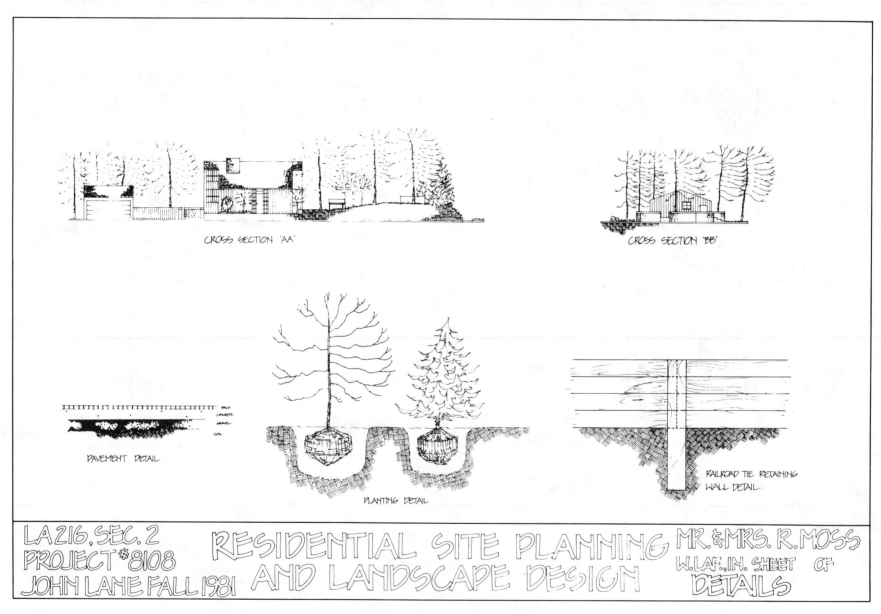

CROSS SECTION 'AA'

CROSS SECTION 'BB'

PAVEMENT DETAIL

PLANTING DETAIL

RAILROAD TIE RETAINING WALL DETAIL.

LA 216, SEC. 2
PROJECT #8108
JOHN LANE FALL 1981

RESIDENTIAL SITE PLANNING
AND LANDSCAPE DESIGN

MR. & MRS. R. MOSS
W. LAF., IN. SHEET OF
DETAILS

FIGURE 12-11
Site details. (Designer: John Lane)

The siting of the residence in the center of the property establishes two separate site areas that can function independently of each other or be used together as the need arises. The northern, upper level of the site is somewhat separated from the street due to the grade change. The garden and "sports" area then are physically and visually separated from street level activities. The design of the garden to the north is necessary to allow maximum sun and minimal shade from existing vegetation. The only possible conflict may be moisture and nutrient competition. New plantings to the south of the house are proposed to provide shade in summer yet allow the warming winter sun to penetrate south-facing windows. The southern half of the site is the proposed family and entertaining area. This area physically and visually relates to the living and dining rooms of the residence and has the least exposure with the residence to the west. This area potentially will have shade and cooling breezes from the existing and proposed deciduous trees to the south. The brick patio material was selected for the surface of the entertaining area to store some heat and warmth from the winter sun. The entry sequence to the east allows guests to park on the street or in the drive adjoining the garage. The entry physically and visually relates to the residences across the street and is sheltered from the northern and westerly winds of winter.

Overall, the plantings and landscape construction materials proposed are extensions of the residence's interior activities and located in accordance with microclimatic conditions. Because the temperate region's weather is so diverse and variable, outdoor activities such as entertaining, relaxing, or gardening will span the months April to November. Site development and use of exterior areas in the Midwest is less common than in warmer regions of the country because of seasonal limitations. Hot humid summers and cold winters dictate a need for site proposals that can provide shade and channel breezes in summer yet buffer winter winds and maximize winter sun. With these inherent characteristics, temperate zone site designs often attempt to include deciduous trees, in the southeast to western portion of a site to shade the hot western sun of summer. Deciduous trees also provide shade beneath their branches and in summer allow the southwestern breezes to cool outdoor and indoor spaces. In the west and northern areas of the site, evergreen windbreaks could provide some buffering from cold northern and western winter winds. In the master plan proposal, the level area to the north of the residence and the proposed evergreen plants help to buffer or shelter the northern end of the house. Due to the proximity of the western property line, a wooden fence rather than ev-

ergreens was suggested to provide partial shelter from the western winds and to be used in conjunction with the screening from the adjoining home. Shade trees have been specified around the eastern and southern edges of the terrace and house to provide a cool activity space for summer yet permit warmth from the winter sun to penetrate active interior living spaces. Beyond these basic considerations, the remaining plantings and construction features are designed to provide privacy, site enclosure, scale, unity, and utility to the site, residence, and use areas.

Planting and Construction Features

Starting at the site's southern edge and working north, the area along the alley is planted in ground cover and trees to enclose and define the property's edges and to shade the garage and play areas. The driveway was proposed to be brick to provide visual interest and scale and to relate to the use of brick in the immediate house area. The scale and design of the garage repeats the lines and details of the residence. The similarity of style between the garage and residence can be seen in the site elevation, Figure 12-9. When looking at the Vine Street (eastern) elevation, notice how the proposed fence attaches to the garage and is designed to visually extend the materials and line of the residence and garage together. The playspace located behind the garage is visually and physically accessible by children and parents from the yard and house. The existing trees also provide a shady location in this site area.

The turf area between the garage and brick patio is a family space. Enclosed by fences for security and privacy it also may provide an overflow area for guests using the patio area. The brick patio provides level access outdoors from indoors with steps and level changes occurring at the patio's edges. The steps relate to the site's topography and also provide a transition between two separate site use areas. Access from the garage to the house for the family would typically be within the yard, thus a brick walk has been proposed. When guests park on the street, the main entry steps at the street sidewalk bring visitors up to a midsite level. The upper site level to the north is accessed by steps adjacent to the front doorway courtyard. The visual appearance of the site from the north and northeast is that of a planted hill. The residence and garage are visible primarily from eastern and southeastern vantages. Secondary access was considered desirable at the northern edge of the site for neighbors or family. It is not intended for guest access due to the indirect sequence and the possible safety hazards at night.

The western area off the dining room is designed as a family eating area. Its physical location connects the southern rear yard and the northern turf area. Since mowers and gardening tools would be stored in the garage, this area and the proposed grassed ramp provide access to and from north to south site areas. Ease of access and maintenance thus results by considering circulation and the interrelated spaces within the site.

The proposed residence is one of many home plans found by the clients in the magazine, *Building Ideas*. Through an evaluation of the basic character and style of the home, building materials were repeated in the selection of landscape construction material to visually tie the residence and site construction together. The scale, proportion, and materials of the home and site construction also relate to the scale and character of the neighborhood and adjoining homes. The primary construction materials used were wood and brick. These were used in site design to unify the residence and site, to reinforce the sense of the landscape's total composition, and to create a feeling of warmth and human scale.

In reviewing this feasibility study, the clients found the master plan and the interrelationships of the proposed residence and site use areas desirable. The clients then decided to continue the site development process and have a *construction package* developed. The four-page construction package is actually an abbreviated version of what would be used as a total construction document. Included are only the construction features that would be included as landscape development. Sheet One of the construction package shown in Figure 12-12 is the title sheet; Sheet Two, Figure 12-13, is the dimensioning plan which shows the basic layout of distances to locate the proposed site components. You will notice slight design changes have occurred since development of the master plan proposal. Figure 12-13 shows the revised plan and the basic changes. The south patio area has been redesigned to extend to the western property line. Physically this change ties the south patio to the small eating/entertaining area off the dining room. The ground surfacing has been changed from turf to pavers with grass dividing strips to provide a more functional and durable area. The cooking area has been moved to be more centrally located between these two use areas. The steps which connect the east entry to the upper turf area have been revised to provide more logical movement. The clients eliminated the northern stair access from the plans due to the additional expense, with the option of adding them later if needed. Also, the garden rows were reoriented north/south to allow maximum sun.

FIGURE 12-12

Construction package title sheet. After a feasibility study is completed, cost estimates and building permits can be obtained if the client decides to implement the proposal. While the feasibility study determines what can be done, working drawings are required to define exactly how the project will be constructed. (Designer: John Lane)

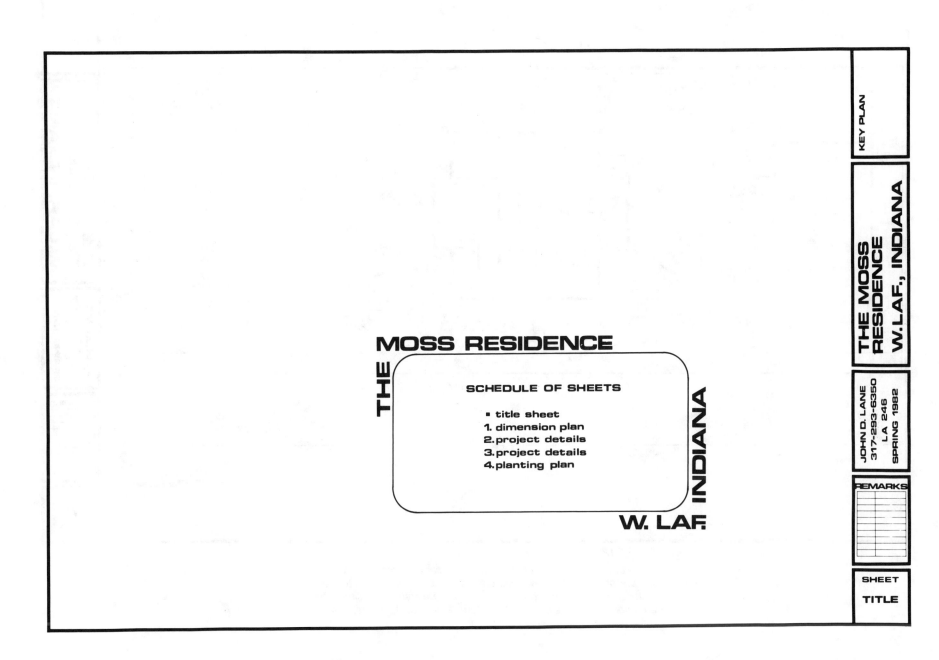

MOSS RESIDENCE

THE

INDIANA

W. LAF.

SCHEDULE OF SHEETS

- title sheet
1. dimension plan
2. project details
3. project details
4. planting plan

KEY PLAN

THE MOSS
RESIDENCE
W.LAF., INDIANA

JOHN D. LANE
317-293-6350
LA 246
SPRING 1982

REMARKS

SHEET

TITLE

379

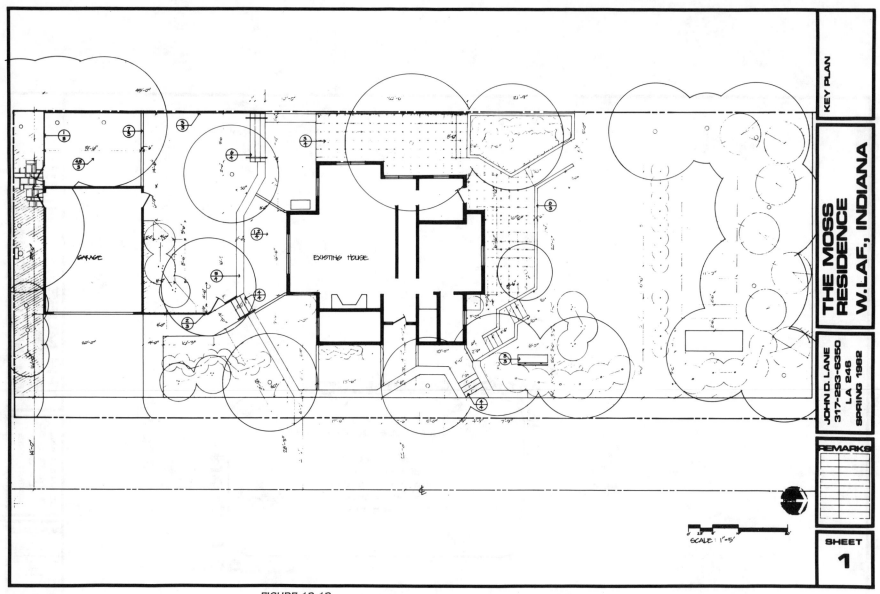

KEY PLAN

THE MOSS
RESIDENCE
W.LAF., INDIANA

JOHN D. LANE
317-293-6350
LA 246
SPRING 1982

REMARKS

SHEET
1

GARAGE

EXISTING HOUSE

SCALE: 1"=5'

FIGURE 12-13

Construction package layout. After the house has been constructed through the use of architectural working drawings, site plantings and constructed features are developed. This site layout plan illustrates how site features are to be implemented. Often site features are measured and referenced to the actual building. (Designer: John Lane)

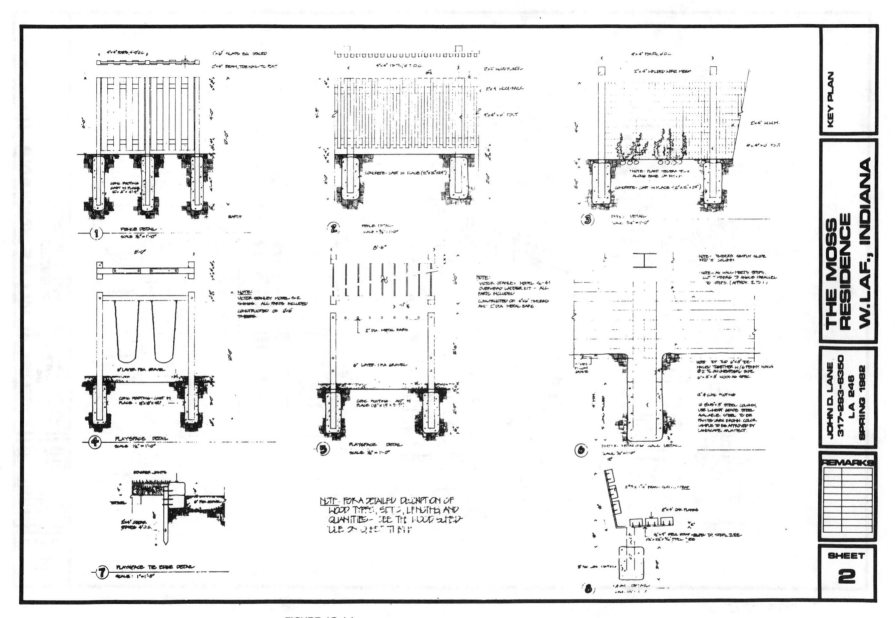

FIGURE 12-14

Construction package details, wooden features. (Designer: John Lane)

THE MOSS RESIDENCE
W. LAF., INDIANA

JOHN D. LANE
317-283-6350
LA 248
SPRING 1982

REMARKS

SHEET
2

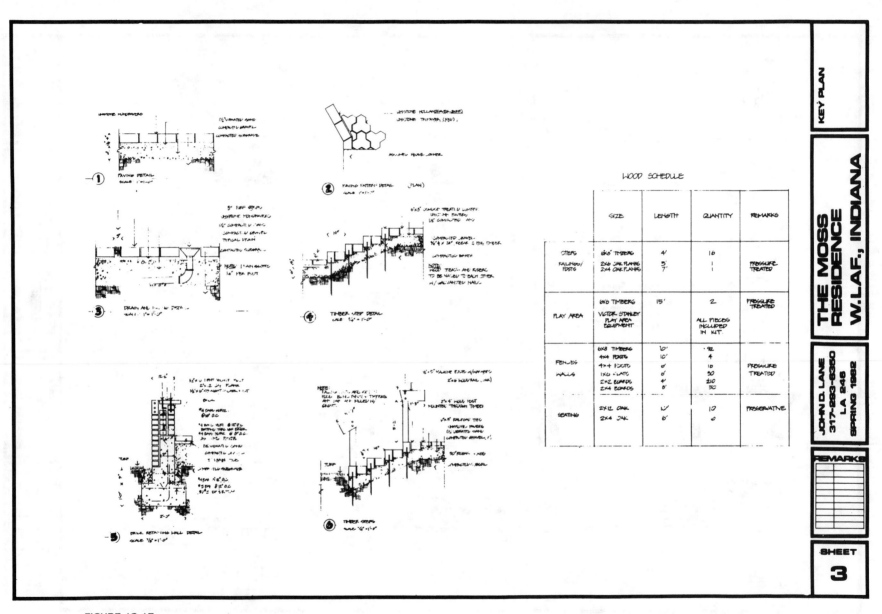

KEY PLAN

THE MOSS
RESIDENCE
W. LAF., INDIANA

JOHN D. LANE
317-283-8350
LA 248
SPRING 1982

REMARKS

SHEET
3

FIGURE 12-15

Construction package details, pavement, steps and walls. While the layout plan defines the location and basic outline of constructed features, enlarge- *ments are often needed to show such details as fences, walls, steps, and pavements. (Designer: John Lane)*

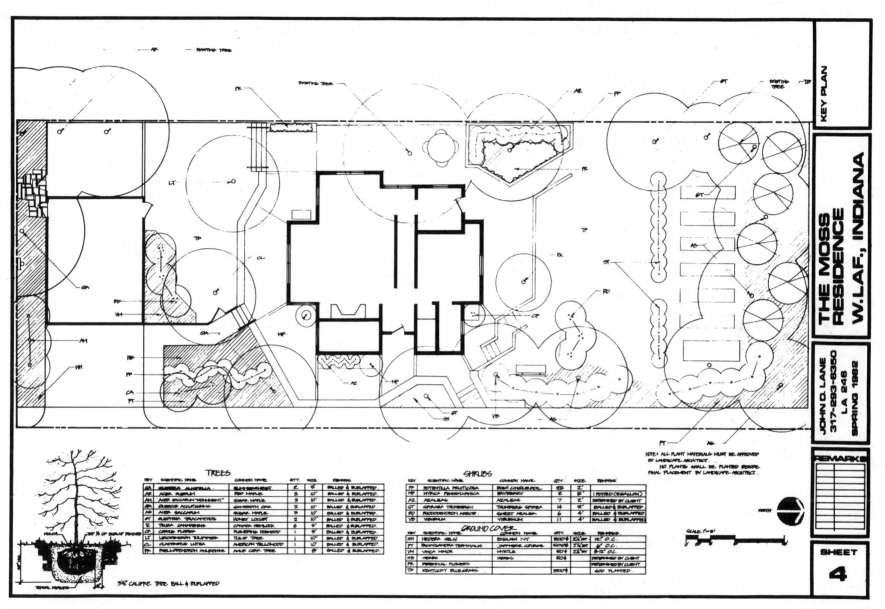

FIGURE 12-16

Construction package planting plan. The planting plan shows both existing
and proposed vegetation. (Designer: John Lane)

When developing a site master plan, remember that changes do occur when projects are implemented. Construction drawings are called working drawings because of the ongoing changes that do occur.

The remaining construction details, Figures 12-14 and 12-15, include fences, walls, edges, benches, steps, drainage, railing, and other landscape features. These include the additional information needed to construct many of the site features. The last sheet, Figure 12-16, is the planting plan. It identifies the species, quantity, size, and location of the proposed plantings. At a larger scale project, details concerning protection and care of existing trees, staking, guying, and planting of new materials and quality specifications may also be included.

SUMMARY

Hopefully, this site planning and landscape design proposal has helped outline and show the applications of the design process. As a landscape designer involved in site development or as a landscape architect involved in site planning, the design of residential sites focuses around the client, site, surrounding and climatic influences. These considerations determine the design opportunities and limitations. They result in design proposals that are not just site plantings but planned sites.

REFERENCES AND READINGS

Booth, Norman. *Basic Elements of Landscape Architectural Design.* New York: American Elsevier Publishing Co., 1983.

Eckbo, Garrett. *Home Landscape: The Art of Home Landscaping.* New York: McGraw-Hill, 1978.

Laurie, Michael. *An Introduction to Landscape Architecture.* New York: American Elsevier Publishing Co., 1975.

Lynch, Kevin. *Site Planning.* Cambridge, MA: MIT Press, 1962.

Rose, James. *Modern American Garden: Designed.* New York: Reinhold Publishing Company, 1967.

Walker, T. D. *Site Design and Construction Detailing.* West Lafayette, IN: PDA Publishers, 1978.

*M*ultifamily site design

The single-family home and the "residential" neighborhood have been traditional focus areas of the landscape industry.
Landscape architects, landscape designers, nurserymen, landscape
maintenance firms, and related sales personnel are all landscape
professionals that support landscape site development. As a reaction
to changing lifestyles, escalating building, operating, and maintenance costs, the forms and density of housing have begun to
change. Homeowners need affordable housing that provides more
multipurpose interiors and exteriors. With design trends toward
housing types other than single-family detached units, landscape design concepts are also changing.

In an article entitled "The Housing Revolution and Its Effect on
the Landscape Industry" (*Landscape and Turf,* Jan/Feb 1982),
R. Tasker discusses the potential future of housing and its related
landscape. He emphasizes that attitudes concerning housing and site
design have caused changes in the landscape industry. "Smaller and
communal, the new home of today is smaller (like our cars), either
attached or on drastically compressed lots, open areas are fre-

quently common instead of private, parking is communal and finishes pre-fabbed and stark" (p. 23).

Housing is a major part of our built environment. If housing demands are to meet the needs of homeowners, simplicity in design and construction and increased densities are some possible solutions. In addition to this trend toward smaller homes and increased densities, homeowners have begun to take advantage of the opportunities available in rehabilitating current housing. (See Chapter 11.) Building on "in-fill" lots not developed in established neighborhoods also has become increasingly popular. (See Chapter 12.) Residential site planning and landscape design has become more responsive to site, its orientation and the influences and uses related to the environment surrounding a home. Interior energy conservation, efficiency and the interior/exterior use relationships have become primary design considerations. The site design opportunities of windbreaks, screening, and shade provided by plantings and constructed features are now primary design objectives. "As houses get smaller and neighborhoods get closer, the need for quality landscaping increases. Large expanses of bluegrass yards used to assure some degree of separation and a fence at the property line were the solutions for privacy and territorial instincts. New solutions will be needed" (Tasker, p. 24).

MULTIFAMILY HOUSING, LANDSCAPE DESIGN OBJECTIVES

Housing of the past included large lots and interiors. In contrast, new housing will have small lots and less interior spaces for activities. As a result, new housing will need proper site planning and landscape design to provide the opportunities for physical and visual extensions of interior activities outdoors. Planning to modify the site's microclimate as a means of reducing energy needs also is a consideration in conjunction with more energy efficient material and design. *Functional design objectives* for new or current site design should consider the use of vegetation to direct breezes and encourage natural ventilation, cooling by shading, natural lighting, passive solar gain in winter, and buffering winter winds. *Aesthetic design objectives* should apply the principles of design such that site spaces visually and physically relate to interior uses and activities. The landform, pavements, and plantings create the site spaces that physically and visually define and extend interiors.

Selection of design materials and plantings appropriate to the locale in terms of hardiness and care also provide a more efficient site landscape. Plantings should be hardy for the region and for the site's microclimatic situation so that extensive care is not needed to maintain them. Selection of more "native" or naturalized species in conjunction with "exotic" species that fit site specific microclimates can be attractive and functional and at the same time reduce the amount of maintenance required. Flexible design elements such as brick, precast patio blocks, or other modular materials can provide functional, durable surfaces that can be removed or revised when repairs or other services must be performed. Also, designing with standard lumber dimensions other than odd lengths reduces waste and increases labor efficiency during the construction phase when wooden design elements are built.

Individuality should be a prime design criteria to include in a residential design proposal. Each client or homeowner has a different personality and image that can be expressed in a site design. This is not to say all sites should stand out in total isolation from other sites, but the opportunity should exist for clients to participate in their site design. Adding seasonal plantings, accessories, or appurtenances to their landscape gives the clients a feeling of involvement. Their image or character is included in the landscape, making it an individual and personalized space.

Landscape design should function as a space and activity definer within which the client lives and accessories are added for individuality and interest. Landscape design is not an end unto itself but a setting or environment for homeowners to live, recreate, and relax. Landscape design is developed through a thought process by which design recommendations are made that reflect the clients' needs, the site, its surroundings, and climatic influences. Landscape design is only as alive and functional as are the imaginations of the designer and clients.

MULTIFAMILY LANDSCAPE DEVELOPMENTS

As the demand for shelter increases, so do the costs and the need for standardization, simplicity, efficiency, and increased densities. To provide housing within the means of the average homeowner at a time when natural resources are quickly being depleted, designers must understand the development of multifamily units. Duplexes, quadplexes, townhouses, apartments and condominiums are housing forms that provide alternatives to more costly single-family detached homes. (See Figures 13-1 [a-c] for examples of "attached" housing.)

FIGURE 13-1(a)

Attached housing. Houston, Texas. Development of attached housing provides denser living conditions and smaller individual yards with the benefits of shared public recreation areas.

FIGURE 13-1(b)

Attached housing streetscape. Columbus, Ohio.

FIGURE 13-1(c)

Attached housing. Tucson, Arizona. A cul-de-sac overview and individual entry way.

FIGURE 13-1(d)

Multifamily housing provides more combined interior living spaces and less outdoor space to maintain, thus it is more efficient inside and out. (Designer: Raymond Paul Strychalski)

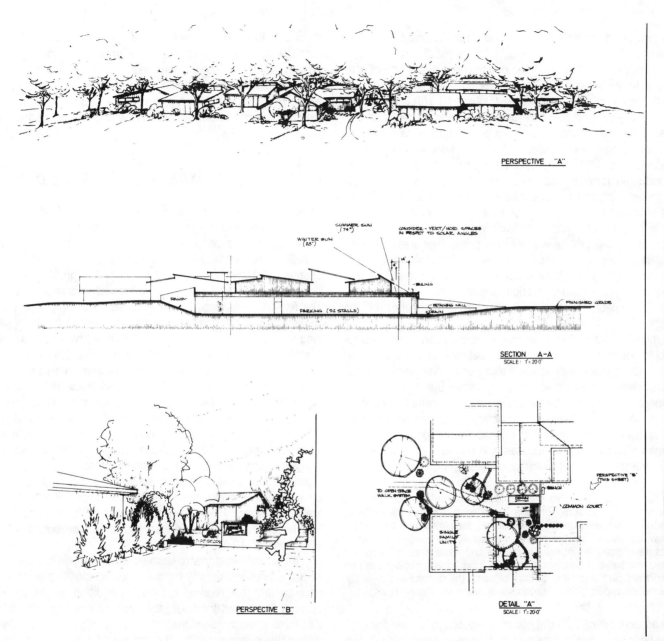

PERSPECTIVE "A"

DEPARTMENT OF
LANDSCAPE ARCHITECTURE
UNIV. OF ILLINOIS
LA 235
JOHN WIENEKE   DEC. 1973
SCALE: AS NOTED   SHEET 9 OF 9

PERSPECTIVES &
DETAILS

SUMMER SUN
(74°)

WINTER SUN
(23°)

CONSIDER - VERT/HORI SPACES
IN RESPECT TO SOLAR ANGLES

CEILING

RAMP

PARKING (32 STALLS)

RETAINING WALL

DRAIN

FINISHED GRADE

SECTION   A-A
SCALE: 1" = 20'-0"

PERSPECTIVE "B"

TO OPEN SPACE
WALK SYSTEM

PERSPECTIVE "B"
(THIS SHEET)

COMMON COURT

UP

SINGLE
FAMILY
UNITS

DETAIL "A"
SCALE: 1" = 20'-0"

HOUSING

FIGURE 13-1(e)

In this multifamily housing proposal, the living units are above a garage level to provide an efficient use of land with minimized sprawl of housing and parking. (Designer: John Wieneke)

As housing densities increase, so does the demand for use and enjoyment of the related grounds outside a home. Successful multifamily developments should include design and development of efficient, usable, and attractive site spaces, in addition to the constructed interior living environments. (Figures 13-1(d) and 13-1(e)) The design objectives considered for the single-family detached residences—functionally and visually extended spaces, energy efficiency, maintenance, and individuality—are also sound objectives for multifamily units. Multifamily developments use more shared open space including facilities such as pools, tennis courts, and recreational spaces. This sharing of public areas provides an overall savings of land and construction costs, thus making these housing developments less costly per unit. Even with these "shared" public facilities, individuals still have a need for private use areas and outdoor spaces immediately next to their units. Site design and development at the larger scale of multifamily housing should consider the project's overall image, function, and efficiency, yet provide individual site spaces relative to the needs and activities of the residents.

In multifamily housing developments, there is often a shared responsibility of care of outdoor spaces between the residents and complex management. Individual dwelling units may have "control" of a small adjoining site space or patios while the majority of the open space is maintained by the management or contracted service specialist. With this shift towards contracted site care, simplicity of design relative to management is critical. The design considers the maintenance objectives with the design concerns. Tasker's observations on the trend toward multifamily housing are worth noting:

> As focus shifts away from the individual residence and more towards the comunal, multifamily projects a propensity towards the exclusive use of a narrow range of easy-to-install plant materials, hardy, fast growing, low maintenance, showy-when-small. . . . Because denser projects mean increased intensity in the use and visual access of landscape areas and because landscaping costs on a per square foot basis can be amortized over a greater number of units, the demand and need for immediate impact plant materials should increase (Tasker, p. 24).

As an example of both the planning and design process for multifamily housing, a duplex site project follows. A townhouse duplex has been selected to illustrate some of the problems associated with increased densities and outdoor spaces in order to avoid the complexity of an entire townhouse or multifamily development. To show a contrast in site developments yet permit the same site and surrounding conditions to apply, the project site found in Chapter 12 will be used. The site planning proposal is again a feasibility study to identify how a duplex and related site spaces could be developed on the site. If the project were to proceed towards construction, more formalized drawings would then be developed.

DUPLEX SITE PLANNING AND LANDSCAPE DESIGN

As an opportunity to see how an in-fill site could be developed to serve changing housing needs, the Moss site was used as an exercise for a landscape architectural housing design class. The site, surrounding, and climatic influences are the same as those described in Chapter 12. However, the client in this sketch problem, rather than being the actual homeowner or user, was a developer/contractor. The feasibility study explores the construction of a duplex and the resulting site areas and landscape design details. In the initial planning stages the contractor selected a linear, two-story townhouse. It was selected for its scale and shape in relation to the site and neighborhood. The basic design program development that was utilized included two attached two-story townhouse units, each having a one-car garage and one guest parking space on the drive and private, individualized outdoor living spaces. The basic considerations of privacy, microclimate, and views to interior and exterior use areas were included. Figure 13-2 is the designer's site inventory and analysis information used in the siting of the three design options. Figures 13-3, 13-4, and 13-5 show the siting options that were considered for development. The pros and cons of each alternative are listed. Figure 13-6 shows the specific design objectives and rationale for the site master plan and details developed in Figures 13-7 through 13-12.

When reviewing this townhouse proposal, you begin to see that with the increased density from one to two dwelling units the siting opportunities are reduced greatly. In addition to the decrease in building and access locations, the need increases greatly for design details to provide for individuality and privacy between the units. Within this design situation, the proposed landscape design features do function to serve both dwelling units and thus require more evaluation in the selection and location of plants and constructed features.

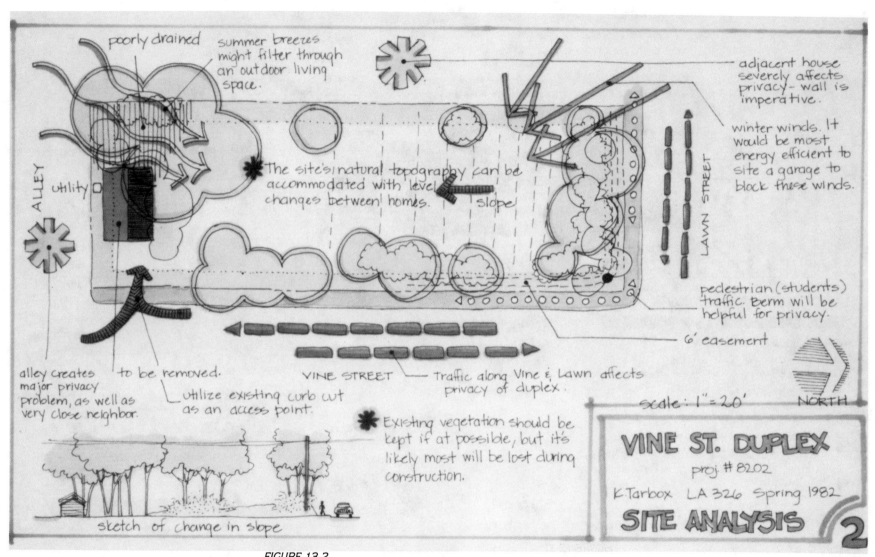

Within the figure:

poorly drained

summer breezes might filter through an outdoor living space.

adjacent house severely affects privacy – wall is imperative.

winter winds. It would be most energy efficient to site a garage to block these winds.

ALLEY

utility

The site's natural topography can be accommodated with level changes between homes.

slope

LAWN STREET

pedestrian (students) traffic. Berm will be helpful for privacy.

6' easement

alley creates major privacy problem, as well as very close neighbor.

to be removed.

utilize existing curb cut as an access point.

VINE STREET

Traffic along Vine & Lawn affects privacy of duplex.

Existing vegetation should be kept if at possible, but it's likely most will be lost during construction.

scale: 1" = 20'

NORTH

sketch of change in slope

VINE ST. DUPLEX
proj. # 8202
K. Tarbox   LA 326 Spring 1982
SITE ANALYSIS   2

FIGURE 13-2

Duplex feasibility study, site analysis. Just as in the single-family feasibility study in Chapter 11, a site inventory and analysis are again used to record and direct the planning and design of the site. (Designer: K. Tarbox)

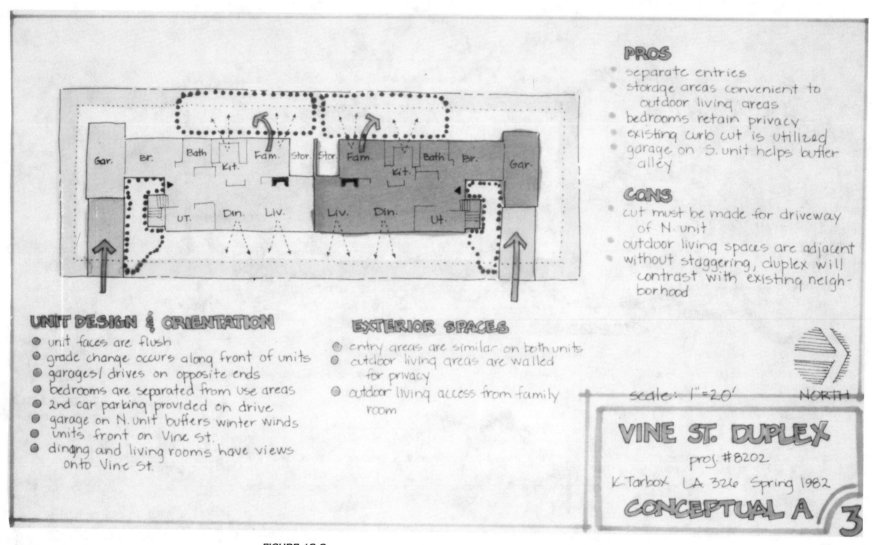

PROS
- separate entries
- storage areas convenient to outdoor living areas
- bedrooms retain privacy
- existing curb cut is utilized
- garage on S. unit helps buffer alley

CONS
- cut must be made for driveway of N. unit
- outdoor living spaces are adjacent
- without staggering, duplex will contrast with existing neighborhood

UNIT DESIGN & ORIENTATION
- unit faces are flush
- grade change occurs along front of units
- garages/drives on opposite ends
- bedrooms are separated from use areas
- 2nd car parking provided on drive
- garage on N. unit buffers winter winds
- units front on Vine St.
- dining and living rooms have views onto Vine St.

EXTERIOR SPACES
- entry areas are similar on both units
- outdoor living areas are walled for privacy
- outdoor living access from family room

scale: 1"=20'   NORTH

VINE ST. DUPLEX
proj. #8202
K. Tarbox   LA 326 Spring 1982
CONCEPTUAL A   3

FIGURE 13-3

Duplex feasibility study, conceptual plan. Here and in the other two siting options shown (Figures 13-4 and 13-5), the same basic units are used yet sited differently to show the options of the resulting site spaces. (Designer: K. Tarbox)

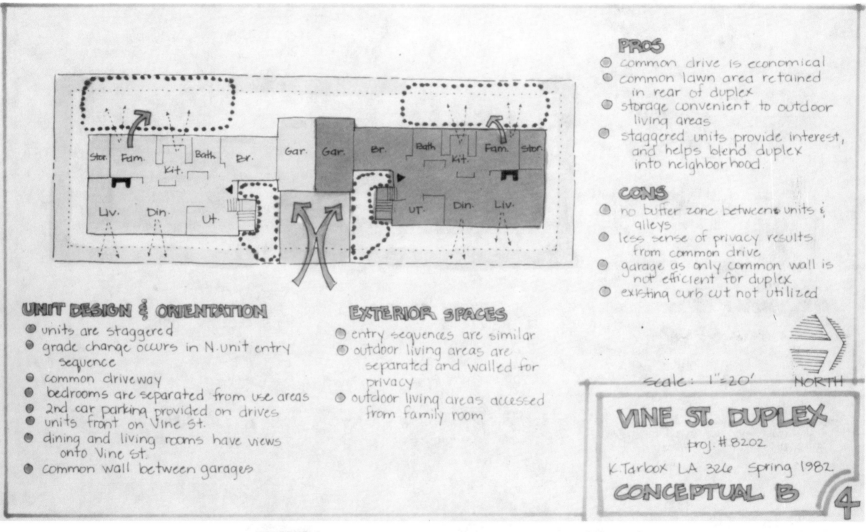

PROS
- common drive is economical
- common lawn area retained in rear of duplex
- storage convenient to outdoor living areas
- staggered units provide interest, and helps blend duplex into neighborhood.

CONS
- no buffer zone between units & alleys
- less sense of privacy results from common drive
- garage as only common wall is not efficient for duplex
- existing curb cut not utilized

UNIT DESIGN & ORIENTATION
- units are staggered
- grade change occurs in N. unit entry sequence
- common driveway
- bedrooms are separated from use areas
- 2nd car parking provided on drives
- units front on Vine St.
- dining and living rooms have views onto Vine St.
- common wall between garages

EXTERIOR SPACES
- entry sequences are similar
- outdoor living areas are separated and walled for privacy
- outdoor living areas accessed from family room

scale: 1"=20'   NORTH

VINE ST. DUPLEX
proj. #8202
K. Tarbox LA 326 Spring 1982.
CONCEPTUAL B 4

FIGURE 13-4
This conceptual plan pulls the drives and entry areas together creating a more unified and efficient entry from the street for residents and guests.

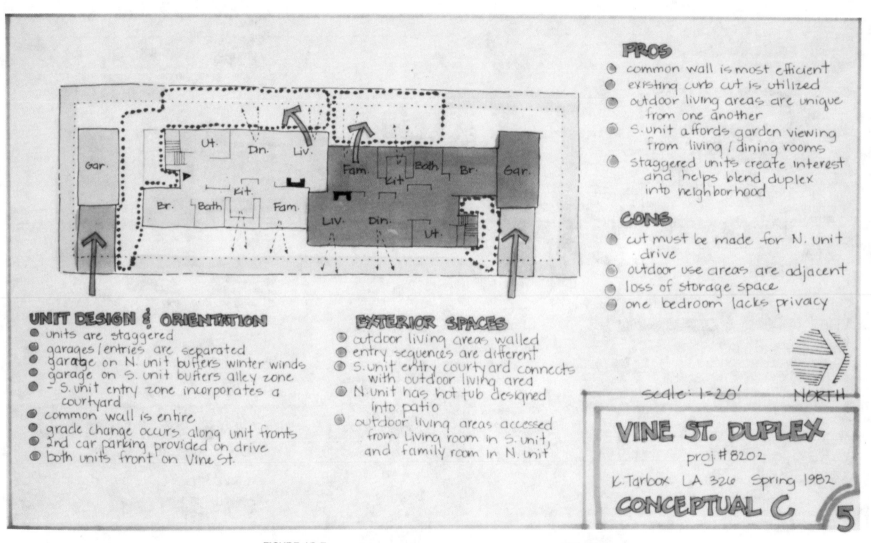

PROS
- common wall is most efficient
- existing curb cut is utilized
- outdoor living areas are unique from one another
- S. unit affords garden viewing from living / dining rooms
- staggered units create interest and helps blend duplex into neighborhood

CONS
- cut must be made for N. unit drive
- outdoor use areas are adjacent
- loss of storage space
- one bedroom lacks privacy

UNIT DESIGN & ORIENTATION
- units are staggered
- garages / entries are separated
- garage on N. unit buffers winter winds
- garage on S. unit buffers alley zone
- S. unit entry zone incorporates a courtyard
- common wall is entire
- grade change occurs along unit fronts
- 2nd car parking provided on drive
- both units front on Vine St.

EXTERIOR SPACES
- outdoor living areas walled
- entry sequences are different
- S. unit entry courtyard connects with outdoor living area
- N. unit has hot tub designed into patio
- outdoor living areas accessed from living room in S. unit, and family room in N. unit

scale: 1=20' NORTH

VINE ST. DUPLEX
proj #8202
K. Tarbox LA 326 Spring 1982
CONCEPTUAL C 5

FIGURE 13-5

This conceptual plan is similar to Figure 13-3 yet provides more outdoor living space for the unit to the south of the site.

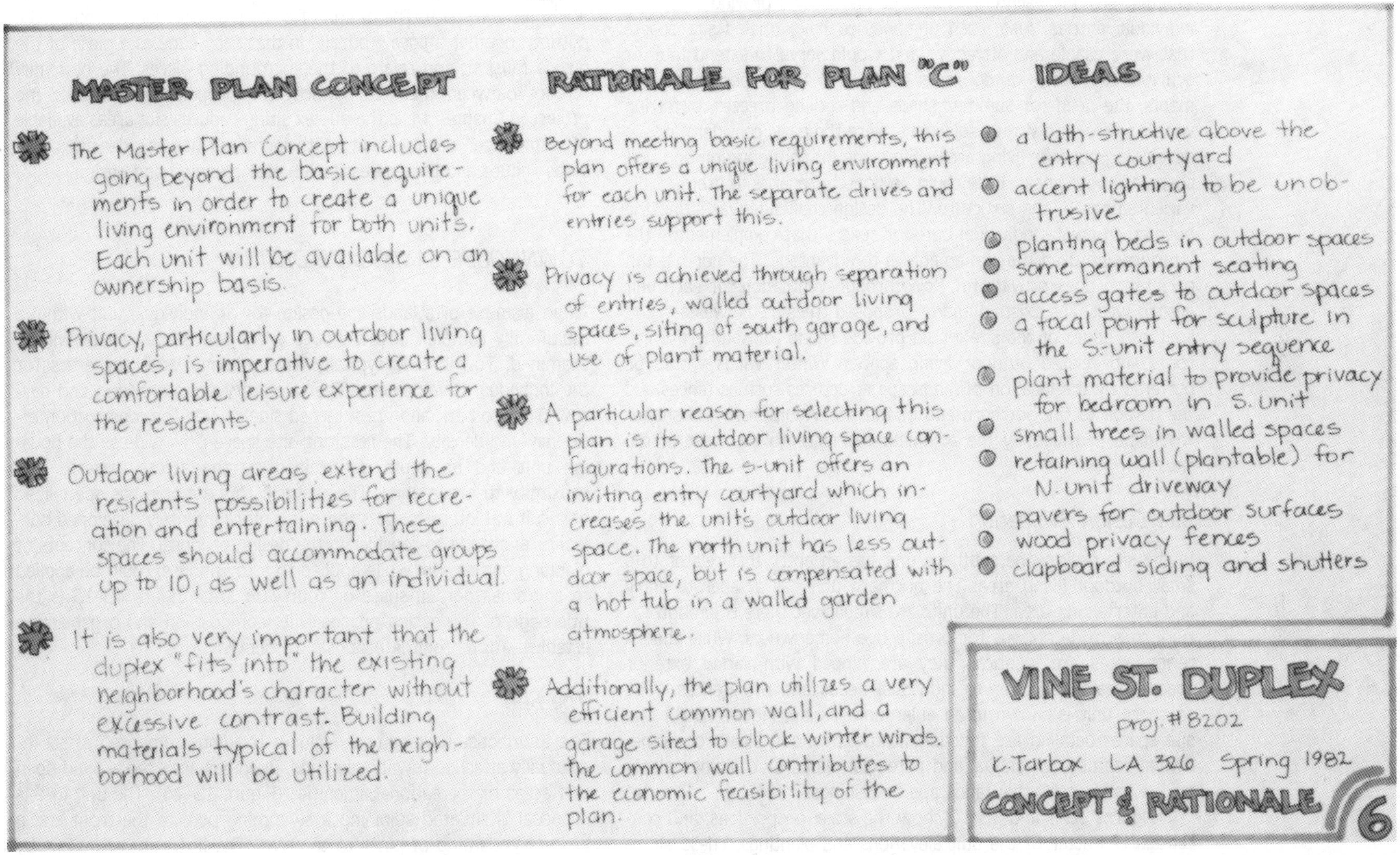

MASTER PLAN CONCEPT

✳ The Master Plan Concept includes going beyond the basic requirements in order to create a unique living environment for both units. Each unit will be available on an ownership basis.

✳ Privacy, particularly in outdoor living spaces, is imperative to create a comfortable leisure experience for the residents.

✳ Outdoor living areas extend the residents' possibilities for recreation and entertaining. These spaces should accommodate groups up to 10, as well as an individual.

✳ It is also very important that the duplex "fits into" the existing neighborhood's character without excessive contrast. Building materials typical of the neighborhood will be utilized.

RATIONALE FOR PLAN "C"

✳ Beyond meeting basic requirements, this plan offers a unique living environment for each unit. The separate drives and entries support this.

✳ Privacy is achieved through separation of entries, walled outdoor living spaces, siting of south garage, and use of plant material.

✳ A particular reason for selecting this plan is its outdoor living space configurations. The s-unit offers an inviting entry courtyard which increases the unit's outdoor living space. The north unit has less outdoor space, but is compensated with a hot tub in a walled garden atmosphere.

✳ Additionally, the plan utilizes a very efficient common wall, and a garage sited to block winter winds. The common wall contributes to the economic feasibility of the plan.

IDEAS

◉ a lath-structure above the entry courtyard
◉ accent lighting to be unobtrusive
◉ planting beds in outdoor spaces
◉ some permanent seating
◉ access gates to outdoor spaces
◉ a focal point for sculpture in the S-unit entry sequence
◉ plant material to provide privacy for bedroom in S. unit
◉ small trees in walled spaces
◉ retaining wall (plantable) for N. unit driveway
◉ pavers for outdoor surfaces
◉ wood privacy fences
◉ clapboard siding and shutters

VINE ST. DUPLEX

Proj. # 8202

K. Tarbox   LA 326   Spring 1982

CONCEPT & RATIONALE   6

FIGURE 13-6

Design concept. After review of the three siting concepts, a listing of design concepts and ideas are generated for inclusion in the final master plan. (Designer: K. Tarbox)

Master Plan Evaluation

The concepts used in the master plan development reflect the fact that the site was to be developed for two, single-family units and, these units were to be purchased rather than rented (Figure 13-7). The designer felt each unit should be private and provide separated individual entries. Also, each unit was to have related site spaces that were usable and attractive and would serve to extend interior activities and views outdoors. In addition to these specific requirements, the need for summer shade and cooling breezes, buffering winter winds, and winter solar gain were the basic considerations in developing outdoor living areas. Since the lot configuration and unit shape are both linear, little could be done in regards to dramatically varied sitings of the structure. The design challenge was siting the building to create individual outdoor spaces that complemented the interiors and used the site amenities to advantage. The north/south orientation does provide for flow-through ventilation for each unit east to west. The existing and/or proposed trees at the western and southern edges of the site would provide shade for southern units' roofs and related outdoor living spaces. Winter winds would be buffered by the location of landscape structures such as fences and the garage to the northern end of the site. Additional wind shelter would be provided by the adjoining residence to the west of the site.

Site Design Evaluation

In the site design, the southern unit has an entry that relates to a small outdoor living area. The northern unit has a separate entry and entertaining area. The units are similar yet there is enough variety to provide options for prospective homeowners. While the interior areas are identical, they are flipped with varied exterior spaces created to cater to individual needs and preferences. (The southern unit is shown in an enlargement plan, Figure 13-8.) The site spaces detailed are functional, attractive, and allow for homeowner additions of annual and perennial plants or container plants on the patio with other landscape furnishings.

Figures 13-9 and 13-10 show the scale, proportions, and conceptual character of the unit elevations and plantings. These elevations are only concepts relative to the planting plan and landscape constructional details that could be developed. At this feasibility study stage of design, the plantings have been defined only as to deciduous and evergreen trees and related specimen and ground cover plants. (See Figures 13-11 and 13-12 for the plan showing the planting concept and construction details.) When the planning and design processes proceed, specific plants would be selected as to their appropriate location, function, installation size, and species. In design situations where site spaces are physically at a minimum, landscape design has to be planned and efficient to provide maximal utility for the space. The design of a small garden space is much like putting together a jigsaw puzzle, in that each edge as a piece of the puzzle must fit and relate to the surrounding pieces. The basic difference between this site development proposal and that of the project in Chapter 11 is the duplex siting reduces site areas available of "landscape" development. With increased housing densities, site areas reduce and thus necessitate better planning and design.

TOWNHOUSE LANDSCAPE DESIGN

As an example of a landscape design for an individual unit within a multifamily complex, a townhouse entry and garden space will be examined. Townhouses typically have minimal landscape areas for the individual development. The two-story units are long and narrow front to back and are attached side to side for construction efficiency and density. The resulting site space is as wide as the housing unit and its depth determined by the access patterns and proximity to other units. The client in this example has specialized horticultural interests; thus there is a more intensely developed horticultural criteria to consider in the design proposal. The concepts of planning and design, while applied to a townhouse, could be applied to any small garden space or courtyard area. Figure 13-13 is the title page of the design proposal. Its composition and organization establish a tone for the proposal to follow.

The Site

The townhouse development includes buildings composed of six individually attached townhouse units. Buildings are sited around open turf areas or recreational amenities (Figure 13-14). The unit in this proposal is situated adjoining a swimming pool to the front and a boundary planting of pines to the rear. The unit is basically 20' by 30', with a potential entry planting space of $10' \times 20'$ and a rear outdoor space available for development of $20' \times 24'$. The residence's main entry is from the front, with a parking area located beyond a view of the swimming pool. The rear entry is for access to the outdoor space and trash collection.

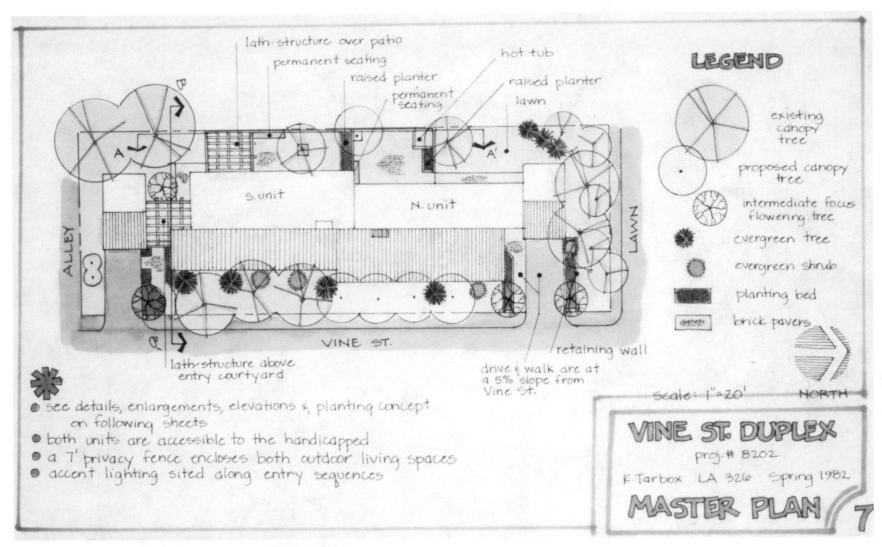

FIGURE 13-7

Duplex master plan. After the basic design process, the master plan and support sheets are developed to communicate the character and details of the envisioned project. After review of this design stage, the process may include construction drawings for implementation. (Designer: K. Tarbox)

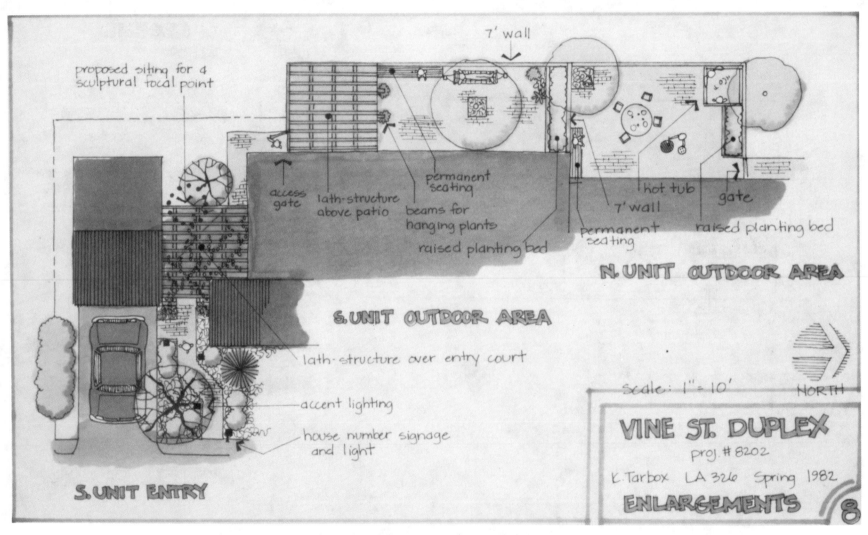

proposed siting for 4
sculptural focal point

7' wall

access
gate

lath-structure
above patio

permanent
seating

beams for
hanging plants

raised planting bed

7' wall

permanent
seating

hot tub

gate

raised planting bed

N. UNIT OUTDOOR AREA

S. UNIT OUTDOOR AREA

lath-structure over entry court

accent lighting

house number signage
and light

S. UNIT ENTRY

scale: 1" = 10'

NORTH

VINE ST. DUPLEX
proj. # 8202
K. Tarbox   LA 326   Spring 1982
ENLARGEMENTS   8

FIGURE 13-8
Entry enlargement, south unit. (Designer: K. Tarbox)

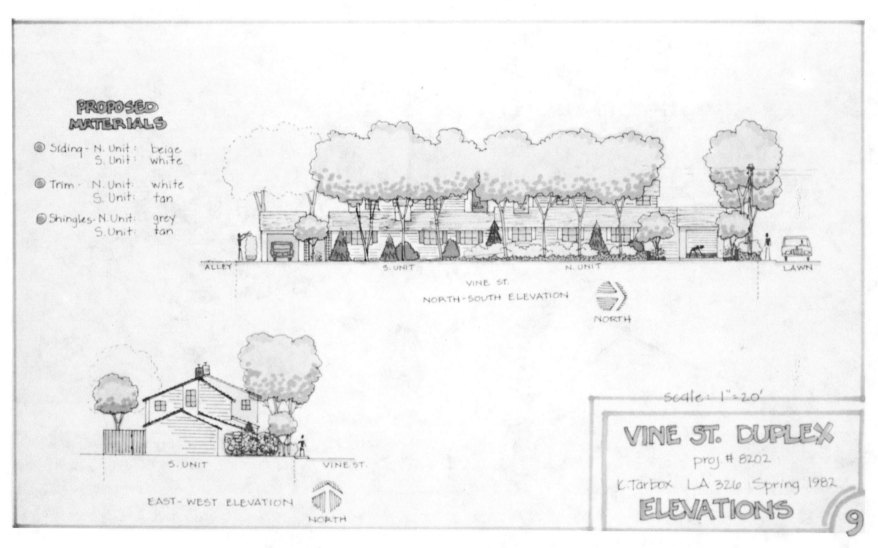

PROPOSED MATERIALS

- ⦿ Siding - N. Unit: beige
  S. Unit: white

- ⦿ Trim - N. Unit: white
  S. Unit: tan

- ⦿ Shingles - N. Unit: grey
  S. Unit: tan

ALLEY

S. UNIT

N. UNIT

LAWN

VINE. ST.

NORTH-SOUTH ELEVATION

NORTH

S. UNIT

VINE ST.

EAST-WEST ELEVATION

NORTH

Scale: 1"=20'

VINE ST. DUPLEX
proj. # 8202
K. Tarbox LA 326 Spring 1982
ELEVATIONS

9

FIGURE 13-9
Duplex elevation. (Designer: K. Tarbox)

N-S CROSS SECTION

NORTH

E-W CROSS SECTION

NORTH

B   B'

scale: 1"=10'

VINE ST. DUPLEX
Proj. #8202
K-Tarbox   LA 326   Spring 1982
SECTIONS   10

FIGURE 13-10
Duplex section elevations. (Designer: K. Tarbox)

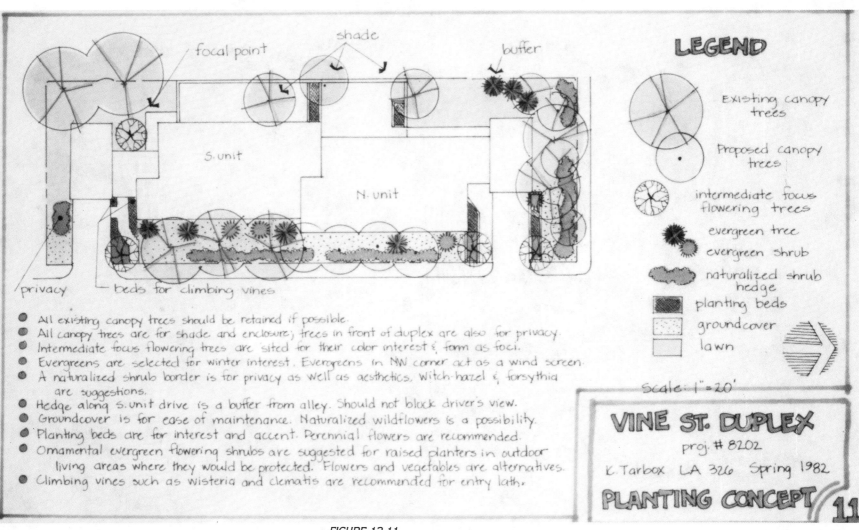

Legend labels:
- focal point
- shade
- buffer
- LEGEND
- S. unit
- N. unit
- privacy
- beds for climbing vines

Legend:
- Existing canopy trees
- Proposed canopy trees
- intermediate focus flowering trees
- evergreen tree
- evergreen shrub
- naturalized shrub hedge
- planting beds
- groundcover
- lawn

Scale: 1"=20'

VINE ST. DUPLEX
proj. # 8202
K. Tarbox   LA 326   Spring 1982

PLANTING CONCEPT   11

- All existing canopy trees should be retained if possible.
- All canopy trees are for shade and enclosure; trees in front of duplex are also for privacy.
- Intermediate focus flowering trees are sited for their color interest & form as foci.
- Evergreens are selected for winter interest. Evergreens in NW corner act as a wind screen.
- A naturalized shrub border is for privacy as well as aesthetics. Witch-hazel & forsythia are suggestions.
- Hedge along s. unit drive is a buffer from alley. Should not block driver's view.
- Groundcover is for ease of maintenance. Naturalized wildflowers is a possibility.
- Planting beds are for interest and accent. Perennial flowers are recommended.
- Ornamental evergreen flowering shrubs are suggested for raised planters in outdoor living areas where they would be protected. Flowers and vegetables are alternatives.
- Climbing vines such as wisteria and clematis are recommended for entry lath.

FIGURE 13-11
Duplex planting plan. (Designer: K. Tarbox)

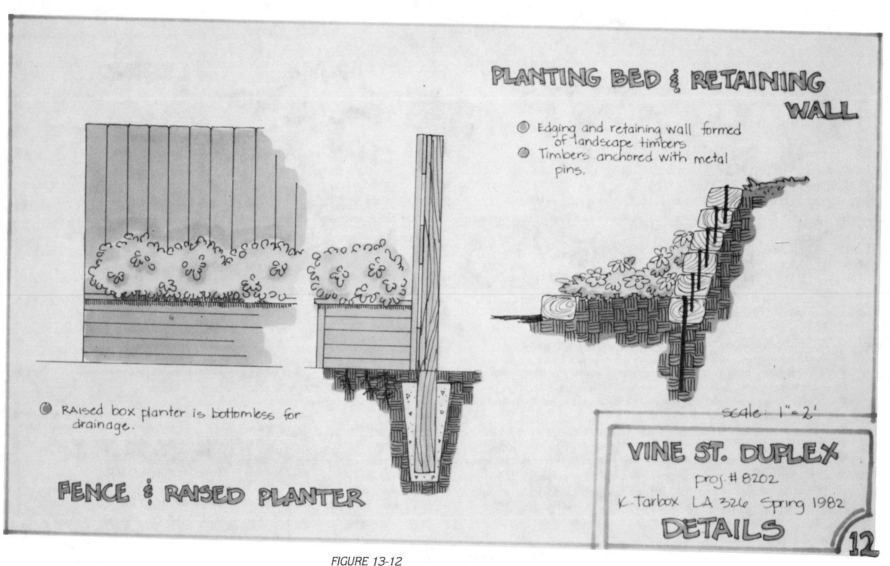

PLANTING BED & RETAINING WALL

- Edging and retaining wall formed of landscape timbers
- Timbers anchored with metal pins.

- Raised box planter is bottomless for drainage.

FENCE & RAISED PLANTER

scale: 1"=2'

VINE ST. DUPLEX
proj. # 8202
K. Tarbox LA 326 Spring 1982
DETAILS

12

FIGURE 13-12
Duplex construction details. (Designer: K. Tarbox)

FIGURE 13-13
Townhouse planting design, title page. (Designer: Virginia Swain Smith)

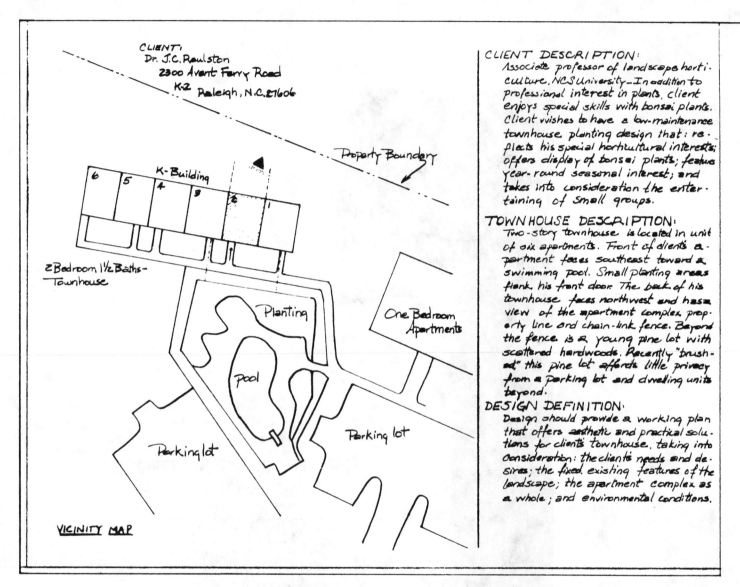

CLIENT:
Dr. J.C. Raulston
2300 Avent Ferry Road
K-2 Raleigh, N.C. 27606

Property Boundary

6 5 K-Building 4 3 2 1

2 Bedroom 1½ Baths –
Townhouse

Planting

One Bedroom
Apartments

Pool

Parking lot

Parking lot

VICINITY MAP

CLIENT DESCRIPTION:
Associate professor of landscape horticulture, NCS University – In addition to
professional interest in plants, client
enjoys special skills with bonsai plants.
Client wishes to have a low-maintenance
townhouse planting design that: reflects his special horticultural interests;
offers display of bonsai plants; feature
year-round seasonal interest; and
takes into consideration the entertaining of small groups.

TOWNHOUSE DESCRIPTION:
Two-story townhouse is located in unit
of six apartments. Front of client's a-
partment faces southeast toward a
swimming pool. Small planting areas
flank his front door. The back of his
townhouse faces northwest and has a
view of the apartment complex, property line and chain-link fence. Beyond
the fence is a young pine lot with
scattered hardwoods. Recently "brush-
ed" this pine lot affords little privacy
from a parking lot and dwelling units
beyond.

DESIGN DEFINITION:
Design should provide a working plan
that offers aesthetic and practical solutions for client's townhouse, taking into
consideration: the client's needs and desires; the fixed, existing features of the
landscape; the apartment complex as
a whole; and environmental conditions.

Sheet Subject: Vicinity Map; General Info.
Client: Dr. J.C. Raulston
Designer: Virginia Smith – NCSU /HS414
Project # 7601
Date: March 6, 1976
Sheet # 1 of 12 Sheets
Scale: (approximate) 1" = 20

FIGURE 13-14

*Townhouse proposal, vicinity plan. In this design proposal, the designer has
included the client, location, and design statements in conjunction with the
location plan. From this overview the remaining sheets focus on the area
immediately surrounding the townhouse. (Designer: Virginia Swain Smith)*

The entry design, when developed, needs to consider the visual relationship of the adjoining units and the view of the pool from living spaces on the first and second floors. The rear yard space is the occupant's primary outdoor living space, thus enclosure, privacy, and access should be the most important design considerations.

The Client

The resident, a professor of landscape horticulture, has a special interest in bonsai plants and needs an outdoor space to display, work with, and enjoy his bonsai collection. He also wants to entertain and relax outdoors. In conjunction with the bonsai display, the garden space should be private, secure, and intimate. It should be an extension of the townhouse's scale, its interiors, and the building's construction materials. At the time of the design proposal, no budget was established to limit the design possibilities. This does not mean the design solutions should not be realistic.

The entry design proposal needs to relate more physically and visually to the adjoining units and should complement existing plantings and construction features. The rear outdoor living proposal could repeat the materials at the entry, but since it is seen separately from the entry, variations could occur.

The Planting Design Proposals

THE ENTRY DESIGN.   In the entry, an existing holly and a juniper were used as focal elements in the proposed development. The holly, trained into an upright form, helps tie the townhouse unit to the adjoining unit in conjunction with a mass of azaleas proposed to visually balance the existing specimen juniper. (See Figures 13-15 and 13-16 for the proposed entry elevation and details.) The ground area is proposed to be ground covers and bulbs for seasonal interest and to unite the space with the adjoining planting strip along the walk. The planting zone between the walk and pool area wall is filled with a low evergreen shrub and ground covers to visually tie the townhouse entry planting across the walk. A wooden screen has been proposed for the side of the unit's entry to enclose and define the entry. The screen is also the first step in establishing an identity and theme to the garden materials that will come at the rear of the unit.

THE REAR GARDEN PROPOSAL.   The landscape design recommendations for the rear garden/entertaining space included both struc-

tural and plant features. (See Figures 13-17 and 13-18 for plans and details.) A wooden deck was selected for the primary surfacing and side enclosure to repeat the wood siding of the townhouse unit and for ease of construction by the client. The deck space is level with interior floors, thus creating planting pockets at the natural ground level just below the deck level. (Figures 13-19 and 13-20 show the proposed space with side elevations looking at the north end of the townhouse and side views.)

Since the space is on the northern side of the townhouse, it has an advantage in being partially shaded by the building and thus cooler in the summer. The proposed tree forms have been selected to provide an outdoor ceiling in the case of the canopy tree and as a focus or specimen in the case of the Japanese maple. The actual plant list and design rationale is found in Figure 13-21. Figures 13-22 and 13-23 are a planting and construction summary for the entry and rear area proposals from which a phased development was determined.

One of the design objectives for the rear garden area was to provide seasonal interest through blossom, berry, leaf, and fragrance. A color theme was developed using white blossoms primarily as a reflective foil at night, the main entertaining time for the client. Maintenance was also a consideration. Plants were selected that would survive in the area and remain in scale with the space. In this design proposal, much of the normal site design opportunities for climate control were focused on physically and visually extending interior spaces outdoors with passive solar gain from the south, front area space.

SUMMARY

When applying site planning concepts to landscape design proposals, part of the design process is to determine the primary objectives most realistic for the site and client situation. Site design should try to satisfy the client's needs and be responsive to the site, its surroundings, and climatic conditions.

As a landscape designer involved with residential site design, the future possibilities and opportunities are expanding more and more. Homeowners desire quality landscape proposals that reflect good planning and competent design. The attached multifamily market will become a definite design focus for designers in the future. Physical space that is designed to be functional as well as attractive is an objective to consider in multifamily site development. Public use areas should provide for flexible use by all the residents, while private garden areas can offer the opportunity for individuality, pri-

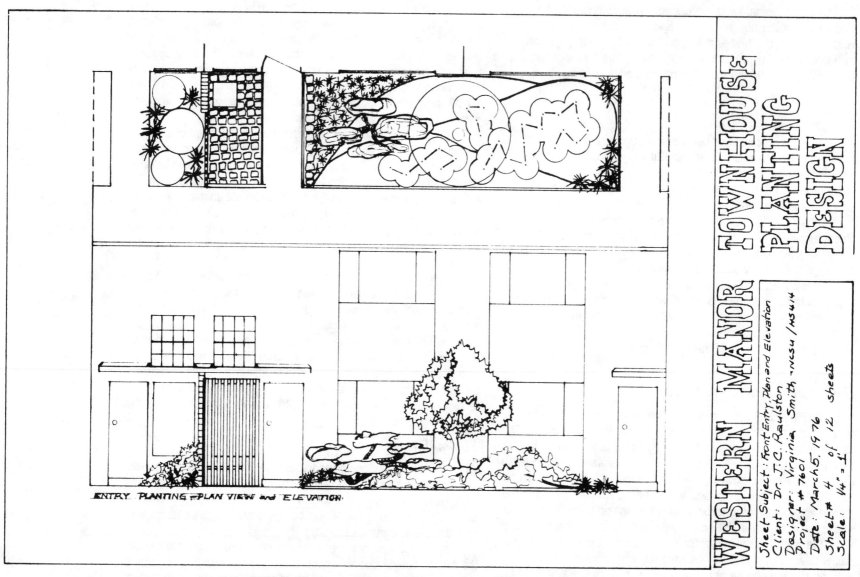

ENTRY PLANTING PLAN VIEW and ELEVATION

FIGURE 13-15

Townhouse proposal, entry proposal, plan and elevation. Since the townhouse proposal includes only a front and rear yard for development, the
proposal illustrates the entry design separate from the rear yard area. The
plan and elevation then illustrate the plant and constructed features proposed for the entry. (Designer: Virginia Swain Smith)

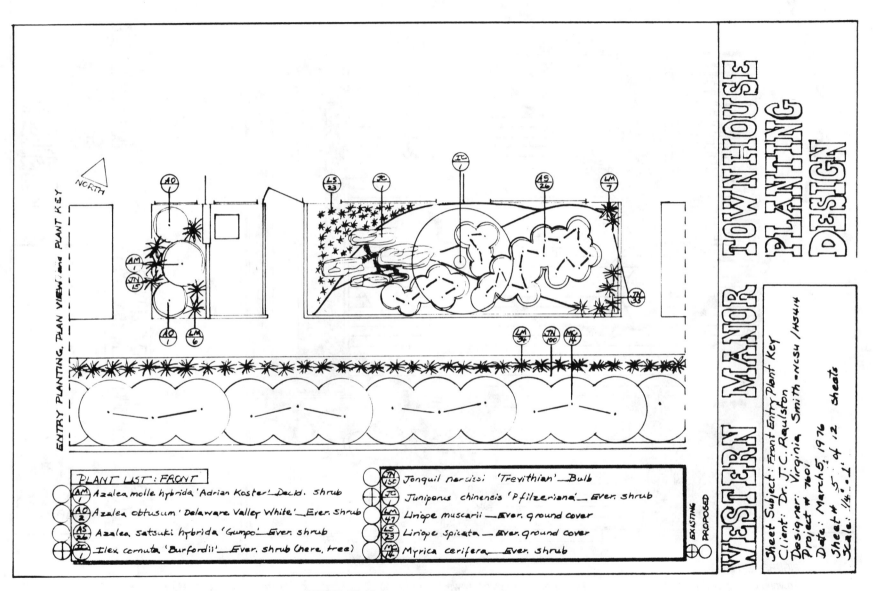

FIGURE 13-16
Entry area enlargement. (Designer: Virginia Swain Smith)

407

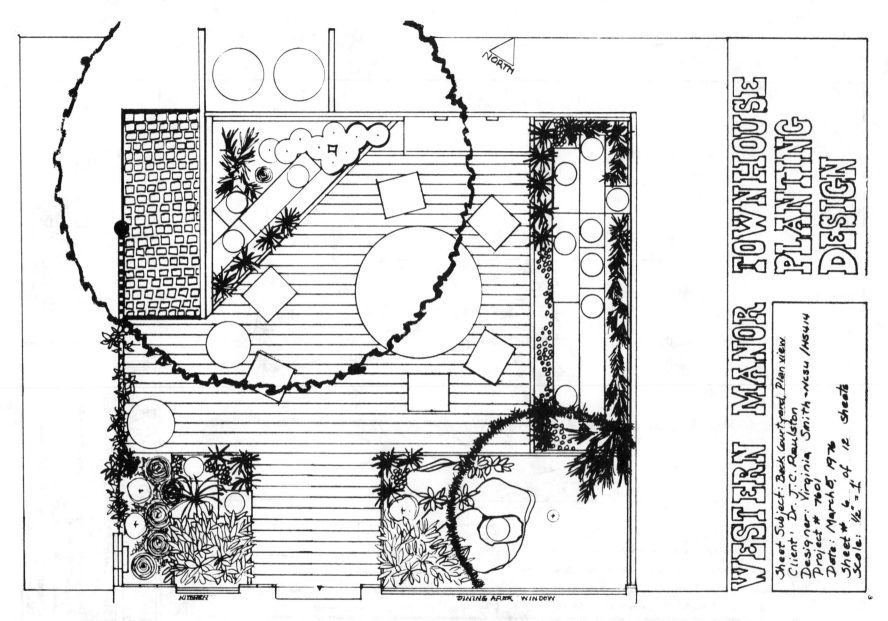

Within the image:
WESTERN MANOR TOWNHOUSE PLANTING DESIGN

NORTH

KITCHEN

DINING AREA WINDOW

Sheet Subject: Back Courtyard Plan View.
Client: Dr. J.C. Raulston
Designer: Virginia Smith—NCSU /HS414
Project # 7601
Date: March 5, 1976
Sheet # 6 of 12 sheets
Scale: 1/2" = 1'

FIGURE 13-17

Townhouse proposal—entertaining area. The entertaining area plans shown here and in Figure 13-18 are identical except one is the illustrative plan and the other is the plan that includes labels and descriptions of what is to be proposed. Two plans such as this would be developed using sepias. The plans then emphasize the outdoor composition and specific design elements separately. (Designer: Virginia Swain Smith)

408

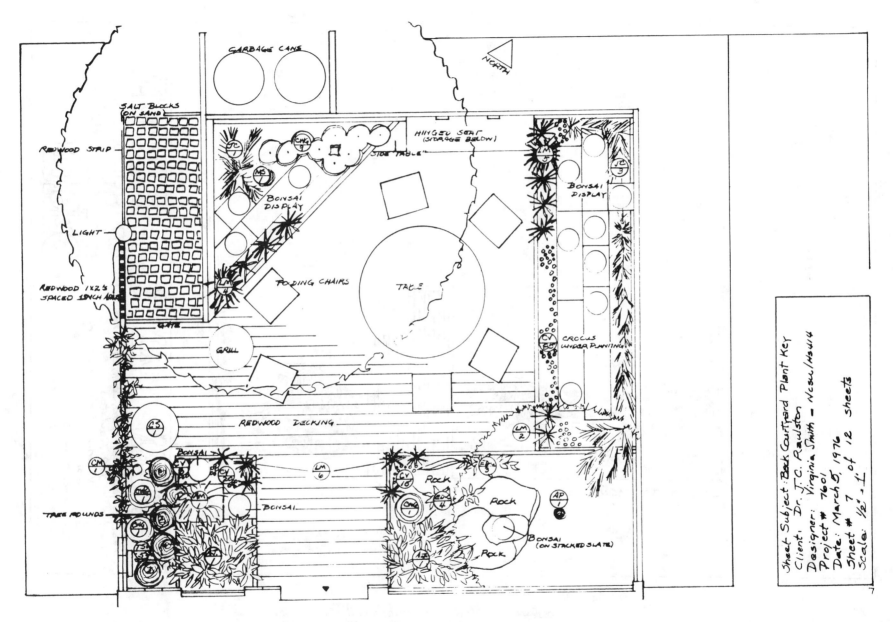

GARBAGE CANS

NORTH

SALT BLOCKS
(ON SAND)

REDWOOD STRIP

HINGED SEAT
(STORAGE BELOW)

SIDE TABLE

BONSAI
DISPLAY

BONSAI
DISPLAY

LIGHT

REDWOOD 1×2's
SPACED 1 INCH APART

FOLDING CHAIRS

TABLE

GATE

CROCUS
UNDER PLANTING

GRILL

REDWOOD DECKING

BONSAI

BONSAI

TREE ROUNDS

BONSAI

ROCK

ROCK

ROCK

BONSAI
(ON STACKED SLATE)

Sheet Subject: Back Courtyard Plant Key
Client: Dr. J.C. Rawlston
Designer: Virginia Smith — NCSU/HSU/IL
Project # 7601
Date: March 5, 1976
Sheet # 7 of 12 sheets
Scale: ½" = 1'

7

FIGURE 13-18
Townhouse proposal—entertaining area. (Continued)

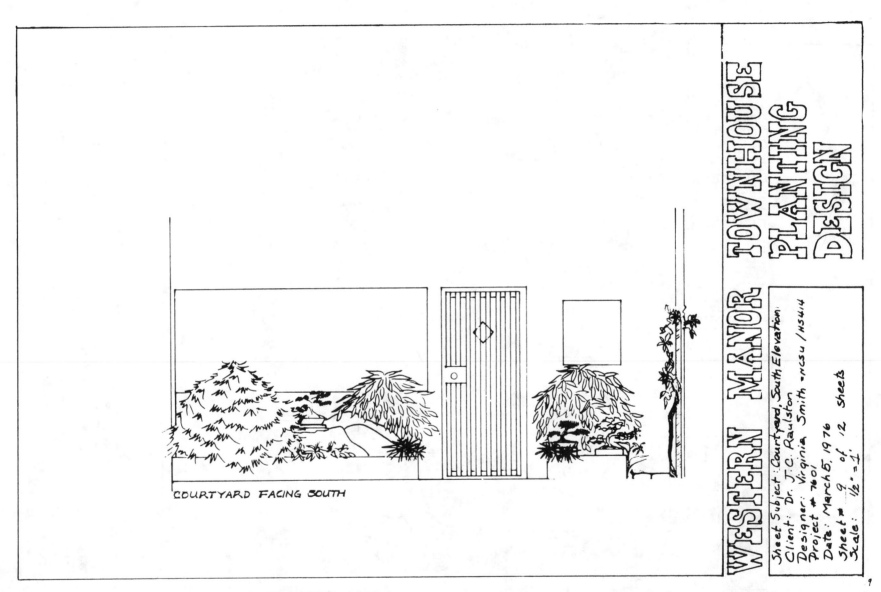

COURTYARD FACING SOUTH

WESTERN MANOR TOWNHOUSE PLANTING DESIGN

Sheet Subject: Courtyard, South Elevation
Client: Dr. J.C. Raulston
Designer: Virginia Smith - NCSU / HS414
Project # 7601
Date: March 5, 1976
Sheet # 9 of 12 sheets
Scale: 1/2" = 1'

FIGURE 13-19

Townhouse proposal—elevation. The elevations shown here and in Figure 13-20 are used to illustrate the four sides of the entertaining area. Note the simplicity yet effectiveness of the elevations. (Designer: Virginia Swain Smith)

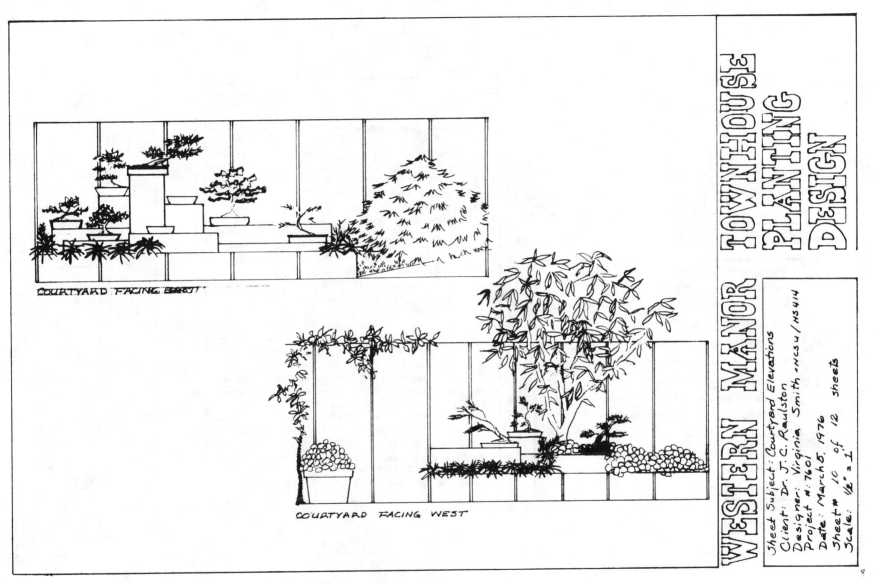

COURTYARD FACING EAST

COURTYARD FACING WEST

WESTERN MANOR TOWNHOUSE PLANTING DESIGN

Sheet Subject: Courtyard Elevations
Client: Dr. J.C. Raulston
Designer: Virginia Smith - NCSU / HS 414
Project #: 7601
Date: March 5, 1976
Sheet # 10 of 12 sheets
Scale: 1/2" = 1'

FIGURE 13-20

Townhouse proposal-elevation. These elevations show the fences and plantings that help enclose the sides of the entertaining area. The platforms offer an ideal location for the client's bonsai collection. (Designer: Virginia Swain Smith)

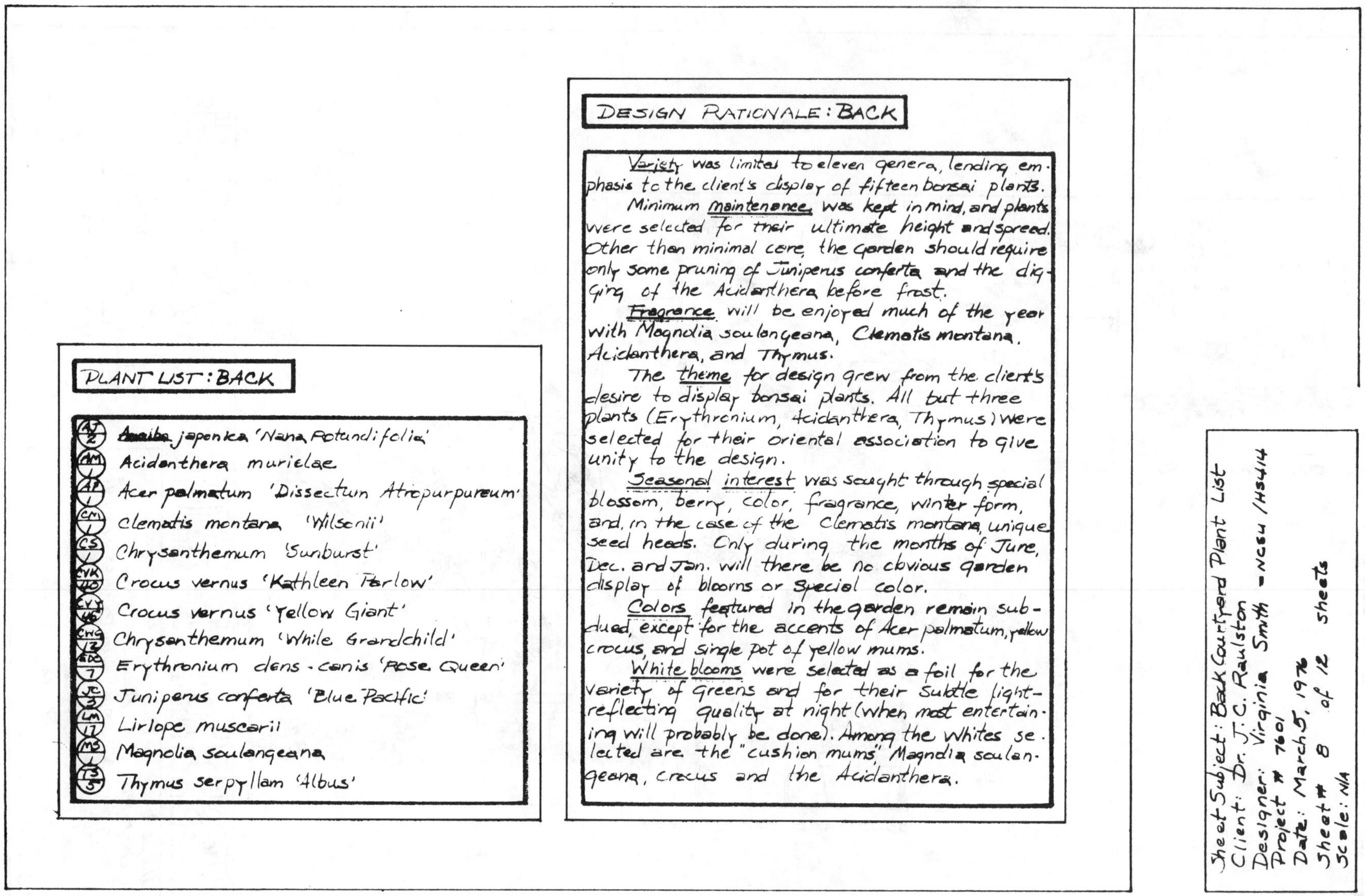

PLANT LIST: BACK

- (AJ/2) Aucuba japonica 'Nana Rotundifolia'
- (AM) Acidanthera murielae
- (AP/1) Acer palmatum 'Dissectum Atropurpureum'
- (CM/1) Clematis montana 'Wilsonii'
- (CS) Chrysanthemum 'Sunburst'
- (YK/10) Crocus vernus 'Kathleen Parlow'
- (YY/10) Crocus vernus 'Yellow Giant'
- (CWG/2) Chrysanthemum 'White Grandchild'
- (ER/7) Erythronium dens-canis 'Rose Queen'
- (JC/2) Juniperus conferta 'Blue Pacific'
- (LM/17) Liriope muscarii
- (MS/1) Magnolia soulangeana
- (TS/3) Thymus serpyllum 'Albus'

DESIGN RATIONALE: BACK

<u>Variety</u> was limited to eleven genera, lending emphasis to the client's display of fifteen bonsai plants.

Minimum <u>maintenance</u> was kept in mind, and plants were selected for their ultimate height and spread. Other than minimal care, the garden should require only some pruning of Juniperus conferta and the digging of the Acidanthera before frost.

<u>Fragrance</u> will be enjoyed much of the year with Magnolia soulangeana, Clematis montana, Acidanthera, and Thymus.

The <u>theme</u> for design grew from the client's desire to display bonsai plants. All but three plants (Erythronium, Acidanthera, Thymus) were selected for their oriental association to give unity to the design.

<u>Seasonal interest</u> was sought through special blossom, berry, color, fragrance, winter form, and, in the case of the Clematis montana, unique seed heads. Only during the months of June, Dec. and Jan. will there be no obvious garden display of blooms or special color.

<u>Colors</u> featured in the garden remain subdued, except for the accents of Acer palmatum, yellow crocus, and single pot of yellow mums.

<u>White blooms</u> were selected as a foil for the variety of greens and for their subtle light-reflecting quality at night (when most entertaining will probably be done). Among the whites selected are the "cushion mums", Magnolia soulangeana, crocus and the Acidanthera.

Sheet Subject: Back Courtyard Plant List
Client: Dr. J.C. Raulston
Designer: Virginia Smith — NCSU / HS414
Project # 7601
Date: March 5, 1976
Sheet # 8 of 12 sheets
Scale: NA

FIGURE 13-21

Townhouse proposal—plant list. As support information for the labeled plan (Figure 13-18), a plant listing is given to the client and the design rationale explained relative to plant selection. Variety, fragrance, seasonal interest, and color were the components considered in the plant selections. (Designer: Virginia Swain Smith)

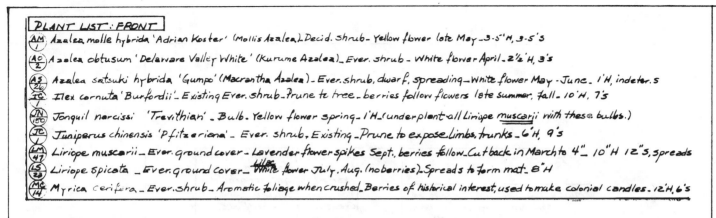

PLANT LIST: FRONT

(AM/1) Azalea molle hybrida 'Adrian Koster' (Mollis Azalea)_ Decid. shrub_ Yellow flower late May_3-5'H, 3-5's

(AO/2) Azalea obtusum 'Delaware Valley White' (Kurume Azalea)_ Ever. shrub_ White flower April_2½'H, 3's

(AS/26) Azalea satsuki hybrida 'Gumpo' (Macrantha Azalea)_ Ever. shrub, dwarf, spreading_White flower May-June_ 1'H, indeter. s

(IC/10) Ilex cornuta 'Burfordii'_ Existing Ever. shrub_ Prune to tree_ berries follow flowers late summer, fall_ 10'H, 7's

(JN/150) Jonquil narcissi 'Trevithian'_ Bulb. Yellow flower spring_1'H (underplant all Liriope muscarii with these bulbs.)

(JC/1) Juniperus chinensis 'Pfitzeriana'_ Ever. shrub. Existing_Prune to expose limbs, trunks_6'H, 9's

(LM/47) Liriope muscarii_ Ever. ground cover_ Lavender flower spikes Sept. berries follow_Cut back in March to 4"_ 10'H 12"s, spreads

(LS/22) Liriope spicata _ Ever. ground cover_ lilac White flower July, Aug. (no berries)_Spreads to form mat_ 8"H

(MC/14) Myrica cerifera _ Ever. shrub_ Aromatic foliage when crushed_ Berries of historical interest, used to make colonial candles_ 12'H, 6's

PLANT LIST: BACK

(AJ/2) Aucuba japonica 'Nana Rotundifolia'_ Ever. shrub_ Red berries (Plant male & female) 3'H

(AM/1) Acidanthera murielae_ Bulb_ Orchid-like bloom, fragrant white-purple blossom Aug. (Dig bulb before frost, store dry) 2½'H

(AP/1) Acer palmatum 'Dissectum Atropurpureum'_ Decid. Dwarf tree_ Delicately cut, deep red leaves_ 4-6'H

(CM/1) Clematis montana 'Wilsonii'_ Decid. vine_ Fragrant white flower April-May_Interesting seeds winter persisting_30'H

(CS/1) Chrysanthemum 'Sunburst' ("cushion mum")_Yellow flower Aug.-frost_ 1'H, 1's_Perennial

(CVK/40) Crocus vernus 'Kathleen Parlow'_ Bulb_ White flower with orange stamen late winter-spring

(CYV/45) Crocus vernus 'Yellow Giant'_ Bulb_ Yellow flower late winter-spring

(CWG/12) Chrysanthemum 'White Grandchild'_ Perennial ("cushion mum")_White flower Aug.-frost_ 1'H, 1's

(ERQ/7) Erythronium dens-canis 'Rose Queen'_ Perennial_(Bulb) Rose flower spring_ 6"H

(JC/3) Juniperus conferta 'Blue Pacific'_ Ever. Ground cover_ (variety named more compact than sp.)_1'H, indeter. S

(LM/17) Liriope muscarii_ Ever. Ground cover_ Lavender flower spikes Sept._ Black berries follow (See above)_ 10"H, 12"s

(MS/1) Magnolia soulangeana_ Decid. tree_ Fragrant, white-purple flowers March_ 20'H, 15-20's

(TS/5) Thymus serpyllum 'Albus'_ Perennial_ Fragrant herb (when crushed)_White flower May-June_prostrate, spreading.

Sheet Subject: Detailed Plant Information
Client: Dr. J.C. Raulston
Designer: Virginia Smith - NCSU/HS 414
Project # 7601 JCR
Date: March 5, 1976
Sheet 11 of 12 Sheets

FIGURE 13-22

Townhouse proposal—plant list. As a summary to the design proposal, the plantings included in front and back areas were listed and their specific characteristics defined. The constructed features were also listed and outlined to help establish guidelines for implementation. (Designer: Virginia Swain Smith)

413

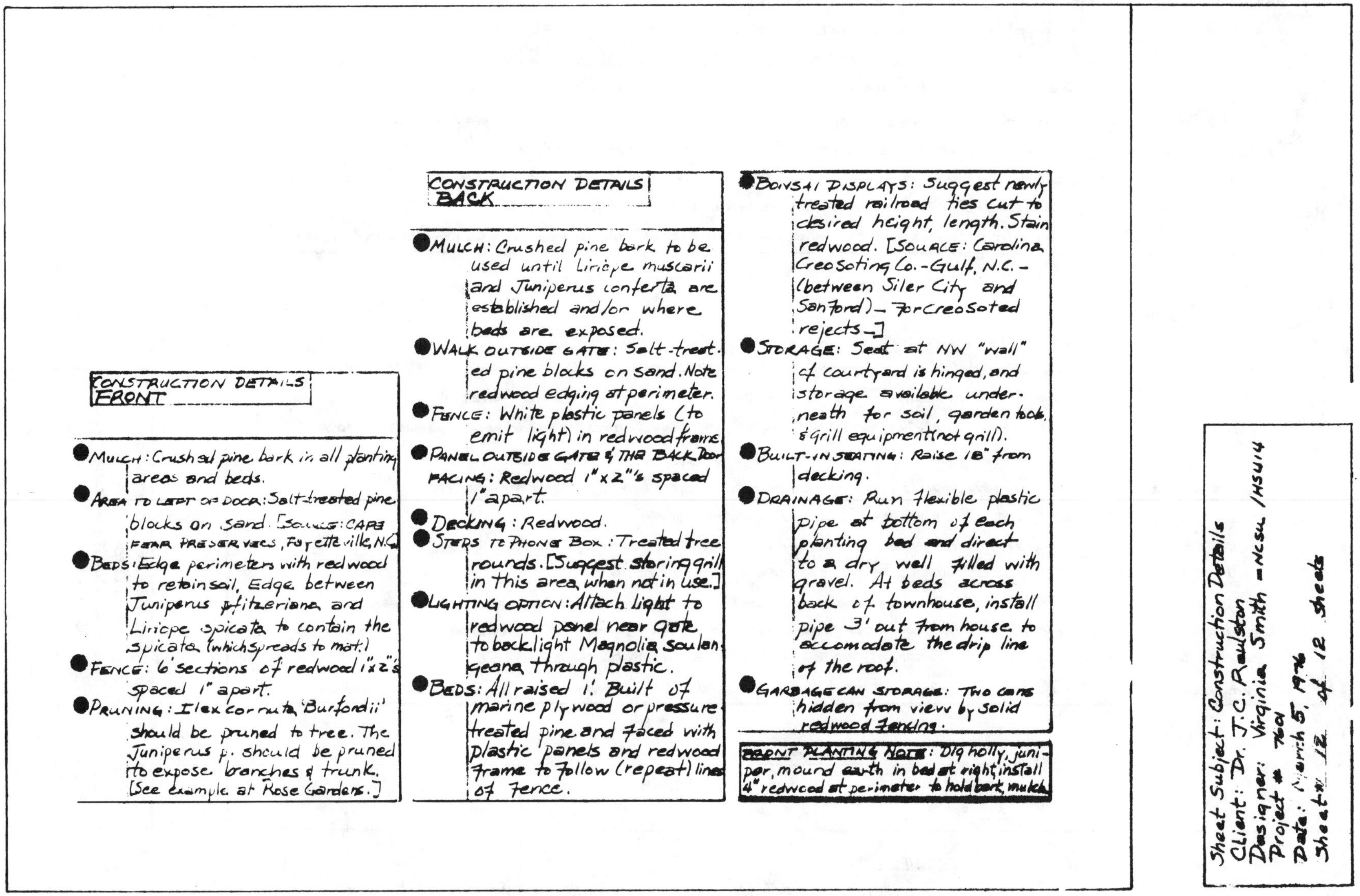

CONSTRUCTION DETAILS FRONT

- MULCH: Crushed pine bark in all planting areas and beds.
- AREA TO LEFT OF DOOR: Salt-treated pine blocks on sand. [SOURCE: CAPE FEAR PRESERVES, Fayetteville, N.C.]
- BEDS: Edge perimeters with redwood to retain soil. Edge between Juniperus pfitzeriana and Liriope spicata to contain the spicata (which spreads to mat).
- FENCE: 6' sections of redwood 1"x2"s spaced 1" apart.
- PRUNING: Ilex cornuta 'Burfordii' should be pruned to tree. The Juniperus p. should be pruned to expose branches & trunk. [See example at Rose Gardens.]

CONSTRUCTION DETAILS BACK

- MULCH: Crushed pine bark to be used until Liriope muscarii and Juniperus conferta are established and/or where beds are exposed.
- WALK OUTSIDE GATE: Salt-treated pine blocks on sand. Note redwood edging at perimeter.
- FENCE: White plastic panels (to emit light) in redwood frame.
- PANEL OUTSIDE GATE & THE BACK DOOR FACING: Redwood 1"x2"s spaced 1" apart.
- DECKING: Redwood.
- STEPS TO PHONE BOX: Treated tree rounds. [Suggest storing grill in this area when not in use.]
- LIGHTING OPTION: Attach light to redwood panel near gate to backlight Magnolia soulangeana through plastic.
- BEDS: All raised 1'. Built of marine plywood or pressure-treated pine and faced with plastic panels and redwood frame to follow (repeat) line of fence.

- BONSAI DISPLAYS: Suggest newly treated railroad ties cut to desired height, length. Stain redwood. [SOURCE: Carolina Creosoting Co. - Gulf, N.C. - (between Siler City and Sanford) - for creosoted rejects.]
- STORAGE: Seat at NW "wall" of courtyard is hinged, and storage available underneath for soil, garden tools, & grill equipment (not grill).
- BUILT-IN SEATING: Raise 18" from decking.
- DRAINAGE: Run flexible plastic pipe at bottom of each planting bed and direct to a dry well filled with gravel. At beds across back of townhouse, install pipe 3' out from house to accomodate the drip line of the roof.
- GARBAGE CAN STORAGE: Two cans hidden from view by solid redwood fencing.

FRONT PLANTING NOTE: Dig holly, juniper, mound earth in bed at right, install 4" redwood at perimeter to hold bark mulch.

Sheet Subject: Construction Details
Client: Dr. J.C. Raulston
Designer: Virginia Smith = NCSU/HSU14
Project #: 7601
Date: March 5, 1976
Sheet: 12 of 12 sheets

FIGURE 13-23
Townhouse proposal construction materials listing. (Designer: Virginia Swain Smith)

vacy, and occupant involvement. In this trend towards increased densities, simplicity, and standardization of units, site development needs to relate the units to site spaces and to provide the versatility that the structures themselves do not.

REFERENCES AND READINGS

Booth, Norman. *Form Evolution: Site Design Considerations in a Multi-Family Residential Community.* Columbus, OH: Ohio State University, Department of Landscape Architecture, 1976.

Engstran, Pottman. *Planning and Design of Townhouses and Condominiums.* Washington, D.C.: Urban Land Institute, 1979.

Jensen/Holt Associates. *Zero-Lot-Line Housing.* Washington, D.C.: Urban Land Institute, 1981.

Robinette, G. O., *Landscape Planning for Energy Conservation.* Reston, VA: Environmental Design Press, 1977.

Untermann and Small. *Site Planning for Cluster Housing.* New York: Van Nostrand Reinhold Company, 1977.

Walker, T. D. *Site Design and Construction Detailing.* West Lafayette, IN: PDA Publishers, 1978.

Summary

The phrase "residential landscape design" to landscape
designers is an idea, a plan on paper, and finally, the finished proposal completed on site. In each instance, the definition and concept
of landscape design relates to one's professional involvement, concerns, and training in landscape design. As a professional, awareness
and understanding of other specialties in the landscape industry provide a means to better communicate and develop a common front.
Professional landscape development is the concern of all the landscape industry.

In the design process starting with the initial client inquiry for
a design through the establishment and maintenance of a proposal,
many individuals with expertise and training are involved. Landscape
design should begin with an understanding and communication link
between individuals. To adequately understand a client's needs, site
conditions, and surrounding influences, designers have to understand the principles of planning and design. To communicate planning and design information, designers use graphic, written, and
verbal presentation skills. Presentation skills are an important com-

munication link for designers in that they not only convey ideas and concepts to clients, but define what, how, and where changes and additions are to occur when landscapes are installed.

While landscape architects or landscape designers are involved in various phases of planning and design, other professionals within the landscape industry provide materials and expertise for its development. Landscape nurserymen, contractors, sales people, and maintenance firms are trained to produce, sell, install, and care for the landscape proposals after they are designed. Without these support professionals in the landscape industry, the efforts of planning and designing a proposal would be hard to implement.

The concepts and principles relating to landscape design have changed greatly from the early emphasis on "foundation planting" to today's functional and attractive landscapes that combine plants, architecture, and the site with the natural landscape. No matter what the landscape style, landscape design is an extension of site planning and the design process. While landscape design is the selection of plants and construction materials as proposals to site specific situations, site planning explores the interrelationships among landforms, buildings, vegetation, and patterns of movement within the site by people and vehicles. Together, the processes of site planning and landscape design make up the design process.

In the case of a landscape design for a newly constructed home or established residence, the landforms, building, vegetation, and circulation ways are established. To adequately propose changes or modifications (landscape design) to these existing features, the designer must evaluate the site situation relative to the client's needs (the design program). When a site is being considered for development, as in a feasibility study, the landscape architect evaluates the design situation as to landform changes, drainage, building location, circulation ways, and removal or conservation of vegetation through the site planning process. Landscape design then proposes the changes and additions relative to these features. To illustrate the application of planning and design in residential landscape design, two large-scale residential design proposals have been selected for discussion. These professional design proposals have been developed by the Ted Baker Group of Coral Gables, Florida, a landscape architectural firm involved in site planning and landscape design. In reviewing the illustrations, please keep in mind that the concepts and principles used in these site planning and landscape design proposals apply to all scales of residential development. It is not the size of the project that counts, it is the quality and character that occurs.

RESIDENTIAL LANDSCAPES

The two design projects included are examples of detailed residential landscapes. While designed by landscape architects, the installation and maintenance were performed by other landscape industry professionals. The plans and photos represent site development through the use of design process. In the design stages that occur prior to the drawing of final plans and implementation, the designer's understanding of the design process provides a logical and efficient collection, evaluation, and utilization of client and site information. First the designer meets with the client to identify the type of design problem and the site's location. After the problem has been established and an agreement made relative to the anticipated design product and fee, the design process continues. The next component generated is the design program which identifies the character, function, and details to be established in the proposal. As shown in the illustrations the function and character of the site developments are distinctly different.

Case Study One

In the first example, the contemporary residence is sited on a property surrounded by other residences. The home and site have been strongly integrated in the design relationships created between indoor and outdoor spaces. Figures 14-1, 14-2, 14-3, and 14-4 are the design sheets used to identify the site's topography, building, interior room locations, and exterior activity areas. Note the matching line notations as to alignment of common edges. The original design sheets were 24" × 36", drawn at an architectural scale of ¼" = 1'0". This large scale permits the use of much detail. The larger scale also results in the presentation of the site plan on four pages. Information on these sheets include the site's grading for proper drainage and proposed pavement levels and site dimensions to define the location of edges, the building, walks, walls, and constructed features. The total design proposal included additional sheets such as irrigation plans and construction details for pavements, walls, and other structural elements. In this discussion these additional sheets were left out to allow space to review the overall planting plan. Figures 14-5, 14-6, 14-7, and 14-8 illustrate the planting plan and the actual completed site design. As in the case of the grading and dimensioning plan, the site's planting is also presented on four sheets.

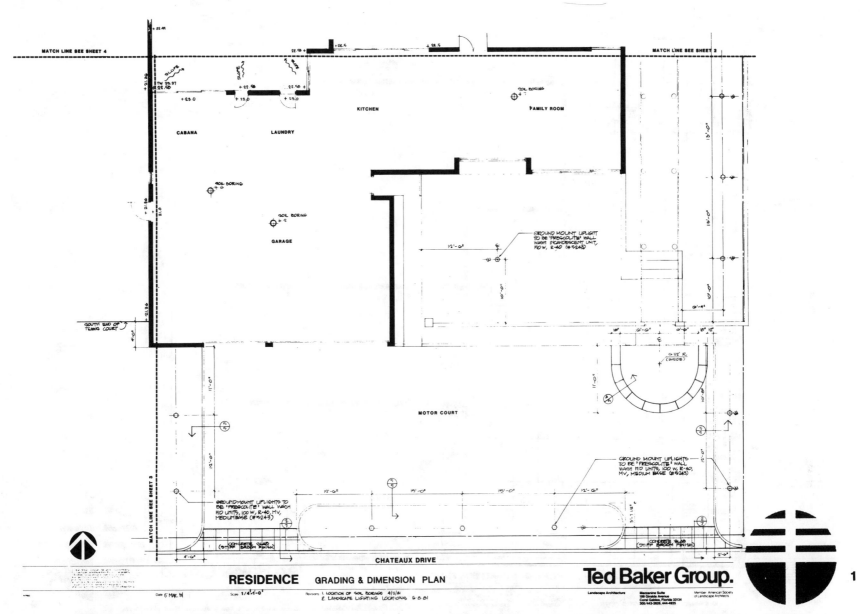

RESIDENCE   GRADING & DIMENSION PLAN

FIGURE 14-1

Residential site development proposal. As shown here and in Figures 14-2 to 14-4, the scale of the proposal, size of the site, and maximum sheet size dictated the use of four sheets rather than one to develop the design. At the original scale of ¼" = 1'-0", the drawings also doubled as construc-

tion documents. In the preliminary stages of design, the entire site would be designed at a different scale using one sheet. It is only at the last stages of design that the plan is cut and drawn to show greater detail for implementation. Please notice the match lines which reference these four sheets. (Designers: T. Baker/Susan Jellison)

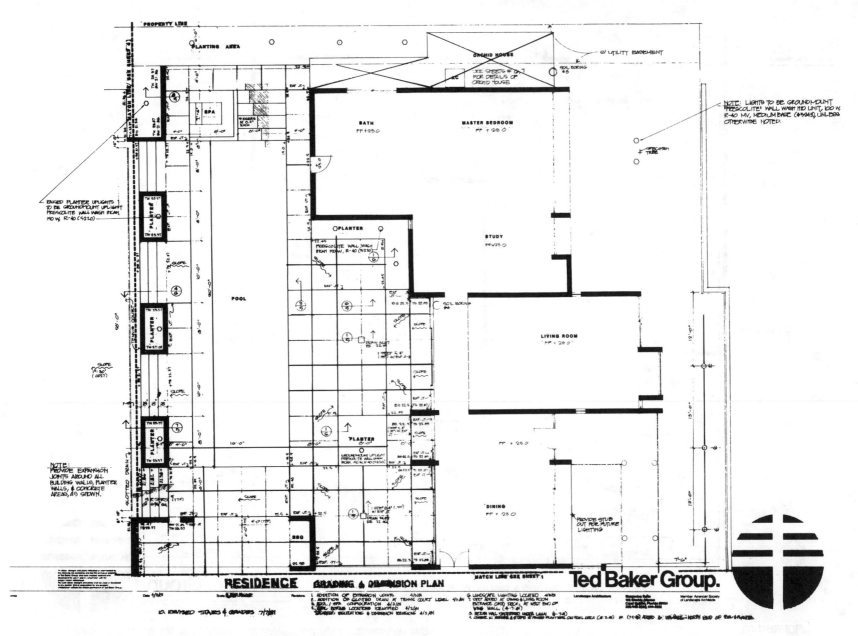

FIGURE 14-2

Residential site development proposal. This sheet shows the rear portion of
the residence and adjoining pool. Please note "match lines" at the bottom
and left-hand edges of the plan.

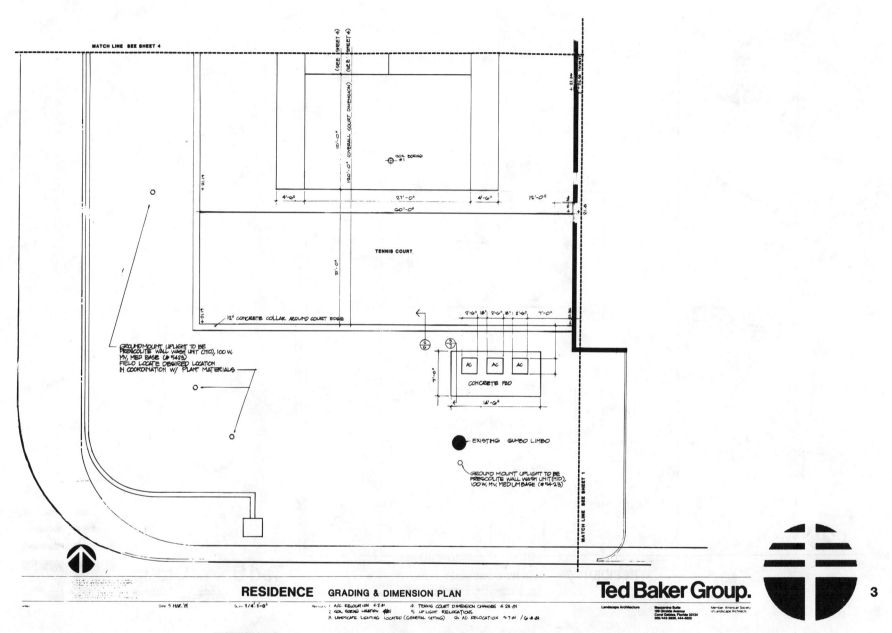

TENNIS COURT

SOIL BORING #1

12" CONCRETE COLLAR AROUND COURT EDGE

GROUND MOUNT UPLIGHT TO BE
PRESCOLITE WALL WASH UNIT (HID), 100 W,
MV, MED BASE (# 5423)
FIELD LOCATE DESIRED LOCATION
IN COORDINATION W/ PLANT MATERIALS

AC   AC   AC

CONCRETE PAD

EXISTING   GUMBO LIMBO

GROUND MOUNT UPLIGHT TO BE
PRESCOLITE WALL WASH UNIT (HID),
100 W, MV, MEDIUM BASE (# 54-23)

RESIDENCE GRADING & DIMENSION PLAN

Ted Baker Group.

3

Date 5 MAR. '81   Scale 1/4"=1'-0"

1 A/C RELOCATION 4-2-81   4 TENNIS COURT DIMENSION CHANGES 4-28-81
2 SOIL BORING LOCATION 4/81   5 UP LIGHT RELOCATIONS
3 LANDSCAPE LIGHTING LOCATED (GENERAL SITING)   6 A/C RELOCATION 5-7-81 / 6-8-81

Landscape Architecture   Mezzanine Suite   Member American Society
199 Giralda Avenue   of Landscape Architects
Coral Gables, Florida 33134
305/443-2828, 444-4925

FIGURE 14-3

*Residential site development proposal. This drawing matches with the left-hand side of Figure
14-1 showing the property's corner and a portion of the tennis court.*

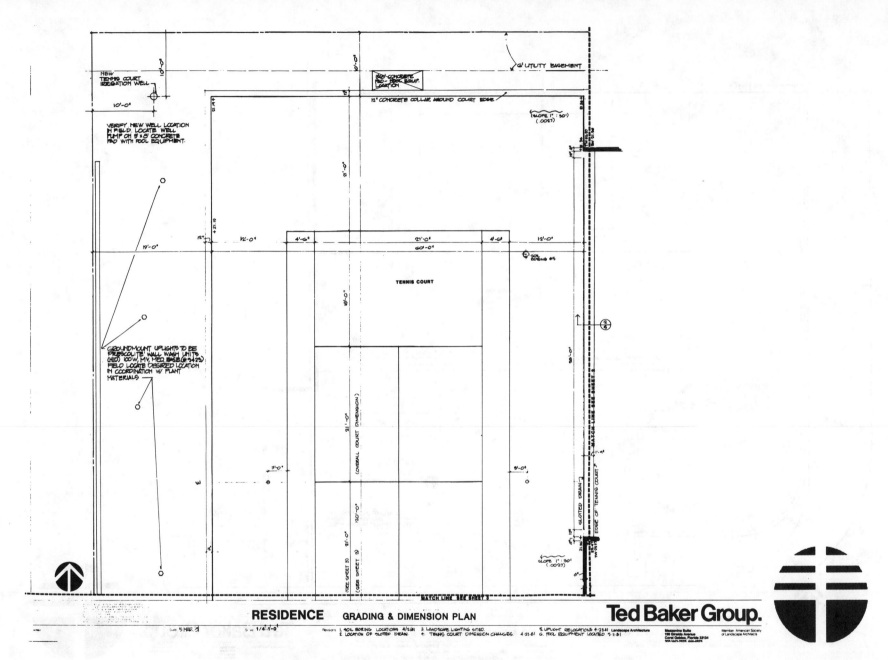

RESIDENCE   GRADING & DIMENSION PLAN

Ted Baker Group.

FIGURE 14-4

Residential site development proposal. This final sheet shows the rear corner of the property which relates to the side yard of the house and pool area. Note: Match lines at the bottom and right-hand edges of the plan.

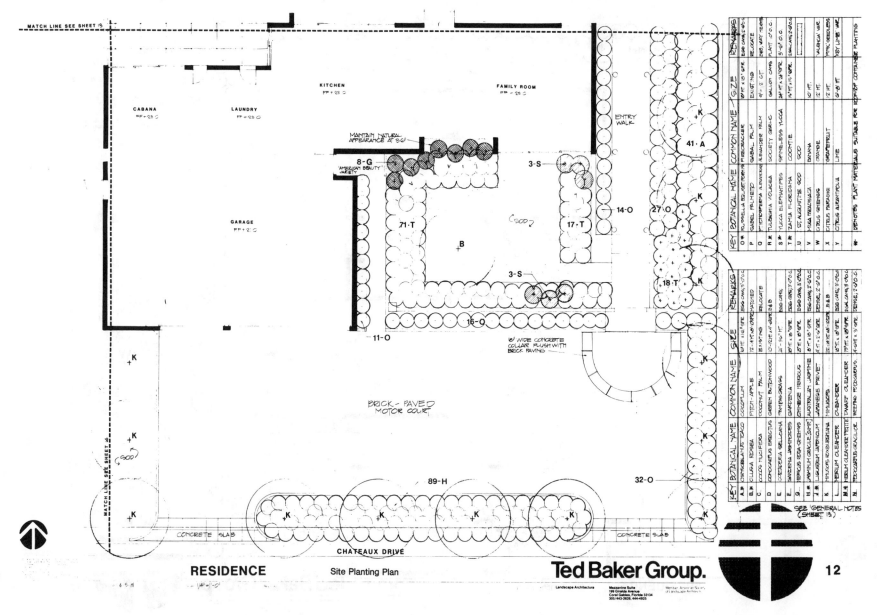

FIGURE 14-5

Site master plan. Here and in Figures 14-6, 14-7, and 14-8 are shown the actual working drawings for the proposed site plantings. From these sheets, bids could be developed to determine the material and installation costs. They can also be used as a field guide for plant establishment and identification. (Designers: T. Baker/Susan Jellison)

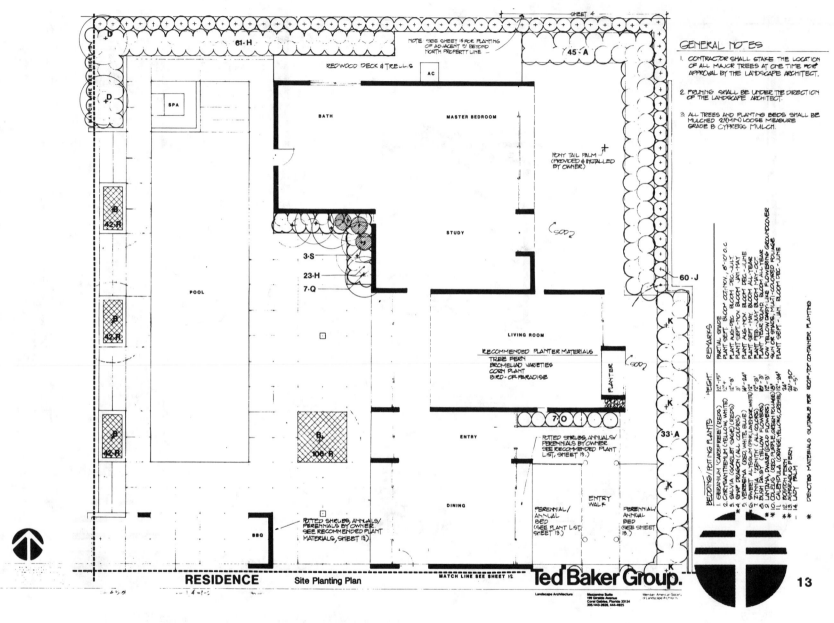

FIGURE 14-6

Site master plan. The entry, pool and yard planting areas.

424

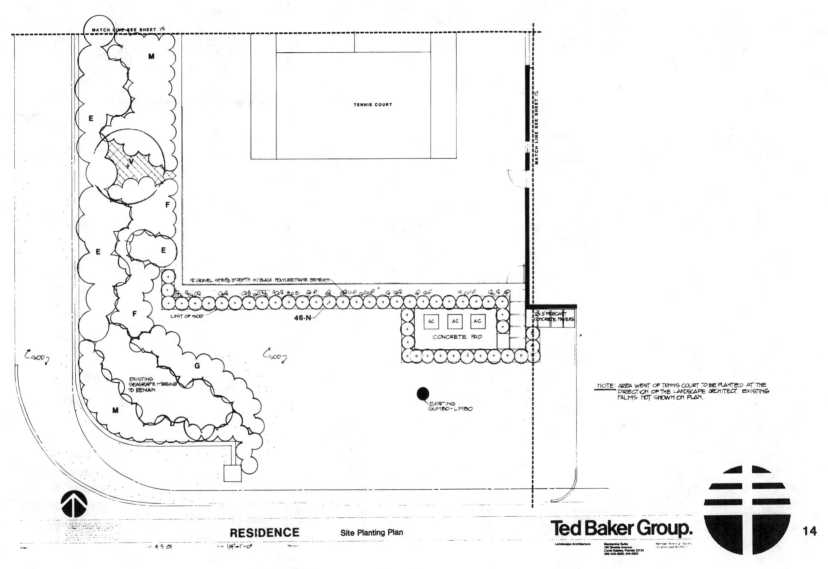

MATCH LINE SEE SHEET 15

M

E

F

E   E

F

G

M

TENNIS COURT

MATCH LINE SEE SHEET 12

1½" GRAVEL STRIP 3" DEPTH W/ BLACK POLYURETHANE BENEATH

LIMIT OF SOD

46·N

AC   AC   AC

CONCRETE PAD

2x 3' PRECAST
CONCRETE PAVERS

EXISTING
SEAGRAPE MASSING
TO REMAIN

EXISTING
GUMBO-LIMBO

NOTE: AREA WEST OF TENNIS COURT TO BE PLANTED AT THE
DIRECTION OF THE LANDSCAPE ARCHITECT. EXISTING
PALMS NOT SHOWN ON PLAN.

RESIDENCE   Site Planting Plan

Ted Baker Group.   14

Landscape Architecture

Mezzanine Suite
199 Giralda Avenue
Coral Gables, Florida 33134
305/443-3626, 444-4925

Member American Society
of Landscape Architects

FIGURE 14-7

*Site master plan. The corner planting for the property and tennis court
screening.*

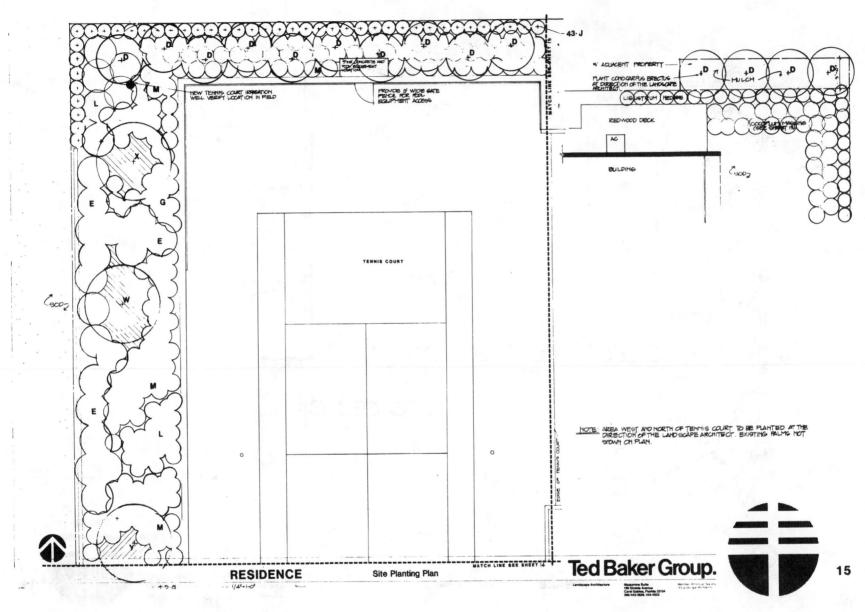

FIGURE 14-8

Site master plan. The continued tennis court screening and rear yard plantings.

The plantings and constructed landscape features in the design establish an inward focus around the terrace, pool, and tennis activity areas. The overall site plan has been developed to create spaces and subspaces that physically and visually combine indoor spaces with outdoor uses and activities. In Figures 4-9(a) and 4-9(b) the entry zone has been developed such that guests move from the street to the motor court subspace, then to the intimate scale and detail of the entry corridor. Through the design of these subspaces, the designer creates a mood change from traveling in a car to the scale and excitement of the residence's interior and exterior activities.

As a visitor moves along the entry walk towards the entry door (Figure 14-9(c)), the interplay of plantings along the walk draws the visitor toward the door. Just as the entry door is in view, plantings become more colorful through the use of annuals and peren-

(a)

FIGURE 14-9

The entry court and walk. Photos (a), (b), and (c) illustrate the plantings used in contrast to the architecture in the motor court and covered walkway to the entry. (Photos courtesy of T. Baker) (continued)

(c)

(b)

427

nials. After entering the door, a visual link is created through the house to provide a glimpse of the outdoor areas of the pool and tennis court beyond (Figures 14-9(d) and 14-9(e)).

At this point in the entry sequence, guests may move within the house to the living room or dining areas. These rooms have been designed such that window and wall placements focus one's view and attention to the landscape and recreational activities. The design plantings and landscape construction provide the setting and stage for the various site areas and activities. Some design features are definite focal points in the composition while the majority of the proposal provides enclosure and unifies the various areas of the site. One focal point is the planting bed directly at the end of the axis between the main entry and pool area. Another focus area is the striking planting viewed from the terrace and pool area.

(d)

(e)

FIGURE 14-9 (continued)

The pool area planting. Photos (d) and (e) show the accents and visual relief that the plantings provide in the outdoor entertaining and pool areas of the site. (Photos courtesy of T. Baker)

Case Study Two

In contrast to the contemporary residence just presented, this more traditionally styled residence and site has an outward focus of the bay beyond its boundaries. Figures 14-10 and 14-11 show the site dimension and grading plan for this residence. Please note that one sheet includes the entry and the other the outdoor living areas of the site. The entry sequence and access to this site is to the top of Figure 14-10. The entry is defined from the street by a wall and the building mass of the garage/servant quarters. Between the residence's entry and the street, a motor court is created to establish a sense of arrival once within the site. An elevation of the main entry area and an elevation looking towards the street can be seen in Figure 14-12.

The residence is two-story and is traditional in its design. As seen in the photos of the entry court (Figure 14–13), plantings are simple with accents of sculpture as selected by the clients. The entry planting plan is Figure 14-14. The entry design creates a sense of enclosure while the rear yard is designed to focus on the view of the bay and to define other site activities. As can be seen in Figure 14-15, a visual axis has been developed between the residence and bay. The row of trees planted parallel to the residence provides a sense of enclosure from views towards the residence yet allows focused vistas out when sitting on the patio or upper balcony. (See Figures 14-16(a) and (b)). The design of the rear yard projects the more traditional lines found in the architectural style of the residence.

When inside the house, the immediate focus is towards the pool and the bay (Figures 14-16(c), (d)). When at pool side, the focus can be diverted towards the visual axis developed parallel to the bay and perpendicular to the house. At each end of the pool, a different use area and focal point has been developed: to the left of the sheet or in a westerly direction a specimen tree is surrounded by steps creating an intimate seating area. To the right of the pool a spa and rose garden are included which physically and visually also aligned with the patio off the kitchen area of the house (Figure 14-16(e), (f)).

While much of the line character of the design is formal, the pool decking has been developed with a more informal material to provide visual contrast and as a safe walking surface (Figures 14-16(g), (h)). The greatest variety in design elements occurs in the rear yard. The patio, pool, spa, rose garden, and seating areas, while quite individual design elements, have been integrated through design to provide a total composition that is useful and attractive.

The residential landscape is an environment that includes the site, residence, and client surrounded by other influences such as people, varied intensities of land uses and climatic factors. Current design trends use site planning as a basis for landscape design decisions. As needs, technologies, and lifestyles change, our landscapes also need to change. As a practicing landscape designer, the best means to be responsible to yourself and your profession is to propose site designs that are responsive to the client and site conditions. Landscape design should focus on "site planning," *not* "site plantings" as its driving force and direction.

Now is the time to influence future landscapes by application of design and planning concepts to the development of residential landscapes. Site environments should not only be attractive but functional and energy efficient and provide the opportunity for the extension of interior spaces. *Functional, buildable,* and *visually pleasing* are the key words when proposing landscape designs with durability and personality.

To adequately respond to diverse landscape situations and opportunities, landscape designers should use a systematic process. Design process provides an efficient and logical means to inventory, analyze, and evaluate considerations while working towards an appropriate landscape design solution. An understanding of landforms, vegetation, climate, landscape construction, maintenance and the design of homes are all components included in the training of a landscape professional. Awareness of architectural periods and styles can also help landscape designers react to site situations and develop proposals that are responsive to period architecture, their sites, surroundings, and client needs.

The concepts of functionally integrating indoor and outdoor space and creating visually pleasing site environments have been around a long time. The future of residential landscape design is not in the design of large estates, but in the development of small quality garden spaces that can endure. Collectively these small residential sites make residential neighborhoods and communities more attractive and efficient places to live.

Through an understanding of how an individual site is developed, the designer and client can better evaluate a site, and the impact of its surroundings. While design and development often occurs site by site, the implications of one site or another should always be considered. While one residential site may not have a dramatic impact, when seen as a whole residential homes have visual and physical impacts collectively.

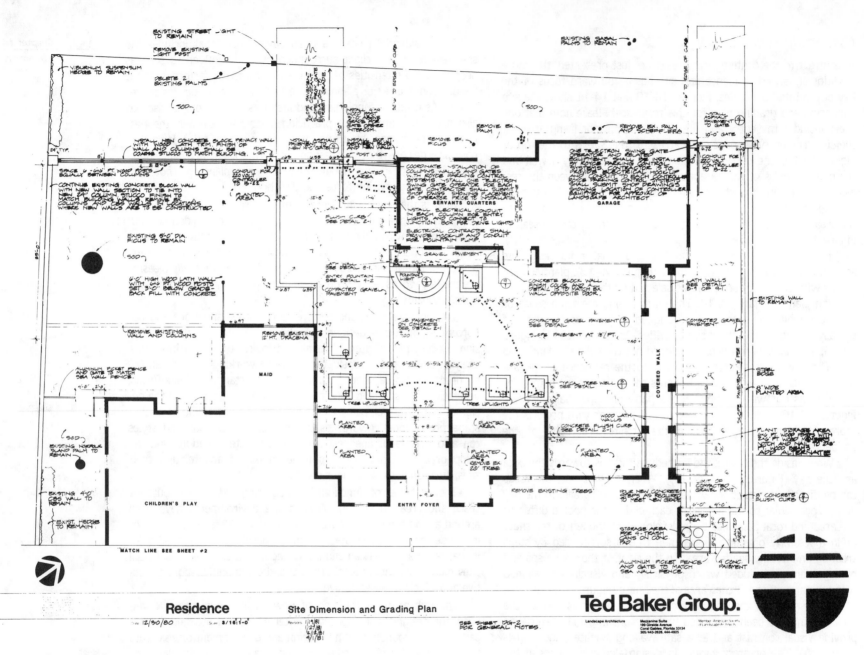

Residence — Site Dimension and Grading Plan

Ted Baker Group.

Date 12/30/80 Scale 3/16:1-0 Revisions 1/19/81

SEE SHEET DG-2 FOR GENERAL NOTES.

Landscape Architecture Mezzanine Suite 100 Giralda Avenue Coral Gables, Florida 33134 305/443-2626, 444-4925 Member American Society of Landscape Architects

FIGURE 14-10

Residential site development proposal. In this more traditional design the house location on the site defined an entry and outdoor living area as the basic areas to be developed. This sheet and the one shown in Figure 14-11 define the structural elements to be added and related dimensions. Please note the sheet match line references. (Designers: T. Baker/Bruce Reinheimer)

430

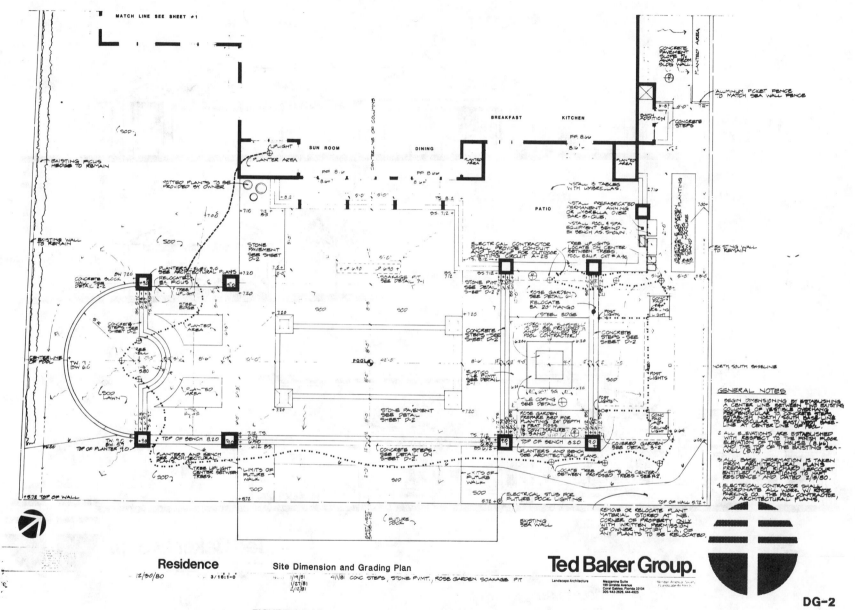

FIGURE 14-11

This sheet shows the rear yard feature and includes the dimension and grading plan information as does Figure 14-10.

431

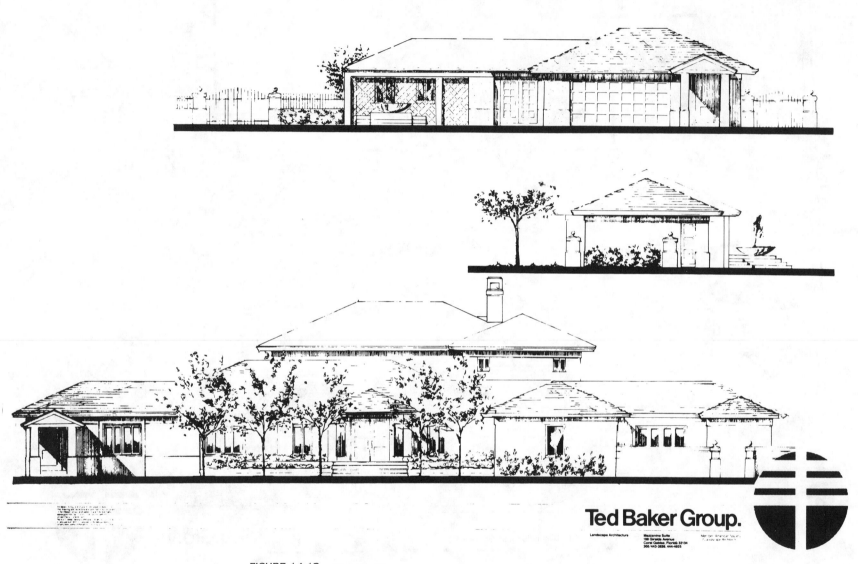

FIGURE 14-12

Entry and motor court elevations. This sheet was developed to show the views a guest may get upon entering the motor court and the vantage looking from the entry towards the street/garage area. (Designers: T. Baker/Bruce Reinheimer)

FIGURE 14-13

Entry court. Photos (a), (b), (c), and (d), show the entry court as developed from the design proposal. Note that the client and designer have also included a collected sculpture as part of the entry design. (Photos courtesy of T. Baker)

(a)

(b)

(c)   (d)

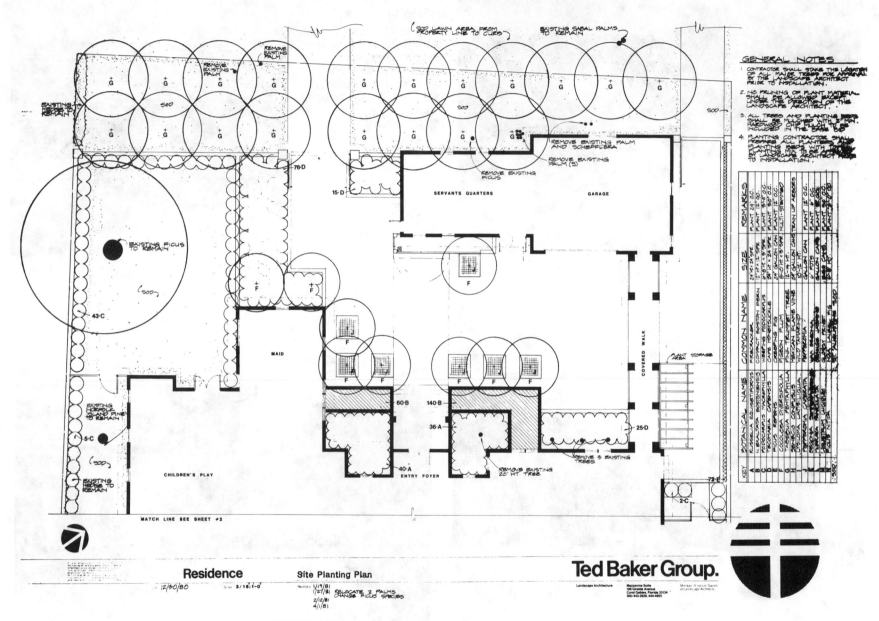

FIGURE 14-14

The entry planting plan illustrates the existing conditions and proposed revisions. From this plan a landscape contractor would implement the proposal. (Designers: T. Baker/Bruce Reinheimer)

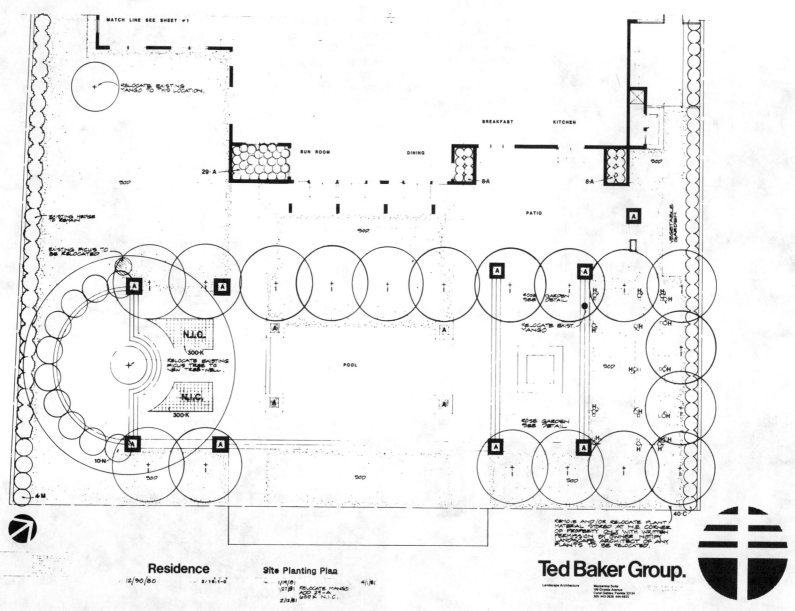

REMOVE AND/OR RELOCATE PLANT MATERIAL STORED AT N.E. CORNER OF PROPERTY ONLY WITH WRITTEN PERMISSION BY OWNER. NOTIFY LANDSCAPE ARCHITECT OF ANY PLANTS TO BE RELOCATED.

Residence   **Site Planting Plan**

12/30/80   3/16:1-0"   1/19/81   4/1/81
1/27/81   RELOCATE MANGO
          ADD 24-A
2/12/81   600 K N.I.C.

Ted Baker Group.

Landscape Architecture   Mezzanine Suite
199 Giralda Avenue
Coral Gables, Florida 33134
305-443-2626 444-4925

FIGURE 14-15

Rear yard and entertaining area planting plan. The second sheet of the planting plan details the changes to occur in the patio and pool areas of the site. In addition to the site grading, dimensions, and planting plans, the design proposal would include irrigation and construction details. (Designers: T. Baker/Bruce Reinheimer)

FIGURE 14-16

Entertaining area. As illustrations of the details developed in the rear yard entertaining areas, the photos show the separate site areas developed. Illustrations (a) and (b) show the balcony patio development, (c), (d), (e) and (f) show the pool deck design and bay view, and (g) and (h) show the patio's transition into the turf and lattice structure adjoining the rose garden. (Photos courtesy of T. Baker)

(a)

(d)

(b) *(c)*

(e)

(g)

(h)

(f)

437

SUMMARY

The design principles used in landscape design are the same as those used in producing any composition. Landscape design is three-dimensional composition in that clients may view it from a particular point yet walk within the composition and view the space from multiple vantages. The scale and proportion of proposed design elements are directly related to the size of the site, the mass of the residence, and the resulting site spaces. Order and unity in a design are based on the visual and physical links between the residence's inherent line, form, color, and textures and proposed landscape design materials. Repetition of design elements and materials can tie the residence and site together. This further reinforces the desirable physical and visual extensions of interior activities outdoors.

Design compositions may be symmetrical or asymmetrical, or a combination, reflecting the lot's configuration, the residence composition, and the physical and visual links interpreted between doors, windows, building edges, and existing landscape features. Landscape design should include rhythm, a recognizable pattern that draws people physically and visually into the design. Landscape composition should be music for our eyes, ears, noses, and fingers as we experience the dynamics of its forms and beauty. We appreciate the wildlife it attracts, the variations of its moods and the activities we enjoy within its boundaries.

While planning and design skills may allow you to go out and install landscape designs, it is often hard to explain how this orchestration will occur without using graphics. Graphics is a basic communication skill that is learned by some designers and is an inherent talent of others. Graphics requires the same mind/body coordination as learning to walk or to write. An understanding of the equipment, process, procedures, techniques, styles, and symbols of landscape design provides a means to visualize and communicate ideas and concepts to others and ourselves. Collecting, tracing, and practicing graphic techniques and styles help individual designers gain a confidence in themselves and in the tools available. After confidence and skills are developed, individual symbols and presentation styles evolve. Landscape design proposals can range from simple line drawings to detailed presentation packages. The end result is the visualization and communication of ideas and concepts that can be implemented and used.

In landscape design education and practice, individuals often have varying degrees of expertise in planning, design, and graphics which reflects their education, experiences, practice, and backgrounds. As a landscape design student or practitioner, an awareness of your interests and strengths helps define your abilities in planning, design, and graphics. Work to strengthen your weaknesses and emphasize your strengths as there is hardly an individual that is an expert at everything. As your exposure and practice in landscape design increase, use your past experiences as departure points for future design proposals. Learn from the past to make a better tomorrow. Landscape design is a very personable profession; remember that the proposals developed are for people and for living.

APPENDICES

*P*ublications and organizations

Publications

American Nurseryman, 310 South Michigan Avenue, Suite 302, Chicago, IL 60604.

Garden Design, 1190 East Broadway, Louisville, KY 40204.

Grounds Maintenance, Intertec Publishing Corporation, 1014 Wyandotte Street, Kansas City, MO 64105

Interiorscape, by Brantwood Publications, Inc., P.O. Drawer 23389 Tampa Airport, Tampa, FL 33623.

Landscape Architecture, 1190 East Broadway, Louisville, KY 40204.

Landscape and Turf, by Brantwood Publications, Inc., P.O. Drawer 23389 Tampa Airport, Tampa, FL 33623.

Nursery Business, by Brantwood Publications, Inc., P.O. Drawer 23389 Tampa Airport, Tampa, FL 33623.

Weeds, Trees and Turf, 1 East First Street, P.O. Box 6049, Duluth, MN 55806.

Organizations

American Association of Nurserymen, 230 Southern Building, Washington, D.C. 20005.

American Society of Landscape Architects, 1733 Connecticut Avenue, N.W. Washington, D.C. 20009.

Associate Landscape Contractors of America, 1750 Old Meadow Road, McLean, VA 22101.

Council of Educators in Landscape Architecture, c/o ASLA due to yearly address changes of executive boards.

Horticultural Research Institute, 230 Southern Building, Washington, D.C. 20005.

International Federation of Landscape Architects, c/o ASLA.

Landscape Architecture Foundation, 1717 N Street, N.W., Washington, D.C. 20036.

Landscape Industry Advisory Council, 230 Southern Building, Washington, D.C. 20005.

National Landscape Association, 203 Southern Building, Washington, D.C. 20005.

*L*andscape architecture programs and licensure information

ACCREDITED PROGRAMS IN LANDSCAPE ARCHITECTURE

The list of Accredited Programs in Landscape Architecture is compiled by the ASLA Council on Education: Landscape Architecture Accreditation Board.

Arizona, University of
Landscape Architecture Program
School of Renewable Natural Resources
Tucson, Arizona 85721
602-626-1004

Ball State University
Department of Landscape Architecture
College of Architecture & Planning
Muncie, Indiana 47306
317-285-1971

California Polytechnic State University
Department of Landscape Architecture
School of Architecture & Environmental Design
San Luis Obispo, California 93407
805-546-1319

California State Polytechnic University
Department of Landscape Architecture
School of Environmental Design
3801 West Temple Avenue
Pomona, California 91768
714-598-4188

California, University of Berkeley
Department of Landscape Architecture
School of Environmental Design
202 Wurster Hall
Berkeley, California 94720
415-642-4022

California, University of Davis
Division of Environmental Planning
& Management
College of Agriculture & Environment Sciences
Davis, California 95616
916-752-6326

City College of New York
Urban Landscape Architecture Program
School of Architecture & Environmental Studies
3300 Broadway
New York City, New York 10031
212-690-4118

Cornell University
Landscape Architecture Program
College of Agriculture & Life Science
230 East Roberts Hall
Ithaca, New York 14853

Florida, University of
Landscape Architecture Program
College of Architecture
Gainesville, Florida 32611
904-392-6098

Georgia, University of
Department of Landscape Architecture
School of Environmental Design
Landscape Architecture Building
Athens, Georgia 30602

Guelph, University of
School of Landscape Architecture
Ontario Agricultural College
Guelph, Ontario N1G 2W1
Canada
519-824-4120 Ext. 3354

Harvard University
Department of Landscape Architecture
Harvard Graduate School of Design
417 Gund Hall
48 Quincy Street
Cambridge, Massachusetts 02140
617-495-2573

Idaho, University of
Landscape Architecture Program
Department of Art & Architecture
Moscow, Idaho 83843
208-885-6272

Illinois, University of
Department of Landscape Architecture
College of Fine & Applied Arts
205 Mumford Hall
Urbana, Illinois 61801
217-333-0176

Iowa State University
Landscape Architecture Program
College of Design
Ames, Iowa 50011
515-294-5676

Kansas State University
Department of Landscape Architecture
College of Architecture & Design
Seaton Hall
Manhattan, Kansas 66506
913-532-5961

Kentucky, University of
Landscape Architecture Program
Department of Horticulture & Landscape Architecture
Agriculture Science Center
Lexington, Kentucky 40506
606-257-2985

Louisiana State University
Department of Landscape Architecture
School of Environmental Design
Room 211, Huey P. Long Field House
Baton Rouge, Louisiana 70803
504-388-1434

Massachusetts, University of
Department of Landscape Architecture and Regional Planning
Amherst, Massachusetts 01003
413-545-2255

Michigan State University
School of Urban Planning & Landscape Architecture
College of Social Science
East Lansing, Michigan 48824
517-353-7880

Michigan, University of
Landscape Architecture–Regional Planning Programs
School of Natural Resources, Dana Building
Ann Arbor, Michigan 48109
313-764-9315

Minnesota, University of
Landscape Architecture Program
Institute of Technology & College of Agriculture
110 Architecture Building
89 Church Street
Minneapolis, Minnesota 55455
612-373-2198

Mississippi State University
Department of Landscape Architecture
College of Agriculture & Home Economics
P.O. Drawer MQ
Montgomery Hall, Room 100
Mississippi State, Mississippi 39762
601-325-4811

North Carolina State University
Landscape Architecture Program
School of Design
P.O. Box 5398
Raleigh, North Carolina 27650
919-737-2206

Ohio State University
Department of Landscape Architecture
School of Architecture
33 Brown Hall
190 West 17th Avenue
Columbus, Ohio 43210
614-422-8263

Oregon, University of
Department of Landscape Architecture
School of Architecture & Allied Arts
216 Lawrence Hall
Eugene, Oregon 97403
503-686-3634

Pennsylvania State University
Department of Landscape Architecture
College of Arts & Architecture
127 Sackett Building
University Park, Pennsylvania 16802

Pennsylvania, University of
Department of Landscape Architecture & Regional Planning
Graduate School of Fine Arts
119 Graduate School
Philadelphia, Pennsylvania 19104
215-243-6591

Purdue University
Landscape Architecture Option
Department of Horticulture
College of Agriculture
Horticulture Building
West Lafayette, Indiana 47907
317-494-1309

Rhode Island School of Design
Department of Landscape Architecture
Division of Architectural Studies
2 College Street
Providence, Rhode Island 02390
401-331-3511

Rutgers University
Landscape Architecture Section
Cook College
Blake Hall
P.O. Box 231
New Brunswick, New Jersey 08903
201-932-9317, 9313

State University of New York
School of Landscape Architecture
College of Environmental Sciences and Forestry
Syracuse, New York 13210
315-473-8741

Texas A&M University
Department of Landscape Architecture
College of Architecture & Environmental Design
321 Langford Architecture Center
College Station, Texas 77843
713-845-1019

Texas Tech University
Landscape Architecture Program
Department of Park Administration and Landscape Architecture
College of Agricultural Science
P.O. Box 4169
Lubbock, Texas 79409
806-742-2858

Utah State University
Department of Landscape Architecture & Environmental Planning
College of Humanities, Arts & Social Sciences
U.M.C. 12
Logan, Utah 84322
801-752-4100

Virginia Polytechnic Institute State University
Landscape Architecture Program
College of Architecture & Urban Studies
202 Architecture Annex
Blacksburg, Virginia 24061
703-961-5582

Virginia, University of
Division of Landscape Architecture
School of Architecture
Campbell Hall
Charlottesville, Virginia 22903
804-924-3957

Washington State University
Landscape Architecture Program
Department of Horticulture & Landscape Architecture
College of Architecture
Johnson Hall 149
Pullman, Washington 99164
509-335-9502

Washington, University of
Department of Landscape Architecture
College of Architecture & Urban Planning
348 Gould Hall
Seattle, Washington 98105
206-543-9240

University of Wisconsin
Department of Landscape Architecture Environmental Awareness Center
School of Natural Resources
College of Agricultural and Life Sciences
Madison, WI 53706
608-263-7300

NON-ACCREDITED SCHOOLS

Program in Landscape Architecture
School of Architecture
University of Arkansas
Fayetteville, Arkansas 72701

Program in Landscape Architecture
School of Architecture and Fine Art
Auburn University
Auburn, Alabama 36830

Department of Plant and Soil Science
College of Agriculture
University of Vermont
Burlington, Vermont 05401

Department of Architecture and Planning
School of Engineering & Architecture
University of Miami
Coral Gables, Florida 33124

Program in Landscape Architecture
Department Plant Science
North Carolina A&T University
Greensboro, North Carolina 27411

Program in Landscape Architecture
Department of Recreation Res.
Colorado State University
Fort Collins, Colorado 80523

Department of Horticulture
College of Architecture
University of Missouri—Columbia
Columbia, Missouri 65211

Conway School of Landscape Design,
Delabarre Avenue
Conway, Massachusetts 01341

Landscape Architecture
College of Resource Development
University of Rhode Island
Kingston, Rhode Island 02881

Department of Horticulture and Landscape Design
Temple University
Ambler, Pennsylvania 19002

Program in Landscape Architecture
School of Architecture and Environmental Design
University of Texas
Arlington, Texas 76019

Landscape Coordinator
The N.Y. Botanical Garden
Bronx, New York 10458

The Arts, UCLA Extension
Room 640
10995 Le Conte Avenue
Los Angeles, California 90024

Department of Art and Architecture
University of Idaho
Moscow, Idaho 83843

LANDSCAPE ARCHITECTURE LICENSURE BY STATE

Licensure refers to state licensing of individuals who, upon fulfillment of specified requirements of training, education, apprenticeship or internship, examination, or a combination, are proven or deemed qualified and competent to do something, the hazards of which are not obvious to the general public. Holding a license represents a legal right to engage in activity otherwise prohibited by law—the right or privilege being conferred by some agency of government. Within professional licensing itself, there are two main types of licensure laws:

1. *Practice Act:* when provisions are properly executed, no unqualified individual *may perform the work* of a landscape architect.
2. *Title Act:* under provisions of this type of act, no persons may *call themselves* a landscape architect without a license. However, an individual can go ahead and do the work under another title or some other designation.

The matrix identifies laws by title and practice act in those states regulating the profession. The matrix was compiled by the Council of Landscape Architectural Registration Boards (CLARB) and is accurate to the best possible information as of January 1, 1982. However, you should contact CLARB or your state licensure board to obtain the most recent information.

LICENSURE REQUIREMENTS BY STATE

State	† Type of Law T	P	State	† Type of Law T	P
Alabama	X	X	Montana		X
Alaska			Nebraska	X	X
Arizona		X	New Hampshire		
Arkansas	X		New Jersey		
California		X	New Mexico		
Colorado			New York	X	X
Connecticut	X	X	Nevada	X	X
Delaware	X	X	North Carolina	X	
Florida		X	North Dakota		
Georgia	X	X	Ohio	X	
Hawaii		X	Oklahoma	X	X
Idaho	X		Oregon	X	
Illinois			Pennsylvania	X	X
Indiana	X		Rhode Island	X	X
Iowa	X		South Carolina	X	X
Kansas	X	X	South Dakota		
Kentucky		X	Tennesee	X	
Louisiana		X	Texas	X	X
Maine	X		Utah		
Maryland	X	X	Vermont		
Massachusetts	X		Virginia*		
Michigan	X		Washington	X	
Minnesota		X	West Virginia	X	
Mississippi	X	X	Wisconsin		
Missouri			Wyoming		

† T designates Title.   P designates Practice.
* Optional State Certification
Source: 1982 ASLA members handbook

Residential landscape design questions and discussion

The purpose of a site, residence, and client inventory is to establish and define what is existing and what changes need to occur relative to the client's needs and priorities. To provide an outline of the information needed prior to development of a site design, the following questions are included. It should be noted that this information is only an outline of questions to be considered in the gathering of data for a residential site design. This listing is not meant to be comprehensive or to be applicable to all design situations. Remember that each site, residence, and client is different and the questions and information collected should be specific to a site/design situation.

CLIENT CONTACT AND DESIGN SERVICES REQUESTED

The client is the person who initiates the design process. This initial contact may be through a phone call, person-to-person, or referral by another client. During an initial conversation, it is important that the designer identify what services the client is requesting and define exactly what services can be provided. A basic consensus of expectations and services should be established between the client and designer before a meeting is arranged.

This early determination saves much embarrassment, time, and frustration both for the client and the designer. When the services provided are not what the client had expected or at the cost envisioned, problems can result.

Questions To Be Answered during an Initial Client Contact

1. Client's name, address, and phone?
2. Anticipated design services being requested? You may need to explain services available before a response is received.
3. How did the client happen to contact you as a designer?
4. Design and installation time schedule?
5. Anticipated budget and fee expectations? This may or may not be a point of discussion at this time.

Discussion

With these questions, the designer has identified the caller and ascertained his or her address. The caller's name and location can provide a mental reference for the designer with respect to other clients or completed designs. This reference can then provide additional information to discuss later in the conversation. The questions pertaining to time schedule and budget can help the designer evaluate the size of the project and any possible timing conflicts with other scheduled or pending proposals. Lack of an accurate date for completion of the design or installation often is a major complaint of design clients. The longer a client waits beyond the promised date for a proposal, the more likely he or she will be unhappy with the designer. After these basic informational questions, the client or designer can establish an appointment to review the site, residence, and family data. A second option may be to delay or even stop the request if the client or designer feels other services or another designer would better serve his or her needs. At this time, the client and designer should understand the design problem, potential range of services, fees, and what will occur at their first meeting. If the client and designer feel comfortable with the overall verbal request and anticipated services discussed, a written contract can be drafted to formalize their conversation. Oftentimes, an on-site review is required to evaluate the request before a contract is drawn up.

Before this on-site visit, it should be determined if the review will cost the clients anything and exactly what will be done. Clients may occasionally request an on-site review to evaluate the project and solutions, then stop the process cold while planning to use your ideas. Before you get too involved in an on-site review, define the design policies you work under and let the clients know your professional services are to generate site ideas for a fee, and not free. A direct yet professional explanation is normally all that is necessary in this regard. Normally, clients' questions are honest and well intended. However, the occasional problem client does exist.

While en route to the site or while returning, the designer should note the neighborhood and surrounding influences that may affect the specific site's design. The site's proximity to major streets, shopping, schools, and related community facilities may influence a site development. The immediate site surroundings including adjoining residences, vegetation, topography, and utilities are also part of a site's review. The relation of a site to the sun and prevailing winds, basic climatic data, soils, and plant hardiness should also be part of the background information.

BASIC SITE/BUILDING INFORMATION

1. Define accurate property line locations through the use of a survey plat, actual field review, or both. From this basic information, a drawing scale can be selected relative to the sheet size on which the design will be presented. Often, field notes are taken on graph paper then drafted to scale at a later date. Field notes may be at a different scale than the final presentation. Slides of the existing site as an inventory record are also helpful when the actual design begins.
2. Identify the relationship between the residence and established property lines. The actual house outline should be drawn in the field to establish its shape, window and door locations, and other details such as roof overhangs, downspouts, steps, window wells, and so forth. After the house configuration is established, the major building corners are referenced to the property lines, sidewalks, and/or street edges.
3. Note the topographic changes on site. Include low and high points, wet areas, drainage swales, drain inlets, and surrounding landforms. When evaluating a relatively flat site, the landform variation from the house to the edges of the property may be the only data collected. The amount of topographic variation within a site's limits can easily be checked using a hand-held level and measuring rod. A site's topography is important in that its evaluation provides information concerning surface drainage and the need for any retaining walls, steps, and/or drainage features.
4. After the site, house location, and topography have been defined, other site features such as existing walks, walls, fences, utility poles, and vegetation should be located and recorded.
5. After these basic site elements are defined, the surrounding conditions such as adjoining roads, signs, lights, topography, residences, and vegetation should be noted as they may influence the site development. After the site inventory, the client interview can proceed.

CLIENT INFORMATION AND DESIGN PROGRAM

After you have an overview of the site, its surroundings, and the inherent features, you need to define how the clients see the site and their ideas concerning its potential development. At this stage of the inventory, the interior floor plan can be established and the physical and visual relationships among the residence, the interior rooms, and the site can be recorded.

CLIENT QUESTIONNAIRE. Actual client questions include a listing of family members, ages, and the site activities associated with those individuals. Don't overlook pets as an inventory element; they also have an impact on a site's development. In collecting parent information, identify how they perceive the existing site conditions and what are their anticipated uses in the future. Consider both immediate and long-term needs relative to their expected ownership of the site. Often, if clients' occupations require frequent moves, their needs and priorities may be quite different from homeowners who plan to establish a "permanent" residence. Within this listing of needs and considerations, try to define the clients' priorities and ideas concerning the installation of their plans. In defining a clients' priorities, the designer can better understand the direction to take in solving the design problems. In reference to installation of the design, if the clients anticipate developing the proposal themselves, the designer will have to ask additional questions about their skills and knowledge of plants and construction design elements. If the project is to be contracted, the designer will then need to define what and how each element and phase of the project should be implemented.

CLIENT MOTIVATION. Question the clients about their reasons for the development of a residential landscape design proposal. Their answers may include the following:

a. *Utility*—outdoor living areas, child's play area, garden and planting locations, easy maintenance, protection from weather, sun and winds, privacy.

b. *Aesthetics*—better composition (if so, what theme is desired—angles, curves) or seasonal interest.

c. *Other*—to create a better setting for the residence and site activities, to tie the residence physically and visually to the site and surroundings, or to develop a landscape in keeping with the architectural style/period established.

CHILDREN. If children are a part of the family, their ages and related activities will have an impact on the eventual design proposal. If younger children are to be included, a play area easily supervised by parents may be a design consideration. For older children, lawn area for running and court games may be a need. If children are grown, the design may need to include adequate parking for "family cars." All in all, as the ages and needs of the children vary, so does their impact on the landscape and site development. If as a designer you are unaware of what activities to include relative to play and children, contact a local elementary school or research play in a local library. (See design of a playspace in Chapter 11.)

OVERALL DESIGN NEEDS. Generally, design requests pertain to three main areas: (1) the entry area, (2) outdoor living area, and (3) boundary areas/property lines. Clients want the entry or public area within the residential landscape to be developed with an inviting or outward orientation. The view or perspective of a visitor or neighbor is important as is the establishment of an attractive view from indoors. The rear yard, on the other hand, is developed most often with an inward orientation. The spaces, activities, and elements established relate to the resident's interior rooms and activities. Utility, attractiveness, and privacy are the main design considerations. If a site's location has an outstanding view or potential vista beyond its limits, the design and development then may reinforce this outward relationship and minimize the inward focus.

The boundary areas of the site are the areas that are developed to provide screening, enclosure, and separation between adjoining residences and to modify the influences of prevailing winds and sun. With the scale of the typical residential site, privacy and screening plants and/or construction usually fit best at the edges of the property to allow the center portion of the site to be used as an activity area. With respect to shading, trees and/or constructed features should occur as closely as possible to the area needing shade as in the summer shadows fall almost directly below the tree or structure providing the shade.

Often at the edge of a site, an easement is defined to provide access for utilities, sewer lines, or as a drainage way. Before developing any design proposal, check with the local municipal government for setback, zoning, or covenant restrictions relative to site development. Besides an easement that may be established, construction setbacks may also exist that limit the extent to which fences, walls, or decks can be constructed on a site. Subdivision covenants may define or restrict the use of various constructed features such as fences and/or the use of various plantings.

When discussing the overall design and development of the project the clients may express an interest in, for example, attracting wildlife to the site, carrying out a particular design theme or installing native plants. This is important information to ascertain at the outset of the design process.

SPECIFIC SITE NEEDS/THE DESIGN PROGRAM. The landscape design needs to define the exact elements the clients desire in the proposal. Start by being general, then become more specific to identify details. For instance, if an outdoor living area is desired, will a patio or deck be more desirable for the clients' use and what are the physical residence/site relationships to consider? If an activity area is to be defined, its location should consider the interior rooms and related activities. Within this outdoor area, what activities will occur? Relaxing? Entertaining? How many people maximum? Times of day? Day of week?

Do the clients want to be able to barbecue? If so, check to see if prevailing summer winds will cause smoke to blow across the activity area. Also, if a *permanent* barbecue is to be considered, what is the best orientation relative to prevailing winds to allow adequate drafts for the chimney to function properly? Will movable or permanent seating be required in the entertaining area? Permanent benches can be desirable additions to any entertaining area as seating is readily available upon demand. If movable seating is to be also used, allow enough space for a table (or tables) and chairs and also for easy passage. If the entertaining area is to be used at night, lighting is a design component that should be included in any master plan.

Other general considerations include the relationship of the outdoor entertaining area to the adjoining yards, which may necessitate screening or enclosure. Seasonal shading of sun and the buffering of winds to maximize the utility of the space may also be necessary.

Other site areas that may need definition as to their function and appearance include the public entry area, site boundaries, garden area, service area, play area, and open lawn areas. While no plan is exactly the same, these are typical elements that can be found in any residential landscape.

BUDGET, MAINTENANCE, AND PHASING. After the site and client inventory have identified what is existing and what site changes are desirable, some outline of the anticipated budget, time for maintenance, and stages for installation is needed.

In discussing budget, the total dollar value available will help define what materials will be selected and the installation schedule to consider. A budget should be established to help define plant and construction material selection and phasing, not the overall design. If the budget defines the limits of the design, the result is often a collection of unrelated parts not a total composition. An entire site plan provides an outline within which time, money, and labor are used efficiently.

Maintenance often is a neglected criteria in a landscape's design and development. While the design proposal and newly constructed project may look great, it is the establishment and long-term care that affect the overall quality and enjoyment of the development. Landscape design, including constructed features and plantings, requires maintenance because of the impact of the sun, winds, precipitation, and seasonal variations of temperature. Landscape construction requires the same type of care that is customarily given to the exterior of a residence. Plantings, however, often require much more care. Plantings are living elements and thus watering, feeding, and grooming are part of their needs. No landscape is "maintenance free," yet the selection of appropriate plantings and constructed features greatly reduces the maintenance time required.

Ground cover plants, including turf and planting beds, would probably be the quickest and easiest to establish but require the greatest maintenance. In the planting of shrubs, small trees, and large trees, the establishment period is longer, but minimal care is necessary after establishment except for watering and pruning. If a savings in maintenance time is desired, it would probably be focused on the selection of ground plane plantings. While turf and ground covers take similar amounts of time to establish, turf requires more time, energy, and funds to maintain its quality. Turf not only requires watering and feeding, but mowing which necessitates a mower,

gasoline, and so on. Ground covers require similar care along with weeding, yet their maintenance component requires less energy and economic resources. However, they do not provide a durable playing surface if an intense activity or use area is needed. One option if developing a flat site may be to phase plantings to include turf and canopy trees to stabilize erosion and provide for shade and enclosure. As the family's needs and activities change, slowly phase out the turf to the sunnier areas and establish ground covers that survive better in shade. It should also be noted that turf is not the best plant species to select for sites that are wooded. It is a waste of time, money, and effort to attempt to establish turf in an environment that is shaded and has competition for water and nutrients. If durable activity areas are needed in wooded sites, shredded bark or pea gravel may be better ground surfacing choices.

While turf and ground covers require extensive maintenance during their establishment and growing season, trees and shrubs require some additional end of the season care. For example, deciduous trees provide shade during the summer, but lose their leaves in the fall. This annual leaf drop requires raking to reduce the ground litter. If possible, a compost area should be included within the property so that these decomposing leaves can be collected and used later as organic matter on site. If leaves fall in a non-activity area, they can remain as a mulch for winter protection, then be raked to the compost area in spring.

The installation of a landscape construction is not only related to budget but to the priorities and sequence of development. If possible, major features such as primary walks, retaining walls, and patios or decks should be defined and/or installed before plantings occur. With constructed features installed, less damage occurs to new plantings. If existing vegetation or plantings are to survive during a site's development, protection of the plant and surrounding soil should occur prior to construction. If heavy equipment is to be used on site, protection of existing vegetation and the surrounding soil is imperative. One of the major losses of vegetation at a construction site is soil compaction and physical damage to trunks and/or branches. Snow fences installed at or beyond the drip line of vegetation can help prevent construction damage. If a construction limit has to occur close to a major tree or planting, the remaining portion has to be protected to help insure survival. Besides soil compaction, changing the soil level by adding or taking soil from around a tree is also harmful. Retaining walls or tree wells should be used before grading begins. Lastly, no material storage or fires should occur under a tree as these too can be harmful and cause damage.

From an establishment standpoint, a lawn should be installed before landscape plantings. During the installation and establishment period, a lawn, either sod or seed, requires large amounts of water. If the soil is of a clay consistency, it retains the moisture and if installed, the landscape plants often drown. The ideal phasing would be to establish the ground plane plantings, turf and/or ground covers, then install the landscape plants after the turf or other ground covers are established. In an overall installation/phasing scheme, the ground plane should be established, then the plantings that are to provide shade, enclosure, background, a focus, or screening. The last plants to be installed would be the plantings for mass and visual interest, such as small ornamental trees, shrubs, vines.

DESIGN THEME, STYLE, AND CONCEPTS. Lastly, a discussion should occur regarding the design theme and style to be developed. Often the architectural style helps define the theme or style of the landscape. In any proposal, the lines, construction materials, and composition should relate to the residence/site's conditions. Landscape design should visually and physically extend and blend the site and residence together. As a rule of thumb, the area immediately surrounding the house should tend to be more angular and relate to the building's edges and site spaces. To provide some visual and physical transition between the vertical aspect of the house and horizontal character of the site, an area at least as wide as the side wall's height should be developed. This guideline is only an outline and has to be interpreted site to site. Pyramidal forms, if used, often reinforce the vertical aspect of the corner rather than soften it, thus a rounded form would be more suitable.

The basic function of the foundation's development should be to help create a pleasing entry space that is visually and physically an extension of the entry and related guest sequence from the street. If the residence is sited close to the street, the planting of canopy trees in the area of the curb helps establish some foreground and thus frames the view, giving an illusion of depth. Background trees are also important, as they help screen the sites of the residence and/or blend the residence and site with the surrounding homes.

SUMMARY. After the process of collecting the initial client, site program, and design information, the designer works through the *design process* as identified in Chapter 8 of the text. It is important to emphasize to the client that design is a logical process and the proposal generated can be only as useful and attractive as the information collected. After the site and client inventories, it may be desirable to again walk the site and to discuss the opportunities and limitations of the site's design with the client.

After the site review and evaluation, preliminary ideas can be developed. If the design situation permits, it is desirable to discuss the concepts with the client before a final proposal is drafted. With this review, the client can react to the ideas before the final proposal is begun.

$\mathcal{G}$lossary

Accent Plant Any plant, placed in contrast to its surroundings, which by reason of distinctive form, foliage, texture, or color calls special attention to itself.[1]

Accessory A subordinate or supporting item in building or land development; i.e., sculpture, bench, stepping stones, etc.[1]

Acclimatization The adjustment of a plant to a climatic zone or area to which the plant is not native.[1]

Aesthetic Design for the purpose of enhancing the beauty of a landscape. Since landscape architecture or design may be defined as the science or art of space utilization, and inasmuch as beauty which gives enjoyment is an important use of space in a landscape, it follows that beauty is a prime aim of landscape design. Dictionaries define aesthetics as the science of beauty.[2]

Aggregate An inert material, such as sand, gravel, shell, or bro-

---

[1]Horticultural Research Institute, Inc., Washington, D.C.

[2]*Landscape Vocabulary*, Warner L. Marsh, Miramar Publishing Co., Los Angeles, CA, 1964.

[3]*Websters World Dictionary*. The World Publishing Company, Cleveland and New York, 1974.

455

ken stone, or combination thereof, with which a cementing material is mixed to form a concrete or macadam.[1]

Annual A plant that completes its life cycle in one year, germinating from seed, producing seed, and dying in the same growing season.[1]

Arbor An open structure, usually consisting of a horizontal framework supported by columns, on which vines or other plants are trained. A pergola. A leafy bower under trees or vines.[1,2]

Arboretum A place where trees are grown for scientific or educational purposes, either by themselves or in association with other plants. Arboretums are botanical gardens in which trees and other woody plants predominate. Much of our knowledge regarding the culture of trees and shrubs has originated in arboretums.[2]

Arboriculture The growing of, and caring for, trees for aesthetic purposes, such as specimen trees, street trees, and shade trees.[1]

Arborist One who is versed in the art of arboriculture, including tree surgery, the prevention and cure of tree diseases, and the control of insects.[1]

Architect A practitioner of the design profession of architecture.[1]

Architecture The art and science of designing enclosed structures to control the environment for human activities.[1]

Ashlar A rectangular block of dressed stone. Also applied to a masonry wall constructed of, or faced with, such stones.[2]

Asymmetrical Plan Unequal or unlike objects balanced on either side of a visual axis.[1]

Atrium A small, roofless, planted court enclosed within a building.[1]

Axis A line, actual or assumed, which divides the parts in a symmetrical arrangement. In garden design the term may be used where the planting and other parts are asymmetrical, if the axis line is the center line of a vista, or terminates in a garden feature.[2]

B&B An abbreviation. (See Balled and Burlapped.)[1]

B.R. An abbreviation. (See Bare Rooted.)[1]

Backfill 1. The replacement of excavated material as into a pit or trench, against a structure, over and around culverts, and around plant material, etc. 2. The replacement material.[1]

Balled and Burlapped Plants prepared for transplanting by digging them so that the soil immediately around the roots re-

mains undisturbed. The ball of earth is then bound up in burlap or a similar mesh fabric. Abbreviated B&B.[1]

Bare Rooted Harvested plant material from which the growing medium has been removed. Abbreviated B.R.[1]

Bench Mark A fixed point of reference, chiefly for elevations, which is given either an arbitrary elevation or an elevation in direct relation to some common datum. Mean sea level is usually considered as zero.[1]

Berm 1. A narrow space or ledge. The shoulder of a road or the gradual transition slope around a paved area. 2. An elongated mound.[1]

Biennial A plant which produces leaves the first year of its life and flowers, fruit, and seeds the second year, and then dies.[1]

Blueprint 1. A negative cyanotype made by exposing to light, a drawing on translucent paper in contact with a paper coated with a preparation of ammonium ferric citrate or oxalate, and potassium ferricyanide. The light causes a chemical reaction, forming a compound of blue ferrous ferricyanide which is insoluble. The other compounds formed are soluble and are washed out by water. The term *blueprint* is now applied to many different processes of making negative and positive contact prints which are not blue. 2. The term blueprint is often used as a synonym for plan or design.[2]

Bonsai The art of growing miniature trees.[1]

Border The heavy or continuous planting about the boundaries of a site, lawn, or garden space.[1]

Botanical Garden A garden devoted to the cultivation of plants for scientific or educational purposes.[1]

Boulder A large rounded rock.[1]

Boundary A line in space which marks or defines a limit.[1]

Boundary Screen Plant or construction materials on the boundary of a site which provide protection or concealment.[1]

Brick A building block, generally a rectangular prism, of clay or shale which has been fused in a kiln or sundried. Brick and bricklike building blocks are also made of many materials, such as slag, cement, lime, etc. For the landscape architect, bricks have many uses, for paving, garden walls, and other garden and landscape features.[2]

Buffer Strip An area utilized to reduce undesirable effects from the surrounding area. A space between different land uses to reduce the impact of the uses on each other.[1]

Caliper In landscape and nursery usage, the diameter of a trees trunk is measured six inches above the groundline including trees up to a four-inch caliper. If of a larger caliper than 6 inches, the measurement is made 12 inches above the ground-line. In forestry, the caliper is measured four and a half feet above ground level.[1]

Canopy 1. The overhanging part of a tree which shades the ground. 2. An awning or structure for shade purposes.[1]

Character Plant Unique, atypical, or distinctly different plants either in form or density because of pruning or other cultural manipulation. In landscaping, a character plant may be used as a focal point or accent subject.[1]

Chromatic Color A pure spectral hue. The sensation to the eye caused by a specific wavelength of solar radiation.[2]

Circulation 1. Movement of air through an area. 2. Traffic routes which are utilized between points.[1]

Clearing 1. A natural open area within a forest or woodland, or an area which has been cleared for cultivation or human occupation. 2. The removal of trees, brush, or other vegetation, boulders, etc., prior to earthwork operations.[1]

Client One who employs a professional to perform a service, hence the patron of a profession. The relationship between the client and the professional practitioner involves some confidential service and tends to be closer than the relationship between employer or employee, or between customer and merchant.[2]

Climate A generalization of the weather conditions of a specific area. The climate of an area is a major factor in the environment of the organisms which inhabit the area. The weather phenomena observed and recorded pertain to atmospheric temperature, freezing, humidity, precipitation, wind, and storm occurrence. Landscape architects are continually concerned with the climates of areas in which they work, not only in their broad aspects, but with regard to local variations, or microclimates.[2]

Collector Street A major traffic route for a neighborhood.[1]

Collector Walks A sidewalk which carries heavy pedestrian traffic coming from several areas.[1]

Color A phenomenon resulting from reactions of matter and light, whereby light rays (radiations) are separated as to wavelengths, some being absorbed and others reflected. (See Chromatic Color.)[2]

Conifer A plant which bears seeds in a cone; with the exception of the larches and the bald cypress, practically all conifers are evergreens. Needle-bearing plants, as the pine, spruce, and the fir.[1]

Conservatory A glazed room or structure where plants are grown for display under controlled conditions of humidity and temperature.[1]

Construction The process of fabricating and erecting the various elements of a structure or area of land.[1]

Construction Details Drawings of plans, sections, and elevations of individual elements of site plans; such as roads, walks, curbs, gutters, drain inlets, paving patterns, fences, etc.[1]

Contour An imaginary line or its representation on a map of all points of the same height above or below a given datum. Mean sea level (zero elevation) is generally the given datum.[1]

Contractor A person who undertakes to perform specific works for specific compensation. In the United States and in many other countries, contractors engaged in construction projects are licensed and regulated by law.[2]

Cost Plus A contractual arrangement where the purchaser agrees to pay all costs plus a specified percentage of the total cost to the contractor for work done.[1]

Course Any single or horizontal layer of material.[1]

Courtyard An unroofed area, surrounded or partially surrounded by a dwelling or other structures.[1] The Spanish name for courtyard is "patio."[2]

Cross section 1. A cutting or section, or a piece of something cut off, at right angles to an axis. 2. A transverse section at right angles with the longitudinal axis of the object, structure, or item of construction through which the section is taken.[1]

Crown 1. Upper branches of a tree. 2. A measure of elevation of the center of a road in relation to outside edges of road surface.[1]

Cul-de-Sac 1. Passage or place with only one outlet; such as a dead-end street or circular turnaround. 2. A French name for a short street or passageway, open only at one end. Literally the term means "bottom of a bag."[1, 2]

Cyanotype A photographic print made on paper sensitized by a cyanide.[3]

Deciduous Plants that shed all their leaves at the end of the growing season and remain leafless during winter or dormant periods.[1]

Design   1. To fashion according to a plan or idea. 2. A term often used as a synonym for plan or in common usage, as a synonym for intent.[1,2]

Diagram   A graphic presentation of an object, situation, or operation.[2]

Dry Wall   A wall of stone or rubble laid without mortar. Dry walls are used as low retaining walls or freestanding walls in gardens. The crevices in dry walls are frequently filled with soil and planted with alpines or other suitable plants.[2]

Dry Well   Collection pit for drainage, often filled with stone rubble.[1]

Dwarf   Small-sized plant for its age, but nevertheless a plant with normal vigor and in a healthy condition.[1]

Dwelling   A place of abode. A residence. Most of the area of cities is occupied by dwellings. The term *dwelling unit* has come to mean a structure or part of a structure occupied by a single family which may consist of one or more persons living independently of other individuals.[2]

Earthwork   The movement of earth materials to alter surface levels. Earthworks include excavation, embankment, cut and fill, leveling, trenching, terracing, etc. Earthworks not only change surface levels, but alter natural drainage systems, and require the construction of artificial drainage structures.[1,2]

Easement   1. An acquired right of use which one may have in the land of another. 2. A right-of-way for public or quasi-public use. Easements are used for public utilities, bridle paths, parkways, floodways, and other purposes.[1,2]

Environ   To enclose or surround. The areas surrounding a city or town are its environs.[2]

Environment   The assemblage of materials, situations, and conditions surrounding an organism and its component parts. Also called the *surround.*[1,2]

Environmental Factor   A constituent of an environment considered separately from other constituents. Environmental factors in the landscape may be classified into four major groups: (1) biotic, (2) climatic, (3) edaphic, and (4) topographic.[2]

Espalier   1. Method of training plants to grow flat against a wall or trellis in a desired shape or form. 2. A tree or other plant trained to grow flat on a wall or a trellis. It is useful where space is limited, but it requires perseverance and skill on the part of the gardener.[1,2]

Establishment Period   Time necessary after installation of a plant to assure continued growth.

Esthetic   See Aesthetic.

Evergreen   Retaining foliage throughout the year. This term is applied to many conifers and broadleaf plants which have this characteristic. Deciduous plants drop their foliage during cold weather (winter). Almost all tropical and semitropical plants are evergreen.[2]

Excavation   Act of taking out materials; the hollow or depression after materials are removed.[1]

Exotic   Plant or other organism which has been introduced from other regions and is not native to the region to which it is introduced.[1]

Extensional Landscape   The landscape beyond boundaries of a property. The macrolandscape.[1,2]

Face Planting   Frontal planting to taller groups of plants or structures.

Fence   An artificial barrier used to enclose an area and generally to restrict movement by man, animals, and machines. Sometimes used only for ornament. Fences are used as boundary markers and are important factors in the cultural landscape.[1,2]

Filler Tree or Shrub   Temporary tree or shrub of fast-growing habit utilized to give density to a planting, which is later removed when desired plants mature sufficiently to give the desired density.[1]

Finish Grade   Final earthwork which leaves the terrain at the designated elevation as required by the site grading plans.[1]

Flagstone   Any stone which can be split into large flat slabs, suitable for paving or for stepping stones. Most flagstones are fine grained sandstones with shaly partings in the bedding planes.[2]

Footing   Enlargement at lower end of a wall, pier, or column to distribute load over a larger ground surface.[1]

Formal Garden   A symmetrically arranged garden where the plantings, walks, fountains, pools, pergolas, and other structures are arranged symmetrically on one or more axes. Simple geometrical forms—rectangles, triangles, circles, etc., reminiscent of formal gardens—are frequently incorporated into garden structures and plantings, these being arranged asymmetrically upon a visible or an implied axis.[1,2]

Foundation Planting Planting of shrubs, ground covers, and sometimes small trees near the foundation of a building.[1]

Fountain A natural or artificial spring of water, particularly any ornamental device arranged to throw jets or sprays of water into the air and returning the water to a basin or pool.[1,2]

Frame Structure for plants with a covering of glass or plastic to control humidity and temperature and for some kind of shading, as a lath or plastic screen to control light.[1]

Freeform 1. Having an irregular, nonrectangular, or curvilinear form or outline. 2. Spontaneous or unrestrained.[1]

Freestanding Object which relies only upon itself for its form and support.[1]

French Drain Method of providing temporary surface drainage when the quantity of water to be removed is small and the amount of sediment would likely clog surface inlets.[1]

Front Setback A condition usually set forth by a zoning ordinance which regulates the distance the structure must be from the front property line.[1]

Garden 1. A piece of ground for the cultivation of herbs, fruits, flowers, or vegetables. 2. A place where plants are cultivated for pleasure or domestic use. In gardens, the plants are arranged in an orderly or planned fashion.[1,2]

Gazebo A Dutch name for a summer house or garden shelter from which a view can be enjoyed.[2]

Grade 1. A ground level (noun). 2. To alter the ground level (verb). 3. Sometimes used as a synonym for gradient.[2]

Grading Modifications of ground surface by either cuts and/or fills.[1]

Grading Plan Plan showing existing and proposed elevations, which establishes levels for buildings, roads, retaining walls, outside steps or ramps, and other ground surface areas.[1]

Graphic Scale A graphic device used on maps or drawings to indicate the ratio between the size of the elements of the map or drawing and the area of things depicted.[2]

Gravel Unconsolidated, sedimentary deposits of pebbles and sand particles. Gravel deposits vary greatly in composition. They are frequently lens shaped and mixed with other sedimentary deposits. Consolidated gravel deposits form conglomerate rock.[2]

Ground Cover 1. Plants, usually of low height, used to cover areas, to exclude undesirable plants or to prevent erosion. 2. Also inert materials used for the same purpose.[1]

Habit of Growth Mode of growth, confirmation, or general appearance of a plant, including the changes which take place seasonally during its life cycle.[1]

Hardiness The adaptation of a plant or other organism to the rigors of a climate, particularly to the occurrence of freezing, although conditions of moisture, extreme heat, etc., may also affect the ability of a plant or organism to survive.[1,2]

Hardy Capable of living over winter without artificial protection.[1]

Hedge Plants growing close to each other in a row to form a continuous mass of foliage, either trimmed or allowed to grow naturally. Although hedges require more land area than do fences, they are frequently preferred for their aesthetic values, to provide protection, and to reduce soil erosion.[1,2]

Herbaceous Plant Plant which does not develop woody persistent tissue, as that of a shrub or tree, but is more or less soft or succulent.[1]

Horticulture 1. Art and science of growing fruits, vegetables, and ornamental plants. 2. The art and science of propagating and cultivating plants for their produce or for ornament.[1,2]

Hue The name of any one of the chromatic colors as they appear in the spectrum of sunlight. The recognized hue names are violet, blue, green, yellow, orange, and red. Many thousands of tints and shades of these hues are recognized and named. (See Color.)[2]

Informal Garden Garden employing asymmetrical or occult balance.[1]

Land The solid part of the earth's surface which is not covered by water.[2]

Land Form The shape into which a land surface area is sculptured by natural forces. The configuration of the land. Landforms may be classified as depositional, diastrophic, erosional, or residual.[1,2]

Landscape 1. That portion of the earth's surface which is visible from any point on or above the land surface, which the eye can comprehend in a single view, especially in its pictorial aspect. If we accept this understanding of the term, we find ourselves, when out-of-doors, always in the midst of a landscape composed of nature's pristine works, or in a cultural landscape, where these works have been altered, modified, or replaced by the hand of man.

Landscape Architect   A practitioner of the science and art of designing and developing landscapes and gardens. In some states the right to use this designation is restricted by law to licensees.[1,2]

Landscape Architecture   1. The art of arranging land and the objects upon it for human use and beauty. 2. The art of space utilization in the landscape. Landscape architecture is concerned with the use to which landscape space is put, the creation of controlled environments within the landscape space, the adaptation of organisms to both the natural and controlled environment, and the conservation of the aesthetic values and resources of the landscape.[1,2]

Landscape Construction   Alteration of existing ground conditions together with construction and development of ground features including minor structures.[1]

Landscape Contractor   Contractor who specializes in work dealing with all phases of landscape planting and construction.[1,2]

Landscape Design   Creative environmental problem-solving process to organize external space and attain an optimum balance of natural factors and human needs.[1]

Landscape Garden   1. An area designed and built to contain the natural and man-made elements for man to enjoy. 2. A naturalistic style of garden popular in the latter part of the eighteenth, and the nineteenth centuries. The landscape garden style had perhaps its finest development in England under Humphrey Repton, and later in America under Andrew Jackson Downing, the elder Frederick Law Olmsted, and Jens Jensen.[1,2]

Landscape Nursery   A firm whose activities are devoted to all phases of landscape planting and construction, often including design and maintenance services, and often growing a portion of plants installed.[1]

Landscaping   The improvement of the landscape by design, construction, and plantings.[1]

Layout Plan   A plan which locates accurately by dimensions all buildings, walks, roads, parking areas, planting areas, etc.

Macro-landscape   A term coined by the editor[2] to convey the concept of landscape not limited by boundaries. The whole landscape as visible from any point on or above the surface of the earth.[1,2]

Maintenance   1. The upkeep of property, equipment, etc., 2. To sustain. The landscape is not static, but subject to all the forces of nature. Rain falls, the wind blows, the sun heats and dries, trees and plants grow, mature, and die, soils erode, structures weather and disintegrate. [1,2]

Map   A representation of the physical, cultural, and political features of the surface of an area, such as the earth, a country, state, etc. [1]

Master Plan   1. A plan which covers all existing conditions and proposed development for an area. 2. In common usage, any plan which pretends to be comprehensive, or to depict or describe an ultimate development.[1,2]

Microclimate   The climate of localized areas and of the lower layer of the atmosphere near the ground. The published climatic data of any area deal with the averages of temperature, moisture, etc., of a number of included microclimates plus data concerning the upper layers of the atmosphere. The occurrence of these microclimates is a matter of common observation. All of us are aware of the variations from sun to shade, the variations of frost, the differences between forests, clearings, and open field.[1,2]

Micro-landscape   A term coined by the editor[2] to convey the concept of a landscape unit definitely limited by boundaries. A garden is a micro-landscape.

Mulch   A layer of leaves, straw, manure, litter, or other more or less decomposed organic materials used as a thin protective covering on the surface of the soil. Mulches reduce water losses from the soil by reducing evaporation. They also reduce runoff of water, prevent erosion, improve soil structure by reducing compaction, control weeds, and prevent freezing. Artificial materials, such as paper and inorganic materials, such as rocks and vermiculite may also be used as mulches.[1,2]

Mulching   Application of a protective cover to the soil to conserve moisture, lessen temperature variation, protect against runoff and erosion and surface compaction by rain, improve aeration, and discourage weeds.[1]

Native   Plant that grows naturally in a region, not introduced nor naturalized.[1]

Natural Form   1. General plant shape which develops when outside influences such as crowding, pruning, dwarfing, etc., are absent. 2. The complex and constantly changing curves in line and plane which are classified as restful forms of beauty and nature.[1]

Naturalize   Adapt to an area in which it is not native.[1]

Neighborhood   An area or a location containing an association or population of organisms.[2]

Nursery   1. A place where trees, shrubs, vines, and other plants are grown. 2. Enterprise which grows trees, shrubs, vines, and other plants.[1]

Nurseryman   One who engages in the business of growing nursery stock.[1]

Nursery Stock   Plant materials grown in and/or obtained from a nursery.[1]

Ornamental   A plant grown for beauty of its form, foliage, flowers, or fruit rather than food, fiber, or other uses.[1]

Ornamental Horticulture   Art and science of growing ornamental plants.[1]

Parkway   Street or highway established with a right-of-way and which has been planted with trees, shrubs, and/or flowers, or on which natural vegetation has been retained; or an elongated park often used to connect parks in a system and usually associated with a road or highway.[1]

Patio   The Spanish name for a paved, enclosed, or partially enclosed courtyard adjoining a dwelling.[1,2]

Pavement   Any hard surfacing material on a roadway or other area. Rock, concrete, and asphalt are paving materials in common use.[2]

Perennial   Plant that continues to live from year to year. In cold climates the tops may die but the roots and rhizomes persist.[1]

Pergola   An open garden structure consisting of a framework held aloft by posts or columns and over which vines or other plants are trained.[2]

Plan   A graphic presentation, usually in the form of drawings and descriptive writing, to convey the data essential to the construction, development, or accomplishment of a project. Sometimes the term *plan* is applied to the drawing, and *specifications* to the descriptive writing, but they are not separable. In reality, the plans are the ideas which the drawings and writings represent. The purpose of plans is to convey ideas from the mind of the planner to the minds of all others, especially clients.[2]

Plane   A smooth, flat surface.[2]

Planning   Any activity which projects an enterprise into the future belongs in the category of planning.[2]

Plant Form   Each species' unique "expression" which is determined by the size that is natural to it, mode of branching, form of top, twig characters, · bark, foliage, flower, and fruit characters.[1]

Plant List   List of plant materials indicating quantities and sizes called for on a planting plan.[1]

Plant Pit   Excavated hole in which the plant material is placed.[1]

Planting Plan   Plan which locates and identifies all items of plant material to be used and any existing materials to be preserved or removed.[1]

Planting Saucer   Saucer shape of soil (man-made) surrounding the immediate area of newly planted tree, for purpose of water concentration. Also planting basin.[1]

Planting Strip   Area between the sidewalk and the curb.[1]

Plat   Map, plan, or chart of a city, town, section, or subdivision indicating the location and boundaries of individual properties.[1]

Plot   1. Small, limited area. 2. A lot. 3. A plan (noun). 4. To plan (verb).[1,2]

Project   Any enterprise which advances toward a goal. The term is most frequently applied to enterprises which require planning as a major means in advancing toward the ultimate goal.[2]

Ramp   An inclined plane serving as a way between two different levels.[1]

Retail Nursery   A firm primarily engaged in retail selling of plants and related supplies which also grows plant material, most of which it sells at retail. Also retail grower.[1]

Retaining Wall   Wall to retain an embankment or an abrupt change in surface levels.[1]

Right-of-Way   Total strip of land within which there is public control and common right of passage, and within which all pavements and utility lines are located, if possible. (See Easement.)[1]

Rock Garden   A garden where rocks are associated with plants in natural or formal compositions.[2]

Rough Grading   Stages of earthwork operations, cuts and fills preliminary to final work.[1]

Scale   1. Size of a plan, map, drawing, or model compared with what it represents. A reference to the relative size of things. The size of man, the human scale, is the standard reference for the size of all things in his culture and in the universe. 2. Feeling of size a person gets within a landscape. 3. Any of several plant insects with a shield-like covering. 4. Protective covering of a leaf bud.[1, 2]

Scheme   A term frequently employed as a synonym for design or plan.[2]

Service Area   1. An area set aside for outdoor storage and household utilities, such as clotheslines, incinerators, etc. Usually separated from garden areas by walls, fences, or hedges. 2. Area served by a utility. 3. Area developed for delivery of goods and services.[1, 2]

Setback   Distance between property line and a line authorized by local ordinances and codes, which designates how close a building can be built to the property line.[1]

Shade   The partial or complete obstruction of direct sunlight. Shading is one of the ways that large plants affect the environment of smaller plants and other organisms which live in association with them.[2]

Shrub   Woody perennial plant, usually smaller than a tree and generally with multiple stems arising from the roots.[1]

Site   A location.[2]

Site Analysis   The collection and organization of data pertinent to the landscape design and development of a site. Such data include information regarding boundaries, drainage, topography, soil, vegetation, proposed uses, surroundings, etc.[1, 2]

Site Factors   Environmental factors which are present at a specified location.[1]

Site Planning   Design process which explores relationships between building masses, vehicular and pedestrian circulation, ground forms, vegetation, and appropriate use of all the land to produce an aesthetic and functional development.[1]

Slope   Face of an embankment or cut section; any ground whose surface makes an angle with the plane of the horizon.[1]

Sod   1. Grassy surface of the ground. 2. Section cut from grassland, containing the top growth, rhizomes, roots, and the soil clinging to the roots. (See Turf.)[1]

Soil   The weathered, and biologically altered, upper part of the regolith. To a farmer or a landscape architect, the soil is the part of the surface of the earth which supports the growth of plants. It supports plant growth when it contains the proper amounts of air, water, and nutrients. Soils also give mechanical support to plants.[2]

Solar Energy   The energy received on the surface of the earth from the sun.[2]

Space   That which has length, breadth, and height. For practical purposes, the three-dimensional working area within which landscape architects may construct gardens and landscapes. Landscape architecture is the art of space utilization.[2]

Specification   Written document stipulating kind, quality, and sometimes quantity of materials and workmanship required for any construction or work.[1]

Specimen   1. Exceptionally heavy, well-shaped plants. 2. Sample of a particular plant species.[1]

Specimen Plant   1. In appearance, an ornamental plant which approaches the optimum form and density characteristics for the particular species and variety. 2. In landscape usage, any plant which is displayed to its best advantage either singly or in multiple plantings. 3. Atypical or distinctly different plant either in form or density because of pruning or other cultural manipulation. (See Character Plant.)[1]

Stagger   1. To plant alternately at equal distances in a row on either side of a middle line (as in the planting of hedges). 2. To arrange over any area at equal distances without any reference to any definite line.[1]

Subdivision   The dividing of land into parcels.[2]

Substitute Plant   A plant allowed to be substituted for one originally selected, for reasons of supply, season, suitability, etc.[1]

Surveying   The determination of the relative location of point on the surface of the earth. Precise measuring instruments and trigonometry are the principal tools used by surveyors. Much surveying today is accomplished with the aid of aerial photography and photogrammetry, supplementing the establishment of control points in the field.[2]

Symmetry   Exactly similar parts of components on opposite sides of an axis, point, or plane.[1]

Tanbark   A byproduct of the tanning industry, sometimes used on paths, around playground equipment, or as a mulch.[1]

Terrace   An essentially level and defined area, often raised, either paved or planted, forming part of a garden or building setting.[1]

Thinning   Removal of some of the plants in a row, or trees in a stand, in order to avoid crowding.[1]

Topography   1. Configuration of a land surface including its relief, the position of its streams, roads, etc. 2. A term applied to the surface features or relief of the earth, or to a graphic description of these features.[1,2]

Transplant   Move a plant from one growing area or medium to another.[1]

Tree   Woody perennial plant usually having a single main axis or stem (trunk) usually exceeding 10 feet in height at maturity. Trees are the largest organisms on earth.[1,2]

Tree Canopy   Overstory provided by tree foliage.[1]

Tree Well   Device constructed to maintain the original grade around an existing tree.[1]

Trellis   An open framework or lattice used as a support for growing vines or other plants.[2]

Turf   1. The live dense top growth with the upper stratum of earth and vegetable mold filled with roots of grass and other small plants, so as to form a kind of mat. 2. Thick matting of low plants, mostly grasses, on the surface of the ground. (See Sod.)[1,2]

Understory   The small trees, shrubs, and other vegetation growing beneath the canopy of forest trees.[2]

Utility Map   Map which shows utility easements, rights-of-way, location, size, and invert elevations of existing sanitary sewers, storm drains and open drainage channels, light poles, railroad lines, etc.[1]

Vegetation   The plant life that covers land areas of the earth.[2]

Walk   A graded, surfaced thoroughfare intended for pedestrian use.[1,2]

Wind   A horizontal current of air in the atmosphere.[2]

Windbreak   A planting composed of plants placed in such location as to shield certain areas from undesirable winds, usually the cold northwest winds of winter.[1]

Working Drawings   Drawings which show all details required for construction of a project.[1]

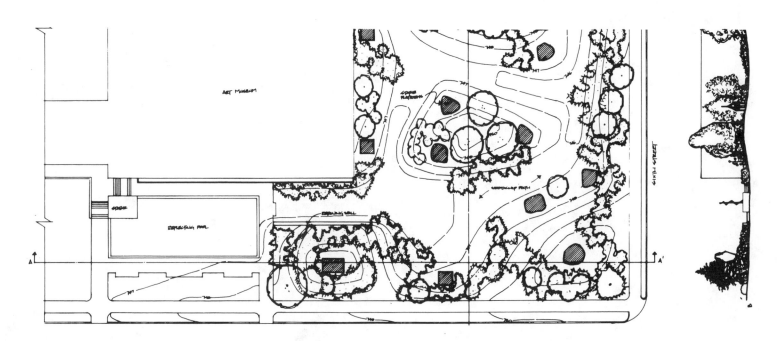

Index

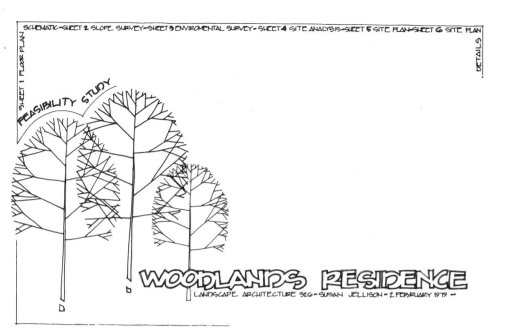
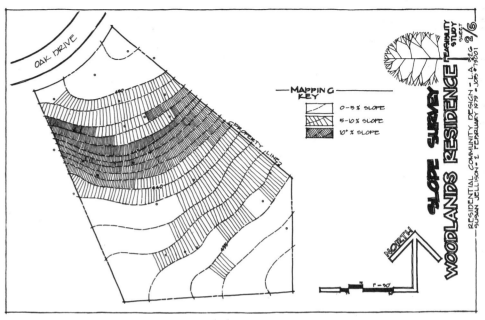
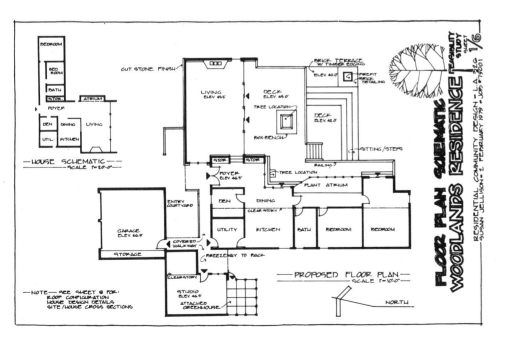
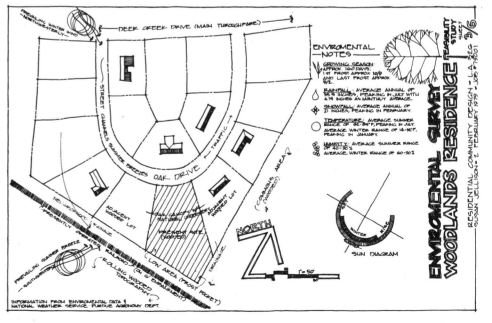